BEGINNING ASP.NET 4.5

FOREWORD xxxi

INTRODUCTION xxxiii

CHAPTER 1   Getting Started with ASP.NET 4.5. 1

CHAPTER 2   Building an ASP.NET Website 33

CHAPTER 3   Designing Your W eb Pages. 65

CHAPTER 4   Working with ASP.NET Server Controls. 107

CHAPTER 5   Programming Your ASP.NET Web Pages. 145

CHAPTER 6   Creating Consistent Looking Websites 207

CHAPTER 7   Navigation 253

CHAPTER 8   User Controls 285

CHAPTER 9   Validating User Input. 311

CHAPTER 10   ASP.NET AJAX 349

CHAPTER 11   jQuery. 385

CHAPTER 12   Introducing Databases 421

CHAPTER 13   Displaying and Updating Data. 453

CHAPTER 14   LINQ and the ADO.NET Entity Framework 497

CHAPTER 15   Working with Data — Advanced Topics. 553

CHAPTER 16   Security in Your ASP.NET 4.5 Website. 603

CHAPTER 17   Personalizing Websites. 643

CHAPTER 18   Exception Handling, Debugging, and Tracing 679

CHAPTER 19   Deploying Your Website. 729

APPENDIX A   Exercise Answers. 767

APPENDIX B   Configuring SQL Server 2012 793

INDEX. 807

D1377188

BEGINNING

ASP.NET 4.5

BEGINNING

ASP.NET 4.5

IN C# AND VB

Imar Spaanjaars

WILEY

John Wiley & Sons, Inc.

Beginning ASP.NET 4.5: in C# and VB

Published by
John Wiley & Sons, Inc.
10475 Crosspoint Boulevard
Indianapolis, IN 46256
www.wiley.com

Copyright © 2013 by John Wiley & Sons, Inc., Indianapolis, Indiana

Published simultaneously in Canada

ISBN: 978-1-118-31180-6
ISBN: 978-1-118-38799-3 (ebk)
ISBN: 978-1-118-33202-3 (ebk)
ISBN: 978-1-118-33530-7 (ebk)

Manufactured in the United States of America

10 9 8 7 6 5 4 3 2 1

For general information on our other products and services please contact our Customer Care Department within the United States at (877) 762-2974, outside the United States at (317) 572-3993 or fax (317) 572-4002.

Wiley publishes in a variety of print and electronic formats and by print-on-demand. Some material included with standard print versions of this book may not be included in e-books or in print-on-demand. If this book refers to media such as a CD or DVD that is not included in the version you purchased, you may download this material at http://booksupport.wiley.com. For more information about Wiley products, visit www.wiley.com.

Library of Congress Control Number: 2012944686

—To Niek

ABOUT THE AUTHOR

IMAR SPAANJAARS graduated in Leisure Management at the Leisure Management School in the Netherlands, but he quickly changed his career path to the Internet world.

After working in the Internet business at various web agencies for over twelve years, he now runs his own company called De Vier Koeden (http://devierkoeden.com), a small Internet agency specializing in consultancy and development of Internet and intranet applications with Microsoft technologies such as ASP.NET 4.5.

Imar has written books on ASP.NET and Macromedia Dreamweaver, all published under the Wrox brand. He is also one of the top contributors to the Wrox Community Forum at p2p.wrox.com, where he shares his knowledge with fellow programmers.

Imar has received Microsoft's Most Valuable Professional (MVP) award each year since 2008 for his contributions to the ASP.NET community. In early 2012, Imar joined the ASPInsiders, a small group of international professionals that provide feedback and direction on new features for future versions of ASP.NET.

Imar lives in Utrecht, the Netherlands, with his girlfriend Fleur and his son Niek. You can contact him through his personal web site at http://imar.spaanjaars.com or by e-mail at imar@spaanjaars.com.

CREDITS

ACKNOWLEDGMENTS

ALTHOUGH THE JUMP IN VERSION NUMBER by only 0.5 seems to suggest that there's not much new in ASP.NET 4.5 or Visual Studio 2012, you'd be surprised at the number of changes—small and large—that made their way into these products. I spent the past couple of months working on updating this book from the .NET 4 release to the new .NET 4.5 release. I discovered new features and functionality every day. Some of those changes are really small, but could mean a boost in productivity on a day-to-day basis. Others are much bigger and affect the way you built or deploy your web sites. I tried to incorporate as many of the new features found in ASP.NET and Visual Studio as long as they make sense for you, someone with no or limited experience with ASP.NET.

I have also made a lot of changes to the book based on reader feedback. Just as with the previous versions of the book, I went over all the errata that have been submitted as well as over the hundreds of forum posts that were made, identifying areas in the book that readers had difficulties with, and finding ways to improve it. If you have the previous edition and posted a question in the Wrox forums: thanks for your valuable feedback; you've really helped to make this book better.

Besides my readers, I owe a lot to other people who helped me write this book.

First of all, a big thanks goes out to Brian Herrmann and Kim Cofer for their editorial work. Once again, it was a pleasure to work with you! I also want to thank Damien Foggon for his many useful suggestions he provided as a technical editor. All of you really helped shape this book. Many thanks also to the people from Wrox for their support and contributions to this book.

Another person I owe a lot to is my friend Anne Ward from Blue Violet, a UK-based web and graphic design company. Anne has done most of the new designs used in this book and I highly appreciate her input. Thanks again, Anne! The concert pictures you see in this book come from Nigel D. Nudds, who kindly let me use pictures from his collection.

Finally, I would like to thank my lovely girlfriend Fleur for her support during this project. With her help, writing a book with our newborn son Niek around wasn't as hard as I expected it to be.

CONTENTS

FOREWORD   *xxxi*

INTRODUCTION   *xxxiii*

CHAPTER 1: GETTING STARTED WITH ASP.NET 4.5   1

Microsoft Visual Studio Express for Web   2
  Getting Visual Studio   3
  Installing Visual Studio Express (VSEW)   3
Creating Your First ASP.NET 4.5 Website   5
An Introduction to ASP.NET 4.5   10
  Understanding HTML   11
    HTML Elements and Tags   11
    HTML Attributes   14
    HTML Comments   14
    The Rules of HTML5   14
  A First Look at ASP.NET Markup   16
A Tour of the IDE   16
  The Main Development Area   17
    Choosing Your Development Profile   17
    The Main Menu   18
    The Toolbar Area   18
    The Toolbox   18
    The Solution Explorer   18
    The Database Explorer   19
    The Properties Grid   19
    The Document Window   19
    The Start Page   20
  Informational Windows   22
    The Error List   22
    The Output Window   22
    The Find Results Window   23

Customizing the IDE   **23**

Rearranging Windows   23

Modifying the Toolbox   24

Customizing the Document Window   26

Customizing Toolbars   27

Enabling and Disabling Toolbars   27

Editing Existing Toolbars   27

Creating Your Own Toolbars   27

Customizing Keyboard Shortcuts   27

Resetting Your Changes   28

Resetting the Window Layout   28

Resetting the Toolbox   28

Resetting All Settings   28

The Sample Application   **28**

Practical Tips on Visual Studio   **30**

Summary   **31**

CHAPTER 2: BUILDING AN ASP.NET WEBSITE   **33**

Creating Websites with Visual Studio 2012   **34**

Different Project Types   34

Web Application Projects   34

Web Site Projects   34

Choosing between Web Site Projects and Web Application Projects   35

Choosing the Right Website Template   35

ASP.NET Web Forms Site   36

ASP.NET Web Site (Razor v1 / Razor v2)   36

ASP.NET Empty Web Site   36

ASP.NET Dynamic Data Entities Web Site   36

WCF Service   36

Creating and Opening a New Website   37

Creating New Websites   37

Opening Existing Websites   39

Working with Files in Your Website	**40**
The Many File Types of an ASP.NET 4.5 Website	41
Web Files	41
Code Files	43
Data Files	44
Adding Existing Files	44
Organizing Your Site	46
Special File Types	47
Working with Web Forms	**47**
The Different Views on Web Forms	47
Choosing between Code Behind and Pages with Inline Code	49
Adding Markup to Your Page	54
Inserting and Formatting Text	54
Adding Tables and Other Markup	57
Connecting Pages	60
Practical Tips on Working with Web Forms	**62**
Summary	**63**

CHAPTER 3: DESIGNING YOUR WEB PAGES	**65**

Why Do You Need CSS?	**66**
Problems of HTML Formatting	66
How CSS Fixes Formatting Problems	67
An Introduction to CSS	**67**
CSS — The Language	72
The Style Sheet	72
Selectors	73
Properties	75
Values	76
Using Shorthand	77
The CSS Box Model	78
Adding CSS to Your Pages	85
Choosing among External, Embedded, and Inline Style Sheets	86

Working with CSS in Visual Studio   **87**
  Using the CSS Editor   88
  Creating Embedded and Inline Style Sheets   93
  Applying Styles   98
  Managing Styles   100
Practical Tips on Working with CSS   **102**
Summary   **103**

**CHAPTER 4: WORKING WITH ASP.NET
SERVER CONTROLS**   **107**

Introduction to Server Controls   **108**
A Closer Look at ASP.NET Server Controls   **112**
  Defining Controls in Your Pages   112
  Common Properties for All Controls   113
Types of Controls   **116**
  Standard Controls   116
    Simple Controls   116
    List Controls   117
    Container Controls   123
    Other Standard Controls   130
  HTML Controls   132
    How to Choose between Standard and
    HTML Controls   132
  Data Controls   132
  Validation Controls   133
  Navigation Controls   133
  Login Controls   133
  Ajax Extensions   133
  WebParts   133
  Dynamic Data   134
The ASP.NET State Engine   **134**
  What Is State and Why Is It Important?   134
  How the State Engine Works   135

Not All Controls Rely on View State 139
A Note about View State and Performance 140
Practical Tips on Working with Controls **141**
Summary **142**

CHAPTER 5: PROGRAMMING YOUR ASP.NET WEB PAGES 145

Introduction to Programming **146**
Data Types and Variables **147**
Converting and Casting Data Types 150
Using Arrays and Collections 153
Defining and Working with Arrays 153
Defining and Working with Collections 154
An Introduction to Generics 156
Statements **157**
Operators 158
Assignment Operators 158
Arithmetic Operators 158
Comparison Operators 161
Concatenation Operators 163
Logical Operators 164
Making Decisions 166
If, If Else, and Elself Constructs 166
Select Case/switch Constructs 168
Loops 173
The For Loop 173
The For Each/foreach Loop 175
The While Loop 175
Exiting Loops Prematurely 176
Organizing Code **177**
Methods: Functions and Subroutines 177
The App_Code Folder 180
Organizing Code with Namespaces 184

Writing Comments   186
    Commenting Code Inline   186
    Writing XML Comments   187
Object Orientation Basics   **189**
    Important OO Terminology   189
        Objects   189
        Classes   190
        Fields   190
        Properties   191
        Methods   194
        Constructors   195
        Inheritance   197
        Access Modifiers   200
    Events   201
Practical Tips on Programming   **202**
Summary   **203**

CHAPTER 6: CREATING CONSISTENT LOOKING WEBSITES 207

Consistent Page Layout with Master Pages   **208**
    Creating Master Pages   210
    Creating Content Pages   212
        A Closer Look at Master Pages   215
        Nesting Master Pages   216
        Master Page Caveats   217
Using a Centralized Base Page   **218**
    An Introduction to the ASP.NET Page Life Cycle   219
    Implementing the Base Page   221
    Creating Reusable Page Templates   225
Themes   **229**
    Different Types of Themes   230
    Choosing Between Theme and StyleSheetTheme   230
    Applying Themes   230
    Extending Themes   235
    Dynamically Switching Themes   238

Skins   **245**

    Creating a Skin File   246

    Named Skins   248

    Disable Theming for Specific Controls   249

Practical Tips on Creating Consistent Pages   **249**

Summary   **250**

CHAPTER 7: NAVIGATION   253

Different Ways to Move Around Your Site   **254**

    Understanding Absolute and Relative URLs   254

      Relative URLs   255

      Absolute URLs   256

    Understanding Default Documents   257

Using the Navigation Controls   **257**

    Architecture of the Navigation Controls   258

    Examining the Web.sitemap File   258

      Key Elements of the Web.sitemap File   259

    Using the Menu Control   261

      Using the Rendering Mode   262

      Creating a Basic Version of the Menu Control   262

      Styling the Menu Control   265

    Using the TreeView Control   270

    Using the SiteMapPath Control   274

Programmatic Redirection   **276**

    Programmatically Redirecting the Client to a Different Page   276

    Server-Side Redirects   279

Practical Tips on Navigation   **281**

Summary   **282**

CHAPTER 8: USER CONTROLS   285

Introduction to User Controls   **286**

    Creating User Controls   287

    Adding User Controls to a Content Page or Master Page   290

    Sitewide Registration of User Controls   293

User Control Caveats 295

Understanding and Managing Client IDs 295

Introducing ClientIDMode 296

Adding Logic to Your User Controls **296**

Creating Your Own Data Types for Properties 297

Implementing View State Properties 302

View State Considerations 308

Practical Tips on User Controls **308**

Summary **309**

CHAPTER 9: VALIDATING USER INPUT **311**

Gathering Data from the User **312**

Validating User Input in Web Forms 313

The ASP.NET Validation Controls 313

A Warning on Client-Side Validation 314

Using the Validation Controls 314

Using the HTML5 Data Types 317

The Standard Validation Controls 320

The CustomValidator and ValidationSummary Controls 327

Understanding Request Validation 332

Processing Data at the Server **334**

Sending E-mail from Your Website 334

Configuring Your Website for Sending E-mail 334

Creating E-mail Messages 336

Reading from Text Files 340

Practical Tips on Validating Data **345**

Summary **346**

CHAPTER 10: ASP.NET AJAX **349**

Introducing Ajax **350**

Using ASP.NET AJAX in Your Projects **351**

Creating Flicker-Free Pages 352

The UpdatePanel Control 352

A Closer Look at the UpdatePanel 355

The ScriptManager Control 356

Providing Feedback to Users   358
    The UpdateProgress Control   358
The Timer Control   362
Using Web Services and Page Methods in Ajax Websites   **363**
What Are Web Services?   364
    Introducing WCF   364
    Calling Services from Client-Side Code   365
    Exchanging Complex Objects with WCF   366
Creating Web Services   369
    Configuring the ScriptManager   372
Introducing Page Methods   378
Practical Ajax Tips   **381**
Summary   **382**

CHAPTER 11: JQUERY   **385**

An Introduction to jQuery   **386**
Introducing NuGet   387
    Using the Manage NuGet Packages Dialog Box   387
    Using the Package Manager Console   389
Choosing the Location for Your jQuery Reference   391
Different Ways to Include the jQuery Library   392
jQuery Syntax   **395**
jQuery Core   396
Selecting Items Using jQuery   397
    Basic Selectors   397
    Basic Filters   400
    Advanced Filters   402
Modifying the DOM with jQuery   **404**
CSS Methods   404
    css(name, value)   404
    css(name)   404
    css(properties)   404
    addClass, removeClass, and toggleClass   404
    attr(attributeName)   405
    attr(attributeName, value)   405

Handling Events   405
Miscellaneous jQuery Functionality   407
Common Mistakes When Working with jQuery   408
   Your ID Selectors Don't Work   408
   Your ID Selectors Don't Work, Even with a Hash Symbol   408
   None of Your Code Seems to Run   408

Effects with jQuery   **408**
jQuery and Validation   **414**
Practical Tips on jQuery   **418**
Summary   **418**

CHAPTER 12: INTRODUCTION TO DATABASES   421

What Is a Database?   **422**
Different Kinds of Relational Databases   **423**
  Installing SQL Server 2012 Express   424
Using SQL to Work with Database Data   **425**
Retrieving and Manipulating Data with SQL   **428**
  Reading Data   428
   Selecting Data   428
   Filtering Data   429
   Ordering Data   430
   Joining Data   434
  Creating Data   437
  Updating Data   438
  Deleting Data   438
Creating Your Own Tables   **441**
  Data Types in SQL Server   441
  Understanding Primary Keys and Identities   442
  Creating Relationships Between Tables   446
Practical Database Tips   **450**
Summary   **451**

CHAPTER 13: DISPLAYING AND UPDATING DATA   453

Data Controls   **453**
  Data-Bound Controls   454
   List Controls   454

Single Item Controls 455
Paging Controls 455
Data Source Controls 456
Other Data Controls 456

Data Source and Data-bound Controls Working Together 456
Displaying and Editing Data with GridView 456
Inserting Data with DetailsView 463
Storing Your Connection Strings in Web.config 464
Filtering Data 466

Customizing the Appearance of the Data Controls 472
Configuring Columns or Fields of Data-bound Controls 473

Updating and Inserting Data 479
Using DetailsView to Insert and Update Data 479

Practical Tips for Displaying and Updating Data 493
Summary 494

CHAPTER 14: LINQ AND THE ADO.NET ENTITY FRAMEWORK 497

Introducing LINQ 498
LINQ to Objects 499
LINQ to XML 499
LINQ to ADO.NET 499

Introducing the ADO.NET Entity Framework 500
Mapping Your Data Model to an Object Model 501
Introducing Query Syntax 507
Standard Query Operators 507
Select 508
From 508
Order By 508
Where 509
Sum, Min, Max, Average, and Count 509
Take, Skip, TakeWhile, and SkipWhile 509
Single and SingleOrDefault 510
First, FirstOrDefault, Last, and LastOrDefault 511
Shaping Data with Anonymous Types 511

Using Server Controls with LINQ Queries   **517**

Using Data Controls with the Entity Framework   517

Introducing the EntityDataSource Control   517

Introducing the ListView Control   524

Using Strongly Typed Data-Bound Controls   536

Introducing the DataPager Control   544

A Few Notes about Performance   549

Practical LINQ and ADO.NET Entity Framework Tips   **550**

Summary   **550**

**CHAPTER 15: WORKING WITH DATA —
ADVANCED TOPICS**   **553**

Formatting Your Controls Using Styles   **554**

An Introduction to Styles   555

Combining Styles, Themes, and Skins   559

Handling Events   **563**

The ASP.NET Page and Control Life Cycles Revisited   564

The ASP.NET Page Life Cycle and Events in Data Controls   569

Handling Errors that Occur in the Data Source Controls   574

Hand-Coding Data Access Code   **579**

Caching   **589**

Common Pitfalls with Caching Data   589

Avoiding Stale Data   590

Don't Rely on the Data Being There   590

Different Ways to Cache Data in ASP.NET Web Applications   590

Output Caching   591

Caching with Data Source Controls   592

Programmatic Caching   593

Practical Data Tips   **600**

Summary   **600**

**CHAPTER 16: SECURITY IN YOUR ASP.NET 4.5
WEBSITE**   **603**

Introducing Security   **604**

Identity: Who Are You?   604

Authentication: How Can You Prove Who You Are? 604
Authorization: What Are You Allowed to Do? 605
An Introduction to the ASP.NET
Application Services 605
Introducing the Login Controls **607**
The Login Controls 612
Login 612
LoginView 614
LoginStatus 615
LoginName 615
CreateUserWizard 617
PasswordRecovery 621
ChangePassword 621
Configuring Your Web Application 624
The Role Manager **627**
The Role Manager Configuration 627
Managing Users with the WSAT 628
Configuring the Web Application to Work with Roles 632
Programmatically Checking Roles 636
Practical Security Tips **640**
Summary **641**

CHAPTER 17: PERSONALIZING WEBSITES **643**

Understanding Profile **644**
Configuring the Profile 645
Creating Simple Profile Properties 645
Creating Profile Groups 646
Using Non-Standard Data Types 647
Using the Profile 652
Other Ways of Dealing with Profile **670**
Anonymous Identification 670
Cleaning Up Old Anonymous Profiles 671
Looking at Other Users' Profiles 672
Practical Personalization Tips **675**
Summary **675**

CHAPTER 18: EXCEPTION HANDLING, DEBUGGING, AND TRACING   679

Exception Handling	**680**
Different Types of Errors	680
Syntax Errors	680
Logic Errors	681
Runtime Errors	682
Catching and Handling Exceptions	682
Global Error Handling and Custom Error Pages	690
The Basics of Debugging	**698**
Tools Support for Debugging	**701**
Moving Around in Debugged Code	701
Debugging Windows	702
Watching Variables	702
Other Windows	704
Debugging Client-Side Script	**709**
Debugging with the Page Inspector	**712**
Introducing the Page Inspector	712
Using the Page Inspector	713
Tracing Your ASP.NET Web Pages	**718**
Using the Standard Tracing Capabilities	719
Tracing with Individual Pages	719
Tracing the Entire Website	720
Adding Your Own Information to the Trace	723
Tracing and Performance	725
A Security Warning	725
Practical Debugging Tips	**725**
Summary	**726**

CHAPTER 19: DEPLOYING YOUR WEBSITE   729

Preparing Your Website for Deployment	**730**
Avoiding Hard-Coded Settings	730
The Web.config File	731
Expression Syntax	731
The WebConfigurationManager Class	732

Introducing Bundling and Minification **738**

Copying Your Website **741**

    Creating a Simple Copy of Your Website 742

    Publishing Your Website 745

Running Your Site under IIS **746**

    Installing and Configuring the Web Server 746

        Making Sure IIS Is Installed 747

    Installing and Configuring ASP.NET 748

    Understanding Security in IIS 753

    NTFS Settings for Planet Wrox 754

    Troubleshooting Web Server Errors 757

Moving Data to a Remote Server **759**

    Exporting Your Data to a File 760

    Re-Creating the Database 762

The Deployment Checklist **763**

What's Next **764**

Summary **765**

APPENDIX A: EXERCISE ANSWERS 767

APPENDIX B: CONFIGURING SQL SERVER 2012 793

Configuring SQL Server 2012 **793**

    Terminology and Concepts 793

        SQL Server Authentication 794

        Windows Authentication 794

        Choosing between Windows and Server Authentication 795

    Using SQL Server Management Studio 795

        Enabling Remote Connections in SQL Server 795

        Attaching Databases to SQL Server 796

    Connecting Your Application to SQL Server 2012 798

        Scenario 1 — Using SQL Server Authentication 799

        Scenario 2 — Using Windows Authentication with IIS
and the Database on the Same Machine 803

Configuring Application Services **805**

INDEX *807*

FOREWORD

THE ADOPTION RATE OF EMERGING STANDARDS like HTML5 and CSS3 grows every day. Things that were only possible on thick client apps are becoming a reality on the web. With browsers getting faster and better each day, with more common tasks becoming available as reusable libraries, and with open sourcing of nearly all big web frameworks, our world wide web is a happening place. Penetration of mobile devices and the varied mobile app development technologies are making developers further consider the open and accessible web as their medium of expression.

During this time, client side libraries like jQuery and jQuery mobile, and server-side technologies like ASP.NET are making typically difficult and cumbersome tasks approachable. On top of all this, free tools like Visual Web Developer 2012 make web development more fun than ever before. It is indeed a joy to be a web developer these days, and it is nice to see this book come out and make becoming web developer approachable for everyone.

Imar Spaanjaars, the author of this book, has been a Microsoft MVP in ASP.NET since 2008, and this time around we also had him join the ASP.NET Insiders group, in which we bounce feature ideas and pre-release products even before they ever get to public beta. Imar has been a constant source of feedback for the team during the development process and I am certain he will continue to be so even in the future.

In *Beginning ASP.NET 4.5: in C# and VB* he starts slow, goes deep, builds concepts, and covers the latest features of both ASP.NET 4.5 and Visual Studio 2012. Whether you are just starting web development or upgrading to ASP.NET 4.5, this book is certainly worth adding to your toolbox.

It is my pleasure to know Imar, and I want to thank him for his contribution to our community. His insights and thoughts were invaluable the product team behind ASP.NET and Visual Studio. I hope his insights will help you too.

VISHAL R. JOSHI
Principal Program Manager Lead
Windows Azure Group, Microsoft Corporation
http://vishalrjoshi.com

INTRODUCTION

TO BUILD EFFECTIVE AND ATTRACTIVE database-driven websites, you need two things: a solid and fast framework to run your web pages on and a rich and extensive environment to create and program these web pages. With ASP.NET 4.5 and Visual Studio 2012 you get both. Together they form *the* platform to create dynamic and interactive websites.

ASP.NET 4.5 builds on top of its popular predecessors ASP.NET 2.0, 3.5, and 4.0. While maintaining backward compatibility with sites built using these older versions, ASP.NET 4.5 and Visual Studio 2012 introduce new, exciting features and bring many smaller, but much needed changes to the framework and development tools.

With each new release of Visual Studio since Visual Studio 2003, I am surprised by the sheer amount of new functionality and changes Microsoft has been able to put in the product. Visual Studio 2012 is no exception. If you're familiar with earlier versions, you'll notice the new design as a big change. The UI of Visual Studio has been updated to the Windows 8 design look and feel to better align with other products from Microsoft.

You'll also find many changes—small and large—in both the ASP.NET Framework and Visual Studio. Some of these changes are the improved CSS and JavaScript editors (discussed in Chapter 3 and Chapter 10, respectively), the strongly typed data-bound controls (discussed in Chapter 14), the inclusion of NuGet, discussed in Chapter 11, and the introduction of bundling and minification, discussed in Chapter 19.

My favorite new feature is probably the Page Inspector that helps you debug client-side as well as server-side code at the same time. I discuss the Page Inspector in Chapter 18.

If you're familiar with earlier versions of ASP.NET, you'll be happy to find many small gems in the new version of the framework that will make your life as a developer easier. I mention and discuss these new features throughout this book where appropriate. For a complete list of all new features in ASP.NET, check out the following white paper at the official ASP.NET website:

```
http://www.asp.net/vnext/overview/whitepapers/whats-new
```

If this link no longer works by the time you read this book, search www.asp.net for "What's new in ASP.NET 4.5."

Probably the best thing about Visual Studio Express 2012 for Web is its price: it's available for free. This makes Visual Studio and ASP.NET probably the most attractive and compelling web development technologies available today.

WHO THIS BOOK IS FOR

This book is for anyone who wants to learn how to build rich and interactive websites that run on the Microsoft platform. With the knowledge you gain from this book, you create a great foundation to build any type of website, ranging from simple hobby-related websites to sites you may be creating for commercial purposes.

Anyone new to web programming should be able to follow along because no prior background in web development is assumed, although it helps if you do have a basic understanding of HTML and the web in general. The book starts at the very beginning of web development by showing you how to obtain and install Visual Studio. The chapters that follow gradually introduce you to new technologies, building on top of the knowledge gained in the previous chapters.

Do you have a strong preference for Visual Basic over C# or the other way around? Or do you think both languages are equally cool? Or maybe you haven't made up your mind yet and want to learn both languages? Either way, you'll like this book because *all* code examples are presented in both languages!

Even if you have some experience with prior versions of ASP.NET, you may gain a lot from this book. Although many concepts from previous versions are brought forward into ASP.NET 4.5, you'll discover there's a lot of new stuff to be found in this book, including the strongly typed data controls, smarter code editors, new debugging facilities, and more.

WHAT THIS BOOK COVERS

This book teaches you how to create a feature-rich, data-driven, and interactive website called Planet Wrox. Although this is quite a mouthful, you'll find that with Visual Studio 2012, developing such a website isn't as hard as it seems. You'll see the entire process of building a website, from installing Visual Studio in Chapter 1 all the way up to putting your website on a live server in Chapter 19. The book is divided into 19 chapters, each dealing with a specific subject:

- ➤ **Chapter 1, "Getting Started with ASP.NET 4.5."** In this chapter you see how to obtain and install Visual Studio Express 2012 for Web, the free version of Visual Studio 2012 to build ASP.NET websites. You are also introduced to HTML5, the latest standard for defining web pages. The chapter closes with an overview of the customization options that Visual Studio gives you.

- ➤ **Chapter 2, "Building an ASP.NET Website."** This chapter shows you how to create a new website and how to add new items like pages to it. Besides learning how to create a well-structured site, you also see how to use the numerous tools in Visual Studio to create HTML and ASP.NET pages.

- ➤ **Chapter 3, "Designing Your Web Pages."** Visual Studio comes with a host of tools that enable you to create well-designed and attractive web pages. In this chapter, you see how to make good use of these tools. Additionally, you learn about CSS, the language that is used to format web pages.

➤ **Chapter 4, "Working with ASP.NET Server Controls."** ASP.NET Server Controls are one of the most important concepts in ASP.NET. They enable you to create complex and feature-rich websites with very little code. This chapter introduces you to the large number of server controls that are available, explains what they are used for, and shows you how to use them.

➤ **Chapter 5, "Programming Your ASP.NET Web Pages."** Although the built-in CSS tools and the ASP.NET Server Controls can get you a long way in creating web pages, you are likely to use a programming language to enhance your pages. This chapter serves as an introduction to programming with a strong focus on programming web pages. Best of all: all the examples you see in this chapter (and the rest of the book) are in both Visual Basic and C#, so you can choose the language you like best.

➤ **Chapter 6, "Creating Consistent-Looking Websites."** Consistency is important to give your website an attractive and professional appeal. ASP.NET helps you create consistent-looking pages through the use of master pages, which enable you to define the global look and feel of a page. Skins and themes help you to centralize the looks of controls and other visual elements in your site. You also see how to create a base page that helps to centralize programming code that you need on all pages in your site.

➤ **Chapter 7, "Navigation."** To help your visitors find their way around your site, ASP.NET comes with a number of navigation controls. These controls are used to build the navigation structure of your site. They can be connected to your site's central site map that defines the pages in your website. You also learn how to programmatically send users from one page to another.

➤ **Chapter 8, "User Controls."** User controls are reusable page fragments that can be used in multiple web pages. As such, they are great for repeating content such as menus, banners, and so on. In this chapter, you learn how to create and use user controls and enhance them with some programmatic intelligence.

➤ **Chapter 9, "Validating User Input."** A large part of interactivity in your site is defined by the input of your users. This chapter shows you how to accept, validate, and process user input using ASP.NET Server Controls. Additionally, you see how to send e-mail from your ASP .NET website and how to read from text files.

➤ **Chapter 10, "ASP.NET AJAX."** Microsoft ASP.NET AJAX enables you to create good-looking, flicker-free web pages that close the gap between traditional desktop applications and websites. In this chapter you learn how to use the built-in Ajax features to enhance the presence of your web pages, resulting in a smoother interaction with the website.

➤ **Chapter 11, "jQuery."** jQuery is a popular, open source and cross-browser JavaScript library designed to make it easier to interact with web pages in the client's browser. In this chapter you learn the basics of jQuery and see how to add rich visual effects and animations to your web pages.

➤ **Chapter 12, "Introduction to Databases."** Understanding how to use a database is critical to building websites, because most modern websites require the use of a database. You learn the basics of SQL, the query language that enables you to access and alter data in a database. In addition, you are introduced to the database tools found in Visual Studio that help you create and manage your SQL Server databases.

➤ **Chapter 13, "Displaying and Updating Data."** Building on the knowledge you gained in Chapter 12, this chapter shows you how to use the ASP.NET data-bound and data source controls to create a rich interface that enables your users to interact with the data in the database that these controls target.

➤ **Chapter 14, "LINQ and the ADO.NET Entity Framework."** LINQ is Microsoft's solution for accessing objects, databases, XML, and more. The ADO.NET Entity Framework (EF) is Microsoft's new technology for database access. This chapter shows you what LINQ is all about, how to use the visual EF designer built into Visual Studio, and how to write LINQ to Entities queries to get data in and out of your SQL Server database. You also see how to work with strongly typed data controls to make it easier to write code with fewer errors.

➤ **Chapter 15, "Working with Data—Advanced Topics."** Whereas earlier chapters focus mostly on the technical foundations of working with data, this chapter looks at the same topic from a front-end perspective. You see how to change the visual appearance of your data through the use of control styles. You also see how to interact with the data-bound controls and how to speed up your website by keeping a local copy of frequently accessed data.

➤ **Chapter 16, "Security in Your ASP.NET 4.5 Website."** Although presented quite late in the book, security is a first-class, important topic. This chapter shows you how to make use of the built-in ASP.NET features related to security. You learn about a number of application services that facilitate security. You also learn how to let users sign up for an account on your website, how to distinguish between anonymous and logged-on users, and how to manage the users in your system.

➤ **Chapter 17, "Personalizing Websites."** Building on the security features introduced in Chapter 16, this chapter shows you how to create personalized web pages with content targeted at individual users. You see how to configure and use ASP.NET Profile, which enables you to store personalized data for known and anonymous visitors.

➤ **Chapter 18, "Exception Handling, Debugging, and Tracing."** You need good debugging tools to understand, improve, and fix the code you write for your ASP.NET web pages. Visual Studio ships with great debugging support that enables you to diagnose the state of your application at run time, helping you find and fix problems before your users do. You also get a good look at the Page Inspector that has been introduced in Visual Studio 2012.

➤ **Chapter 19, "Deploying Your Website."** By the end of the book, you should have a website that is ready to be shown to the world. But how exactly do you do that? What are the things you need to know and understand to put your website out in the wild? This chapter gives the answers and provides you with a good look at configuring different production systems in order to run your final website. You also see how to implement bundling and minification to improve the performance of your website.

HOW THIS BOOK IS STRUCTURED

This book takes the time to explain concepts step by step using working examples and detailed explanations. Using the famous Wrox Try It Out and How It Works sections, you are guided through a task step by step, detailing important things as you progress through the task. Each Try It Out task is followed by a detailed How It Works section that explains the steps you performed in the exercise.

At the end of each chapter, you find exercises that help you test the knowledge you gained in this chapter. You can find the answers to each question in Appendix A at the end of this book. Don't worry if you don't know all the answers to the questions. Later chapters do not assume you followed and carried out the tasks from the exercise sections of previous chapters.

Because this is a beginner's book, I can't go into great detail on a number of topics. For nearly every chapter in this book, you'll find numerous other books that exclusively deal with the topic discussed. Where appropriate, I have included references to these books so you can easily decide where to go to next if you want to deepen your knowledge on a specific subject.

WHAT YOU NEED TO USE THIS BOOK

This book assumes you have a system that meets the following requirements:

➤ Capable of running Visual Studio. For the exact system requirements, consult the readme file that comes with the software.

➤ Running Windows 7 or Windows 8 (at least the Home Premium edition), or one of the Windows Server 2008 R2 or 2012 editions.

Chapter 1 shows you how to obtain and install Visual Studio 2012, which in turn installs the Microsoft .NET Framework version 4.5 and SQL Server Express LocalDB edition; then all you need is a good operating system and the drive to read this book!

CONVENTIONS

To help you get the most from the text and keep track of what's happening, a number of conventions are used throughout the book.

TRY IT OUT   Conventions

The Try It Out is an exercise you should work through, following the text in the book.

1. They usually consist of a set of steps.

2. Each step has a number.

3. Follow the steps through with your copy of the code.

4. Then read the How It Works section to find out what's going on.

How It Works

After each Try It Out, the actions you carried out and the code you've typed in are explained in detail.

> **NOTE** *Boxes like this one hold important, not-to-be forgotten information that is directly relevant to the surrounding text.*

> **COMMON MISTAKES** *Mistakes that are easily made while following the exercises are presented in a box like this. Be sure to read these carefully when you get stuck in an exercise.*

As for styles in the text:

➤ New terms and important words are *italicized* when they are introduced.

➤ Code within the text is presented like this: `Request.QueryString.Get("Id")`

➤ URLs that do not start with www are prefixed with `http://` to make it clear it's an Internet address. URLs within the text are presented like this: `http://imar.spaanjaars.com`.

➤ You'll see many URLs that start with `tinyurl.com` or `bit.ly`, which are handy, online services to make URLs shorter (and thus easier to type). Entering a `tinyurl.com` or `bit.ly` address in your browser should take you to its final destination.

➤ Menu items that require you to click multiple submenus have a special symbol that looks like this: ⇨ . For example: File ⇨ New ⇨ Folder.

➤ Code or content irrelevant to the discussion is either left out completely or replaced with ellipsis points (three dots) and a comment, like this:

```
<tr>
  <td style="white-space: nowrap;">
    ... Menu items go here; not shown
  </td>
</tr>
```

The three dots are used regardless of the programming language used in the example, so you'll see it for C#, Visual Basic, HTML, CSS, and JavaScript. When you see it in code you're instructed to type into the code editor, you can simply skip the three dots and anything that follows them on the same line.

➤ Code shown for the first time, or other relevant code, is in the following format:

```
Dim roles As New ArrayList()
roles.Add("Administrators")
roles.Add("ContentManagers")
```

To put emphasis on a block of code surrounded by other code, I use a bolded font like this:

```
<appSettings>
  <add key="FromAddress" value="planetwrox@example.com"/>
</appSettings>
```

The surrounding code is used to make it easier to see where the bolded code should be placed.

➤ Quite often, white space in code is irrelevant, as is mostly the case with ASP.NET markup and HTML. To fit code within the boundaries of this book, I often wrap code over multiple lines and indent the part that should have been on the previous line like this:

```
Dim result As String =
        WebConfigurationManager.AppSettings.Get("FromAddress")
```

If you're typing this code yourself, you can put it all on one line, or use the same line breaks if you prefer. The sample code that comes with this book has the code typically on a single line.

➤ Text that appears on-screen often has Each Word Start With A Capital Letter, even though the original screen text uses a different capitalization. This is done to make the screen text stand out from the rest of the text.

SOURCE CODE

As you work through the examples in this book, you may choose either to type in all the code manually or to use the source code files that accompany the book. All of the source code used in this book is available for download from the book's own page on the Wrox website at www.wrox.com/remtitle.cgi?isbn=1118311809. If somehow this link no longer works, go to www.wrox.com and locate the book either by using the Search box or by using one of the title lists. Click the Download Code link on the book's detail page to obtain all the source code for the book.

> **NOTE** *Because many books have similar titles, you may find it easiest to search by ISBN; for this book the ISBN is 978-1-118-31180-6.*

You can download the full source for this book as a single file for each programming language used in the book (C# or Visual Basic). You can decompress these files with your favorite decompression tool. If you extract the source, make sure you maintain the original folder structure that is part of the code download. The different decompression tools use different names for this feature, but look for a feature like Use Folder Names or Maintain Directory Structure. Once you have extracted the files from the code download, you should end up with a folder called Source and a folder called Resources. Then create a new folder in the root of your C drive, call it BegASPNET, and move the Source and Resources folders into this new folder so you end up with folders like C:\BegASPNET\Source and C:\BegASPNET\Resources. The Source folder contains the source for each of the 19 chapters of this book and the final version of the Planet Wrox website. The Resources folder contains files you need during some of the exercises in this book. If everything turned out correctly, you should end up with the structure shown in Figure I-1.

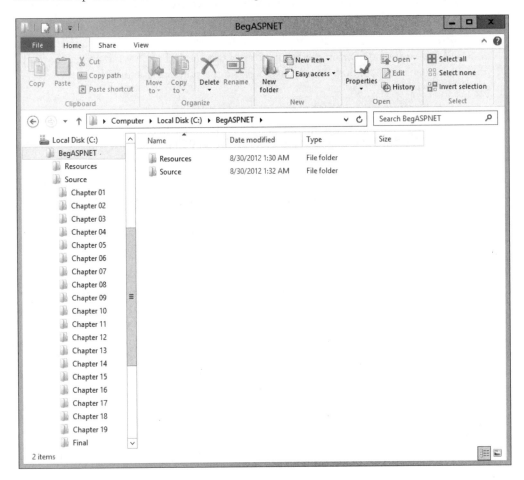

FIGURE I-1

Later chapters have you create folders called Site and Release inside the same C:\BegASPNET folder, giving you a folder structure similar to that in Figure I-2.

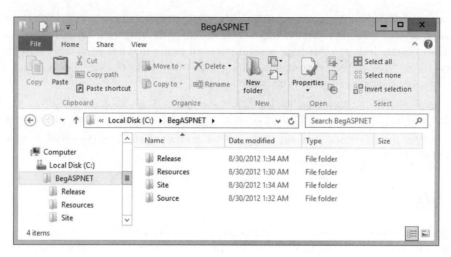

FIGURE I-2

The `Site` folder contains the site as you'll build it throughout this book, and the `Release` folder will contain your final version at the end of this book. Whenever you're stuck with some examples in this book, you can take a peek in the `Source` folder to see how things should have ended up.

If you want to run the site for a specific chapter to see how it works, be sure to open the chapter's folder in Visual Studio as a website. So, you should open a folder such as `C:\BegASPNET\Source\Chapter 12` directly rather than opening its parent folder `C:\BegASPNET\Source`.

If you want to follow along in both programming languages, create a second folder called `C:\BegASPNETVB` or `C:\BegASPNETCS` to hold the files for the other version. This way, the two sites can coexist without any problems. If you create a folder specifically for the C# language, don't include the hash symbol (#) because that's an invalid character in the pathname for a website.

Sticking to this structure ensures a smooth execution of the Try It Out exercises in this book. Incorrectly mixing or nesting these folders makes it harder to carry out the exercises and may even lead to unexpected situations and errors. Whenever you run into an issue or error that is not explained in this book, ensure that your site structure is still closely related to the one presented here.

ERRATA

I have made every effort to ensure that there are no errors in the text or in the code. However, no one is perfect, and mistakes do occur. If you find an error in this book, such as a spelling mistake or a faulty piece of code, I'd be very grateful for your feedback. By sending in errata you may save another reader hours of frustration and at the same time you will be helping me provide even higher quality information.

To find the errata page for this book, go to www.wrox.com/remtitle.cgi?isbn=1118311809 or go to www.wrox.com and locate the title using the Search box or one of the title lists. Then, on the book details page, click the Errata link. On this page you can view all errata that has been submitted for this book and posted by Wrox editors. A complete book list including links to each book's errata is also available at www.wrox.com/misc-pages/booklist.shtml.

If you don't spot "your" error on the book's Errata page, go to www.wrox.com/contact/techsupport.shtml and complete the form there to send us the error you have found. I'll check the information and, if appropriate, post a message to the book's errata page and fix the problem in subsequent editions of the book.

P2P.WROX.COM

For author and peer discussion, join the P2P forums at p2p.wrox.com. The forums are a web-based system for you to post messages relating to Wrox books and related technologies and interact with other readers and technology users. The forums offer a subscription feature to e-mail you topics of interest of your choosing when new posts are made to the forums. I am a frequent visitor of the Wrox forums, and I'll do my best to help you with any questions you may have about this book.

At p2p.wrox.com you will find a number of different forums that will help you not only as you read this book, but also as you develop your own applications. To join the forums, just follow these steps:

1. Go to p2p.wrox.com and click the Register Now link.

2. Read the terms of use and click Agree.

3. Complete the required information to join as well as any optional information you wish to provide and click Submit.

4. You will receive an e-mail with information describing how to verify your account and complete the joining process.

You can read messages in the forums without joining P2P but in order to post your own messages, you must join (which is free).

After you join, you can post new messages and respond to messages other users post. You'll find this book's own forum under the ASP.NET 4.5 category that is available from the homepage. You can read messages at any time on the web. If you would like to have new messages from a particular forum e-mailed to you, click the Subscribe to this Forum icon by the forum name in the forum listing.

For more information about how to use the Wrox P2P, be sure to read the P2P FAQs for answers to questions about how the forum software works as well as many common questions specific to P2P and Wrox books. To read the FAQs, click the FAQ link on any P2P page.

BEGINNING

ASP.NET 4.5

1

Getting Started with ASP.NET 4.5

WHAT YOU WILL LEARN IN THIS CHAPTER:

➤ How to acquire and install Visual Studio Express 2012 for Web and Visual Studio 2012

➤ How to create your first website with Visual Studio Express 2012

➤ How an ASP.NET page is processed by the server and sent to the browser

➤ How you can use and customize the development environment

Ever since the first release of the .NET Framework 1.0 in early 2002, Microsoft has put a lot of effort and development time into ASP.NET, the part of the .NET Framework that enables you to build rich web applications. This first release meant a radical change from the older Microsoft technology to build websites called *Active Server Pages (ASP)*, now often referred to as *classic ASP*. The introduction of ASP.NET 1.0 and the associated Visual Studio .NET gave developers the following benefits over classic ASP:

➤ A clean separation between presentation and code. With classic ASP, your programming logic was often scattered throughout the HTML of the page, making it hard to make changes to the page later.

➤ A development model that was much closer to the way desktop applications are programmed. This made it easier for the many Visual Basic desktop programmers to make the switch to web applications.

➤ A feature-rich development tool (called Visual Studio .NET) that enabled developers to create and code their web applications visually.

➤ A choice between a number of *object-oriented programming (OOP)* languages, of which Visual Basic .NET and C# (pronounced as C-Sharp) are now the most popular.

➤ Access to the entire .NET Framework, which for the first time meant that web developers had a unified and easy way to access many advanced features to work with databases, files, e-mail, networking tools, and much more.

Despite the many advantages of ASP.NET over the older model, using ASP.NET also meant an increase in complexity and the knowledge needed to build applications with it, making it harder for many new programmers to get started with ASP.NET.

After the initial release in 2002, Microsoft released another version of the .NET Framework (called .NET 1.1) and the development IDE (called Visual Studio .NET 2003). Many people saw this as a service pack for the initial release, although it also brought a lot of new enhancements in both the framework and the development tools.

In November 2005, Visual Studio 2005 and ASP.NET 2.0 were released. To the pleasant surprise of many developers around the world, Microsoft had again been able to drastically improve and expand the product, adding many features and tools that helped reduce the complexity that was introduced with ASP.NET 1.0. New wizards and smart controls made it possible to reduce the code required to build an application, decreasing the learning curve for new developers and increasing their productivity.

In November 2007, Microsoft released Visual Studio 2008 and the ASP.NET 3.5 framework, followed by Visual Studio 2010 and ASP.NET 4 in March 2010. Both versions added a lot of new functionality, including LINQ (discussed in Chapter 14), the integration of the AJAX Framework (which you learn more about in Chapter 10), the ADO.NET Entity Framework (discussed in Chapter 14), the inclusion of jQuery (discussed in Chapter 11), and more.

The current versions, Visual Studio 2012 and ASP.NET 4.5, build on top of the successful Visual Studio 2010 and ASP.NET 4 releases, leaving many of the beloved features in place while adding new features and tools in other areas.

Over the next 19 chapters, you learn how to build full-featured ASP.NET websites using Visual Studio Express 2012 for Web, Microsoft's free development tool for ASP.NET web applications, which is also part of the full Visual Studio 2012 suite. This book guides you through the process of creating a fully functional, database-driven website, starting with a bare-bones website in the next chapter, all the way down to the deployment of it to a production environment in Chapter 19.

The sample site that comes with this book and all the examples are built with Visual Studio Express 2012 for Web (VSEW), so it's important that you have it installed on your development machine. The next section shows you how to acquire and install VSEW. Once you have it up and running, you see how to create your first website, followed by an extensive tour through the many features of VSEW.

MICROSOFT VISUAL STUDIO EXPRESS FOR WEB

Although you could theoretically write ASP.NET web applications with Notepad or another text editor alone, you really want to install a copy of Microsoft Visual Studio (VS). VS hosts an enormous number of tools that will help you in rapidly creating complex ASP.NET web applications.

Visual Studio comes in two flavors: as a standalone and free version called Microsoft Visual Studio Express 2012 for Web, and as part of the larger development suite called Visual Studio 2012, which is also available in different editions, each with its own price tag. With the commercial editions of Visual Studio, the web components are fully integrated. You just start Visual Studio 2012 and then create a Web Site Project or a Web Application Project, which in turn enables the web components of Visual Studio.

Although the Express edition of Visual Studio is free, it contains all the features and tools you need to create complex and feature-rich web applications. All the examples you find in the book can be built with the free Express edition, so there's no need to shell out big bucks for the commercial versions of Visual Studio 2012 to follow along with this book.

I'll use the term Visual Studio (VS) to refer to both the commercial and free versions of Visual Studio. When talking about the free edition specifically, I'll use the terms Express edition or Visual Studio Express 2012 (VSEW).

Getting Visual Studio is easy. You can download it from the Microsoft site as discussed next.

Getting Visual Studio

You can get the free Visual Studio Express 2012 for Web from the Microsoft site at `www.microsoft.com/express/`. On the Express homepage, follow the Downloads link until you reach the page that offers the downloads for the Express products, including VSEW. From this page, you can download VSEW as a Web Install, where you download only the installer, while the remaining files are downloaded during the installation process. Make sure you choose Visual Studio Express 2012 for Web from the page, and not one of the other free Express products or one of the older editions of Visual Studio.

Don't be fooled by the file size of the Web Install download, which is just a few megabytes. The file you download is just the installer that downloads the required files over the Internet. The total download depends on your current system and will be somewhere between 180 MB and 270 MB.

If you want to try out the full version of Visual Studio 2012, which also contains the web components, you can sign up for a free trial on the Microsoft site at `http://msdn.microsoft.com/vstudio`. You can choose to download an ISO image that you'll need to burn on a DVD or choose to download the Web Installer.

Finally, you can download VSEW with the *Microsoft Web Platform Installer (WPI)* application available for download at `www.microsoft.com/web/platform` and at `www.asp.net/downloads/`. Besides VSEW, this tool also gives you easy access to many other web development–related tools and programs. The WPI is an excellent tool to get a whole bunch of web development–related programs and tools in one fell swoop. I often use it to get up and running real quick on a clean development machine.

Installing Visual Studio Express (VSEW)

Installing VSEW is a straightforward, although somewhat lengthy, process. Depending on your installation method, your computer, and your Internet connection speed, installing VSEW may take anywhere between 20 minutes and an hour — or even more.

TRY IT OUT Installing Visual Studio Express 2012 for Web

This Try It Out exercise guides you through installing VSEW on your computer. It assumes you're using the Web Platform Installer option as explained earlier, although the process for installing the Express edition from a DVD is almost identical. The steps you need to perform to install the full versions of Visual Studio 2012 are similar as well, although the screens you'll see will be somewhat different.

No matter how you install VSEW, it's important that you also install Microsoft SQL Express LocalDB Edition 11.0 — a required component if you want to follow along with many of this book's examples. It should be installed automatically when you install VSEW, but in case it's not installed, you'll find instructions at the end of this exercise to make sure it's properly installed.

1. Start by browsing to www.microsoft.com/express/ and follow the instructions to download VSEW 2012. Make sure you install Visual Studio Express 2012 for Web, and not one of the other free Express editions or older versions. If this link is ever changed or no longer provides direct access to the VSEW download, search the web for "install Visual Studio Express 2012 for Web" and you'll be taken to a download page where you can start the installation.

2. Depending on how you started the installer, you have a few options. If you started the VSEW download, you should see a screen similar to Figure 1-1.

FIGURE 1-1

Click Install to initiate the installation and related components.

If you started the Web Platform Installer instead, find Visual Studio Express 2012 for Web in the list of tools and select it. Finally, start the installation process.

3. In both cases, you get a screen that lists the components to be installed. In addition, you need to agree to the license terms for the software. Once you agree, you should see a screen similar to Figure 1-2.

4. After a while you should see a message indicating that VSEW has been installed successfully. The installer may need to reboot your machine during or after the installation. Once the installer has

finished, VSEW is ready for use. To check if SQL Express LocalDB has installed correctly, start the Web Platform Installer from the Windows Start menu or Start screen. Next, under the Products item, find Microsoft SQL Express LocalDB Edition 11.0 and install it if it hasn't been installed already.

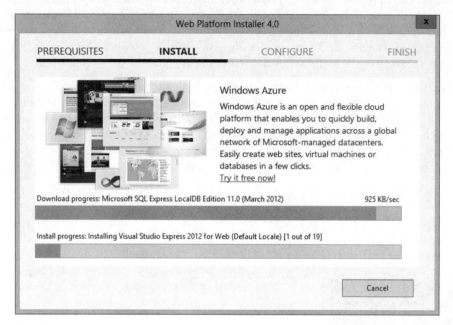

FIGURE 1-2

How It Works

The straightforward installation process guided you through the setup of VSEW using the Web Platform Installer. During installation, the WPI also installed a copy of Microsoft SQL Express LocalDB Edition 11.0, Microsoft's free version of its SQL Server 2012 database engine. SQL Server 2012 is discussed and used a lot in this book, starting with Chapter 12. Appendix B shows you how to configure security settings for the various versions of SQL Server 2012.

Now that VSEW is installed, it's time to fire it up and start working with it. The next section shows you how to create your very first site in VSEW. You see how to create a site, add content to a web page, and view that page in your browser.

CREATING YOUR FIRST ASP.NET 4.5 WEBSITE

You probably can't wait to get started with your first ASP.NET website, so instead of giving you a theoretical overview of websites in VS, the next Try It Out exercise dives right into the action and shows you how to build your first web project. Then, in the How It Works explanation and the section that follows, you get a good look at what goes on behind the scenes when you view an ASP.NET page in your browser.

TRY IT OUT Creating Your First ASP.NET Website

1. Start VS from the Windows Start menu or Start screen if you haven't done so already. Follow the on-screen instructions to register VSEW online and get a key. Enter the key in the VSEW start-up screen and click Next to continue. Note: if you're using the commercial version of Visual Studio, just start Visual Studio 2012 from the Start menu. All web-related components are accessed from the main VS program. The first time you start VS, there might be a delay before you can use it because it's busy configuring itself. Subsequent starts of the application will go much faster.

2. If you're using a commercial version of Visual Studio, you may also get a dialog box that lets you choose between different collections of settings the first time you start Visual Studio. The choice you make on that dialog box influences the layout of windows, toolboxes, menus, and shortcuts. Choose the Web Development settings because those settings are designed specifically for ASP.NET developers. You can always choose a different profile later by resetting your settings, as explained later in this chapter.

3. Once VS is fully configured, you see the main screen appear, as shown in Figure 1-3.

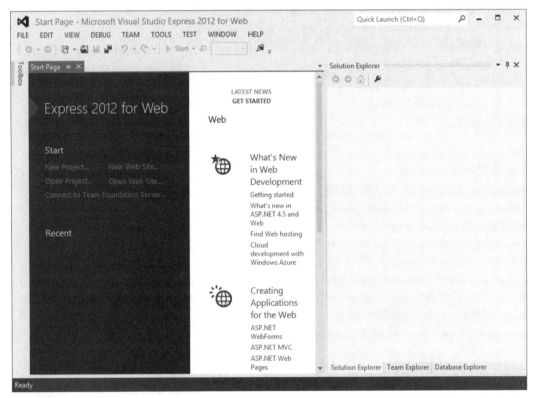

FIGURE 1-3

You get a full description of all the windows, toolbars, panels, and menus in the next section, so for now, just focus on creating a new website. Click the File menu in the upper-left corner and choose New Web Site. If you're using a commercial version of Visual Studio, depending on the settings you chose when starting Visual Studio the first time, you may have to open the submenu New first.

Make sure you don't accidentally use the New Project menu, because that is used to create different types of .NET applications. The New Web Site dialog box appears as shown in Figure 1-4.

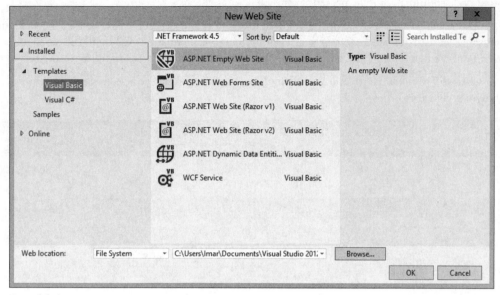

FIGURE 1-4

4. In the Installed Templates section on the left you can choose a programming language you will use for your site. This book shows all examples in both Visual Basic and Visual C# so you can choose a language to your liking.

5. In the list of templates in the middle, click ASP.NET Web Forms Site. Verify that File System is the selected option in the Web Location drop-down list at the bottom left. If you want, you could change the location on disk where the website is stored by clicking the Browse button and choosing a new location on your computer's hard drive. For now, the default location — a folder under your Documents folder — is fine, so you can leave the location as is.

6. Click OK. VS creates a new website for you that includes a number of files and folders (see Figure 1-5) to jump-start your website.

7. Open the file Default.aspx by double-clicking it and remove all the code inside the <asp:Content> block that has its ID set to BodyContent (it starts with <h3> at around line 19 and ends with </ol>) all the way at the bottom. Replace it with the following bolded code:

FIGURE 1-5

```
<asp:Content runat="server" ID="BodyContent" ContentPlaceHolderID="MainContent">
  <h2>Hello World</h2>
  <p>Welcome to Beginning ASP.NET 4.5 on <%: DateTime.Now.ToString() %></p>
</asp:Content>
```

You'll see code formatted like this a lot more in this book. When you are instructed to type in code formatted like this with some code in bold, you only need to type in the bolded code. The other code should already be present in the file.

Don't worry about the code with the angle brackets (<>) and percentage symbol in the welcome message; these are called tags, and you learn more about them later. Although this code may not look familiar to you now, you can probably guess what it does: It writes out today's date and time.

8. Press Ctrl+F5 to open the page in your default web browser. You see a page similar to the one shown in Figure 1-6.

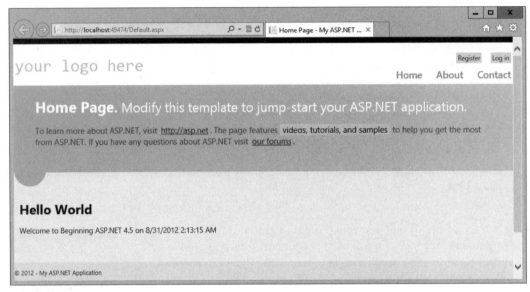

FIGURE 1-6

If you already have some experience with Visual Studio you may be used to pressing F5 instead. If you use that option, the site is opened in debug mode and you may get a dialog asking if you want to enable debugging (which you can safely do). Debugging with F5 is discussed in Chapter 18, and you're advised to use Ctrl+F5 until then.

If you see an information bar warning about intranet settings in Internet Explorer, click Turn on Intranet Settings.

If you don't see the date and time in the page, or if you get an error, look again at the code in the welcome message. It starts with an angle bracket (<) followed by a percentage symbol and a colon. It closes with a single percentage sign and another angle bracket (>). Also, make sure you typed in the code exactly as shown here, including capitalization. This is especially true when you are using C#, because that language is case sensitive.

FIGURE 1-7

9. Notice how a small icon representing *IIS Express* has appeared in the tray bar of Windows, visible in Figure 1-7.

How about English grammar? The grammatical rules are finite. Yet, you can say whatever you want using this finite set of rules. Your linguistic production is limitless, although the grammar is finite. Isn't this amazing? No matter what language we speak, we are all equipped with an amazing skill to use grammar and vocabulary in a very creative fashion. Whether or not you become a fluent Japanese speaker depends on how creatively you can manipulate the language.

Here is an example to show the importance of creativity. One of my students went to Japan and stayed with a Japanese host family. One day her stereo broke, and she needed to have it repaired. She had just begun learning Japanese, so she could not say something like, "My stereo is broken. Could you take this to a radio shop and have them repair it for me?" Instead, what she said was

> *Stereo-ga byoki desu. Isha-ga irimasu.*
>
> "The stereo is sick. It needs a doctor."

Her host family immediately understood what she meant and took it to a shop for repair.

Imagine that you suddenly get ill in Japan and need immediate assistance. You probably would have to use the words you know and try to convey your needs to other people—perhaps together with body language. Life does not always go exactly as you learn it in a textbook. This is why I emphasize creativity as a great survival skill.

Shortcuts to Success

When you start getting accustomed to basic Japanese vocabulary and grammar, try to imagine various unexpected situations and write them down, such as "At the New Tokyo International Airport, an immigration officer incorrectly identifies me as a drug smuggler. How can I convince him I am not a criminal?" Remember, you don't have to know all the words such as "criminal" or "smuggling." What you are asked to do is explain things as much as possible by using limited vocabulary and grammar. You will find this task challenging, but you will also find it a lot of fun. Try it!

Rule 5: Be Japanese!

Last, but not least, keep in mind that you must try to be or act *Japanese* when you learn the language. Language learning begins with imitation. On TV, in movies, or in actual conversations, observe how Japanese people communicate, paying attention to the way they nod, argue, laugh, complain, show their anger, and so on. Try to imitate their intonation. Your friends might find you a little eccentric, but that's okay. This will help you build another personality within yourself—a personality suitable for speaking Japanese.

The title of this chapter is "Can I *Really* Learn Japanese on My Own?" As long as you carry out the Five Golden Rules, you really can learn Japanese on your own. However, keep in mind that you need to communicate with Japanese speakers as much as possible to improve your Japanese.

How to Use This Book

So what do you think? I hope you're starting to think that learning Japanese will be fun, not intimidating. I wrote this book in a specific way so that you will be able to accomplish the Five Golden Rules mentioned previously. Here are five guidelines that you can use to accomplish the Five Golden Rules.

First, this book is organized in a step-by-step fashion, so you can grasp important grammatical and cultural concepts with confidence. Part 2 covers all the fundamental grammatical concepts. If you forget something in subsequent lessons, you can always go back to Part 2 to review these grammatical concepts.

Second, each chapter has a number of relatively easy but extremely useful expressions. I suggest that you try out those expressions on someone who knows Japanese. By doing so, you will gain confidence, gradually erase inhibitions of using the language, and get rid of fear of making mistakes.

Third, I included exercises in many chapters for you to use to self-evaluate your level of understanding and encourage your persistence. Remember, doing exercises over and over is a must for understanding the material. Make sure that you answer *aloud*, in a clear voice—no mumbling! Answering aloud will significantly improve your speaking skills and pronunciation.

Fourth, I made sure that each chapter contains new basic sentence patterns. Underline and memorize them! Mastery of these patterns is extremely important for you to improve your linguistic creativity. With this creativity, you will be able to survive in challenging situations!

Fifth, I included many sidebars. The sidebars (especially the "Green Tea Break" sidebars) give you brief but useful information about Japanese culture and behavioral psychology of Japanese people, as well as help you "Japanize" yourself.

Because the main objective of this book is to improve your conversational skills as effectively as possible, emphasis on the writing system is kept to a minimum. Examples are written in *romaji*, or romanized characters, which is the way a Japanese word would look in English—for example, *karate* and *sushi*. However, those who are interested in learning the writing system are encouraged to look at Appendix A.

The Top Ten Reasons to Learn Japanese

Still not convinced that you will conquer Japanese? Okay, then how about if I give you the top 10 reasons you should learn Japanese?

10. You want to impress a grumpy sushi master by ordering sushi with a perfect Japanese accent.

9. You fell in love with someone from Japan, but he or she does not speak English.

8. You want to be called "King of Karaoke" at a local karaoke bar.

7. You want to be a bilingual business negotiator for your company.

6. You want to try out imported PlayStation games.

5. You want to travel to Japan and broaden your horizons.

4. You're thinking about becoming a Zen master.

3. Your in-laws are Japanese.

2. You have a lot of Japanese friends, and you really want to know what they're talking about.

1. You don't know exactly *why*, but *why not?*

Whatever your reason, learning a foreign language is a rewarding experience. There are a lot of things you can do using Japanese, whether in business, your hobbies, or your personal life. Look at people around you. How many of them can speak Japanese? Not many. By having read this chapter, you're already a step ahead of the crowd. What are we waiting for? Let's get started.

The Least You Need to Know

- Learning Japanese will enrich your life in many ways.
- The keys to success in learning Japanese are confidence, courage, persistence, creativity, and imitation.
- Mistakes are positive experiences that improve your Japanese.
- As long as your interest is there, Japanese is not a difficult language to conquer.

Behind the Language

In This Chapter

- ◆ Facts beyond the language make Japanese easy to learn
- ◆ What Japanese society is like
- ◆ The psychology of the Japanese people

If you are asked what Japan is known for, you might immediately think of cars, stereos, computers, *anime*, sushi, temples, and so on. Japan is certainly known for these. But when describing the country, these things only partially and somewhat superficially suffice. Deeper knowledge of various aspects of Japan will help you learn Japanese with much more ease.

In this chapter, we will explore Japan by looking at the land, people, society, culture, and mind. The more you know about Japan, the less of a culture shock you will experience if you visit. So let's forget about the mere "images" of Japan and learn the facts.

Geographic Facts About Japan

To Westerners in the nineteenth century, Japan was as far to the east of the prime meridian—0° longitude in Greenwich, England—as one could get and still be on dry land.

The Japanese people knew that their nation was located in the Far East long before Westerners said so! In an official document that Japan sent to China in

Huh?

Kanji is a Japanese term for "Chinese characters." *Kan* means "the Han Dynasty," an ancient Chinese dynasty, and *ji* means "characters." Japanese words are written in a combination of these "foreign" characters and native Japanese characters called *kana*.

the seventh century C.E., the Japanese referred to their country as "the Land of the Rising Sun." In fact, the formal name of Japan, *Nippon* or *Nihon*, is written in *kanji* as a combination of the characters for "sun" and "origin."

Japan is an *archipelago* country—a country consisting of a chain of islands. Four main islands, Honshu, Hokkaido, Kyushu, and Shikoku, cover 95 percent of the total land area. Japan is approximately 150,000 square miles in size, slightly smaller than the state of California. Japan is not a big country, but it has 18,490 miles of coastline.

Japan is located in the Far East.

(Courtesy of the General Libraries, University of Texas at Austin)

Green Tea Break

The biggest non-Japanese population in Japan is Korean. The population of Caucasians is extremely small. Two indigenous groups are in Japan—the Ainu people residing in Hokkaido and the Ryukyu people in Okinawa. They each have their own distinctive culture. Even though they speak Japanese as well as their own languages or dialects, some of them refuse to be identified as "Japanese."

Japan.

(Courtesy of the General Libraries, University of Texas at Austin)

Lifesavers

If you live in the United States, you're accustomed to using the Fahrenheit (F) scale. In Japan, however, Celsius (C) is used. To convert Celsius to Fahrenheit, multiply degrees Celsius by 1.8, and then add 32. For example, if it's 25°C, then (25 × 1.8) + 32 = 77°F. Here's a handy conversion chart:

0°C = 32°F	25°C = 77°F
5°C = 41°F	30°C = 86°F
10°C = 50°F	35°C = 95°F
15°C = 59°F	40°C = 104°F
20°C = 68°F	

By the way, your normal body temperature in Celsius should be around 36°C. If your temperature is 40°C, call your doctor!

The population of Japan is roughly 127,000,000. Can you imagine 127,000,000 people squeezed into California? (For comparison, the population of California is 30,000,000.) Even more amazing, because more than 70 percent of Japan is mountainous, the population is concentrated in a few urban areas. There are 12 cities whose population exceeds 1,000,000. Tokyo, the capital of Japan, is the largest among those cities, with more than 8,000,000 people in its central district alone.

There are four distinct seasons almost everywhere in Japan. The winter in northern Japan is severe and snowy, but the summer is pleasantly cool. For example, in Hokkaido, the average temperature in summer is 71°F (21.7°C), and the average temperature in winter is 23°F (–4°C). On the other hand, in southern Japan, such as Kyushu, the average temperature in summer is 82°F (27.8°C), and in winter it is 50°F (10°C). If you go to Okinawa, farther south of Kyushu, you can also enjoy a Hawaiian-like vacation.

Who Are the Japanese?

Japan is geographically isolated from the Asian continent. This factor made Japan's national seclusion policy easier from the early seventeenth century to the mid-nineteenth century, which kept Japan in peace for 215 years. In turn, however, Japan had very little contact with the rest of the world. There was almost no flow of people from outside Japan until the nineteenth century. Because of this, Japan is ethnically very dense—98 percent of the residents of Japan are Japanese.

Huh?

Since the first Westerners (Portuguese) arrived in Japan in 1543, Western civilization—in the form of trading goods, weapons, and Christianity—flowed into Japan at lightning speed. The Tokugawa Shogunate government, fearful of their domestic enemies gaining power through trading with the West, closed the nation to the rest of the world in 1639. This is known as the "National Seclusion Policy." Christianity was automatically banned in Japan under this policy. It was not until 1854 that Japan came out of seclusion and opened itself to diplomatic overtures from the United States and other countries.

The majority of Japanese consider themselves "pure" Japanese. However, the Japanese race is actually a mixture of Pacific islanders and Continental Asian peoples (particularly peoples from areas such as northeastern China, the Korean Peninsula, and Mongolia). This mixture has made the Japanese language unique. The sounds of spoken Japanese resemble the Pacific languages such as Hawaiian and Tahitian, whereas the grammar of Japanese resembles the grammar of languages such as Korean, Mongolian, Manchurian, and even Turkish.

Green Tea Break

Many people think the Japanese and Chinese languages are similar. In fact, they are structurally unrelated to each other because they do not share a common linguistic ancestor. Although they might look alike, Japanese and Chinese are very different languages—far more different from one another than, say, English and German. The only important similarity is in their writing systems because the Japanese adopted characters from the Chinese around the fourth century C.E.

The Japanese Society

A society in which there are a variety of individuals and races tends to evolve into a diverse culture. The United States is a good example. Quite opposite of American society, Japanese society consists of an overwhelming majority of people from the same ethnic group—Japanese. As a result, Japanese society is very uniform and much less diverse than American society. Japanese society tends to be strongly dominated by social protocols and rituals. Getting accustomed to those protocols and rituals is crucial if you want to understand that society and its language.

Let's look at the Japanese culture in terms of interpersonal communication. When you meet a person for the first time, you must figure out who he is, what he does, what social status he has, and so on. This task is important for effective communication in Japanese: You have to adjust your greeting style and subsequent conversational style according to the social hierarchy established between you and him.

For example, there are a variety of ways of saying "I'm going," depending on who you are talking to. Here are three versions of "I'm going," ranging from a casual to a very formal style:

> *Iku.*
>
> *Ikimasu.*
>
> *Mairimasu.*

Many cultural rituals make communication smooth. You can compare this with conversation styles in American English. Casualness is typical in human interaction in a diverse society like America. You feel comfortable meeting with a stranger in a casual setting in which a conversation is carried out in an informal fashion. On the other hand, formality bears heavy weight on human interaction in a *homogeneous* society like Japan.

Living in a homogeneous society, Japanese people feel secure by being a loyal member of a rigid social structure. They feel extremely uncomfortable if placed outside their group. They try to remain in their "place" by obeying social obligations. This is illustrated by the famous old Japanese proverb, *Deru Kui-wa Utareru*—"A nail that sticks out is pounded down." This does not necessarily mean that Japanese people are exclusive or discriminating, however. Because of their group consciousness, they might not open the door to just anybody right away, but they welcome those who respect their social values and culture.

Huh?

By **homogeneous**, I mean "ethnically uniform." Japan is a homogeneous country because the majority of people living in Japan are from the same ethnic group. Note that I will use this term loosely. As I mentioned earlier, there are minority groups of different ethnicity in Japan, too.

In Chapter 1, I said that it is extremely important to "Japanize" yourself if you want to master Japanese. By "Japanize," I mean that you need to become Japanese in thought. You probably know why by now. The most effective way to learn the language is to immerse yourself in the society. If you are resistant to adjusting your way of thinking, you probably will not be able to learn as much as you want to. Try not to compare the Japanese way of thinking to your own standards and be critical about it. Be open-minded to and accepting of the way Japanese people behave.

Communication for Peace and Harmony

The most important characteristic of the Japanese mind is "group consciousness." Having been isolated from the rest of the world for a long period of time, Japan still remains an almost perfectly homogeneous society. Wherever the Japanese go within their country, they see people who resemble them in looks as well as behavior. So to live in peace and harmony, the Japanese developed certain communication strategies. Here are three important principles that you should keep in mind for better communication in Japanese.

Principle 1: No Matter Whom You Talk to, It's Safe to Be Polite

For people like you who want to learn Japanese, it's extremely important to give Japanese people the best possible impression. With a good first impression, they are more likely to help you learn the language. Of course, the Japanese also have casual speech, which they use every day among friends and family members. In fact, because of its wide usage, some Japanese teachers teach their students very casual, informal Japanese. But I don't agree with this. If you were a kid who wanted to be immersed in school right away, sure, this would not be a bad idea at all.

However, I suspect most readers of this book are mature adults. Unlike kids whose first Japanese language encounter might be other kids who speak informal (and impolite) Japanese, chances are that you will encounter a variety of people in Japan—businesspeople, teachers, home-stay families, immigration officers (!), and so on. If I were you, I wouldn't risk being mistaken for an obnoxious, impolite foreigner by picking up this informal form. Another reason I emphasize polite Japanese is because the conjugation of this form is far easier than that of casual speech.

Shortcuts to Success

You might have noticed that Japanese people often say *eh* or *hai* during conversation. Besides "yes"—the common definition of these words—*eh* and *hai* also mean "I am listening to you." Try saying these words as you listen to people. It will make the conversation go more smoothly. Frequent use of these expressions does not mean you agree with who you are speaking with, so don't worry!

Principle 2: Be Humble When Talking—a Good Listener Is a Better Communicator

Japanese people value humility. Remember the proverb "A nail that sticks out is pounded down"? The Japanese are extremely conscious of how they are perceived by other people and behave accordingly so that they will not stand out in a crowd. This characteristic is reflected in verbal communication as well. Japanese people tend to be receptive (and often passive) in communication to avoid confrontation.

In Western societies, verbal communication is active and people are trained to be good at argument and discussion. I remember my college experiences during my first couple of years in the States. I was very uncomfortable being in a discussion group or debate. As a result, I remained silent. My speech professor used to tell me that in America, if you don't speak up, people think you are dumb. It required a lot of courage for me to "speak up." Likewise, you might want to be conscious of your communication style when you speak Japanese. For Japanese, one needs to be less argumentative, even if you're in a disagreement with someone. Try to find agreeable points in your opponent's argument, admire them, and don't be afraid to accept his ideas. You might be amazed at how smoothly your conversations will follow.

Principle 3: Know the *TPO!*

TPO stands for T(ime), P(lace), and O(ccasion):

> **T:** A good speaker knows whether it is the *right time* to say something.
>
> **P:** A good speaker knows whether he or she is in the *right place* with the right audience.
>
> **O:** A good speaker knows whether it is the *right situation* to talk about something.

TPO is synonymous with "courteousness" or "good manners." TPO is the key to success in any language, but especially in Japanese. Japan is a group-conscious society, so speaking in front of the right audience is particularly important. Just make sure that you look around before you speak. Is it the *right time* to say something? That is, are you speaking in turn, not surpassing anybody? Is it the *right place* to say something? That is, are you talking to the right audience? And, are you in the *right situation* to say something? That is, is the situation appropriate?

TPO is meant to help you become aware of the significance of relative social standing. It is *not* to discourage you from speaking up! Just by trying to be modest and paying attention to the situation surrounding you, you can successfully converse in Japanese if you adhere to this principle.

Merely learning Japanese grammar will make you an okay speaker, but knowing the rules of Japanese behavior will make you a better speaker. By being aware of the importance of behavior, your Japanese will sound more "Japanese."

The Least You Need to Know

- ◆ Deeper knowledge of Japan—including familiarity with Japanese geographical, demographical, and psychological facts—will make you a better speaker.

- ◆ Japan is an almost completely homogeneous society; group consciousness is woven throughout every aspect of social life.

- ◆ You will appear and sound natural if you conduct yourself and speak in harmony with the Japanese ways of thinking and behaving.

- ◆ What are the secrets of success in learning Japanese? Be polite! Be receptive! Be conscious of *TPO!*

Japanese Sounds: As Easy as *A, I, U, E, O*

In This Chapter

◆ Japanese sounds are simple!

◆ Become accustomed to Japanese syllables

◆ Difficult sounds for English speakers

◆ Japanese is a *calm* language

Unlike many commonly taught foreign languages, Japanese has a quite simple sound inventory. Japanese has only 14 *consonants* and 5 *vowels*; on the other hand, English has 24 consonants (including the semi-vowels, *y* and *w*) and although it, too, has 5 vowels, it has at least 12 vowel sounds. This is encouraging news for English-speaking students because most Japanese sounds are already in the English sound inventory. On the other hand, many Japanese speakers struggle with English pronunciation because they have to deal with many sounds that don't exist in their language.

Even though Japanese sounds are fairly simple, I don't think it's a good idea to underestimate them, especially when you've just started learning Japanese. Unfortunately, many Japanese textbooks don't tell readers how the Japanese sound system is organized. But without a clear understanding of it, how can you speak and understand Japanese properly?

Huh? _____

Consonants are speech sounds that are characterized by constriction or obstruction of airflow at varying points of the mouth or throat. For example, *t* is a consonant because to pronounce it you use the tongue to block airflow at the edge of the mouth between the upper teeth and the gum.

Vowels are speech sounds that are produced without any obstruction of airflow in the mouth. For example, *i* is a vowel because to pronounce it you push air forward and out smoothly, without using your tongue.

In this chapter, you learn the basics of Japanese pronunciation, including the organization of the sound inventory, vowel lengthening, and accent patterns.

Keep Your Mouth Open, Please: Syllabication

Japanese *syllables* are almost always open-ended. What this means is that they always (with two exceptions—see the following "The Two Standalone Consonants" section) end in a vowel, not a consonant.

In Japanese, a possible syllable is composed of either a vowel alone, like *a, i, u, e, o,* or a consonant plus a vowel, as in *ka, ki, ku, ke, ko.* Each syllable has the same length. Because Japanese has such a restricted sound structure, only 102 syllables are possible in the entire Japanese sound inventory.

Shortcuts to Success _____

Throughout this chapter, and throughout the rest of this book, make sure that you articulate aloud all Japanese words, phrases, and sentences. Never read them silently. Perception of a sound is *not* the same as production of a sound. Clear articulation is the most effective way to make your brain recognize sounds as Japanese sounds. Silent reading does not activate your brain, as numerous research experiments have shown. I also emphasize this method from my own experience. My English learning was awful when I first started studying—because of my silent reading.

Keeping the Japanese style of syllabication in mind is important not only for learning vocabulary, but also for pronunciation. Because each syllable ends with a vowel, they are considered to have the same "weight"—that is, all Japanese syllables sound as though they have the same length.

Let's look at an example. The word *karaoke* has four syllables in Japanese (*ka-ra-o-ke*) and four syllables in English (*car-rie-oh-key*). In Japanese, each syllable sounds as though it has exactly the same length as the others. The syllables are short and open. If you have ever taken a music lesson, you must have seen a metronome—a device that assists a musician's timing by clicking in a perfectly uniform fashion: click, click, click. Japanese syllables are just like the clicks made by a metronome: *ka-ra-o-ke*. On the other hand, English syllables are not characterized by the same length. Listen to the English pronunciation: *car-rie-oh-key*. Perhaps you can hear the slight difference in length between "oh" and "key." Listen to the irregular length of the syllables in other examples like *Eng-lish* or *Jap-a-nese*. Hear the long "nese"?

If you want to sound like a Japanese person, keep your syllables short and even. You might practice Japanese syllables by clapping your hands or snapping your fingers to make sure each syllable is equal in length.

Remember that Japanese syllables are open-ended with vowels. This will help in your pronunciation because it means that your mouth remains open at the end of each sound. In other words, in Japanese your mouth is relaxed when speaking. If you watch Japanese people speak, pay attention to how they move their mouths. You will be surprised by how little their mouths move. This is because of open-ended syllables. To sound Japanese, just relax, try not to move your mouth too much, and keep it open.

Huh?

A **syllable** is a unit of spoken language that consists of a vowel or a vowel-like consonant alone, or a vowel or a vowel-like consonant pronounced with one or more consonant sounds before or after. For instance, the word *consonant* is divided into three syllables—*con-so-nant*.

Green Tea Break

Karaoke is a coined compound word that consists of *kara* and *oke*. Kara means "empty," and *oke* is a shortened word for *ōkesutora*, "orchestra." The result is "empty orchestra"! A clever compound, isn't it? The Japanese not only like adopting Western words but also shortening them—as in dejikame (shortened from *dejitaru kamera*), "digital camera," and hebimeta (shortened from *hebi metaru*), "heavy metal."

All the Possible Japanese Sounds

Following are tables of all possible Japanese syllables and sounds. (The five vowels *a, e, i, o, u* are traditionally listed in the order of *a, i, u, e, o* in Japanese.) Before we look at the tables, let's make sure that you can pronounce each vowel correctly. The five Japanese vowels always make the same five sounds:

[a] is pronounced *ah*, as in English "f<u>a</u>ther."

[i] is pronounced *ee*, as in English "h<u>e</u>."

[u] is pronounced *oo*, as in English "c<u>oo</u>l."

[e] is pronounced *eh*, as in English "b<u>e</u>t."

[o] is pronounced *oh*, as in English "b<u>o</u>re."

Shortcuts to Success

When you pronounce Japanese vowels, try not to open your mouth too wide. By relaxing your mouth, you will be able to pronounce Japanese sounds naturally.

Each sound in the following tables is made by combining a consonant in the top column with a vowel in the leftmost row. For example, when the consonant *k* meets the vowel *i*, it is pronounced *ki*. (ø means that no consonant is attached; these are plain vowels.)

The Japanese Sounds

Track 3
CD-1

	ø	k	s	t	n	h	m	y	r	w
a	a	ka	sa	ta	na	ha	ma	ya	ra	wa
i	i	ki	shi	chi	ni	hi	mi		ri	
u	u	ku	su	tsu	nu	fu	mu	yu	ru	
e	e	ke	se	te	ne	he	me			re
o	o	ko	so	to	no	ho	mo	yo	ro	

	g	z	d	b	p
a	ga	za	da	ba	pa
i	gi	ji		bi	pi
u	gu	zu		bu	pu
e	ge	ze	de	be	pe
o	go	zo	do	bo	po

	ky	sh	ch	ny	hy	my	ry
a	kya	sha	cha	nya	hya	mya	rya
u	kyu	shu	chu	nyu	hyu	myu	ryu
o	kyo	sho	cho	nyo	hyo	myo	ryo

	gy	j (= zy)		by	py
a	gya	ja		bya	pya
u	gyu	ju		byu	pyu
o	gyo	jo		byo	pyo

ah
ee
oo
eh
oh

In traditional Japanese grammar, the Japanese sounds are divided into four separate tables as seen previously. The sounds in the first table are considered "basic" sounds. The second table contains "relatives" of some of the sounds in the first table. **G** is a relative of **k,** **z** of **s, d** of **t,** and **b** and **p** are relatives of **h.**
(In ancient Japanese, the **h** sounded similar to **p,** the "lip" sound.) The third table contains **y** on some of the basic sounds, and the fourth table contains **y** on the sounds in the second table.

Another reason why the Japanese sounds are represented in four separate tables is that Japanese kana characters are best illustrated this way (see Appendix A).

Shortcuts to Success

There are some blanks in the tables, lacking sounds like *yi, ye, wi, wu, we, wo, di,* and *du.* These sounds do not exist in Japanese. For example, *yi* is pronounced the same as *i,* and *du* as *zu.*

The Two Standalone Consonants

In addition to the consonants discussed in the previous section, Japanese has two standalone consonants. A *standalone consonant* is a syllable that does not accompany a vowel. In Japanese, there are only two standalone consonants—the double consonant and *N.* Both are discussed later in the following "Tricky Sounds" section.

Shortcuts to Success

When *y* accompanies a consonant, as in *ky,* the only possible vowels that can be added after the *y* are *a, u,* and *o.*

Tricky Sounds

Although you can accurately pronounce most of the sounds just as they are spelled, there are some tricky sounds, such as the following.

tsu

Pronounce *tsu* just like the English *ts* in *ca<u>ts</u>.* Try the following word:

Track 3
CD-2

    <u>tsu</u>nami

fu

Unlike the English *f* sound, you don't bite your lower lip to make this sound in Japanese. To pronounce this sound, imagine that you're blowing out a candle. This sound is pronounced somewhere between the English *h* and *f* sounds. Try the following word:

Track 3
CD-3

    <u>F</u>ujita   "Fujita (name of the author of this book)"

ra, ri, ru, re, ro

The Japanese *r* is by no means identical to the English *r*. When you make the *r* sound, try to lightly tap the back of your upper front teeth with the tip of your tongue. *Never* curl back the tip of your tongue as you do in English! For example, say "bu<u>tt</u>er" very fast. This *tt* sound is very close to the Japanese *r*. The English upper-class pronunciation of "ve<u>r</u>y" is also close to the Japanese *r*. Try the following words:

Track 3
CD-4–8

<u>r</u>aisu	"rice"
<u>r</u>isa	"Lisa"
hote<u>r</u>u	"hotel"
<u>r</u>efuto	"left"
pu<u>r</u>o	"pro(fessional)"

Position of the tongue for Japanese r *(left) and English* r *(right).*

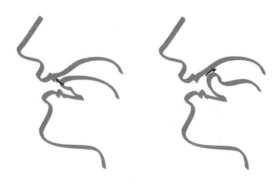

wa

Unlike the English *w*, you don't round your lips when making this Japanese sound. Relax your mouth and keep it half open. Try the following word:

Track 3
CD-9

<u>w</u>atashi   "I; me"

y

In the preceding tables, you see a number of two-consonant sounds containing *y*, such as *kya*, *pyo*. Even though there are two consonants, this chunk of sounds is still considered one syllable. Try to pronounce them in one quick breath—"kya," "pyo"—instead of making two syllables, like "ki-ya" and "pi-yo." Try the following words:

Track 3
CD-10–12

<u>kya</u>Ndoru *(kya-N-do-ru)* (four syllables)   "candle"

<u>hya</u>ku *(hya-ku)* (two syllables)   "hundred"

<u>pyo</u>N<u>pyo</u>N *(pyo-N-pyo-N)* (four syllables)   "hopping"

The Double Consonant

This standalone consonant is a silent sound. You might ask how Japanese can make a silent sound. English has this sound, too. Consider *Uh oh!* Between *Uh* and *oh*, there is a slight pause. The Japanese double consonant is like this slight pause. Look at the following words:

Track 3
CD-13–14

> *ba<u>tt</u>o (ba-t-to)* (three syllables)   "(baseball) bat"
>
> *po<u>pp</u>u (po-p-pu)* (three syllables)   "pop"

Both examples have three syllables, but the actual pronunciation can be described as follows:

> bat-to
>
> pop-pu

Again, the hyphen indicates a momentary break between the syllables.

Remember, this is a standalone consonant, so it carries the same length as a syllable. Make sure that you are able to distinguish *ki<u>tt</u>e*, "stamp," from *kite*, "Come!" The former word has three syllables, and the latter only two.

N

This is also a standalone consonant, which carries the same length as an ordinary syllable. The way you make this sound is quite different from the "regular" *n*. You know that in order to pronounce the regular *n*, the tip of your tongue touches the back of the upper teeth (actually, the edge between the teeth and the gum). On the other hand, pronunciation of this standalone *n* (represented in this book by a capital letter, *N*) requires that your tongue touch *nowhere* in the mouth. The sound is actually made in the throat. Try the following words:

 Lifesavers

> When a vowel follows *N*, make sure that *N* is pronounced separately from the following vowel! For example, one of the common male names, *Shinichi*, is pronounced *Shi-N-i-chi*, not *Shi-ni-chi* (four syllables vs. three syllables). In some cases, this might lead to miscommunication. For example, *shi-N-a-i* means "dear," but *shi-na-i* means "bamboo sword."

Track 3
CD-15–17

> *ho<u>N</u>da (ho-N-da)* (three syllables)   "Honda"
>
> *ko<u>N</u>nichiwa (ko-N-ni-chi-wa)*   (five syllables)   "hello; good afternoon"
>
> *ko<u>N</u>ba<u>N</u>wa (ko-N-ba-N-wa)*   (five syllables)   "good evening"

Please keep in mind that this standalone *N* never appears at the beginning of a word. Throughout this book, the first character of a Japanese word is always written with an uppercase letter. If you see the uppercase *N* at the beginning of any word, it should be pronounced as the regular *n*, not the standalone *N*.

I strongly suggest that you read all the examples aloud in the subsequent chapters, paying attention to the preceding sounds (especially the *r* sound). Remember, silent reading is a waste of time in language learning. *GaNbatte (Ga-N-bat-te)*—"Good luck!"

My Husband Is a Prisoner? Importance of Long Vowels

In Japanese, there are both short and long vowels. A long vowel should be clearly pronounced exactly twice as long as a short vowel.

The length of a vowel is very important. Compare the following pairs. (Note that the macron symbol [¯] indicates a long vowel.)

Track 3
CD-18–19

shujiN (three syllables)   "husband"
shu-ji-N
shūjiN (four syllables)   "prisoner"
shu-u-ji-N

The only difference between *shujin* and *shūjin* is the length of the vowel *u*, but the meaning is so different between the two! (What? No difference?) Here are a few more similar pairs:

Track 3
CD-20–23

obasaN (four syllables)   "aunt"
o-ba-sa-N
obāsaN (five syllables)   "grandmother"
o-ba-a-sa-N
ojisaN (four syllables)   "uncle"
o-ji-sa-N
ojī-sa-N (five syllables)   "grandfather"
o-ji-i-sa-N
Kite! (two syllables)   "Come!"
Ki-te
Kīte! (three syllables)   "Listen!"
Ki-i-te
nyūyoku (four syllables)   "bathing"
nyu-u-yo-ku
nyūyōku (five syllables)   "New York"
nyu-u-yo-o-ku

Remember, Japanese rhythm is uniform, just like a metronome. Practice these pairs by clapping your hands or snapping your fingers to maintain the same interval between syllables.

Japanizing English Words

Japanese words are not cognate to English words, but even as you begin to learn Japanese, you might find some words that are familiar to you. Those words are called *loan words*. Japanese has a lot of Western loan words called *gairaigo*, the majority of which have been borrowed from English.

Huh?

A **loan word** is a word imported from another language's word inventory. In Japanese, there are two types of loan words—*gairaigo* (words that come from Western languages, especially English) and *kango* (words that come from Chinese). Most of *gairaigo* is relatively new to Japanese, whereas the history of *kango* is much longer. Some of the oldest *kango* are probably 1,600 years old.

This is good news for you because it increases your chances that Japanese people will understand common English nouns that you say. But when it comes to you hearing English-based loan words in Japanese, it isn't always good news. Those words are so "Japanized" that they might not sound like English at all.

Because Japanese has fewer sounds than English, many English sounds must be substituted with the closest-possible Japanese sounds. Here are those sounds with substitution examples:

- **L**   English *l* is replaced by *r* in Japanese. So both *blues* and *Bruce* are pronounced as *burūsu*.

- **TH**   English *th* is replaced by *s* or *z* in Japanese. The words *third* and *that* are pronounced as *sādo* and *zatto*, respectively. You might have heard the Japanese saying *saNkyū* for "Thank you."

- **V**   English *v* is replaced by *b* in Japanese. For example, *violin* is pronounced *baioriN*. Both *vest* and *best* are pronounced *besuto*.

- **F**   English *f* is replaced by the Japanese version of *f*. The Japanese *f* does not involve biting the lower lip. Instead, it's somewhere between an *f* and an *h*, very much like the light puff of breath used to blow out a candle. In certain English dialects (like the Southern accent in America), *wh* as in *what* or *which* sounds like the Japanese *f*. Try to pronounce the following words without biting the lower lip: *faN* ("fan"), *fiNraNdo* ("Finland"), *fuji-saN* ("Mt. Fuji"), *kafe* ("café"), *fōku* ("fork" or "folk").

Because of the sound discrepancies between English and Japanese, when it comes to pronunciation, sometimes it's safer and less stressful to regard English-based loan words *not* as English words. Actually, they're on permanent loan, and they're not going to be returned. Most important, when you pronounce English-based loan words, be sure that you obey the following rules:

- ◆ Use Japanese sounds.
- ◆ Attach a vowel to a consonant.
- ◆ Do not use English accents.

Keeping these rules in mind, would you like to try "Japanizing" the following common food-related loan words? Don't look at the answers too quickly!

English Words in Japanese Pronunciation

English Words	"Japanized" Pronunciation
beer	*bīru (bi-i-ru)*
hamburger	*haNbāgā (ha-N-ba-a-ga-a)*
steak	*sutēki (su-te-e-ki)*
soup	*sūpu (su-u-pu)*
salad	*sarada (sa-ra-da)*
dressing	*doresshiNgu (do-re-s-shi-N-gu)*
knife	*naifu (na-i-fu)*
spoon	*supūN (su-pu-u-N)*
fork	*fōku (fo-o-ku)*
plate	*purēto (pu-re-e-to)*
menu	*menyū (me-nyu-u)*
juice	*jūsu (ju-u-su)*
coffee	*kōhī (ko-o-hi-i)*
cola	*kōra (ko-o-ra)*
desert	*dezāto (de-za-a-to)*
cake	*kēki (ke-e-ki)*

Japanese Is a Calm Language

Every language has its unique intonation pattern, and this characteristic makes a language sound musical, strong, harsh, mellow, and so on. To me, English sounds very rhythmical.

This rhythmic characteristic arises from the pattern of strong and weak accents. Even within a word like *television*, there are two accents:

   tél-e-vì-sion

In "television," *tel* has the primary accent, *vi* has the secondary accent, and the syllables *e* and *sion* carry no accents. This regular sequence between an accented syllable and a non-accented syllable makes English very rhythmical.

What do you think about Japanese? How does Japanese sound to you? Does it sound as rhythmical as English? It probably doesn't. Japanese words don't carry as regular an accent-nonaccent sequence as heard in English. Instead, Japanese words are pronounced in a rather monotone, flat fashion. For example, take a look at the words *Yokohama* and *konnichiwa* ("hello"). English speakers tend to pronounce these words like this:

   Yò-ko-há-ma (*há* = primary accent, *Yò* = secondary accent)

   kon-ní-chi-wà (*ní* = primary accent, *wà* = secondary accent)

To Japanese ears, these pronunciations would sound heavily accented. If you want to speak Japanese like the Japanese, first try to forget the English accent pattern, and then *calmly* say the words while maintaining the same length on each syllable.

Track 3
CD-40–41

   Yo-ko-ha-ma

   Ko-N-ni-chi-wa

Lifesavers

Count yourself lucky that Japanese intonation is not like Chinese or Thai, which are strongly tonal languages. In Chinese, depending on what intonation contours you have, a word like *ma* could mean "horse," "mother," "scold," or "hemp"! Of course, there is intonation in Japanese, too, but it is not as strict as in Chinese. As long as you pronounce words clearly and with a much flatter intonation than English, you will be understood.

Some impersonators are amazingly good at sounding just like someone else. But this doesn't mean that they have special vocal cords. They first listen very carefully to people over and over, trying to figure out their intonation, pitch, and pronunciation. Then, they imitate those distinctive patterns.

Shortcuts to Success

One of my students had a very strong accent when speaking Japanese. To help him fix this problem, I told him to "turn down the volume a little bit." The result was incredible. Even he could not believe himself! So if you're a loud speaker, try this method. Even if you aren't, it's worth giving it a try because toning down the volume results in less movement of the mouth, which is essential in articulating natural Japanese sounds.

Language learning is exactly the same as what impersonators do. Listen carefully to how Japanese people talk. If there is no one who speaks Japanese around you, rent a Japanese video. You don't have to try to understand what they say. Close your eyes and concentrate on just listening. Listen to the CD included with this book, and keep listening until you're confident that you can say those phrases like a native Japanese speaker. This will not only improve your oral/aural skills, it will also give you confidence.

The Least You Need to Know

♦ Japanese syllables are uniform in length. Except for two special consonants, the *N* and the double consonant, all syllables are open-ended with a vowel.

♦ Among the 102 Japanese syllables, you should pay special attention to *tsu, fu, ra, ri, ru, re, ro, wa*, double consonants, and *N*.

♦ A long vowel should be clearly pronounced exactly twice as long as a short vowel.

♦ Don't be controlled by your native language when speaking Japanese! Become familiar with Japanese pronunciation and try to eliminate accenting syllables. To do this, avoid putting strong stresses on words and speak calmly.

Part 2

The Survival Skills: Grammar

Language learning can be like mountain climbing. For a fun and safe experience, you must be prepared and fully equipped with all the necessary things, such as food, warm clothing, a sturdy ice ax, rope, and so on.

Like mountain climbing, a new language is full of unexpected events. Besides greetings and idioms, people might not speak exactly the same way you do, nor use exactly the same phrases or words. So how can you be prepared for such unexpected events? The answer is simple: You must be fully equipped, and the most basic, necessary tool is grammar.

With an overview of the grammar, you will be able to not only construct sentences but also understand newly introduced patterns. I guarantee that after carefully going through these chapters, you will find the rest of this book much easier. For those who think grammar is dry and unappealing, I have gone to great efforts to make these chapters as simple and informative as possible.

Speak Like Yoda: Basic Sentence Structure

In This Chapter

- Japanese as a "free word order" language
- Functions of particles
- The concept of topic
- Dropping phrases

"Do or do not, there is no try!"
—Yoda

I'm a big fan of Yoda, a revered Jedi master in the *Star Wars* saga. When George Lukas created this character, he must have had an Asian hermit in mind. Yoda's word order is a little *different*. If Yoda were the author of this book, he would probably say something like, "*Today, something teach you I will. Grammar that is. Ready are you?*"

Was the language model for Yoda Chinese or Japanese? Chinese word order is similar to English word order; Yoda would not speak like that. I think that the language model for Yoda is Japanese. If I translate Japanese into English as literally as I can, it sounds like something Yoda would say.

A bizarre word order in one language might be a perfectly normal word order in another. In this chapter, let's see what Japanese sentences really "look" like. Ready are you? You will be!

Godzilla Ate John, or John Ate Godzilla?

The English language has what is known as a fixed word order. That is, every sentence is arranged in pretty much the same fashion, with the sequence of subject-verb-object. Let's look at the following English example to illustrate a fixed word order:

John gave sushi to Lisa.

If you're a native speaker of English—if you are not Yoda—you probably don't say something like "To Lisa sushi John gave," even though it might make sense (meaning "John gave sushi to Lisa," of course). How about using a different word order, such as "Sushi gave to Lisa John"? Does this mean "John gave sushi to Lisa"? No, this is just gibberish!

In Japanese, however, you can "scramble" words pretty much in any order you like, and this scrambled sentence still means "John gave sushi to Lisa." Let me translate this English sentence into Japanese (*age-mashita* = "gave"):

John-ga Lisa-ni sushi-o age-mashita.	"John to Lisa sushi gave."
John-ga sushi-o Lisa-ni age-mashita.	"John sushi to Lisa gave."
Lisa-ni John-ga sushi-o age-mashita.	"To Lisa John sushi gave."
Lisa-ni sushi-o John-ga age-mashita.	"To Lisa sushi John gave."
Sushi-o John-ga Lisa-ni age-mashita.	"Sushi John to Lisa gave."
Sushi-o Lisa-ni John-ga age-mashita.	"Sushi to Lisa John gave."

Wow! Isn't it amazing? As long as the *verb* stays at the end of the sentence, you can scramble all the other items, and they remain perfectly grammatical! The sentence structure of Japanese is characterized (very basically) by the following statement:

In Japanese, the verb comes last.

A Quick Grammar Review

A quick grammar review might be in order before we talk more about Japanese sentence structure. Don't worry—we don't need to get into a lot of terminology here! We'll keep all definitions on the simplest level.

As you might recall from your grammar class, every sentence is made up of two main parts—a subject and a predicate. The subject is the person, idea, animal, or thing being described; the predicate is the explanation of the action of the subject. Subjects are usually nouns; predicates are usually verbs and the words that go with them to modify the noun. So in the sentence …

John gave sushi to Lisa.

... the predicate is "gave sushi to Lisa." The verb (gave) modifies the subject (John). A good way to find the subject of a sentence, in fact, is to locate the verb and ask who or what is performing the verb's action. In this case, who or what "gave"? The answer is "John." Therefore, "John" is the subject of the sentence.

"John" is also the subject of the following three sentences. Notice that in addition to the verb, the predicate can contain adjectives and nouns as well:

John *ate pizza.*

John *is tall.*

John *is a student.*

The sentence "John gave sushi to Lisa" also provides a helpful refresher on the role of direct and indirect objects. The object of a sentence, in simplest terms (there are some exceptions), is the noun that is *directly* affected by the verb. "John gave," but what did he give? The answer is "sushi," so "sushi" is the direct object.

The indirect object (again, in simplest terms) is the person or thing to whom something is given, said, or shown. It is the noun that is *indirectly* affected by the verb. "John gave sushi," but to whom or what did he give it? The answer is "Lisa," so "Lisa" is the indirect object in this sentence.

Here's an easy way to tell direct and indirect objects apart in English: Indirect objects usually have a *preposition* in front of them (as in "John gave sushi *to* Lisa"), whereas direct objects don't have one (for example, "John ate *pizza*").

Don't worry if you're a little rusty in this area. As you read through the exercises in this book, you'll get stronger at instinctively recognizing the relationship of the nouns to the verbs in a sentence. And, as you'll find out later in this chapter, you sometimes don't even have to include all the nouns in a sentence to be understood!

Huh?

A **preposition** is a connecting word that shows the relationship of a noun or pronoun to some other word in a sentence.

Particles

Did you notice in all of our *"John-ga Lisa-ni sushi-o age-mashita"* examples, that some tiny suffixes were attached to the nouns, such as *-o, -ga, -ni?* Thanks to these markers, we don't get confused no matter what order the nouns are used in a sentence. In a sentence with only two nouns, scrambling the words could be confusing in English:

John Godzilla ate.

Godzilla John ate.

In either case, it isn't clear who did the eating and who got eaten! But the tiny markers make any arrangement in Japanese perfectly clear:

> *Godzilla-ga John-o tabe-mashita.* "Godzilla ate John."
>
> *John-o Godzilla-ga tabe-mashita.* "Godzilla ate John."

The good news is that word order is flexible. The not-so-good news is that a sentence conveys a totally different meaning if you attach a wrong marker to a word, so you have to be diligent about learning particles. Who is the poor victim, John or Godzilla? Whoever it might be, one tiny particle makes a huge difference! Let's learn more about particles.

Particles: Tiny but Mighty!

Learning Japanese will be much easier if you familiarize yourself with those helpful markers called particles. (They're called "particles," as in chemistry, because they're so tiny.) Bear in mind that every noun must accompany the appropriate particle in a Japanese sentence. In other words, particles are noun markers that reveal the relationship of the attached noun to the verb.

Here is a list of important particles. These are not all the particles, but the most basic.

Basic Particles

Particle	Function
-ga	subject marker
-o	object marker
-ni	"toward"; "in" (existence marker)
-mo	"also"
-kara	"from"
-made	"up to"; "until"
-de	"by means of"; "in; at" (activity marker)
-to	"together with"
-wa	topic marker

As I mentioned earlier, each of these particles is attached to a noun, and this noun with the particle indicates its grammatical relation to the verb. Let's look at each particle in depth.

-ga: Subject Marker

"Subject," as I discussed previously, means someone or something of which something is said. The subject particle *-ga* is used in the following three cases:

- ◆ Identification of "doer"
- ◆ Someone/something that exists in a certain location
- ◆ Description of an unexpected or surprising event

Identification of "Doer"

By "doer," I mean a person who causes something to happen. If John throws the ball to Tom, John is the doer (or "subject"), so "John" would get the subject marker *-ga*, as in *John-ga*. Let's consider a simpler sentence. The sentence "John cried" would be …

Track 4
CD-1

> *JoN-ga naki-mashita.*   "John cried."

Look at another example:

> *JoN-ga tabe-mashita.*   "John ate."

Track 4
CD-2

John is the doer of "crying" in the first example, and of "eating" in the second example. Therefore, we attach *-ga* to it.

Someone/Something That Exists in a Certain Location

In English, when you describe someone or something being in a certain location, you use the phrase *there is/are*, such as "*There is a boy in the park*," or "*There are vases in the room*." I will call these verbs "existence verbs." In Japanese, the equivalent existence verbs are *i-masu* and *ari-masu*. When you describe someone or something being in a certain place, the person or thing is marked by *-ga*.

Huh?

Use *i-masu* when referring to the existence of something "animate" (for example, John, person, dog, and so on), and use **ari-masu** when referring to the existence of something "inanimate" (for example, pizza, pencil, and so on).

Track 4
CD 3–4

> *JoN-ga i-masu.*   "John is there."
> *Piza-ga ari-masu.*   "There is pizza."

Description of an Unexpected or Surprising Event

When you want to describe something unexpected or surprising happening, attach *-ga* to the event noun. First, consider such events in English. When you see the bus coming earlier than the scheduled time, you alert your friend by saying, "*Here comes the bus!*" This is expressed in Japanese as follows:

Track 4
CD-5–7

> *Basu-ga ki-mashita!* "(*Lit.*) The bus came!"

Consider another example. Suppose the lights go out. This unexpected event would be described as follows:

> *Raito-ga kie-mashita!* "The lights went out!"
> (*kie-masu* = "go out")

Huh? _____

An **adjective** is a word that describes, or modifies, a noun. For example, in the phrase a *smart dog* and the sentence *My dog is <u>smart!</u>* "smart" is an adjective because it describes the noun "dog."

The preceding examples contain verbs ("come" and "go out"); however, an unexpected or surprising event can be described by an *adjective* as well. Suppose that you go to a pizza parlor in Tokyo and are surprised at its outrageous prices. This would be described in Japanese as follows:

Piza-ga taka-idesu! "Pizza is expensive!"
(*taka-idesu* = "is expensive")

-o: Object Marker

"Object," as discussed earlier, means someone or something that is affected by a certain action. So in *John ate pizza*, "pizza" is the object of "ate," and in *John loves Lisa*, "Lisa" is the object of "loves." An object noun is marked by *-o*, as in the following examples:

Track 4
CD-8–9

> *Piza-o tabe-te!* "Eat pizza!"
>
> *JoN-ga Tomu-o shikari-mashita.* "John scolded Tom."

-ni: "toward"; "in"

This particle has two major functions. One function is to show "destination," which is equivalent to *toward* in English.

Track 4
CD-10–11

> *JoN-ga Pari-ni iki-masu.* "John will go to Paris."
>
> *JoN-ni piza-o age-te!* "Give the pizza to John!"

Notice that in these examples, Paris is the destination of "going" and John is the destination of "giving (pizza)."

The other function is to specify the location in which someone/something exists. This is equivalent to the English *in*.

Track 4
CD-12–13

*JoN-ga kicchiN-**ni** i-masu.*   "John is in the kitchen."
*Piza-ga furīzā-**ni** ari-masu.*   "There is pizza in the freezer."

-mo: "also"

The particle *-mo* means "also." If you want to put "also" on the subject noun, as in *Tom also came*, mark the subject noun with *-mo* instead of the subject marker *-ga*. This is illustrated as follows:

Track 4
CD-14

*JoN-ga ki-mashita. Tomu-**mo** ki-mashita.*   "John came. Tom **also** came."

If you want to put "also" on the object noun, as in *Order fried chicken also*, mark the object noun with *-mo* instead of the object marker *-o*. This is illustrated as follows:

Track 4
CD-15

*Piza-o tanoN-de! Furaido chikiN-**mo** tanoN-de!*
"Order pizza! Order fried chicken, **too!**"

Huh?

The particle *-mo* ("also") replaces the subject particle *-ga* and the object particle *-o*. However, for particles other than subject and object markers, *-mo* is simply added on to the particle:

*JoN-ga Yokohama-ni iki-mashita. Hiroshima-ni-**mo** iki-mashita.*
"John went to Yokohama. He also went to Hiroshima."

Notice that the particle *-ni* remains with *-mo*.

-kara: "from" / -made: "up to"; "until"

The particles *-kara* and *-made* are the same as the English prepositions "from" and "until," respectively. The only difference is, of course, that in Japanese these particles are not *pre*positions, but *post*positions, and they are attached at the end of nouns, just like all Japanese particles:

Track 4
CD-16–17

*JoN-ga Kurisumasu-**kara** BareNtaiNdē-**made** Hawai-ni i-masu.*
"John will be in Hawaii from Christmas to Valentine's Day."

Note that *-made* also means "up to," referring to the destination of some action such as "going." It is similar to the particle *-ni*, but *-made* implies that you do not go beyond that point. *-Kara* and *-made* are often used in a pair, as seen in the next example:

*JoN-ga Pari-**kara** Rōma-**made** iki-masu.*   "John will go from Paris to Rome."

-de: "by means of"; "at"

This particle has two major functions. One is to state "by means of":

Track 4
CD-18

> *JoN-ga basu-de BosutoN-ni iki-masu.* "John will go to Boston by bus."

The other function is to specify the location at which some activity takes place:

Track 4
CD-19

> *KicchiN-de beNkyō shi-te!* "Study in the kitchen."

-to: "together with"

This is straightforward and easy! You simply add *-to* to a person to show the "with" relationship:

Track 4
CD-20

JoN-ga Tomu-to Pari-ni iki-masu.
"John will go to Paris with Tom."

CAUTION
Lifesavers

Note that the other location particle *-ni* specifies "existence," not an activity.

Shortcuts to Success

Because a particle tells the listener the noun's relationship to the verb, particles should not be overlooked. When you speak, just take your time to make sure that you use the correct particles.

Some particles function the same as English prepositions, but remember again that in Japanese they are postpositions. You might need some time to get used to the subject and object markers because they are new concepts to English speakers.

We have quickly covered the basic particles. You might be wondering why I skipped one of the particles— *-wa*, the "topic" particle. I left it out on purpose because it is a very important particle that requires a section of its own for explanation.

Before talking about the "topic" particle *-wa*, how about a short review? I will give you several sentences with blanks. Fill in the appropriate particles. With the translation, you should be able to understand each sentence.

1. "John ate sushi at the restaurant with Tom."
   JoN-_____ resutoraN-_____ Tomu-_____ sushi-_____ tabe-mashita.

2. "John came from Paris."
   JoN-_____ Pari-_____ ki-mashita.

3. "Stay until Christmas!"
   Kurisumasu-_____ i-te!

4. "Please come by bus!"
   Basu-_____ ki-te!

5. "Tom came. John also came."
   Tomu-_____ ki-masita. JoN-_____ ki-mashita.

6. "John ate sushi using a fork."
   JoN-____ fōku-____ sushi-____ tabe-mashita.

How was it? Here are the answers:

1. *-ga, -de, -to, -o*
2. *-ga, -kara*
3. *-made*
4. *-de*
5. *-ga, -mo*
6. *-ga, -de, -o*

For speakers whose native language has a strict word order, it will take some time to get used to the idea of attaching a particle to every noun. However, when you become accustomed, the rest is easy. You can say a sentence pretty much in "free" word order as long as you put the verb at the end.

In a sense, Japanese is an easy language because the word order is not rigid. Don't be afraid. Speak out! You will be amazed at how much Japanese you speak that will be understood by Japanese people.

The Concept of "Topic"

Besides the extensive use of particles, perhaps the most significant feature Japanese has, but English doesn't, is the concept of "topic." When you talk with someone in Japanese, you provide the listener with the "topic" of the dialog by marking it with *-wa*. Because of this characteristic, I call Japanese a "listener-friendly" language.

The "topic" has the following two functions:

- "Topic" lets the listener know that you are going to talk about *X*.
- "Topic" assures the listener that you and he are still talking about *X*.

"Topic" is a new concept to English speakers. It might be helpful to think of Japanese sentence structure in the following way:

Japanese Sentence = TOPIC + COMMENT

> ### Green Tea Break
>
> The topic-comment structure is a manifestation of Japanese psychology. As explained in Chapter 2, Japanese people are conscious of their position in a given conversation. They do their best not to be considered egocentric by the listener, so they listen and speak carefully. The notion of "topic" makes doing the previously mentioned functions easy.

When you state a certain topic, the rest of the sentence is your "comment" about the topic.

Let's look at an example. With the particles you've learned so far, let's translate "John ate cake on Christmas." This sentence has three possible topics—"John," "on Christmas," and "cake." The one you want to talk about is the one you attach *-wa* to. If you want to let the listener know that you're going to talk about John, or if you want to assure the listener that you and he are still talking about John, you must mark John with the topic particle *-wa*:

Track 4
CD-21

> *JoN-**wa** Kurisumasu-ni kēki-o tabe-mashita.*

This sentence means something like "As for John (*or* Speaking of John), he ate cake on Christmas."

Similarly, if you want to talk about "on Christmas," the sentence looks like this:

Track 4
CD-22

> *Kurisumasu-ni-**wa** JoN-ga kēki-o tabe-mashita.*

This sentence means "Let me talk about a particular day, that is, Christmas. On Christmas, John ate cake."

If you want to talk about the "cake," you then should mark the word "cake" with the topic particle *-wa*:

Track 4
CD-23

> *Kēki-**wa** JoN-ga Kurisumasu-ni tabe-mashita.*

This sentence means "Let me talk about a particular food, that is, cake. John ate it on Christmas."

In summary, anything can be made a topic by placing it with the topic particle *-wa* at the beginning of a sentence. Without a topic in Japanese, a sentence might sound unkind or unnatural.

At this point, just be aware of the function of *-wa*. In the rest of the book, you will see numerous examples with *-wa*, so you will eventually get used to it!

Lifesavers

When a subject or an object becomes a "topic," the topic particle *-wa* completely replaces *-ga* and *-o*. In the case of other particles, on the other hand, *-wa* is added on to the existing particle, as in *Kurisumasu-ni-wa*, "on Christmas."

Simple Is Beautiful

Japanese sentences might sometimes appear incomplete because they lack a subject or object. This is illustrated in the next example:

Track 4
CD-24

> *Tōkyō-ni iki-mashita.* "I went to Tokyo."

The English translation shows that the subject is "I," but the Japanese sentence does not have "I" in it; it literally reads something like, "To Tokyo, went." You could add *watashi*, "I," as the topic of this sentence, as seen in the following, but it is not necessary:

Track 4
CD-25

> *(Watashi-wa) Tōkyō-ni iki-mashita.*   "I went to Tokyo."

In Japanese, if a phrase is understood between you and the listener in a given context, you can drop the phrase. In the previous example, you are sure that the listener knows you are talking about yourself, so "I" is omitted. Suppose that you and the listener are talking about "going to Tokyo." In this case, "to Tokyo" is also understood between the two of you, so you can drop it, too, as you can see in the following sentence:

Track 4
CD-26

> *Iki-mashita.*   "(I) went (to Tokyo)."

Wow! Amazing, isn't it? In English, you can't omit phrases even if they are understood. Instead of dropping them, you use pronouns, such as "it," "them," "he," and so on. In reply to a question like "Did you meet Lisa?" you don't say "Yes, I met" or "Yes, met" in English. For this reason, many students of Japanese first think that Japanese is a "broken" language. On the surface, it might appear so, but on the context level, it is not broken at all, just efficient.

Before closing this chapter, take a simple quiz. I will give you English sentences, and your task is to translate them into Japanese. The answers are at the end of the chapter. Don't worry about word order. Just check to see whether you've used the correct particles. The topic phrase is also indicated in each question.

Review Quiz

1. John (= topic) swam in the pool with Tom.

   (swam = *oyogi-mashita*)

   _____

2. As for the pizza (= topic), Lisa ate it.

   (ate = *tabe-mashita*)

   _____

3. I (= topic) went from Chicago up to Boston.

   (went = *iki-mashita*)

   _____

4. John (= topic) was in the bar.

   (was = *i-mashita*)

   _____

5. In the freezer (= topic) there is pizza.

   (there is = *ari-masu*)

   _____

6. (Following number 5) There is *also* ice cream!

   _____

Okay, that's it! As far as basic sentence structure is concerned, you've got it. After you have a good handle on this chapter, you should be able to follow all the sentences in this book.

Answers

Track 4
CD-27–32

1. John (= topic) swam in the pool with Tom.

   JoN-wa pūru-de Tomu-to oyogi-mashita.

2. As for the pizza (= topic), Lisa ate it.

   Piza-wa Risa-ga tabe-mashita.

3. I (= topic) went from Chicago up to Boston.

   Shikago-kara BosutoN-made iki-mashita.

4. John (= topic) was in the bar.

   JoN-wa Bā-ni i-mashita.

5. In the freezer (= topic) there is pizza.

   Furīzā-ni-wa piza-ga ari-masu.

6. (Following number 5) There is *also* ice cream!

   Aisukurīmu-mo ari-masu!

(Because "I" in number 3 is an understood topic, you do not have to mention it.)

The Least You Need to Know

◆ Particles are noun markers that show the relation of nouns to verbs.

◆ As long as you add the correct particle to each noun and put the verb at the end, you can say a Japanese sentence in any word order you want.

◆ The fastest way to master Japanese is to constantly pay attention to "topic." Know what is being discussed in a given dialog and mark it with *-wa*.

◆ English has pronouns (it, them, and so on) to refer to already mentioned phrases, whereas Japanese often drops them.

Everything You Need to Know About Conjugation

In This Chapter

- ◆ The concept of conjugation
- ◆ Verb endings
- ◆ Adjective endings
- ◆ Noun endings

You've learned the sound system (see Chapter 3) and basic sentence structure (see Chapter 4). After you familiarize yourself with some more grammatical items in this and the following chapter, you're ready to start speaking Japanese!

Conjugation Is No Headache!

Those who have learned languages such as Spanish and French might suspect that Japanese conjugation is complicated and painful to master. Is it really? Let's consider Spanish. Although Spanish is known as a relatively easy language to learn, you still have to deal with a complex conjugation system. The conjugation of a verb in Spanish depends on whether the subject is in first, second, or third person and whether the subject is singular or plural. Not to mention that this is just for a particular tense—you need to learn conjugations for other tenses.

Huh? _____

Conjugation is the transformation of a verb in a sentence based on such considerations as number, person, voice, mood, and tense. In English, for example, *walk* is conjugated as *walks* if its subject is third person singular, and *walked* if it is in past tense.

English conjugation is also complicated, but in a different way. Hundreds of "irregular verbs" exist, such as *break, broke,* and *broken!* There is no easy way to systematically learn irregular verbs. You have to memorize each one of them—quite an ordeal!

Will the Japanese *conjugation* system haunt you like other languages? Not a chance! It's comparatively simple. Japanese grammar is not concerned with marking gender (masculine, feminine, or even neutral), number (singular or plural), or person (first, second, or third). For example, *tabe-masu* ("to eat") does not undergo any change whether the subject is *John, Mary, we, you, they,* or whoever!

All you need to know to conjugate words in Japanese is whether the *predicate* is (1) present or past tense, and (2) affirmative or negative. That's all!

Basically, there are three types of predicates in Japanese—verb predicates, adjective predicates, and noun predicates. Here is an English example for each type:

Huh? _____

A **predicate** is the verb or phrase that modifies the subject of a sentence. See Chapter 4 for more information.

John *ate* pizza.	[verb predicate]
John *is tall.*	[adjective predicate]
John *is a student.*	[noun predicate]

In each example, the italicized phrase is the core of the sentence, the *predicate*. As there are three types of predicates in Japanese, there are three types of conjugations. Now, let's look at each predicate in Japanese and its method of conjugation.

Verb Predicate Conjugation

First of all, let's define verbs. Verbs refer to an action or state of being. For example, verbs such as "eat" and "watch" refer to the action of eating and watching, respectively, and verbs such as "be married" and "live" refer to marital status and the state of living somewhere, respectively.

Let's pick up the verb *watch* as an example and look at its conjugation in English. Keep in mind that two considerations affect conjugation: (1) present tense or past tense, and (2) whether the predicate is affirmative or negative. In English, the verb *watch* undergoes the following conjugation:

Conjugation of the Verb "Watch"

	Affirmative	Negative
Present	watch	do not watch
Past	watched	did not watch

Notice that the suffix *-ed* is attached to *watch* in the affirmative past tense. Japanese conjugation is similar to the way *watch-ed* is created. That is, you attach the appropriate suffix for any of the four forms a verb might be conjugated in. In other words, the affirmative present tense, affirmative past tense, negative present tense, and negative past tense each have their own distinctive suffix. The following table shows which suffix follows the verb in verb predicate conjugation:

Conjugation Suffixes for Verbs

	Affirmative	Negative
Present	VERB + *masu*	VERB + *maseN*
	(do)	(not)
Past	VERB + *mashita*	VERB + *maseN-deshita*
	(did)	(not-did)

Note that as indicated in the previous table, *masu* is equivalent to the English "do," *mashita* is equivalent to "did," *maseN* is equivalent to "not," and *maseN-deshita* is equivalent to "not-did." These English words are known as "helping verbs." In Japanese, the helping verbs are "stacked" on to the ending of a verb.

Let's go over each conjugation more thoroughly with an example verb, *mi*, "to watch."

When you use a verb in the *affirmative present tense*, such as *I watch TV*, the suffix *masu* is attached to the verb, as in:

> *mi-masu* ("watch" + "do")

When you use a verb in the *affirmative past tense*, such as *I watched TV*, the suffix *mashita* is attached to the verb, as in:

> *mi-mashita* ("watch" + "did")

When you use a verb in the *negative present tense*, such as *I don't watch TV*, the suffix *maseN* is attached to the verb, as in:

> *mi-maseN* ("watch" + "not")

Finally, when you use a verb in the *negative past tense*, such as *I did not watch TV,* the suffixes *maseN* and *deshita* are attached to the verb, as in:

mi-maseN-deshita ("watch" + "not" + "did")

Verb conjugation is shown in the following table:

Track 5
CD-1

Verb Conjugation

	Affirmative	Negative
Present	*mi-masu* ("watch")	*mi-maseN* ("do not watch")
Past	*mi-mashita* ("watched")	*mi-maseN-deshita* ("didn't watch")

I want to emphasize again that Japanese does not have any grammatical markers for gender, number, or person. The preceding chart is "universal" for any verb.

For verb conjugation, all you have to remember is the ending of each function: *-masu, -mashita, -maseN,* and *-maseN-deshita.* The verb element that attaches to those endings, like *mi-*, is called the "verb stem."

I will give you a few verbs in various endings in this exercise. Try to identify the stem of each example:

Exercise 1

1. *kakimashita* ("wrote")   _____

2. *hanashimaseN* ("does not speak")   _____

3. *ikimaseNdeshita* ("didn't go")   _____

4. *yomimasu* ("reads")   _____

How did you do? Check the answers in the end of this chapter. Here is another exercise. Conjugate each of the following verbs as instructed.

Exercise 2

1. *kaeri* ("to go home") (to negative present form)

   _____

2. *oyogi* ("to swim") (to affirmative past form)

   _____

3. *naki* ("to cry") (to negative past form)

   _____

4. *iki* ("to go") (to affirmative present form)

_____

5. *ne* ("to go to bed") (to negative past form)

_____

6. *hajime* ("to begin") (to negative present form)

_____

The order of conjugation for verbs is schematized as follows:

Verb Stem	+	(Negative)	+	Tense	Translation
mi				*masu*	"watch"
mi				*mashita*	"watched"
mi		*maseN*			"don't watch"
mi		*maseN*		*deshita*	"didn't watch"

Getting back to the original example, let's make actual sentences using "watch TV" (*terebi* = TV).

Track 5
CD-1–5

    *JoN-wa terebi-o mi-**masu.***   "John watches (*or* will watch) TV."

    *JoN-wa terebi-o mi-**mashita.***   "John watch**ed** TV."

    *JoN-wa terebi-o mi-**maseN.***   "John does**n't** watch (*or* won't watch) TV."

    *JoN-wa terebi-o mi-**maseN-deshita.***   "John **didn't** watch TV."

You might have noticed in the examples that *mi-masu* means both "watches" and "will watch," and *mi-maseN* means both "doesn't watch" and "won't watch." In Japanese, present tense takes care of not only present but also future tense. In other words, Japanese tense is either "past" or "*non*past." This makes Japanese conjugation even easier, doesn't it?

In the next exercise, translate the English sentences into Japanese. This time you need to find the words in the dictionary.

Exercise 3

1. "I ate sushi."

_____

2. "John will not go to Japan." (The postposition for "to" is *-ni*.)

_____

3. "John did not take a bath."

_____

4. "I will buy a book."

_____

5. "I don't eat shrimp."

_____

Keep in mind that the most important point of verb conjugation in Japanese is that functions such as "past," "present," "negative," and "affirmative" are indicated by "stacking" these helping verbs on to a verb stem.

In the next sections, we will look at the conjugations of adjective and noun predicates. You will see that the same concept applies to these conjugation systems.

Adjective Predicate Conjugation

A predicate can sometimes function as an adjective, as in _John is smart_ and _It was expensive._ In English, the "helping" verb "be" is placed before an adjective to indicate tense, and "not" is added if it is in negation—as in _is cheap_, _isn't cheap_, _was cheap_, _wasn't cheap_.

In Japanese, helping verbs appear _after_ an adjective. In this way, adjective predicate conjugation is similar to verb conjugation.

Conjugation Suffixes for Adjectives

	Affirmative	**Negative**
Present	Adjective + _idesu_	Adjective + _kuna-idesu_
	(is)	(not-is)
Past	Adjective + _kattadesu_	Adjective + _kuna-kattadesu_
	(was)	(not-was)

As illustrated in the table, the helping verb _idesu_ is equivalent to the English "is," _kattadesu_ is equivalent to "was," and _kuna_ is equivalent to "not." As with verbs, these helping verbs are "stacked" on to the ending of an adjective.

Let's go over each conjugation thoroughly with an example adjective, _yasu_, "cheap."

When you use an adjective in the _affirmative present tense_, such as _It is cheap_, the suffix _idesu_ is attached to the adjective stem, as in:

yasu-idesu ("cheap" + "is")

When you use an adjective in the _affirmative past tense_, such as _It was cheap_, the suffix _kattadesu_ is attached to the adjective, as in:

yasu-kattadesu ("cheap" + "was")

When you use an adjective in the *negative present tense*, such as *It isn't cheap*, the suffixes *kuna* and *idesu* are attached to the adjective, as in:

   yasu-kuna-idesu ("cheap" + "not" + "is")

Finally, when you use an adjective in the *negative past tense*, such as *It wasn't cheap*, the suffixes *kuna* and *kattadesu* are attached to the adjective, as in:

   yasu-kuna-kattadesu ("cheap" + "not" + "was")

Adjective predicate conjugation is shown in the following table:

Track 5
CD-6

Adjective Conjugation

	Affirmative	**Negative**
Present	*yasu-idesu*	*yasu-kuna-idesu*
	"is cheap"	"isn't cheap"
Past	*yasu-kattadesu*	*yasu-kuna-kattadesu*
	"was cheap"	"wasn't cheap"

For adjective predicate conjugation, all you have to remember is the ending of each function: *-idesu*, *-kattadesu*, *-kuna-idesu*, and *-kuna-kattadesu*. The adjective element that attaches to those endings, like *yasu-*, is called the "adjective stem." Following are a few adjectives in various endings. Try to identify the adjective stem of each example:

Exercise 4

   1. *takakattadesu* ("was expensive")   _____
   2. *oishikunaidesu* ("isn't delicious")   _____
   3. *muzukashikunakattadesu* ("wasn't difficult")   _____
   4. *omoidesu* ("is heavy")   _____

Here is another exercise. Conjugate each of the following adjectives as directed.

Exercise 5

   1. *waru* ("bad") (to negative present form)

   _____

   2. *tanoshi* ("enjoyable") (to affirmative past form)

   _____

3. *samu* ("cold") (to negative past form)

_____

4. *hiku* ("low") (to affirmative present form)

_____

5. *tsuyo* ("strong") (to negative past form)

_____

6. *ita* ("painful") (to negative present form)

_____

The order of conjugation for adjectives is schematized as follows.

Adjective Stem	+	(Negative)	+	Tense	Translation
yasu				*idesu*	"is cheap"
yasu				*kattadesu*	"was cheap"
yasu		*kuna*		*idesu*	"isn't cheap"
yasu		*kuna*		*kattadesu*	"wasn't cheap"

Lifesavers _____

Japanese has only one irregular adjective, *i-idesu*, "is good." Its stem is simply *i*.

	Affirmative	Negative
Present	*i-idesu*	*yo-kuna-idesu*
	"is good"	"isn't good"
Past	*yo-kattadesu*	*yo-kuna-kattadesu*
	"was good"	"wasn't good"

Now, let's look at actual sample sentences using the adjective stem *yasu*, "cheap."

Track 5
CD-7–10

*Sono piza-wa yasu-**idesu**.*   "That pizza **is** cheap."

*Sono piza-wa yasu-**kattadesu**.*   "That pizza **was** cheap."

*Sono piza-wa yasu-**kuna-idesu**.*   "That pizza **isn't** cheap."

*Sono piza-wa yasu-**kuna-kattadesu**.*   "That pizza **wasn't** cheap."

In the next exercise, translate the English sentences to Japanese. As with Exercise 3 for verb conjugation, you need to find the words in the dictionary.

Exercise 6

1. "Sushi is delicious."

   _____

2. "Japanese is not difficult!"

   _____

3. "That pizza was not expensive."

   _____

4. "(The) movie was interesting."

   _____

5. "It is not hot today." (_Lit._ "Today is not hot.")

   _____

Noun Conjugation

A predicate can sometimes function as a noun, as in _John is a student_ and _John was a student_. Notice that in English, the "helping" verb "be" is placed before a noun to indicate tense and "not" is added if it is in negation, as in _is a student_, _isn't a student_, _was a student_, and _wasn't a student_.

In Japanese, as with verbs and adjective predicates, helping verbs appear _after_ a noun. The following table shows how a noun conjugates:

Conjugation Suffixes for Nouns

	Affirmative	**Negative**
Present	NOUN + _desu_	NOUN + _jana-idesu_
	(is)	(not-is)
Past	NOUN + _deshita_	NOUN + _jana-kattadesu_
	(was)	(not-was)

You might have noticed that noun conjugation is very similar to adjective conjugation, especially in negative forms.

Let's go over each conjugation thoroughly with an example noun, _kyō_, "today."

When you have a noun in the _affirmative present tense_, such as _It is today_, the suffix _desu_ is attached to the noun, as in:

   kyō-desu ("today" + "is")

When you have a noun in the *affirmative past tense*, such as *It <u>was</u> today*, the suffix *deshita* is attached to the noun, as in:

> *kyō-deshita* ("today" + "was")

When you have a noun in the *negative present tense*, such as *It <u>isn't</u> today*, the suffixes *jana* and *idesu* are attached to the noun, as in:

> *kyō-jana-idesu* ("today" + "not" + "is")

Finally, when you have a noun in the *negative past tense*, such as *It <u>wasn't</u> today*, the suffixes *jana* and *kattadesu* are attached to the noun, as in:

> *kyō-jana-kattadesu* ("today" + "not" + "was")

For noun predicate conjugation, all you have to remember is the ending of each function: *desu*, *deshita*, *jana-idesu*, and *jana-kattadesu*. Because noun conjugation looks similar to adjective conjugation, be sure that you don't get confused between the two!

Noun Conjugation

Track 5
CD-11

	Affirmative	Negative
Present	*kyō-desu*	*kyō-jana-idesu*
	"is today"	"isn't today"
Past	*kyō-deshita*	*kyō-jana-kattadesu*
	"was today"	"wasn't today"

Do the following exercise. Conjugate each of the following noun predicates as directed.

Exercise 7

1. *NihoNjiN* "(be) Japanese" (to negative present form)

   _____

2. *seNsē* "(be a) teacher" (to affirmative past form)

   _____

3. *gakusē* "(be a) student" (to negative past form)

   _____

4. *AmerikajiN* "(be an) American" (to affirmative present form)

   _____

5. *moderu* "(be a) fashion model" (to negative past form)

   _____

6. *ēga sutā* "(be a) movie star" (to negative present form)

_____

The order of negative conjugation for adjectives is schematized as follows:

Adjective Stem	+	(Negative)	+	Tense	Translation
Kyō				*desu*	"is today"
Kyō				*deshita*	"was today"
Kyō		*jana*		*idesu*	"isn't today"
Kyō		*jana*		*kattadesu*	"wasn't today"

Now, let's look at an example for each of the noun conjugations.

Track 5
CD-12–15

*Tesuto-wa kyō-**desu**.*   "The test is today."

*Tesuto-wa kyō-**deshita**.*   "The test **was** today."

*Tesuto-wa kyō-**jana-idesu**.*   "The test **isn't** today."

*Tesuto-wa kyō-**jana-kattadesu**.*   "The test **wasn't** today."

Lifesavers _____

When you're used to the past tense affirmative form for nouns, NOUN + *deshita*, such as *kyō-deshita* ("was today"), it becomes tempting to do the same for adjectives, like *yasu-i-deshita*, "was cheap." This is a very common mistake. Remember that the adjective conjugation is ADJECTIVE + *kattadesu*, for example, *yasu-kattadesu*.

In the next exercise, translate the English sentences into Japanese. Just as with Exercises 3 and 6, you need to find the words in the dictionary.

Exercise 8

1. "I am a student."

_____

2. "This is not my book." ("this (pronoun)" = *kore*; "my" = *watashi-no*)

_____

3. "My car was not a Honda."

_____

4. "This shop used to be a hospital." ("this" (adjective) = *kono*)

_____

5. "I am not a lawyer."

_____

You have seen the conjugation of all the predicates, verbs, adjectives, and nouns. Let's summarize each conjugation in terms of the type of suffixes:

Conjugation: Summary

	Present Affirmative	**Examples**
Verbs	VERB STEM + _masu_	_mi-masu_ ("watch")
Adjectives	ADJECTIVE STEM + _idesu_	_yasu-idesu_ ("is cheap")
Nouns	NOUN STEM + _desu_	_kyō-desu_ ("is today")

	Past Affirmative	**Examples**
Verbs	VERB STEM + _mashita_	_mi-mashita_ ("watched")
Adjectives	ADJECTIVE STEM + _katta-desu_	_yasu-kattadesu_ ("was cheap")
Nouns	NOUN STEM + _deshita_	_kyō-deshita_ ("was today")

	Present Negative	**Examples**
Verbs	VERB STEM + _maseN_	_mi-maseN_ ("don't watch")
Adjectives	ADJECTIVE STEM + _kuna-idesu_	_yasu-kuna-idesu_ ("isn't cheap")
Nouns	NOUN STEM + _jana-idesu_	_kyō-jana-idesu_ ("isn't today")

	Past Negative	**Examples**
Verbs	VERB STEM + _maseN-deshita_	_mi-maseN-deshita_ ("didn't watch")
Adjectives	ADJECTIVE STEM + kuna-kattadesu	_yasu-kuna-kattadesu_ ("wasn't cheap")
Nouns	NOUN STEM + jana-kattadesu	_kyō-jana-kattadesu_ ("wasn't today")

Conjugation can be challenging no matter what language you learn. The good news with regard to learning Japanese is that you don't have to worry about issues such as number, person, and gender. Conjugation is the basic of basics. Make sure that you memorize all the forms correctly!

Answers

Exercise 1

1. _kaki_ ("to write")

2. _hanashi_ ("to speak")

3. *iki* ("to go")

4. *yomi* ("to read")

Exercise 2

1. *kaeri-maseN* ("do[es] not go home")

2. *oyogi-mashita* ("swam")

3. *naki-maseN-deshita* ("did not cry")

4. *iki-masu* ("went")

5. *ne-maseN-deshita* ("did not go to bed")

6. *hajime-maseN* ("do[es] not begin")

Exercise 3

Track 5
CD-16–20

1. "I ate sushi."

   Watashi-wa sushi-o tabe-mashita.

2. "John will not go to Japan."

   JoN-wa NihoN-ni iki-maseN.

3. "John did not take a bath."

   JoN-wa ofuro-ni hairi-maseN-deshita.

4. "I will buy a book."

   Watashi-wa hoN-o kai-masu.

5. "I don't eat shrimp."

   Watashi-wa ebi-o tabe-maseN.

Exercise 4

1. *taka* ("expensive")

2. *oishi* ("delicious")

3. *muzukashi* ("difficult")

4. *omo* ("heavy")

Exercise 5

1. *waru-kuna-idesu* ("is not bad")

2. *tanoshi-kattadesu* ("was enjoyable")

3. *samu-kuna-kattadesu* ("was not cold")

4. *hiku-idesu* ("is low")

5. *tsuyo-kuna-kattadesu* ("was not strong")

6. *ita-kuna-idesu* ("is not painful")

Track 5
CD-21–25

Exercise 6

1. "Sushi is delicious."

   Sushi-wa oishi-idesu.

2. "Japanese is not difficult!"

   NihoNgo-wa muzukashi-kuna-idesu.

3. "That pizza was not expensive."

   Sono piza-wa taka-kuna-kattadesu.

4. "(The) movie was interesting."

   Ēga-wa omoshiro-kattadesu.

5. "It is not hot today." (*Lit.* "Today is not hot.")

   Kyō-wa atsu-kuna-idesu.

Exercise 7

1. *NihoNjiN-jana-idesu* ("is not Japanese")

2. *seNsē-deshita* ("was a teacher")

3. *gakusē-jana-kattadesu* ("was not a student")

4. *AmerikajiN-desu* ("is an American")

5. *moderu-jana-kattadesu* ("was not a fashion model")

6. *ēga sutā-jana-idesu* ("is not a movie star")

Track 5
CD-26–30

Exercise 8

1. "I am a student."

   Watashi-wa gakusē-desu.

2. "This is not my book."

   Kore-wa watashi-no hoN-jana-idesu.

3. "My car was not a Honda."

   Watashi-no kuruma-wa HoNda-jana-kattadesu.

4. "This shop used to be a hospital."

   Kono mise-wa byōiN-deshita.

5. "I am not a lawyer."

   Watashi-wa beNgoshi-jana-idesu.

The Least You Need to Know

◆ Predicate conjugations for verbs, adjectives, and nouns are the heart of grammar. Learn the forms by heart!

◆ In English, helping verbs appear before a verb. In Japanese, helping verbs are stacked on to the end of a verb.

◆ Verb conjugation is summarized by the following examples:

mi-masu "watch," *mi-mashita* "watched," *mi-maseN* "do not watch," and *mi-maseN-deshita* "did not watch."

◆ Adjective conjugation is summarized by the following examples:

yasu-idesu "is cheap," *yasu-kattadesu* "was cheap," *yasu-kuna-idesu* "is not cheap," and *yasu-kuna-kattadesu* "was not cheap."

◆ Noun conjugation is summarized by the following examples:

kyō-desu "is today," *kyō-deshita* "was today," *kyō-jana-idesu* "is not today," and *kyō-jana-kattadesu* "was not today."

Chapter 6

Other Grammar Essentials

In This Chapter

- ◆ *TE*-form
- ◆ How to describe something
- ◆ How to ask questions

You've learned the basic sentence structure and particles in Chapter 4 and conjugation in Chapter 5. There are a few more grammatical concepts that you should be familiar with before starting actual lessons. In this chapter, you first will be introduced to another important conjugation called *TE*-form, which is used in many grammatical constructions. Second, you will learn how to describe a thing or person. And third, you will learn how to ask questions in Japanese.

TE-Form

English has a versatile verb ending, *-ing*, as in *go → going*. This grammatical form is used in many sentence patterns:

> I am <u>studying.</u>
>
> I was <u>studying.</u>
>
> <u>Seeing</u> is <u>believing.</u>
>
> No <u>smoking!</u>

In the first and second examples, the *-ing* form indicates ongoing actions—present progressive in the first example and past progressive in the second example. In the third and fourth examples, the *-ing* form makes verbs function like nouns (called gerunds). The *-ing* form is "required" by the preceding sentence patterns. Because of this requirement, it is not grammatical to say, for example, *I am study* or *See is believe.*

Japanese has a special form known as *TE*-form whose function is similar to the *-ing* form. Like the *-ing* form, the *TE*-form is a "bare" form that is neutral to number, person, and tense. It is also used to indicate continuous action. And just as the last two English sentences in the preceding exercise require the use of *-ing*, certain special Japanese sentence structures (such as expression of a request, asking permission, or indicating a prohibition) require the use of the *TE*-form.

Let's explore some of the uses of the *TE*-form.

Continuous Action

In Chapter 5, we learned to conjugate verb, noun, and adjective predicates. This type of conjugation might be thought of as "simple" conjugation of present, past, or future. We say that something happens, happened, or will happen. In English, we might say "Bob ate" or "Lisa writes."

But what if you want to suggest continuous happening—that is, "Bob was eating" or "Lisa is writing"? In English, you would just add the *-ing*. In Japanese, you switch to the *TE*-form.

TE-form is so called because you generally add *-te* to the verb if you want to indicate a continuous action. (There are some exceptions when you will add *-de* instead, to indicate a slightly different pronunciation.) You also need to add the conjugation suffixes you learned in Chapter 5.

Let's compare the use of the verb "watch," *mi(-masu)*, in simple present and continuous present forms.

Suppose you want to say "John watches TV." As you learned in Chapter 5, you would say:

> *JoN-wa terebi-o mi-masu.*   "John watches TV."

If you want to say that John is watching TV, you would say:

> *JoN-wa terebi-o mi-te i-masu.*   "John is watching TV."

Note that *mi-te* is translated as "watching" and *i-masu* as "is" (*Lit.* "be-present").

That is, you add *-te* to the verb stem *mi* and the verb *i-masu*. This indicates the continuous action of John watching television.

The order of conjugation for the verb "is watching," *mi-te i-masu*, is schematized as follows:

Verb Stem	+	*TE*	+	"Be"	+	Present Tense	Translation
mi		*te*		*i*		*masu*	"is watching"

TE-form can get a little complicated because the shape of the *TE*-form changes depending on the ending of a verb. In order to come up with the right conjugation, you need a verb stem. The verb stem is a "bare" form without -*masu*. For example, the stem of the verb *tabe-masu* ("eat") is *tabe*.

There are two types of verb stem endings, one ending with an [-e] sound and the other ending with an [-i] sound. Let me list a few common verbs here as examples.

Two Types of Verb Endings

[e]-Ending Verb Stems		[i]-Ending Verb Stems	
ne	"sleep"	*mi*	"see"
tabe	"eat"	*ki*	"come"
oboe	"memorize"	*shi*	"do"
oshie	"teach"	*ai*	"meet"
mise	"show"	*machi*	"wait"
tate	"build"	*kaeri*	"go home"
yame	"quit"	*nomi*	"drink"
		yobi	"invite"
		shini	"die"
		kaki	"write"
		oyogi	"swim"
		hanashi	"speak"

There are four different conjugations of *TE*-form, depending on what kinds of stems you have. I call them Type 1, Type 2, Type 3, and Type 4.

Type 1

If the stem (1) is an [e]-ending stem, (2) contains only one syllable, or (3) ends with -*shi*, all you have to do is to add -*te* to the stem:

Track 6
CD-1

ta<u>be</u>	"eat"	→	*tabe-te*
ne	"sleep"	→	*ne-te*
mi	"see"	→	*mi-te*
hana<u>shi</u>	"speak"	→	*hanashi-te*

Type 2

If the stem ends with *-i*, *-chi*, or *-ri*, replace those syllables with the double consonant and add *-te:*

Track 6
CD-2

ai	"meet"	→	*at-te*
machi	"wait"	→	*mat-te*
kaeri	"go home"	→	*kaet-te*

Type 3

If the stem ends with *-mi*, *-bi*, or *-ni*, replace those syllables with *-N* and add *-de:*

Track 6
CD-3

nomi	"drink"	→	*noN-de*
yobi	"invite"	→	*yoN-de*
shini	"die"	→	*shiN-de*

Type 4

If the stem ends with *-ki*, replace that syllable with *-i* and add *-te*. If the stem ends with *-gi*, replace that syllable with *-i* and add *-de*.

Track 6
CD-4

kaki	"write"	→	*kai-te*
oyogi	"swim"	→	*oyoi-de*

Type 1 of the *TE*-form is relatively easy, but you might find Types 2, 3, and 4 a bit challenging. Here is a way to make learning Types 2, 3, and 4 of *TE*-form a little easier and more enjoyable. I am sure you know the song "Clementine" (a.k.a. "Oh My Darling"). With this music, replace the original lyrics with the following *TE*-forms. Ready? Here we go.

i-chi-ri **tte**	*mi-bi-ni* **Nde**	*ki* **ite**	*gi* **ide**
Oh my darling	*Oh my darling*	*Oh my darling*	*Clementine*
[Type 2]	[Type 3]	[Type 4]	[Type 4]

CAUTION **Lifesavers** _____

The only exceptional *TE*-form is *iki-masu*, "go." Its stem ends with *-ki*, but its *TE*-form is *it-te*, not *ii-te*.

Did you get it? I wish I could sing along with you in person! (Actually, I'm a bad singer, so count yourself fortunate!) Anyway, in each phrase you sing the verb-ending syllables together with the appropriate *TE*-forms. Try this simple memory trick to help you learn all the types of *TE*-form.

Exercise 1

Provide the *TE*-form of each of the following verbs:

1. *hashiri-masu*   "run"
2. *aruki-masu*   "walk"
3. *tachi-masu*   "stand up"
4. *ake-masu*   "open"
5. *oshi-masu*   "push"
6. *shini-masu*   "die"
7. *mi-masu*   "see; watch"
8. *tobi-masu*   "jump"
9. *tanomi-masu*   "ask; request"
10. *ai-masu*   "meet"

Connecting Predicates

I mentioned earlier that, aside from indicating ongoing action, *TE*-form is required by a number of grammatical structures, such as "connection of predicates." If you wanted to knit two sentences into one—for example, "John is a student" and "John is an American"—you would use the *TE*-form to do it. There are two important steps to remember:

1. You first need to determine whether your predicates are verb, adjective, or noun.
2. To combine the two, you only need to turn the first predicate into its *TE*-form. The second predicate remains as it is.

Let's connect the following two sentences ending with verb predicates:

JoN-wa tabe-mashita.   "John ate."

JoN-wa ne-mashita.   "John went to bed."

In order to connect the two predicates, *tabe-mashita* and *ne-mashita*, you need to turn the first predicate *tabe-mashita* into the *TE*-form, as in *tabe-te*. The result is seen here:

Track 6
CD-5

TE-Form Connecting Verb Predicates

JoN-wa tabe-te, ne-mashita.   "John ate and (then) went to bed."

Just like verb predicates, noun and adjective predicates also have their *TE*-forms. Let's start with the simpler form—a noun *TE*-form.

TE-Form for Noun Predicates

Let's learn how to convert a noun predicate to its *TE*-form for the purpose of combining two noun predicates.

The Japanese translation of "John is a student" would be …

JoN-wa gakusē-desu. "John is a student."

The noun predicate is *gakusē-desu*. To make the *TE*-form of this predicate, you only need to attach *-de* to the noun, as seen here:

TE-Form for Noun Predicate
(for example, *gakusē-desu*, "to be a student")

*JoN-wa gakusē-**de*** "John being a student"

Huh? _____

In some cases of *TE*-form, *-te* is pronounced *-de*, as seen in the *TE*-form for a noun predicate.

To connect predicates, you must turn the first predicate into the *TE*-form. To illustrate this point, look at the following two noun predicates:

JoN-wa gakusē-desu. "John is a student."

JoN-wa AmerikajiN-desu. "John is an American."

To connect the two predicates, *gakusē-desu* and *AmerikajiN-desu*, you need to turn the first predicate *gakusei-desu* into the *TE*-form, as in *gakusē-de*. The result is seen here:

Track 6
CD-6

TE-Form Connecting Noun Predicates

*JoN-wa gakusē-**de**, AmerikajiN-desu.* "John is a student and (is) an American."

Note that in a combined sentence, the first and second predicates do not have to be the same type. The *TE*-form can connect a noun predicate and verb predicate, as seen here:

JoN-wa gakusē-desu. "John is a student."

JoN-wa okane-ga ari-maseN. "John has no money."

Track 6
CD-7

*JoN-wa gakusē-**de**, okane-ga ari-maseN.* "John is a student and he has no money."

Make sure that the *TE*-form for a noun predicate follows this formula:

Noun stem + *-de* (for example, *gakusē-de*, "being a student")

Now, do the next exercise.

Exercise 2

Connect two noun predicate sentences using the *TE*-form.

1. *Watashi-wa NihoNjiN-desu.*   "I am Japanese."
   Watashi-wa kyōshi-desu.   "I am a teacher."

   _____

2. *Risa-wa KanadajiN-desu.*   "Lisa is a Canadian."
   JoN-wa AmerikajiN-desu.   "John is an American."

   _____

3. *Terebi-wa SONY-desu.*   "My TV is SONY."
   Terebi-wa taka-kattadesu.   "My TV was expensive."

   _____

TE-Form for Adjective Predicates

Now let's look at the *TE*-form for adjective predicates, for the purpose of combining two adjective predicates. First, here's a regular sentence containing an adjective predicate:

   Sono piza-wa yasu-idesu.   "That pizza is cheap."

The adjective predicate is *yasu-idesu*. To make the *TE*-form of this predicate, change *-idesu* to *-kute*, as seen here:

> **TE-Form for Adjective Predicate**
> (for example, *yasu-idesu*, "to be cheap")
> *Sono piza-wa yasu-**kute***   (Lit.) "That pizza being cheap"

I showed in the previous section that the *TE*-form connects two noun predicates. Let's now connect two adjective predicates:

   Sono piza-wa yasu-idesu.   "That pizza is cheap."
   Sono piza-wa oishi-idesu.   "That pizza is delicious."

The *TE*-form connects these two sentences as follows:

> **TE-Form Connecting Adjective Predicates**
> *Sono piza-wa yasu-**kute**, oishi-idesu.*   "That pizza is cheap and (is) delicious."

Make sure you remember the formula for converting an adjective predicate to the *TE*-form:

   Adjective stem + *kute* (for example, *yasu-kute*, "being cheap")

Now, do the next exercise.

Track 6
CD-8

Exercise 3

Connect two sentences using the *TE*-form:

1. *John-wa yasashi-idesu.* "John is kind."
   John-wa atama-ga i-idesu. "John is smart."

   _____

2. *NihoNgo-wa omoshiro-idesu.* "Japanese language is fun."
   NihoNgo-wa yakuni tachi-masu. "Japanese is useful."

   _____

3. *Jon-wa se-ga taka-idesu.* "John is tall."
   Tomu-wa se-ga hiku-idesu. "Tom is short."

   _____

Other Instances When You Want to Use the *TE*-Form

TE-form is useful for situations other than connecting predicates and indicating ongoing action. Without this form, you won't be able to express a lot of basic concepts. Following is a list of three useful patterns that require the *TE*-form:

- Making a request
- Expressing permission
- Expressing prohibition

Let's look at an example of each:

Track 6
CD-9

Making a Request
Tabe-te! or *Tabe-te kudasai!* "Eat!" *or* "Please eat!"
(*tabe-te < tabe-masu*)

Track 6
CD-10

Expressing Permission
Kaet-te mo i-idesu ka? "May I go home?"
(*kaet-te < kaeri-masu*)

Track 6
CD-11

Expressing Prohibition
Koko de noN-de wa, ike-maseN! "You cannot drink here."
(*noN-de < nomi-masu*)
(*koko de* = "here")

Let's sum up what we have learned about the *TE*-form:

- *TE*-form is comparable to the English *-ing* in that it expresses an "ongoing action."
- *TE*-form is used in various grammatical patterns such as "request," "permission," and "prohibition," among others.
- Each predicate type (verb predicate, noun predicate, and adjective predicate) has its own *TE*-form.
- The conjugation of *TE*-form for verb predicates is slightly complicated. I suggest that you go over the section on verb predicates thoroughly. Remember, the song "Clementine" is helpful for remembering the three most difficult endings of the *TE*-form for verbs.

How to Describe Something or Someone

Life would be dull if you could not describe a person or thing in detail. Suppose you want your friend to hand you a particular book from the bookshelf. You might have to say something like "a yellow book," "an expensive-looking book," "an old book," or "a book written in Japanese."

There are three basic ways to describe a thing or person:

- By an adjective
- By a noun
- By a *na*-adjective

No matter which type of describer you use, remember that a describer always comes *before* a thing/person to be described, as seen in the following diagram:

Describer (adjective, and so on) + Thing/Person

Adjectives

You have already seen adjective predicates like *oishi-idesu* ("delicious"), *yasu-idesu* ("inexpensive"), and *i-idesu* ("good"). When you use an adjective as a noun describer, delete **desu** from the adjective predicate:

oishi-idesu	→	*oishi-i*	"delicious"
yasu-idesu	→	*yasu-i*	"cheap"
i-idesu	→	*i-i*	"good"

To describe a noun, simply place an adjective before the noun.

See the following examples using these adjectives:

Track 6
CD-12–14

*oishi-**i** sushi*	"delicious sushi"
*yasu-**i** peN*	"cheap pen"
*i-**i** hoN*	"good book"

Make sure that an adjective ends with *-i* when describing a noun.

Exercise 4

Using the English to Japanese dictionary in Appendix B, describe the following nouns using adjectives. All the adjectives are listed with the *-i* ending.

1. "big bag"

   _____

2. "small clothes"

   _____

3. "dirty room"

   _____

4. "sweet cake"

   _____

5. "difficult language"

   _____

Nouns

When you describe a noun using another noun, the describer is marked by *-no*. Let's describe the nouns *sushi*, *peN*, and *hoN* (book) using noun describers.

Track 6
CD-15–17

*JoN-**no** sushi*	"John's sushi"
*NihoN-**no** peN*	"pen made in Japan"
*Kanada-**no** hoN*	"book about Canada"; "book printed in Canada"

Noun describers are basically the same as adjective describers: They appear before the thing/person to be described. The only difference is that noun describers are marked by *-no*.

Exercise 5

Just like in Exercise 4, describe the following nouns using nouns, using the English to Japanese dictionary in Appendix B. The core noun that is to be described is underlined in the questions.

1. "<u>student</u> of the Japanese language"

   _____

2. "<u>shop</u> in Tokyo"

   _____

3. "<u>John</u> from Toyota"

   _____

4. "Tom's <u>child</u>"

   _____

5. "<u>top</u> of the mountain"

   _____

Na-Adjectives

I said previously that there are three types of describers, and the third one is called "*na-adjectives.*" *Na*-adjectives are "hybrids" that function as adjectives but conjugate exactly like nouns.

Look at the following examples:

Track 6
CD-18–20

JoN-wa heN-desu.	"John is strange."
KoNpyūtā-wa beNri-desu.	"Computers are convenient."
JoN-wa haNsamu-desu.	"John is handsome."

"Strange," "convenient," and "handsome" are all adjectives, but the words *heN*, *beNri*, and *haNsamu* do not look like the familiar adjectives. They look different because they don't end with *-idesu*.

When these "adjectives" describe a noun, they are marked by *-na*, just as their name suggests. Let's see how *na*-adjectives describe nouns:

Track 6
CD-21–23

heN-**na** sushi	"strange-looking sushi"
beNri-**na** peN	"handy pen"
haNsamu-**na** hito	"handsome person"

Green Tea Break

By now you know that there are a lot of Western loan words in Japanese. Most loan words are nouns. However, quite a few loan words are adjectives, as shown here:

haNsamu(-na)	"handsome"
ricchi(-na)	"rich"
eregaNto(-na)	"elegant"
karafuru(-na)	"colorful"
gōjasu(-na)	"gorgeous"

"Colorful pens" would be translated as follows:

karafuru-**na** peN

Exercise 6

Again, using the English to Japanese dictionary in Appendix B, describe the following nouns using *na*-adjectives:

1. "inconvenient telephone"

   _____

2. "favorite book"

   _____

3. "quiet person"

   _____

4. "mean child"

   _____

5. "safe place"

   _____

In short, Japanese has two adjectives, *i*-adjectives and *na*-adjectives. For describing a noun, the only difference is the ending (-*i* or -*na*). However, when it comes to conjugation, *na*-adjectives look quite different from *i*-adjectives. They behave just like noun predicates.

NA-Adjective Predicate Conjugation

	Affirmative	**Negative**
Present	*heN-desu*	*heN-jana-idesu*
	"is strange"	"isn't strange"
Past	*heN-deshita*	*heN-jana-kattadesu*
	"was strange"	"wasn't strange"

I-Adjective Predicate Conjugation

	Affirmative	**Negative**
Present	*yasu-idesu*	*yasu-kuna-idesu*
	"is cheap"	"isn't cheap"
Past	*yasu-kattadesu*	*yasu-kuna-kattadesu*
	"was cheap"	"wasn't cheap"

Noun Predicate Conjugation

	Affirmative	**Negative**
Present	*kyō-desu*	*kyō-jana-idesu*
	"is today"	"isn't today"
Past	*kyō-deshita*	*kyō-jana-kattadesu*
	"was today"	"wasn't today"

Na-adjectives are bizarre, but once in a while you see bizarre grammar in any language!

Asking a Question

Let's learn how to ask a question. As in English, Japanese has two types of questions:

- *Yes-no* questions
- *Wh*-questions (questions containing words like *who, what, where, when,* and so on)

Compared to other languages, asking a question in Japanese is extremely easy because you don't have to shuffle words! If you want to make a question out of "John is a student" in English, you have to bring "is" to the beginning, as in "Is John a student?" *Wh*-questions are even more complex in English. When you ask a question out of "John ate an apple" as to what he ate, you have to insert a question word and add the helping verb "did," as in "What did John eat?"

Huh?

I have stated elsewhere in this book that a Japanese sentence ends with a verb. However, in the case of questions, *-ka* follows the verb. This marker is just like the question mark ("?").

ka

In Japanese, forming a question sentence is easy. For *yes-no* questions, all you have to do is add the question word *ka?* at the end of a sentence.

Track 6
CD-24

Yes-No **Questions**

Q: *JoN-wa AmerikajiN-desu* **ka?** "Is John an American?"

A: *Hai, AmerikajiN-desu.* "Yes, he is an American."

Track 6
CD-25

Q: *Pari-ni iki-masu* **ka?** "Will you go to Paris?"

A: *Īe, iki-maseN.* "No, I will not go to Paris."

Lifesavers _____

Hai means "What you've said is correct," and *īe* means "What you've said is *not* correct." In a negative *yes-no* question, this causes *hai* to mean "no" and *īe* to mean "yes." Suppose you are asked if you *don't* eat pizza:

Q: *Piza-wa tabe-maseN ka?* "You don't eat pizza?"

If you indeed *do not* eat pizza, you should say **Hai**, *tabe-maseN*, because what the speaker said is correct. On the other hand, if you *do* eat pizza, you should say **Īe**, *tabe-masu* because what the speaker said is *not* correct.

Exercise 7

Make question sentences based on the following information. Pay attention to the tense.

1. "Did you eat?"
   ("eat" = *tabe-masu*)

   _____

2. "Is Japanese difficult?"
   ("difficult" = *muzukashi-idesu*)

   _____

3. "Was the movie interesting?"
   ("movie" = *ēga*; "interesting" = *omoshiro-idesu*)

   _____

4. "Are you going home?"
   ("go home" = *kaeri-masu*)

   _____

5. "Is John a student?"
   ("student" = *gakusē*)

   _____

Wh-Questions

For *wh*-questions, you just need to put an appropriate question word where its answer normally appears. Let's look at a couple of examples:

Wh-Questions

Track 6
CD-26

Q: **Nani-o** *tabe-mashita* **ka?** "What did you eat?"

A: **Piza-o** *tabe-mashita.* "I ate pizza."

Q: *JoN-wa **doko-ni** iki-masu **ka?*** "Where will John go?"

A: ***Pari-ni*** *iki-masu.* "He will go to Paris."

Basically, when you answer a *wh*-question, all you need to do is listen to the question carefully and replace the question word with your answer. That's it! You don't have to worry about word order or a helping verb! Isn't that great?

Although you will see a number of questions in the rest of the book, I think it's a good idea to list frequently used question words.

Question Words	
what	*nani* or *naN*
who	*dare*
where	*doko*
when	*itsu*
which one	*dore*
which X	*dono X*
which direction	*dochira*
why	*dōshite* or *naze*
how	*dōyatte*
how much (money)	*ikura*
how much (quantity)	*donogurai*
how old (age)	*naN-sai* or *ikutsu*
what nationality	*nani-jiN*
what language	*nani-go*
what kind of X	*doNna X*
what time	*naN-ji*
how long	*donogurai*
how many	*ikutsu*

Exercise 8

Answer the following questions:

1. *Nani-jiN-desu ka?*
   (American)

   _____

2. *Namae-wa naN-desu ka?*
   (*namae* = "name")

   _____

3. *Kore-wa nanigo-desu ka?*
   (*kore* = "this") (Japanese)

   _____

4. *NihoNgo-no sensē-wa dare-desu ka?*
   (*sensē* = "teacher") (Mr. Fujita)

   _____

5. *AmazoN-wa doko-ni ari-masu ka?*
   (*AmazoN* = "Amazon") (Brazil)

   _____

Review

Before we leave this chapter, let's do a short review to check your grammatical understanding. I've given you the answers at the end of the chapter. I don't expect you to have completely memorized all the things covered in this chapter. Refer to the discussion in Chapters 5 and 6 to answer the questions.

Review Quiz

1. How would you say the following in Japanese?

   a. John is not an American.
      (American = *AmerikajiN*)

      _____

   b. Japan was fun!
      (fun = *tanoshi-idesu*)

      _____

   c. I didn't drink sake.
      (drink = *nomi-masu*)

      _____

   d. Japanese is not difficult!
      (Japanese = *NihoNgo*; difficult = *muzukashi-idesu*)

      _____

   e. I went to Japan.
      (go = *iki-masu*)

      _____

2. Write the *TE*-form for each verb:

    a. *yomi-masu*   "read"   _____

    b. *shi-masu*   "do"   _____

    c. *tsukuri-masu*   "make"   _____

    d. *tame-masu*   "save"   _____

    e. *tsukai-masu*   "use"   _____

    f. *asobi-masu*   "have fun"   _____

    g. *tsuki-masu*   "arrive"   _____

3. Describe the pizza:

    a. healthy pizza
       (healthy = *herushī*)

    _____

    b. John's pizza

    _____

    c. small pizza
       (small = *chīsa-i*)

    _____

Answers

Track 6
CD-28

Exercise 1

1. *hashit-te*	→	*hashiri-masu*	"run"
2. *arui-te*	→	*aruki-masu*	"walk"
3. *tat-te*	→	*tachi-masu*	"stand up"
4. *ake-te*	→	*ake-masu*	"open"
5. *oshi-te*	→	*oshi-masu*	"push"
6. *shiN-de*	→	*shini-masu*	"die"
7. *mi-te*	→	*mi-masu*	"see; watch"
8. *toN-de*	→	*tobi-masu*	"jump"
9. *tanoN-de*	→	*tanomi-masu*	"ask; request"
10. *at-te*	→	*ai-masu*	"meet"

Exercise 2

Track 6
CD-29–31

1. *Watashi-wa NihoNjiN-**de** kyōshi-desu.* "I am Japanese and (am a) teacher."

2. *Risa-wa KanadajiN-**de** JoN-wa AmerikajiN-desu.* "Lisa is a Canadian, and John is an American."

3. *Terebi-wa SONY-**de** taka-kattadesu.* "My TV is SONY and it was expensive."

Exercise 3

Track 6
CD-32–34

1. *John-wa yasashi-**kute** atama-ga i-idesu.* "John is kind and (is) smart."

2. *NihoNgo-wa omoshiro-**kute** yakuni tachi-masu.* "Japanese is fun and (is) useful."

3. *Jon-wa se-ga taka-**kute** Tomu-wa se-ga hiku-idesu.* "John is tall and Tom is short."

Exercise 4

Track 6
CD-35–39

1. *ōki-i baggu* or *ōki-i kabaN*
   "big bag"

2. *chīsa-i fuku*
   "small clothes"

3. *kitana-i heya*
   "dirty room"

4. *ama-i kēki*
   "sweet cake"

5. *muzukashi-i kotoba*
   "difficult language"

Exercise 5

Track 6
CD-40–44

1. *NihoNgo-no gakusē*
   "student of the Japanese language"

2. *Tōkyō-no mise*
   "shop in Tokyo"

3. *Toyota-no JoN*
   "John from Toyota"

4. *Tomu-no kodomo*
   "Tom's child"

5. *yama-no ue*
   "top of the mountain"

Exercise 6

Track 6
CD-45–49

1. *fubeN-na deNwa*

   "inconvenient telephone"

2. *daisuki-na hoN*

   "favorite book"

3. *shizuka-na hito*

   "quiet person"

4. *ijiwaru-na kodomo*

   "mean child"

5. *aNzeN-na basho* or *aNzeN-na tokoro*

   "safe place"

Exercise 7

Track 6
CD-50–54

1. *(Anata-wa) taba-mashita ka?*

   "Did you eat?"

2. *NihoNgo-wa muzukashi-idesu ka?*

   "Is Japanese difficult?"

3. *Ēga-wa omoshiro-kattadesu ka?*

   "Was the movie interesting?"

4. *(Anata-wa) kaeri-masu ka?*

   "Are you going home?"

5. *JoN-wa gakusē-desu ka?*

   "Is John a student?"

Exercise 8

Track 6
CD-55–59

1. *Nani-jiN-desu ka?*   "What nationality are you?"

   Amerika-jiN-desu.   "I'm an American."

2. *Namae-wa naN-desu ka?*   "What is your name?"

   Namae-wa XYZ-desu.   "My name is XYZ."

3. *Kore-wa nanigo-desu ka?*   "What language is this?"

   Kore-wa nihoNgo-desu.   "This is Japanese."

4. *NihoNgo-no sensē-wa dare-desu ka?*   "Who is your Japanese teacher?"

   NihoNgo-no sensē-wa Fujita-seNsē-desu.   "My Japanese teacher is Fujita Sensei." (That's me!)

5. *AmazoN-wa doko-ni ari-masu ka?*   "Where is the Amazon?"

   AmazoN-wa Burajiru-ni ari-masu.   "The Amazon is in Brazil."

Review Quiz

1. a. *JoN-wa AmerikajiN-jana-idesu.*

   b. *NihoN-wa tanoshi-kattadesu!*

   c. *(Watashi-wa) sake-o nomi-maseN-deshita.*

   d. *NihoNgo-wa muzukashi-kuna-idesu.*

   e. *(Watashi-wa) NihoN-ni iki-mashita.*

2. a. *yoN-de*

   b. *shi-te*

   c. *tsukut-te*

   d. *tame-te*

   e. *tsukat-te*

   f. *asoN-de*

   g. *tsui-te*

3. a. *herushī-na piza*

   b. *JoN-no piza*

   c. *chīsa-i piza*

The Least You Need to Know

- *TE*-form is essential because so many expressions require this form.
- A noun can be described by (1) *i*-adjective (ending with *-i*), (2) *na*-adjective (ending with *-na*), or (3) noun (ending with *-no*).
- To make a *yes-no* question, simply add *ka?* at the end of a sentence. To make a *wh*-question, simply insert an appropriate question word in the sentence where its answer normally appears.

Chapter 7

Numbers

In This Chapter

◆ Basic numbers
◆ Really big numbers
◆ Counters

Numbers are an indispensable tool for everyday life. Without numbers, you cannot count objects, tell your age, check prices when shopping, and so on. In this chapter, you will be introduced to basic numbers and the concept of "counters."

Basic Numbers

The following is a table of basic Japanese numbers.

Track 7
CD-1

Basic Numbers 1 Through 10	
0	*zero* or *rē*
1	*ichi*
2	*ni*
3	*saN*
4	*yoN* or *shi*
5	*go*
6	*roku*
7	*shichi* or *nana*
8	*hachi*
9	*kyū* or *ku*
10	*jū*

These numbers are certainly different from the English numbers, but not extremely difficult to learn. When you are comfortable with these basic numbers, the numbers beyond
"10" are relatively easy.

> ### Green Tea Break
>
> In Japan, 4 is the unlucky number (not 13), because the reading *shi* is identical to the
> pronunciation of the word for "death." For this reason, some people prefer saying *yoN*,
> not *shi*.

Shortcuts to Success

You don't have to be in a classroom to learn a language. There are a lot of
places where you can practice Japanese numbers. For example, practice counting to 100 in Japanese while taking a shower or driving to work. If you go to a
gym, count weight-lifting reps in Japanese. In an elevator, count floors in
Japanese. Consistent practice makes perfect.

10 to 99

Japanese numbers beyond *jū* (ten) are simple. For example, "eleven" is *ten one* in Japanese.
First, look at how to count from 11 to 20.

Track 7
CD-2

Numbers 11 Through 20	
11	*jū ichi*
12	*jū ni*
13	*jū saN*
14	*jū yoN* or *jū shi*
15	*jū go*
16	*jū roku*
17	*jū shichi* or *jū nana*
18	*jū hachi*
19	*jū kyū* or *jū ku*
20	*ni-jū*

Simple, aren't they? Notice that 20 is said as *two ten*. Likewise, 20 to 90 are pronounced as
follows:

Track 7
CD-3

Numbers 20 Through 90	
20	*ni-jū*
30	*saN-jū*
40	*yoN-jū*
50	*go-jū*
60	*roku-jū*
70	*nana-jū*
80	*hachi-jū*
90	*kyū-jū*

Now, how would you say the following numbers in Japanese?

1. 72

_____

2. 48

_____

3. 36

_____

4. 83

_____

5. 99

_____

Track 7
CD-4–8

How did you do? Here are the answers:

1. 72 *nana-jū ni*
2. 48 *yoN-jū hachi*
3. 36 *saN-jū roku*
4. 83 *hachi-jū saN*
5. 99 *kyū-jū kyū*

100 to 9,999

Wow, numbers are getting bigger and bigger! We have covered up to 99 so far. Let's first look at the unit of "hundred." Unlike the previous numbers, you will notice that there are three irregular pronunciations, which are boldfaced in the following table.

Track 7
CD-9

Numbers 100 Through 900	
100	*hyaku*
200	*ni-hyaku*
300	***saN-byaku***
400	*yoN-hyaku*
500	*go-hyaku*
600	***rop-pyaku***
700	*nana-hyaku*
800	***hap-pyaku***
900	*kyū-hyaku*

Huh?

The irregular versions of *hyaku* ("hundred") aid in pronunciation of some numbers. For example, pronouncing 600 as *roku-hyaku* would be a tongue twister for Japanese speakers, so it is pronounced as *rop-pyaku*.

Let's do a short practice again. How would you say the following?

1. 172

_____

2. 348

_____

3. 936

_____

4. 840

_____

5. 602

_____

Track 7
CD-10–12

How did you do? Here are the answers:

1. 172 *hyaku nana-jū ni*
2. 348 *saN-byaku yoN-jū hachi*
3. 936 *kyū-hyaku saN-jū roku*

4. 840 *hap-pyaku yoN-jū*

5. 602 *rop-pyaku ni*

Let's move on to the unit of "thousand." Again, there are a couple of irregular pronunciations, 3,000 and 8,000:

Numbers 1,000 Through 9,000

1,000	*seN*
2,000	*ni-seN*
3,000	**saN-zeN**
4,000	*yoN-seN*
5,000	*go-seN*
6,000	*roku-seN*
7,000	*nana-seN*
8,000	**has-seN**
9,000	*kyū-seN*

With the numbers introduced so far, you can say up to 9,999. How would you say the following in Japanese?:

1. 7,380

_____

2. 3,075

_____

3. 2,601

_____

4. 8,004

_____

5. 9,103

_____

How did you do? Here are the answers:

1. 7,380 *nana-seN saN-byaku hachi-jū*
2. 3,075 *saN-zeN nana-jū go*
3. 2,601 *ni-seN rop-pyaku ichi*
4. 8,004 *has-seN yoN*
5. 9,103 *kyū-seN hyaku saN*

Lifesavers _____

Japanese people usually write "big" numbers like "year" or "price" in Arabic numbers rather than Japanese characters.

As an example of practical application of these numbers, you can talk about "years," which use the unit of "thousand." All you need to do is attach the word for "year" (*-neN*) to the end of the number. For example, the year 2002 would be …

ni-seN ni-neN   "year 2002"

Now I will ask you the following question:

Anata-wa naN-neN-ni umare-mashita ka?   "In what year were you born?"
(*umare-masu* = "be born")

The word *naN-neN* is the question word for "what year." If you were born in 1971, the answer would be …

SeN kyū-hyaku nana-jū ichi-neN-ni umare-mashita.   "I was born in 1971."

What is your birth year?

Answer: _____

Shortcuts to Success

Notice that the topic phrase for "I" is missing in the answer of the dialog. As explained in Chapter 4, you can omit any item in a sentence if it is understood by both speaker and listener.

Beyond 10,000

You will find the expression *ichi-maN* (10,000) to be particularly useful because it is the denomination of the largest bill in Japanese money. As we did previously, you count by saying "two 10,000," "three 10,000," and so on.

Numbers 10,000 Through 100,000			
10,000	(= 1,0000)	*ichi-maN*	1 × 10,000
20,000	(= 2,0000)	*ni-maN*	2 × 10,000
30,000	(= 3,0000)	*saN-maN*	3 × 10,000
40,000	(= 4,0000)	*yoN-maN*	4 × 10,000
50,000	(= 5,0000)	*go-maN*	5 × 10,000
60,000	(= 6,0000)	*roku-maN*	6 × 10,000
70,000	(= 7,0000)	*nana-maN*	7 × 10,000
80,000	(= 8,0000)	*hachi-maN*	8 × 10,000
90,000	(= 9,0000)	*kyū-maN*	9 × 10,000
100,000	(= 10,0000)	*jū-maN*	10 × 10,000

Track 7
CD-21

Track 7
CD-22

Track 7
CD-23

Track 7
CD-24

How would you say the following "big" numbers in Japanese?

1. 24,720

_____

2. 98,254

_____

3. 70,541

_____

4. 10,039

_____

5. 50,902

_____

Track 7
CD-25–29

How did you do? Here are the answers:

1. 24,720 *ni-maN yoN-seN nana-hyaku ni-jū*
2. 98,254 *kyū-maN has-seN ni-hyaku go-jū yoN*
3. 70,541 *nana-maN go-hyaku yoN-jū ichi*
4. 10,039 *ichi-maN saN-jū kyū*
5. 50,902 *go-maN kyū-hyaku ni*

Because a new unit appears every four digits, *one million*, or 1,000,000, is 100,0000 in Japanese:

> *hyaku-maN* "1,000,000" (= 100,0000 in Japanese)

Track 7
CD-30

> **Green Tea Break**
>
> The idea that a counting unit changes every four digits (as opposed to every three digits, common in Western countries) originated in China. Japan's adoption of this system was a result of the country's aggressive importation of Chinese civilization about 1,600 years ago.

Really Big Numbers

The most likely setting in which you might have to deal with very big numbers is counting money when you are shopping. As of February 2002, U.S. $1 is about 130 *yen*. This means that if you exchange U.S. $100 for Japanese currency, you will have 13,000 *yen* in hand.

Track 7
CD-31

> *ichi-maN san-zeN eN*   "13,000 *yen*"
>
> (Literally: 1 ten-thousand and 3 thousand yen)

Note that the Japanese monetary unit is pronounced *eN*, not *yen*. Its international symbol is ¥.

What Is a "Counter"?

In English, when you count "uncountable" substances such as paper, rice, and coffee, you use words such as "one <u>sheet</u> of paper," "two <u>scoops</u> of rice," or "three <u>cups</u> of coffee." These underlined words are called "counters." When you count objects in Japanese, the appropriate counter must accompany them. Just as English has a number of counters such as *sheets*, *scoops*, and *cups*, Japanese has numerous counters that refer to particular types of objects.

You will learn several basic counters in this book; however, to illustrate the concept in this chapter, I will explain one such counter now.

When you count objects that are "thin and flat," you use the counter *-mai*. Can you think of any "thin and flat" objects? Paper, CDs, postcards, stamps, mouse pads, windowpanes, pizza, plates, T-shirts—all are examples of thin, flat objects.

If you want to say "I ate two sheets (not slices!) of pizza," the sentence should look like this:

> *Watashi-wa piza-o ni-mai tabe-mashita.*   "I ate two sheets of pizza."

Here is the complete list of this "thin and flat" counter for numbers from 1 to 10:

Track 7
CD-32

Counter for Thin and Flat Objects	
1	*ichi-mai*
2	*ni-mai*
3	*saN-mai*
4	*yoN-mai*
5	*go-mai*
6	*roku-mai*
7	*nana-mai*
8	*hachi-mai*
9	*kyū-mai*
10	*jū-mai*
How many?	*naN-mai*

Suppose that you want to buy 10 stamps at the post office. You might expect the following dialog to take place:

Track 7
CD-33

You:	*Kitte-o kudasai.*	"Stamps, please."
Clerk:	*NaN-mai-desu ka?*	"How many?"
You:	*Jū-mai kudasai.*	"Ten, please."

Here are some commonly used counters.

Common Counters

Objects	Counter	Examples
Bound objects	*-satsu*	books, magazines ...
Long objects	*-hoN*	pens, carrots, sticks ...
Small objects	*-ko*	fruits, erasers, marbles ...
Machinery	*-dai*	cars, computers ...
Small animals	*-hiki*	dogs, cats, rabbits ...
Large animals	*-tō*	lions, elephants, horses ...
People	*-niN*	

Memorizing numbers might take time, but what you can do with numbers is unlimited—you can shop without going over your budget, read the calendar, count things, and so on.

Before concluding this chapter, let's do some review exercises. How would you say the following in Japanese?

Review

1. 98

_____

2. 276

_____

3. 901

_____

4. 3,476

_____

5. 2,003

_____

6. 54,192

_____

7. 28,505

_____

8. 110,000

_____

9. Year 1986 (with the appropriate counter)

_____

10. 25,048 *yen* (with the appropriate counter)

_____

Answers

**Track 7
CD-34**

1. 98

    kyū-jū hachi

2. 276

    ni-hyaku nana-jū roku

3. 901

    kyū-hyaku ichi

4. 3,476

    saN-zeN yon-hyaku nana-jū roku

5. 2,003

    ni-seN saN

6. 54,192

    go-maN yoN-seN hyaku kyū-jū ni

7. 28,505

    ni-maN has-seN go-hyaku go

8. 110,000

    jū ichi-maN

9. Year 1986

    seN kyū-hyaku hachi-jū roku-neN

10. 25,048 *yen*

    ni-maN go-seN yoN-jū hachi-eN

The Least You Need to Know

- ◆ Master the basic numbers so that you can count objects, tell your age, check prices when shopping, and so on.
- ◆ In Japanese, counting units change every four digits, not three digits as is common in Western countries.
- ◆ When you count objects, you must use the appropriate "counter" for the noun being counted.

Part  3

Getting to Know People

Even if you are a shy person, getting to know people is not a difficult task at all if you learn the expressions for greetings and self-introductions. These phrases are fixed or "ritualized"—mechanical and simple, yet very effective. Take a close look at the next few chapters and learn those expressions as conversation starters.

After you master greetings and self-introductions, you will want to know more personalized expressions so that you can talk more about yourself and ask other people more questions. Politeness is important in Japanese, and I will show you how to carry out these conversations without being perceived as rude or nosy.

At the end of these chapters, you will also learn how to invite people to various activities, and you will be given a few tips that make your invitations hard to resist. Don't miss them!

Chapter **8**

Greetings

In This Chapter

◆ Greeting expressions

◆ How to express thanks and apologies

◆ Other useful expressions

For a student of Japanese, it's important to give the listener the best possible first impression. If you sound rude or disrespectful from the start, the conversation is likely to stop there. If the listener finds you polite and friendly, the dialog might go on. And, who knows, this person might become a great Japanese tutor or even lifelong friend—just because of the first encounter!

Don't take this chapter on greetings too lightly. Greetings are very effective and can give people a good first impression of you. In this chapter, you learn how to use the proper greetings for the appropriate occasions. Try them out as you learn them. Even though you can't speak much Japanese at this point, greetings are powerful enough to draw people's attention and start a conversation, so don't be shy!

The expressions in this chapter are all "ritualized" or "fixed" expressions. When you say *hello*, you don't think about what this word means, do you? Likewise, don't worry about the meanings behind Japanese *ritualized expressions*. Instead, accept them as they are and pay attention to which expression to say in a given situation. With proper use of fixed expressions, your Japanese will sound more natural.

Greetings Around the Clock

Let's think about English greetings first. English has very handy greeting words such as *hi* and *hello*. You can say these to pretty much anyone at any time, be it friends, acquaintances, or strangers. These greetings can also be used whether it is morning, afternoon, or night.

Huh?

As the phrase suggests, **ritualized expressions** are expressions of social protocol. Most such expressions have been used for daily greetings, and the original meanings were lost over time.

I wish I could say that Japanese has a handy word like *Hi!* Japanese people are particular about greetings. You must remember to use the right greeting at the appropriate time:

Track 8
CD-1–3

Good morning!	*Ohayō gozaimasu!*
Good afternoon!	*KoNnichiwa!*
Good evening!	*KoNbaNwa!*

Did you actually move your mouth and say these words aloud rather than read them silently? Remember, silent reading does not improve your speaking skill.

Lifesavers

Remember, when you speak Japanese, try not to add any strong accents or stress to the words. For example, if you stress a certain syllable, as in *koNníchiwa*, your Japanese will sound very foreign! It's good to keep in mind that you should always speak calmly. To review speech patterns, see Chapter 3.

Let's imagine that you're staying with a Japanese family. You'll hear a lot of ritualized or fixed expressions at home. Let's learn those expressions as they are used in specific situations.

At the Dining Table

Eating is an important part of Japanese daily life. Food is considered a gift from God (or gods, in Japan), and, therefore, we express our thanks not only before we begin eating, but when we finish:

Track 8
CD-4–5

Before you eat:	*Itadakimasu.*
After you eat:	*Gochisōsama.*

The French say *Bon appétit!* before eating. *Bon appétit!* means "good appetite," whereas *itadakimasu* literally means "I will humbly accept (the food)." *Itadakimasu* was originally a very religious expression, although most Japanese probably have never thought about its origin because it's so ritualized. *Gochisōsama* means "That was a feast!" Again, it is a ritualized expression, so you say this even if what you've just eaten was not a "feast."

What if your host offers you food, but you can't eat any more? You can say either of the following:

Track 8
CD-6–7

No, thank you.   *Īe, kekkō-desu.*

I am full.   *Onaka-ga ippai-desu.*

If you're still hungry, you can accept the offer by saying the by-now-familiar *itadakimasu* because you are "humbly accepting" the food.

And remember, it's always nice to give the host a compliment for her or his cooking:

Track 8
CD-8

That was delicious!   *Oishi-kattadesu!*

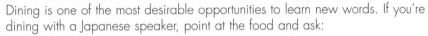

Shortcuts to Success

Dining is one of the most desirable opportunities to learn new words. If you're dining with a Japanese speaker, point at the food and ask:

Kore-wa naN-desu ka?   "What is this?"

There is no doubt that the best way to learn a new word is by association, and tasting delicious food is a wonderful way of association! So don't be afraid to try exotic foods!

Leaving Home and Coming Home

When you leave for work in the morning, what do you say to your family and what does your family say to you in English? You probably say something like *See you, Later,* or *I love you!* The expression varies from person to person.

In Japanese, on the other hand, no matter what circumstances you're in, the following dialog is exchanged between the one leaving and the one seeing her or him off:

Track 8
CD-9–10

Person leaving: *Itte kimasu.*   "I am going." (*Lit.* "I am going and coming back.")

Person seeing her or him off: *Itte rasshai.*   "See you." (*Lit.* "Please go and come back.")

The bottom line is that it would be extremely rude to leave home or to see someone off without saying a word.

After long hours of work, you get home. What do you say to your family then? In English, perhaps you say *Hi* or maybe *Honey, I'm home!* Again, in Japanese, the expressions are fixed, and 99 percent of people—if not 100 percent—say the following:

Person getting home: *Tadaima.*   "I'm home." (*Lit.* "I am here right now.")

Family, welcoming you home: *Okaeri nasai.*   "Welcome back." (*Lit.* "Please come home.")

Notice that the literal translations are somewhat bizarre, but that's what "ritualized" expressions are all about.

These four phrases are musts if you don't want to be perceived as a rude person!

At the End of the Day

Your long day with your host family is near the end, and it's time to say *good night*. But before you say *good night*, it would be a good idea to indicate or imply to the family that you're sleepy. This kind of "communication buffer" is really important in Japanese. Without an extra *buffer expression*—a little hint before you say something directly—you will appear blunt and self-centered.

Huh?

By **buffer expressions**, I mean "filler" expressions uttered before making a point. This is to avoid direct statements and subsequently portray yourself as a self-centered person. For example, if you are hungry, you would utter a seemingly unrelated expression before saying "I'm hungry," like "What time is it?" This way, you can give the listener a "hint" as to what you are going to say afterward. This is a very important communication strategy in Japanese.

Here are some "buffer" expressions suitable for this particular situation:

Chotto tsukare-mashita.   "I am a bit tired."

Ashita-wa haya-idesu.   "I must wake up early tomorrow."

Then you can finally say this:

Oyasumi nasai.   "Good night!"

These around-the-clock expressions are all daily essentials. Practice and use them. If you have a Japanese-speaking friend near you, that's great! Even if you don't, say these words to a friend anyway. You will gain more this way rather than mumbling to yourself!

Thanks, Sorry, and Excuse Me

When I was a child, my mother used to tell me that there is never too much of saying *thanks*, even for a tiny favor. She was absolutely right. Whether you speak English or Japanese, thanking doesn't hurt a person's feelings. Here is the Japanese way of saying *thanks*:

Track 8
CD-15–16

> *Arigatō.*   "Thanks!"
>
> *Dōmo arigatō.*   "Thank you!"

In a formal setting, or if you want to sound polite, say the following:

Track 8
CD-17

> *Dōmo arigatō gozaimasu.*   "Thank you very much!"

In a very casual setting, simply saying *dōmo* is also acceptable. You might also hear *saNkyū* among young people—the Japanized loan word for *thank you*.

If someone says *arigatō* to you, reply to him by saying …

Track 8
CD-18

> *Dō itashi mashite.*   "You're welcome!"

When I was learning English in Japan, my English teacher taught me that I should not say *sorry* unless I acknowledge my fault. I was shocked at that comment because in Japanese, "sorry" is used in a much broader sense. The word for "sorry" in Japanese is …

> *(Dōmo) SumimaseN.*

Track 8
CD-19

> ⚠ CAUTION **Lifesavers** _____
>
> *Dōmo*, which literally means "indeed" or "truly," is a very handy word. In a casual setting, you can say *dōmo* when meeting people, excusing yourself, entering a room, and so on. Because it's a context-sensitive word, pay attention to when Japanese people use *dōmo*.

It might not be a good idea for me to simply translate *sumimaseN* as "sorry" because it can sometimes mean "thank you" as well! For example, when someone works very hard on your behalf, you should thank her or him by saying *sumimaseN*, rather than *arigatō*.

Japanese people use *sumimaseN* when they think they are causing the other party some kind of trouble or inconvenience. Suppose that your friend spent hours fixing your kitchen sink. You think that you caused him trouble, even though he volunteered to do so. This feeling makes you say *sumimaseN*.

If someone says *sumimaseN* to you in order to show her or his apology, reply by saying either of the following:

Track 8
CD-20

> *Ie ie* or *Īe.*   "No problem!"

On the other hand, if she or he says *sumimaseN* to "thank" you, reply by saying

Track 8
CD-21

> *Dō itashi mashite.*   "You're welcome!"

The borderline between "sorry" and "excuse me" is also vague in Japanese. For instance, when you must walk in a hurry through a crowd of people, you would say *excuse me* in English. In Japanese, you would use *sumimaseN*. Then, when should you use "excuse me"? Here are some clear situations in which you should use "excuse me" in Japanese:

Green Tea Break

When you say *ie* or *ie ie* as the reply to a person's apology, you should shake your head from side to side.

- ◆ When entering a room
- ◆ When leaving a room
- ◆ When excusing yourself (for going to the bathroom, for example)
- ◆ When saying good-bye (in a formal setting)

In these cases, you should say …

Track 8
CD-22

> *Shitsurē shimasu.*   "Excuse me."

Here are typical replies to someone saying *shitsurē shimasu*. When someone (1) enters your room or (2) asks for permission to temporarily excuse her- or himself saying *shitsurē shimasu*, you should say …

Track 8
CD-23

> *Dōzo.*   "Please come in."

When someone at work says *shitsurē shimasu* for "Good-bye" at the end of the day, you should reply as follows:

Shortcuts to Success

Because of the *shi* and *tsu* sounds combined, you might find it difficult to pronounce *shitsurē shimasu*. You might want to say the word slowly, by dividing it into syllables: *shi-tsu-re-e shi-ma-su*. Even if you do so, you would not sound awkward to Japanese ears at all.

Track 8
CD-24

> *Otsukaresama-deshita.*   "Good-bye."
> (*Lit.* "You must be exhausted [due to hard work].")

We quickly went through the words for "thanks," "sorry," and "excuse me." Among these words, pay special attention to *sumimaseN* because the usage of this phrase is so wide.

Good-Bye!

There are many ways to say *good-bye* in Japanese, and each use depends on the degree of formality and the type of parting. If parting is short and you expect to see that person soon, you could say any of the following, ranging from a formal to a casual style:

Shitsurē shimasu. [formal]

Soredewa.

↓

Sorejā.

Jā! or *Jāne!* [casual]

If you are going to see this person tomorrow, you can attach *mata ashita* ("again tomorrow") to some of the preceding expressions:

Soredewa mata ashita.

Sorejā mata ashita.

Jā mata ashita!

If you part from someone for a longer period of time, the following would be appropriate:

Mata oai shimashō. "I will see you again."

Sayōnara or *Sayonara.* "So long."

You might know *sayonara*, but once you arrive in Japan, you will notice that it isn't used as often as you might expect. It's a rather formal and "heavy" word for parting. In a formal parting, you might want to add the following phrase to *sayōnara*:

Sayōnara, ogeNkide. "So long, I wish you the best!"

In daily conversation, probably the most common expression for good-bye is *sorejā*. It's neither too casual nor too polite—a neutral expression that can be used on any occasion.

> ### Green Tea Break
>
> The word *sayōnara* came from classical Japanese, meaning "if that is the case." As you know by now, Japanese people prefer an indirect or implicit expression. By *sayōnara*, the ancient Japanese people implied, "It is not easy to part from you, but *if it's the case that you must go*, I must say good-bye."

The Magic Words

The beauty of ritualized expressions is that even one tiny phrase can easily and effectively convey your feelings to the listener. Those magic words literally work "magic" in that they make conversation run smoothly. Let's learn some more useful expressions.

Making a Request

There are a number of ways to ask for a favor, but they boil down to one simple expression. The magic phrase is …

Track 8
CD-30

Onegai shimasu. "Please."

This is an extremely powerful phrase. Even in the worst-case scenario, when you can't remember any appropriate Japanese sentences, body language and using this expression might save you (just like I survived in Paris with only *s'il vous plaît*—"Please!").

Situations in which this phrase can be used are countless. Here are some examples for when to use *onegai shimasu:*

> **Situation 1:** When you buy something, you can point at it and say, *Onegai shimasu.*
>
> **Situation 2:** When you submit a document to someone (such as an immigration officer at the airport), say *Onegai shimasu.* You will give him or her a much better impression of you!
>
> **Situation 3:** When you want someone to pass the salt, you can point at it and simply say, *Onegai shimasu.*

Think about any suitable situations, and practice this phrase in preparation.

In a situation in which you must ask for a big favor, or simply when you want to make a request politely, you can add the by-now-familiar magic word *sumimaseN* to *onegai shimasu:*

Track 8
CD-31

SumimaseN. Onegai shimasu. "Excuse me. Please (do it)."

You'll learn more about making a request in Chapter 12.

Giving and Receiving

If you plan to visit someone in Japan, you might be thinking about taking a gift with you. Here is a very easy dialog that you can practice in such a situation:

Track 8
CD-32

| Giver: | *Dōzo.* | "Here you are." |
| Receiver: | *Dōmo (arigatō).* | "Thank you." |

You can use this very handy *dōzo/dōmo* dialog in any giving/receiving situation—not just for gift giving.

You can also use *dōzo* whenever you offer some kind of service to someone. Suppose that you're sitting in a crowded train and you see an elderly woman standing near you. You can offer her your seat by saying *dōzo.* Similarly, when you're in line and kindly let someone go ahead of you, you can use *dōzo,* meaning "After you, please."

Survival Phrases

What if you didn't catch what the other party said, and you want her or him to repeat it? Here is a list of useful phrases:

**Track 8
CD-33–38**

Mō ichido onegai shimasu.	"One more time, please."
Mō ichido it-te kudasai.	"Please say one more time."
Yukkuri it-te kudasai.	"Please say it slowly."
Wakari-maseN.	"I don't understand."
Ēgo-de i-idesu ka?	"Is English okay?"
Ēgo-de onegai shimasu.	"In English, please."

You can make these requests more politely by adding *SumimaseN* at the beginning of each phrase.

You might think the last two phrases are kind of "cheating" because this is a book about Japanese. However, in a really urgent situation, you might desperately need to communicate in English. You will be pleasantly surprised that many Japanese do understand English. Make sure that you speak English slowly and clearly.

> **Green Tea Break**
>
> When you give a gift to someone in Japan, always hand it to her or him *with both hands.* Likewise, when you receive a gift, never receive it with one hand because you will be considered rude. This principle also applies when you exchange business cards (*mēshi*).

CAUTION

Lifesavers _____

If you need assistance from Japanese people in English, you have a better chance of success by asking in writing rather than speaking. Make sure to use plain English when you write. When you ask someone to write something down, say the following:

Kai-te kudasai.   "Please write it down."

Summary: Essential Expressions

Wow, you've learned quite a few expressions in this chapter! As a summary, here are some of the most essential:

Ohayō gozaimasu.	"Good morning."
KoNnichiwa.	"Good afternoon."

KoNbaNwa.	"Good evening."
Oyasumi nasai.	"Good night!"
Itadakimasu.	Expression before eating
Gochisōsama.	Expression after eating
Dōmo arigatō.	"Thank you."
Dō itashi mashite.	"You're welcome!"
SumimaseN.	"Sorry for the trouble."; "Thanks for your hard work."
Sorejā.	"See you."
Onegai shimasu.	"Please."
Dōzo.	"Here you are."
Mō ichido it-te kudasai.	"Please say it one more time."
Yukkuri it-te kudasai.	"Please say it slowly."
Wakari-maseN.	"I don't understand."

The Least You Need to Know

♦ Greetings are a great way to start conversation—if you're careful to make a good first impression.

♦ Bowing is essential for greetings in Japan, but a big bow is not necessary. A slight bow will do.

♦ Use buffer expressions—little hints before you say something directly—or you will appear blunt and self-centered.

♦ Be comfortable with magic words such as *sumimaseN* (excuse me), *onegai shimasu* (please), and *dōzo* (here you are).

♦ *Sayonara* is a rather formal and heavy word for "good-bye." In daily conversation, probably the most common expression for good-bye is *sorejā*.

♦ Don't be afraid to use ritualized expressions. Practice makes proficient!

Chapter 9

Meeting People

In This Chapter

◆ Meeting people for the first time

◆ Exchanging names

◆ Useful conversation starters

Greetings are great conversation starters. With the greeting expressions that you learned in Chapter 8, you will have more success on first meetings. However, you don't want your conversation to stop there just because you lack something to talk about. You should get to know more about the person you're talking to, and subsequently you need to have her or him learn more about you. In this chapter, you learn a number of sentences and questions useful when meeting people for the first time.

My Name Is ...

Suppose that you're meeting someone for the first time. Because you don't know who he or she is, it's safe to start a conversation by exchanging formal greetings.

Hajime mashite. "How do you do?"

Track 9
CD-1

The phrase *Hajime mashite* literally means "for the first time." At this point, if this is a business setting, you might encounter the ritual of a business card exchange. If that's the case, as I pointed out in Chapter 8, make sure that you give out your card (*mēshi*), as well as receive the other person's business card, with both hands.

Naturally, the next step is to introduce yourself. Let's suppose that your name is Brown.

Track 9
CD-2

> *BurauN-desu.* "I am Brown."

This sentence is a shorter version of the following:

Track 9
CD-3

> *Watashi-wa BurauN-desu.* "I am Brown."

Because you are introducing yourself, it is obvious that the "topic" of the sentence— "I"—is understood by the listener. So you can omit *watashi*, as seen in the first example.

Alternatively, you can introduce yourself using a more formal pattern, *[Your Name Here] to mōshi-masu,* as shown in the following example:

Track 9
CD-4

> *BurauN to mōshi-masu.* "I am Brown."

X-wa Y-desu

In the sentence *Watashi-wa BurauN-desu,* I start the dialog with "I," *watashi,* as the topic. What follows the topic is the speaker's comment on the topic, that is, "Brown," *BurauN.* This "X is Y" kind of equation sentence is very common, and you should be familiar with its structure, as shown here:

> *X-wa Y-desu.* "X is Y."

Let's look at a few examples of the *X-wa Y-desu* pattern:

Track 9
CD-5–7

> *Amerika-wa ōki-idesu.* "America is big."
> *Toyota-wa nihoN-no kaisha-desu.* "Toyota is a Japanese company."
> *Sushi-wa oishi-idesu.* "Sushi is delicious."

In all these examples, *-wa* serves as the bridge between the topic and the comment. For instance, in the first example, the equation [America = big] is established by *-wa.*

Watashi-wa XYZ-desu

Another helpful sentence pattern to be learned here is *Watashi-wa XYZ-desu*. With the sentence pattern *watashi-wa XYZ-desu*, not only can you identify your name, but you can also talk about anything concerning "you," as in the following examples:

Track 9
CD-8–9

> *Watashi-wa [AmerikajiN/KanadajiN/IgirisujiN]-desu.*   "I am a(n) [American/Canadian/British]."
>
> *Watashi-wa jānarisuto-desu.*   "I am a journalist."

And You Are ...?

After you have identified your name, the next step is to ask the listener what her or his name is.

Track 9
CD-10

> *SumimaseN ga, o-namae-wa naN to osshai-masu ka?*   "Excuse me. What is your name?"

Because this is a question sentence, the question marker *ka* is attached at the end, as explained in Chapter 6. Note that to sound even more natural, you can omit *naN to osshai-masu ka*:

Track 9
CD-11

> *SumimaseN ga, o-namae-wa?*   "Excuse me. Your name is?"

Huh?

The Japanese word for "name" or "given name" is *namae*. If you refer to someone else's name, you should attach the polite marker *o-* to *namae*, as in *o-namae*, in order to show your respect to that person. Don't attach *o-* when you refer to your own name because you don't have to show respect to yourself.

By the way, the word for "family name" (or "last name") is *myōji*.

In Chapter 6, you learned how to ask a question. Remember, in Japanese we don't move a question word to the beginning of a sentence, as in ***What** is your name?* in English. Instead, its Japanese counterpart is more like *Your name is **what?*** This is what you see in the preceding example: The question word for "what," *naN*, does not appear at the beginning of the sentence, but toward the end.

Now, let's practice asking each other's names. My name is Fujita. Suppose that your family name is *Brown*.

Me: *SumimaseN ga, o-namae-wa?* "Excuse me. What is your name?"

You: *BrauN to mōshi-masu. O-namae-wa?* "My name is Brown. And your name is?"

Me: *Fujita to mōshi-masu.* "(My name is) Fujita."

Green Tea Break

In English, you usually introduce yourself by your first name. In Japanese, on the other hand, you go by your last name first. When Japanese people refer to their full names, they say their family name first, and then their given name, as in …

> *Watashi-wa Fujita Naoya-desu.* "I am Naoya Fujita."

However, if you have a Western name, either order is acceptable: Japanese people will honor your custom.

Notice that in your part of the dialog, when you ask me what my name is, you simply say *O-namae-wa?* It's an incomplete sentence when translated into English, but a perfect sentence in Japanese. This is because in Japanese, you can omit whatever is understood in the context, as explained in Chapter 4. For the same reason, in response to the question *O-namae-wa?* I said *Fujita to mōshi-masu* instead of answering with a full sentence.

Beyond Exchanging Names

I believe that the most important factor for successful language learning is curiosity. Curiosity makes you ask people questions. A willingness to know something makes you listen to people more carefully. Even if you consider yourself a quiet person when speaking English, don't despair! I know many quiet or shy people who are learning a foreign language. Interestingly, many of them turn out to be quite talkative when speaking a foreign language. In language learning, there is nothing to lose, so don't be shy.

In the rest of this chapter, I will introduce to you useful questions that serve as appropriate and effective "ice breakers" for meeting someone for the first time. Most of the questions fall into the *X-wa* + predicate + *ka?* pattern, such as *O-namae-wa naN to osshai-masu ka?* ("What is your name?"). Ask these questions over and over. Repetition is the fastest way to become fluent in Japanese.

In the following section, just pay attention to question patterns and don't worry about answering the questions. I don't want to keep you too busy here. We'll get into answering questions in Chapter 10.

Occupations

The Japanese word for "job" is *shigoto*. If you refer to someone else's job, you should make the word sound polite by attaching *o-*, as in *o-shigoto*. Now, let's ask what the other party's occupation is. Because it's a somewhat personal question, it's a wise idea to first say *SumimaseN ga* ("Sorry for my rudeness").

Track 9
CD-13

> *SumimaseN ga, o-shigoto-wa nani-o sarete i-masu ka?*
> "Sorry for my rudeness. What do you do?"

For business people, *kaisha* ("company") is an important word. If you're curious where she or he works, ask the following question:

Track 9
CD-14

> *Dochira-no kaisha-ni otsutome-desu ka?*
> "Where do you work?"

Huh?

The question word *dochira* ("where") is the polite version of *doko*.

Suppose that the person mentioned the name of the company she or he works for, but you don't know what kind of business that company engages in. You can ask a question by combining the question word *naN* ("what") and the noun *kaisha* ("company"):

Track 9
CD-15

> *NaN-no kaisha-desu ka?*
> "What company is it?"

Notice that this sentence does not have the topic "your company" because it is mutually understood between you and the listener. In other words, it is not there because it would be redundant if included.

Huh?

When the question word *naN* ("what") precedes a noun such as *kaisha* ("company"), the noun connector particle *-no* is attached to the question word as in *naN-no*. For the explanation of *-no*, see the section "How to Describe Something or Someone" in Chapter 6.

Where Are You From?

It might be rude to ask the age or marital status of the person, but asking where she or he is from is certainly safe. You have just learned *dochira* ("where"). Using this question word, ask the following:

Track 9
CD-16

> *XYZ-saN-no goshusshiN-wa dochira-desu ka?*   "Where do you come from?"
> (*goshusshiN* = birth place)

Notice that this question contains *XYZ-saN*. It is common practice to use *-saN* with the person's name instead of using the second-person pronoun *anata*, "you." In fact, you hardly hear personal pronouns in Japanese. The Japanese prefer calling or being called by

Lifesavers _____

Remember, when you introduce yourself, do not add -san to your own name. This is a big no-no! You would sound very eccentric because you would be showing respect to yourself.

their names rather than "you." Likewise, you can omit the topic *XYZ-saN* in the preceding example.

At a private setting such as a party, asking where someone lives might be acceptable. Again, we can use the same question word, *dochira*. The new word you should know is *o-sumai* ("residence"):

Track 9
CD-17

O-sumai-wa dochira-desu ka?
"Where do you live?"

Essential Party Greetings

If the first encounter with a person takes place where eating is involved, such as at a party or restaurant, there are a lot of things you can talk about and use as a conversation starter. You can give a compliment on the food served or ask whether she or he likes a certain food. Let's first learn how to give a compliment on the food:

Track 9
CD-18

*Kore-wa oishi-idesu **ne!***   "This is delicious, **isn't it?**"

Huh? _____

Because these particles, *ne* and *yo*, appear only at the end of a sentence, they are called "sentence-final particles" and are distinct from other particles that attach to nouns. The question marker *ka* is also a sentence-final particle.

Oishi-i means "delicious." Did you notice the tiny particle at the end of the sentence, *ne?* This particle functions as a kind of exclamation. Use *ne* when you expect an agreement from the listener. I call *ne* the "agreement-seeking particle."

Let me introduce another useful sentence-final particle, *yo*. I call *yo* the "information-giving particle." By attaching *yo*, you are giving the listener new information. So if you want to tell the listener that the food is delicious, say the following:

Track 9
CD-19

*Kore-wa oishi-idesu **yo!***
"**I tell you** this is delicious!"

Shortcuts to Success _____

A good language student never fears to use conversational lubricants called "interjections," such as the English *Oh, my, Oops, You know, Right?* and so on. The Japanese "agreement-seeking particle" *ne* and "information-giving particle" *yo* are also interjections. Try using them when you speak. Such tiny additions make your Japanese sound more Japanese.

Sometimes, conversation begins when you show interest in the food that the listener is eating. Here is how to ask what something is in reference to what the listener has:

> *Sore-wa naN-desu ka?*   "What is that?"

So far, we have seen *kore* ("this one") and *sore* ("that one"). Let me list all the "pointing" words. Please note that there are two kinds of "that one" in Japanese, as seen in the following table.

"Pointing" Words

Object in speaker's domain	*kore*	"this one"
Object in listener's domain	*sore*	"that one"
Object away from speaker and listener	*are*	"that one over there"
Question word	*dore?*	"which one?"

Notice that I use the term "domain" such as "listener's domain." This does *not* necessarily mean the listener's possession. As long as it is *near* the listener, you can refer to that object by using *sore*.

If you want to know what something is that is away from you and the listener, point to it and say …

> *Are-wa naN-desu ka?*   "What is that over there?"

If she or he does not know which one of several things you're referring to, she or he would say …

> *Dore-desu ka?*   "Which one?"

Pointing words are all nouns. When you want to use a pointing word together with another noun, such as *that person (over there)*, you need to use a different form, as shown in the following table.

"Pointing" Adjectives

In speaker's domain	*kono X*	"this X"
In listener's domain	*sono X*	"that X"
Away from speaker and listener	*ano X*	"that X over there"
Question word	*dono X*	"which X?"

Here are examples of each expression:

> *Kono hoN-wa yasu-idesu.*   "This book is cheap."
>
> *Sono hoN-wa dare-no-desu ka?*   "Whose is that book (near you)?"
>
> *Ano hito-wa dare-desu ka?*   "Who is that person over there?"

Dono hoN-o kai-masu ka?   "Which book are you going to buy?"
(*kai-masu* = "buy")

Huh?

To remember all the "pointing" words, remember *"ko-so-a-do."* All four pointing words start with one of these syllables as in the following examples based on "place":

*ko*ko   "this place; here; where I am"

*so*ko   "that place; there; where you are"

*a*soko   "that place away from us; over there"

*do*ko?   "which place?; where?"

Oops! Let's get back to the dining table. Let's imagine that a girl sitting next to you at the table keeps eating *sushi*. Let's ask if she likes it:

Track 9
CD-27

O-sushi-ga o-suki-desu ka?   "Do you like *sushi*?"

If her answer is *hai* or *ē* ("yes"), and you also like *sushi*, great! You have something in common to talk about. Definitely, *o-suki-desu ka* is one of the most frequently used phrases.

Shortcuts to Success

For *suki-desu* ("like"), its object (such as *sushi*) must be marked by *-ga*, not the object marker *-o*. This is an exception.

Note that *o-*, which is attached to *suki-desu*, is an honorific prefix. Attach *o-* when you are addressing someone. However, when you refer to yourself, as in "I like X," simply say *X-ga suki-desu*, without *o-*.

Even if the answer is *Īe* ("no"), you might still continue the conversation, perhaps by asking "Then, what kind of food do you like?" Important words here are *doNna* ("what kind of") and *tabemono* ("food"):

Track 9
CD-28

Jā, doNna tabemono-ga o-suki-desu ka?   "Then, what kind of food do you like?"

If it's a beverage, the word is *nomimono*:

Track 9
CD-29

Jā, doNna nomimono-ga o-suki-desu ka?   "Then, what kind of drink do you like?"

In this chapter, we have looked at useful conversation expressions. As in Western societies, it isn't a good idea to ask overly personal questions, such as the person's age or marital status, at first meetings. The rule of thumb is, before asking any personal questions of someone, talk about yourself first. In Chapter 10, I introduce a number of useful patterns to use when talking about yourself.

Summary: Essential Expressions

Here are some of the most essential expressions you should know:

Hajime mashite.	"How do you do?"
Watashi-wa XYZ-desu.	"I am XYZ (name)."
Watashi-wa XYZ to mōshi-masu.	"I am XYZ (name)." (formal)
O-namae-wa?	"What is your name?" (informal)
O-namae-wa naN to osshai-masu ka?	"What is your name?" (formal)
O-shigoto-wa nani-o sarete i-masu ka?	"What do you do?"
Dochira-no kaisha-ni otsutome-desu ka?	"Where do you work?"
GoshusshiN-wa dochira-desu ka?	"Where do you come from?"
Sore-wa naN-desu ka?	"What is that?"
X-ga o-suki-desu ka?	"Do you like X?"
DoNna X-ga o-suki-desu ka?	"What kind of X do you like?"

The Least You Need to Know

- A proper self-introduction will make the rest of the conversation go smoothly.
- Japanese people usually do not shake hands when greeting, nor do they hug, kiss, or sport big smiles. Polite bowing is all you need to do.
- The *X-wa Y-desu* pattern is very useful for making "X is Y" statements.
- Never add *-san* to your own name when introducing yourself.
- Some basic questions such as *Hajime mashite* (How do you do?) can be used as effective "ice-breakers."
- Use the *ne* particle when you expect an agreement from the listener and *yo* when imparting information to him.
- Be sensitive to others when asking questions.

Chapter 10

Talking About Yourself

In This Chapter

- ◆ Sharing personal information
- ◆ Talking about your hobbies
- ◆ Talking about your family

There is no doubt that you will master Japanese much more quickly if you consistently participate in actual conversation. You can't just wait for an opportunity to try out your Japanese. You need to make an opportunity! In Chapter 9, you learned how to make such an opportunity by using conversation starters. In this chapter, you learn how to elaborate on the conversation by talking about yourself.

Purpose of Your Visit to Japan

Again, let's assume that you're visiting Japan. Perhaps the person you're talking with is curious to know the purpose of your visit. She or he might ask you the following question:

Track 10
CD-1

NaN-de nihoN-ni ki-mashita ka?   "What made you come to Japan?"

The question word *naN-de* means "for what (purpose)." There could be many possible reasons; here are some common ones:

Track 10
CD-2

business	*shigoto*
business trip	*shucchō*
fun/pleasure	*asobi*
sightseeing	*kaNkō*
sightseeing trip	*kaNkō ryokō*
study abroad	*ryūgaku*
traveling	*ryokō*

Do you remember how to answer a question (see Chapter 6)? In Japanese, it's important to listen to the question carefully and simply replace the question word, such as *naN* ("what"), with your answer word without changing the word order. So in reply to the previous question, *NaN-de nihoN-ni ki-mashita ka?* if your answer is "for sightseeing" (*kaNkō*), you would say the following:

Shortcuts to Success

Remember that any element that is understood by speakers within the context of the conversation can be omitted in Japanese. You can even omit the verb by replacing it with *-desu:*

KaNkō(-de) desu.
"For sightseeing."

Track 10
CD-3

KaNkō-de ki-mashita.
"I came for sightseeing."

The words *ryokō* ("traveling"), *kaNkō* ("sightseeing"), and *shigoto* ("business") are all nouns. What if you want to answer with a verb such as "to study Japanese" or "to meet friends," instead of a noun? All you need to do is attach the particle *-ni* to the "stem" of that verb. The "stem" is always the verb without *-masu* (see Chapter 5 for details). Let's find stems of these verbs:

NihoNgo-o beNkyō shi-masu   "study Japanese"
*NihoNgo-o beNkyō **shi***
Tomodachi-ni ai-masu   "meet friends"
*Tomodachi-ni **ai***

Using these stems, your answers should look like the following:

Track 10
CD-4–5

*NihoNgo-o beNkyō **shi-ni** ki-mashita.*   "I came to study Japanese."
*Tomodachi-ni **ai-ni** ki-mashita.*   "I came to see my friends."

The use of the stem for "purpose" is very handy with motion verbs like *ki-masu* ("to come"). You can also use other motion verbs like *iki-masu* ("to go"):

Track 10
CD-6

Q: *Kyōto-ni nani-o **shi-ni** iki-masu ka?*   "For what purpose will you go to Kyoto?"
A: *Tomodachi-ni **ai-ni** iki-masu.*   "To see my friends."

Let's practice this pattern. Answer the following question using the helpful tips provided. The answers are at the end of this chapter.

Exercise 1

Q: *NihoN-ni nani-o **shi-ni** iki-masu ka?*   "For what purpose will you go to Japan?"

A1: _____

"To eat delicious sushi" ("eat" = *tabe-masu;* "delicious" = *oishi-i*)

A2: _____

"To sing karaoke" ("sing" = *utai-masu*)

A3: _____

"To buy a Nikon camera" ("buy" = *kai-masu;* "camera" = *kamera*)

Talk About Your Background

Although it might be rude to ask the listener a personal question, it is okay to discuss something personal about yourself. In this section, you will learn how to talk about:

◆ Where you live

◆ Your marital status

◆ Your job

Huh? _____

Alternatively, you can say:
Osumai-wa dochira-desu ka?
"Where do you live?"
(*Lit.* Where is your residence?)
Dochira is a formal version of *doko,* "where." This option is more formal than *Doko-ni suNde i-masu ka?*

Where You Live

The verb "to live" is *suNde i-masu* in Japanese. Look at an example:

Track 10
CD-7

*Tōkyō-**ni** suNde i-masu.*   "I live in Tokyo."

Make sure that you attach the "existence" particle *-ni* to the place name. By the way, if you want to ask where the listener lives, use *doko* ("where"):

Track 10
CD-8

*Doko-**ni** suNde i-masu ka?*   "Where do you live?"

On a related note, here is how you mention your birthplace:

Track 10
CD-9–10

*Kanada-**de** umare-mashita.*   "I was born in Canada."
ShusshiN-wa Kanada-desu.   "My birthplace is Canada."

Marital Status

Now let's move on to your marital status. The verb "married" is *kekkoN shite i-masu* in Japanese. If you are married, say …

KekkoN shite i-masu. "I am married."

Track 10
CD-11

If you are not, then say …

KekkoN shite i-maseN. "I am not married."

Track 10
CD-12

These two forms refer to your current status. If you want to refer to the future, as in "I will marry," you must use a slightly different form, *kekkoN shi-masu:*

(Watashi-wa) raineN kekkoN shi-masu. "I will marry next year."

Track 10
CD-13

Occupation

In Chapter 9, you learned how to ask the listener what her or his job is …

O-shigoto-wa nani-o sarete i-masu ka? "What do you do?"

Track 10
CD-14

Now it's your turn to say what you do. The pattern is simply …

[Your Occupation Here]-desu. "I'm XYZ."

For example, if you are a journalist, say:

Jānarisuto-desu. "I'm a journalist."

Track 10
CD-15

Here is a list of some occupations.

Occupations

English	Japanese
actor/actress	*haiyū*
artist	*ātisuto*
athlete	*supōtsu seNshu*
chef	*shefu*
company worker	*kaishaiN*
counselor	*kauNserā*
designer	*dezainā*
driver	*uNteNshu*

English	Japanese
(fashion) model	*moderu*
hair designer	*biyōshi*
homemaker	*shufu*
journalist	*jānarisuto*
lawyer	*beNgoshi*
medical doctor	*isha*
missionary	*seNkyōshi*
musician	*myūjishaN*
pastor	*bokushi*
pilot	*pairotto*
priest	*shiNpu*
professor	*kyōju*
rabbi	*rabi*
researcher	*kenkyūiN*
salesperson	*ēgyō*
self-employed	*jiēgyō*
stewardess	*suchuwādesu*
student	*gakusē* (general term) *daigakusē* (university) *daigakuiNsē* (graduate school) *kōkōsē* (high school)
teacher	*kyōshi*

Using this list, let's practice a couple of basic dialogs. Suppose that you're an English teacher, but the person you're talking with mistakenly believes that you're a student. The following dialogs make use of noun predicate conjugation. Before looking at the dialogs, let's quickly review noun predicate conjugation.

Noun Predicate Conjugation

	Affirmative	Negative
Present	*gakusē-desu* "is a student"	*gakusē-jana-idesu* "isn't a student"
Past	*gakusē-deshita* "was a student"	*gakusē-jana-kattadesu* "wasn't a student"

Okay, here is the dialog:

Track 10
CD-16

Q: *Gakusē-desu ka?* "Are you a student?"

A: *Īe, gakusē-jana-idesu.* "No, I'm not a student."

ēgo-no kyōshi-desu. "I'm an English teacher."
(*ēgo* = "English")

What if you're asked whether you *were* a teacher back in your home country? Let's answer that you were not a teacher, but you *were* a college student. Pay attention to the tense.

Track 10
CD-17

Q: *Amerika-de-wa kyōshi-deshita ka?* "Were you a teacher in America?"

A: *Īe, kyōshi-jana-kattadesu.* "No, I was not a teacher."

Daigakusē-deshita. "I was a college student."

If you're learning Japanese with a partner, practice these dialogs with her or him. For an even better result, if there is a Japanese speaker around you, ask her or him to take one of the parts in the dialog!

Lifesavers

Sensē also means "teacher." The word *sensē* is an honorific (or polite) version of the general term *kyōshi*, so don't use *sensē* when referring to yourself.

Green Tea Break

In a formal setting, it's best to say *dochira* instead of *doko*:

Dochira-ni o-tsutome-desu ka? "Where do you work?"

Notice that the polite version of *tsutomete i-masu* is *o-tsutome-desu*.

Do you want to tell people exactly where you work, rather than what type of job you do? The word for "to be employed" is *tsutomete i-masu*. Suppose that you work for SONY:

Track 10
CD-18

Watashi-wa SONY-ni tsutomete i-masu. "I work for SONY."

Of course, using this pattern, you can ask the question "Where do you work?"

Track 10
CD-19

Doko-ni tsutomete i-masu ka? "Where do you work?"

Suppose that you're asked where your company is located. The question you're most likely to hear takes the following pattern (note that your name is indicated as *XYZ*). The key word in this sentence pattern is *ari-masu*, which literally means "exist."

Track 10
CD-20

XYZ-saN-no kaisha-wa doko-ni ari-masu ka? "Where is your company located?"

Let's answer this question. It should be easy by now, right? Keep the verb, omit what is understood, drop *ka*, and replace the question word *doko* with your answer:

Track 10
CD-21

Shikago-ni ari-masu. "It is in Chicago."

I omitted the topic "my company" in the example because it is understood. You could keep it, of course.

Talk About Your Hobbies

If you're looking for a good conversation topic, try talking about each other's hobbies, *shumi*. How would you say "What is your hobby?" in Japanese? Using the by-now-familiar question pattern *X-wa naN-desu ka?* it looks like this:

Track 10
CD-22

> *Shumi-wa naN-desu ka?*   "What is your hobby?"

In reply to this question, all you need to do is insert your answer where *XYZ* appears in the following sentence pattern:

Track 10
CD-23

> *Watashi-no shumi-wa XYZ-desu.*   "My hobby is XYZ."

Here is a list of some common hobbies.

Hobbies

English	Japanese
anime (animation)	*anime*
antique	*aNtīku*
art	*āto*
carpentry	*nichiyōdaiku*
chess	*chesu*
coin collection	*koiN shūshū*
comics	*maNga*
computer	*koNpyūtā*
computer game	*koNpyūtā gēmu*
cooking	*ryōri*
drawing (picture)	*kaiga*
driving	*doraibu*
fishing	*tsuri*
gardening	*gādeniNgu*
Internet	*iNtānetto*
karaoke	*karaoke*
sports	*supōtsu*
movies	*ēga*

continues

Hobbies (continued)

English	Japanese
music	*oNgaku*
reading	*dokusho*
sewing/knitting	*shugē*
shopping	*kaimono*
stamp collection	*kitte shūshū*
studying Japanese	*nihoNgo-no beNkyō*
traveling	*ryokō*

If I say to you "My hobby is sports," what would be the next question you might ask me?

Track 10 CD-24

> *DoNna supōtsu-ga suki-desu ka?* "What kind of sports do you like?"

Or:

Track 10 CD-25

> *DoNna supōtsu-o shi-masu ka?* "What kind of sports do you play?"

If you have a particular sport you're crazy about—for example, skating—and you want to find out if the listener also likes it, here's how you ask the question using *suki-desu* ("like"):

Track 10 CD-26

> *Sukēto-wa o-suki-desu ka?* "Do you like skating?"

If she likes skating, she will say:

Track 10 CD-27

> *Hai, suki-desu.* "Yes, I do."

If she doesn't like it, unfortunately, the answer will be:

Track 10 CD-28

> *Īe, (amari) suki-jana-idesu ga …* "No, (not much)."

Huh?

For any sport-related words, the verb for "play" is *shi-masu*, which literally means "to do."

In a negative answer like this, I suggest that you use *amari*, "not much; not very." By adding this word, your answer becomes softened and doesn't sound rude. The addition of *ga …* at the end of the sentence softens the tone, too.

Because most sports are of Western origin, you can just say the English words as "loan words." Here is a list of some common sports. Notice that some sports names are not loan words.

Sports

English	Japanese
baseball	*yakyū*
basketball	*basuketto*
bicycling	*saikuriNgu*
dancing	*daNsu*
golf	*gorufu*
(scuba) diving	*daibiNgu*
exercise in general	*uNdō*
hiking	*haikiNgu*
jogging	*jogiNgu*
mountain climbing	*tozaN*
rugby	*ragubī*
skating	*sukēto*
skateboarding	*sukēto bōdo*
skiing	*sukī*
soccer	*sakkā*
swimming	*suiē*
surfing	*sāfiN*
tennis	*tenisu*
volleyball	*barē*

As you probably already know, some sports originated in Japan:

jūdō	judo
karate	karate
sumō	sumo
keNdō	kendo
aikidō	aikido

Green Tea Break

Japanese sports were heavily influenced by England in the nineteenth century. This might be why rugby is more popular in Japan than American football.

Perhaps you practice or once practiced a Japanese sport like *judo* or *karate* (probably not *sumo*). If so, try stopping by a local *dojo* (exercise hall) when you visit Japan. It's nice to meet "comrades" in the same discipline, and this would be a great opportunity to get to know people. With something in common to talk about, you will feel more comfortable speaking Japanese with people.

Talk About Your Family

Family-related topics also facilitate conversation. These topics allow you to expand conversation simply because you have more people to talk about and the listener can relate to the topics easily.

Lifesavers

Remember that syllable length is important in Japanese. The four-syllable *ojisaN* means "uncle," but the five-syllable *ojīsaN* means "grandfather."

Before we take a look at frequently used family terms, understand that there are two types of family terms. In Japanese, many nouns have polite counterparts. For example, the polite versions of *doko* ("where") and *kyōshi* ("teacher") are *dochira* and *sensē*, respectively. The same rule applies to family terms. The word for "family" is *kazoku*, and its polite version is *go-kazoku*. When you talk about *your own family*, you use the plain form, but when you talk about *someone else's family*, you use the polite form.

Family Members

English	Your Family (Plain)	Someone's Family (Polite)
grandfather	*sofu*	*ojīsaN*
grandmother	*sobo*	*obāsaN*
father	*chichi*	*otōsaN*
mother	*haha*	*okāsaN*
uncle	*oji*	*ojisaN*
aunt	*oba*	*obasaN*
older brother	*ani*	*onīsaN*
older sister	*ane*	*onēsaN*
husband	*shujiN* or *otto*	*goshujiN*
wife	*kanai* or *tsuma*	*okusaN*
younger brother	*otōto*	*otōtosaN*
younger sister	*imōto*	*imōtosaN*
sibling	*kyōdai*	*gokyōdai*
child	*kodomo*	*okosaN*
son	*musuko*	*musukosaN*
daughter	*musume*	*musumesaN*
grandchild	*mago*	*omagosaN*
cousin	*itoko*	*oitokosaN*
nephew	*oi*	*oigosaN*
niece	*mei*	*meigosaN*

In the rest of this chapter, you will learn the following tasks:

- ◆ Telling people what your family is like
- ◆ Counting family members
- ◆ Counting the age of your family members
- ◆ Talking about your family members in detail

My Family Is ...

First, let's tell the listener whether your family is big or small:

Track 10
CD-29

> *Watashi-no kazoku-wa dai-kazoku-desu.*
> "My family is big."

Dai-kazoku is a compound word, literally meaning "big family." If you want to say "My family is *not* big," you need to use the negative form of the noun "big family." Do you remember noun conjugation from Chapter 5? Here is the table.

Shortcuts to Success

Negative form is extremely handy when you can't remember a certain word. For example, even if you can't come up with the adjective for "big," as long as you know the adjective for "small" (*chīsa-i*), you can convey the message by saying "not small" (*chīsa-ku-na-i*).

	Affirmative	**Negative**
Present	*dai-kazoku-desu*	*dai-kazoku-jana-idesu*
	"is a big family"	"isn't a big family"
Past	*dai-kazoku-deshita*	*dai-kazoku-jana-kattadesu*
	"was a big family"	"wasn't a big family"

The sentence should look like this:

Track 10
CD-30

> *Watashi-no kazoku-wa dai-kazoku-jana-idesu.* "My family is not big."

Now, let's learn how to say "I have a such-and-such family member." In Japanese, when you refer to "having" family members as in "I have children," you use the verb *i-masu* ("exist"). For example, if you have a son (*musuko*), you say:

Track 10
CD-31

> *Watashi-wa musuko-ga i-masu.*
> "I have a son."

Counting People

Japanese does not have a plural marker like the English -s in "sons." In the previous example, there is no way for the listener to find out if I have one son or more. Let's learn how to ask "how many people" there are. The question word for "how many people" is *naN-niN*.

MusukosaN-ga **naN-niN** *i-masu ka?* "How many sons do you have?"

Track 10
CD-32

The question word *naN-niN* consists of two parts, *naN* ("how many") and *niN* ("people"). In Japanese, when you count someone or something, you must use the appropriate "counter"—in this case, the counter for "human beings"—*niN*. (Refer to Chapter 7 for a review of the basic number words.) There are two exceptions, as you can see in the following table. Notice that "one person" and "two people" are *hitori* and *futari*, respectively.

Track 10
CD-33

Counting People	
1	*hitori*
2	*futari*
3	*saN-niN*
4	*yo-niN*
5	*go-niN*
6	*roku-niN*
7	*shichi-niN*
8	*hachi-niN*
9	*kyū-niN*
10	*jū-niN*
11	*jū ichi-niN*
How many?	*naN-niN*

If you have three sons, answer in the following way:

Track 10
CD-34

(Watashi-wa) **musuko-ga saN-niN** *i-masu.* "I have three sons."

Huh?

For "seven people," *nana-niN* is possible. Similarly, for "nine people," *ku-niN* is okay.

This sentence illustrates the basic pattern used when including a number in a sentence:

Noun-Particle + Number-Counter + Predicate

In this example, the noun-particle is *musuko-ga*, then comes the number-counter *saN-niN*, then the verb *i-masu*.

Let's look at a little more complicated case. What if you have three sons *and* four daughters? You'll need the noun connector *to* ("and"):

> *Musuko-ga saN-niN* **to** *musume-ga yo-niN i-masu.*
> "I have three sons and four daughters."

Now, how about a mini-test? How would you say the following? It's perfectly okay to go back to the preceding tables. The answers are at the end of this chapter.

Exercise 2

1. _____

   I have five siblings.

2. _____

   I have two uncles and one aunt.

Ages

You've learned how to count people. Now, let's learn how to say the age of a person. The counter for "age" is *-sai*. I list the ages between 1 and 10 in the following table. As usual, for numbers above 10, we repeat the same counting system. Again, there are some irregularities in pronunciation, which are indicated in bold.

Counting Ages	
1	*is-sai*
2	*ni-sai*
3	*saN-sai*
4	*yoN-sai*
5	*go-sai*
6	*roku-sai*
7	*nana-sai*
8	**has-sai**
9	*kyū-sai*
10	**jus-sai**
11	**jū is-sai**
How old?	*NaN-sai?* or *Ikutsu?*

Asking the listener's age might be rude, but it's okay for you to tell her or him *your* age! Suppose that you're 36 years old. Here is how you tell your age:

> *Watashi-wa saN-jū roku-sai-desu.*   "I'm 36 years old."

For the sake of practice, may I ask your age?

> *NaN-sai-desu-ka?* "How old are you?"

Or even more politely:

> *SumimaseN ga, o-ikutsu-desu ka?* "Excuse me, but how old are you?"

Notice that I'm trying to make my question polite by using *sumimaseN ga.* Now, tell me your age:

> *Watashi-wa* _____ *-sai desu.*

Putting Everything Together

We've covered a lot of topics in this chapter:

- ◆ Residence
- ◆ Marital status
- ◆ Occupations
- ◆ Hobbies
- ◆ Family members
- ◆ Ages

You could, of course, give these information bits separately, sentence by sentence, but you might be tempted to put them together in one sentence. This task can be done by using the conjugation form called *TE*-form, explained in Chapter 6.

First, let's review some of the useful verbs covered in this chapter, along with their *TE*-forms:

	Regular Form	***TE*-Form**
"to live"	*suNde i-masu*	*suNde i-**te***
"to be married"	*kekkoN shite i-masu*	*kekkoN shite i-**te***
"to work"	*tsutomete i-masu*	*tsutomete i-**te***
"my hobby is XYZ"	*shumi-wa XYZ-desu*	*shumi-wa XYZ-**de***
"is XYZ years old"	*XYZ-sai-desu*	*XYZ-sai-**de***

Suppose that you want to put together the following bits of information:

> I live in Tokyo. And I work for IBM.

All you need to do is change the first verb, "live," into the *TE*-form:

Track 10
CD-40

Watashi-wa Tōkyō-ni <u>suNde i-te</u>, IBM-ni tsutomete i-masu.

"I live in Tokyo and work for IBM."

> **CAUTION** **Lifesavers** _____
>
> You might have been tempted to use the connector -to ("and"). But remember, this is a noun connector and never connects sentences. For example, you can say JoN-<u>to</u> Risa ("John and Lisa") but you can *never* say:
>
> *Watashi-wa Tōkyō-ni <u>suNde i-masu</u> to, IBM-ni tsutomete i-masu.*
> "I live in Tokyo and work for IBM."

Connecting sentences using the *TE*-form is extremely useful as seen previously. Most important, with this connector, your Japanese will sound more sophisticated!

Before closing this chapter, do the following exercise for sentence connection. Because this is not a memorization test, it's perfectly okay to refer to the rest of the chapter to find the correct words. As usual, the answers are given at the end of the chapter.

Exercise 3

1. _____

   My father is 62 years old, and his hobby is golf.

2. _____

   I am John and (I) have four children.

3. _____

   My older brother works for SONY and is not married.

4. _____

   I am married and my wife's name is Lisa.

This chapter might have seemed intensive. Although there are many new words, the grammatical structures introduced here are pretty simple. I suggest that you first become familiar with the grammatical patterns, and then gradually increase your vocabulary.

Answers

Track 10
CD-41

Exercise 1

A1: *Oishi-i sushi-o tabe-ni iki-masu.*

A2: *Karaoke-o utai-ni iki-masu.*

A3: *NikoN-no kamera-o kai-ni iki-masu.*

Track 10
CD-42, 44–45

Exercise 2

1. *Watashi-wa kyōdai-ga go-niN i-masu.*

2. *Watashi-wa oji-ga futari to oba-ga hitori i-masu.*

Track 10
CD-43, 46–49

Exercise 3

1. *Chichi-wa roku-jū ni-sai -de, shumi-wa gorufu-desu.*

2. *Watashi-wa JoN-de, kodomo-ga yo-niN i-masu.*

3. *Ani-wa SONY-ni tsutomete i-te, kekkoN shite i-maseN.*

4. *Watashi-wa kekkoN shite i-te, kanai-no namae-wa Risa-desu.*

The Least You Need to Know

◆ Don't be afraid to talk about your personal background, such as hobbies and family, using the patterns and vocabulary in this chapter.

◆ Use the question word *naN-de* when you want to ask someone "for what (purpose)?"

◆ Use the polite counterparts of nouns when you talk about someone else's family, but use the plain form when you talk about your own family.

◆ Use negatives when you can't remember a certain word. For example, if you can't come up with the adjective for "big," as long as you know the adjective for "small" (*chīsa-i*), you can convey the message by saying "not small" (*chīsa-ku na-i*).

◆ Count people and talk about age using the appropriate "counters." The counter for "human beings" is *-niN* (except for *hitori* and *futari*, "one" and "two"). The counter for "age" is *-sai*.

◆ Use the *TE*-form to connect sentences.

Chapter 11

Extending Invitations

In This Chapter

- ◆ Two ways to ask people out
- ◆ Make your invitation tempting
- ◆ How to turn down invitations

As I emphasized in Chapter 10, it's extremely important to "create" opportunities to practice Japanese with native speakers. You learned in Chapter 10 how to initiate conversations in Japanese. In this chapter, you learn how to ask people to dinner, a movie, and so on so that you can create a language learning opportunity.

Polite Invitation

If you want to ask the listener to do something together, such as go to dinner or a movie, use the following pattern:

Verb Stem + *maseN ka?*   "Won't you …?"

As you can see, the invitation pattern uses the negative form of a verb. Here's an example using this pattern:

Track 11
CD-1

ResutoraN-ni iki-maseN ka?   "Won't you go to the restaurant (with me)?"

Shortcuts to Success

To make the *-maseN ka* pattern sound natural, add a slight rising intonation toward the end of the sentence.

Of course, you can use verbs other than *iki-masu* in this pattern, but let's stick to *iki-masu* for the time being because this is probably the most common verb to use when asking people out.

Here is a list of place names you might find common when inviting your friend to go somewhere with you:

Places to Go

English	Japanese
amusement park	*yūeNchi* or *amyūzumeNto pāku*
art museum	*bijutsukaN*
bar	*bā*
beach	*bīchi*
bookstore	*hoNya*
club	*kurabu*
concert	*koNsāto*
concert hall	*koNsāto hōru*
department store	*depāto*
dining	*shokuji*
driving	*doraibu*
fishing	*tsuri*
for a walk	*saNpo*
hiking	*haikiNgu*
karaoke	*karaoke*
karaoke studio	*karaoke bokkusu*
lake	*mizūmi*
live house (for music)	*raibu hausu*
mall (shopping)	*mōru*
mountain	*yama*
movie	*ēga*
movie theater	*ēgakaN*
museum	*hakubutsukaN*
park	*kōeN*
party	*pāti*
picnic	*pikunikku*
play (theater)	*eNgeki*
pub/tavern (Japanese style)	*izakaya*

English	Japanese
restaurant	*resutoraN*
sea	*umi*
shopping	*kaimono*
sport game	*shiai*
swimming pool	*pūru*
traveling	*ryokō*

Now let's practice this pattern. Please try to take your friend to the following places.

Exercise 1

1. Movie (*ēga*)

   _____

2. Shopping (*kaimono*)

   _____

3. Dining (*shokuji*)

   _____

Instead of putting a "destination" phrase into the pattern *XYZ-ni iki-maseN ka?* you could put a "purpose" phrase in the pattern, meaning "Won't you go out *for doing XYZ?*" You learned this pattern in Chapter 10. Simply replace XYZ with a verb stem, as seen in the following example:

Track 11
CD-2

>   *Ēga-o **mi**-ni iki-maseN ka?*

>   "Won't you go out to watch a movie?"

This pattern is very useful because by using an activity verb, you can make your invitation more specific. Here are some more verbs that can be used in this pattern.

> ### Green Tea Break
>
> In the previous table, you find *izakaya*. An *izakaya* is a casual-style pub or tavern where beverages and delicious Japanese foods are served at reasonable prices. It's worth checking out.

⚠ CAUTION Lifesavers

The verb *shi-masu* is handy. By adding *shi-masu* to a western loan word, you can turn it into one of the verbs you see here:

doraibu	*shi-masu*	"to drive (for fun)"
ekusasaizu	*shi-masu*	"to exercise (for fitness)"
jogiNgu	*shi-masu*	"to jog"

Activity Verbs

English	Verb Stem
buy	*kai*
dance	*odori*
do, play (sports)	*shi; yari*
drink	*nomi*
eat	*tabe*
have fun	*asobi*
listen	*kiki*
swim	*oyogi*
sing	*utai*
watch	*mi*

Now with a place name and an activity verb combined, you can ask a more elaborate question. Suppose that you want to go to the beach (*bīchi*) to swim (*oyogi-masu*):

Track 11
CD-3

> *Bīchi-ni oyogi-ni iki-maseN ka?*   "Won't you go to the beach to swim with me?"

Remember that Japanese word order is flexible. In addition to the previous sentence, you could also say the following:

Track 11
CD-4

> *Oyogi-ni bīchi-ni iki-maseN ka?*

Let's do a short exercise here. For each of the following questions, ask the listener out to do the indicated activity. The answers are given at the end of this chapter.

Exercise 2

1. _____

   to the art museum to see the *Mona Lisa*

2. _____

   to the sushi bar to eat delicious sushi (sushi bar = *sushiya*; delicious = *oishi-i*)

3. _____

   to the live house to listen to jazz

So far, we have focused on *iki-masu* ("to go") for the *-maseN ka* pattern. Here are some examples with other commonly used invitational verbs:

Track 11
CD-5–6

> *Uchi-ni ki-maseN ka?*   "Won't you come to my house?"
> *XYZ-o tabe-maseN ka?*   "Won't you eat XYZ?"

XYZ-o nomi-maseN ka?   "Won't you drink XYZ?"

Isshoni kaeri-maseN ka?   "Won't you go home with me?"

Notte iki-maseN ka?   "Need a ride?"

Isshoni XYZ-o mi-maseN ka?   "Won't you watch XYZ (with me)?"

"Let's ... !" and "Shall We ...?"

The pattern you have just learned, *-maseN ka*, is a modest way to ask people out to do something. Let's look at a couple other ways.

Let's

If you're pretty sure that the listener would be all for your invitation, you could use a different pattern, which is equivalent to the English "Let's ...!" The pattern looks like this:

Verb Stem + *mashō!*   "Let's ...!"

Here is an example:

Ēga-ni iki-mashō!   "Let's go to a movie!"

As you can see, we combined the verb stem *iki* with *mashō*.

To make sure that you are comfortable with this pattern, do the following exercise.

Exercise 3

1. _____

    Let's go home! ("go home" = *kaeri-masu*)

2. _____

    Let's eat! ("eat" = *tabe-masu*)

3. _____

    Let's take a rest here! ("take a rest" = *yasumi-masu*; "here" = *koko-de*)

Just as with the *-maseN ka* pattern, you can combine a destination phrase (like *ēgakaN*) with an activity verb (like *ēga-o mi-masu*):

ShiNjuku-no ēgakaN-ni ēga-o mi-ni iki-mashō!   "Let's go to the movie theater in Shinjuku to watch a movie!"

(*Shinjuku* is a business and entertainment district in Tokyo.)

What if you feel like making a suggestion, but you aren't sure exactly what to do? Useful words you can count on are "something (to do)," *nanika*, and "some place (to go to)," *dokoka*. For example, when your friends all look bored, you can make a suggestion by saying the following:

> *Nanika shi-mashō!*   "Let's do something!"
>
> *Dokoka iki-mashō!*   "Let's go somewhere!"

If your friends look hungry, what suggestion would you make?

> *Nanika tabe-mashō!*   "Let's eat something!"

Or in an even more sophisticated way:

> *Nanika tabe-ni iki-mashō!*   "Let's go eat something!" (*iki-masu* = "go")

Huh?

The word *nanika* ("something") is made of *nani* ("what") and *ka* (question particle). *Dokoka* ("somewhere") is made of *doko* ("where") and *ka*. You can make a "some-" word by attaching *ka* to a question word:

dare ("who") + *ka*	*dareka*	"someone"
itsu ("when") + *ka*	*itsuka*	"someday"
ikura ("how much") + *ka*	*ikuraka*	"some amount"
naze ("why") + *ka*	*nazeka*	"for some reason"

Shall We?

With the *-mashō* pattern, you make a strong suggestion. However, by attaching the question marker *ka* at the end of this pattern, you make it sound less forceful:

> Verb Stem + *mashō ka?*   "Shall we …?"

Let's look at one example. Imagine a situation in which you and your friends are wondering what kind of food you should eat for dinner (*ryōri* = "cuisine"):

> *NihoN ryōri-o tabe-mashō ka?*   "Shall we eat Japanese food?"

Unlike other question sentences, the *-mashō ka?* pattern has falling intonation toward the end of a sentence.

The *mashō ka?* pattern is used with a question word as well. This way, instead of making a suggestion, you can ask for a suggestion from your listener(s). Here are some frequently used suggestion-seeking questions:

Track 11
CD-18-22

> *Nani-o shi-mashō ka?*   "What shall we do?"
> (*nani* = "what")
>
> *Nani-o chūmoN shi-mashō ka?*   "What shall we order?" (at a restaurant)
> (*chūmoN shi-masu* = "order food")
>
> *Doko-ni iki-mashō ka?*   "Where shall we go?"
> (*doko* = "where")
>
> *Doko-de ai-mashō ka?*   "Where shall we meet?"
> (*ai-masu* = "meet")
>
> *NaN-ji-ni* VERB STEM-*mashō ka?*   "What time shall we ...?"
> (*naN-ji-ni* = "at what time")

For more question words, refer to Chapter 6.

Wow, we've seen lots of examples! If you're feeling a little overwhelmed, try memorizing a core dialog. When you become comfortable with the core dialog, you can try to apply it to other verbs. Let's look at a core dialog involving the *-mashō ka?* pattern.

Track 11
CD-23

> Q: *Nani-o tabe-mashō ka?*
>   "What shall we eat?"
>
> A1: *Sushi-o tabe-mashō!*
>   "Let's eat sushi!"
>
> Or:
>
> A2: *Sushi-o tabe-mashō ka?*
>   "Shall we eat sushi?"

Shortcuts to Success

Whenever you learn a new grammatical pattern, don't be satisfied with given examples. Instead, try to say the pattern using other words. This "substitution exercise" is a very simple task, but it surely is the shortcut to mastering newly introduced patterns as well as memorizing vocabulary.

Declining the Invitation

So far you have learned invitational questions. When you hear these question patterns, you can easily recognize them and answer properly. Suppose that your friend asks you the following question. Can you figure out what she is saying?

Track 11
CD-24

> *Sushi-o tabe-ni iki-maseN ka?*

You got it! This means "Wanna go out to eat sushi?" If you want to go, your answer looks like this:

> *Hai, iki-mashō!*   "Yes, let's go!"

Or:

> *I-idesu ne! Iki-mashō!*   "Sounds good! Let's go!"
> (*i-idesu* = "good")

What if, for some reason, you must turn down the invitation? Here is the easiest way to decline the invitation:

> *SumimaseN, kyō-wa chotto …*   "Sorry, I cannot make it today …"

Here are some more useful expressions of declination, in case you want to make your answer more specific:

> *SumimaseN, chotto tsugō-ga warukute …*   "Sorry, I have some conflict …"
> *SumimaseN chotto yōji-ga arimashite …*   "Sorry, there is something I have to take care of …"

Chotto can mean many things; I can't give you the exact definition of the word. In this case, *chotto* functions as a "hesitation" marker.

Green Tea Break

Here are other functions of *chotto*:

- Getting someone's attention, equivalent to "Hey!"
  Example: *Chotto mi-te!*   "Hey! Look!"
- Asking people to wait for you.
  Example: *Chotto mat-te!*   "Wait!"
- Meaning "a little."
  Example: Q: *Samu-idesu ka?*   "Are you cold?"
            A: *Ē, chotto.*   "Yes, a little."

Perhaps you think that the *chotto* expressions are not sufficient to decline the offer, and you feel like adding a more specific excusable reason. Then I suggest that you use *kara*, which means "therefore; so." Here is the sentence pattern when *kara* connects the reason sentence with the main sentence:

[REASON *kara* RESULT]

Suppose that you want to decline the listener's invitation because you have another appointment (*yakusoku*):

Track 11
CD-30

Yakusoku-ga ari-masu kara chotto …   "I have an appointment, so I cannot …"
(*ari-masu* = "have")

What other excuses can you think of? Here are a few:

Track 11
CD-31–35

"I have some more work to do."   *Shigoto-ga ari-masu kara chotto …*

"I am busy."   *Isogashi-idesu kara chotto …*

"I don't feel well."   *Guai-ga waru-idesu kara chotto …*
(*guai* = "feeling," *waru-i* = "bad")

"I'm allergic to XYZ."   *XYZ arerugī-desu kara chotto …*

"I must wake up early tomorrow."   *Ashita haya-idesu kara chotto …*
(*ashita* = "tomorrow," *haya-i* = "early")

If you must decline the invitation, it would be nice to thank her for the kindness:

Track 11
CD-36

Arigatō gozaimasu. Mata koNdo onegai shimasu.   "Thank you. Please let me know next time."

Make Your Invitation Hard to Resist!

When you ask the listener out to do something, just saying *Iki-maseN ka?* might not be appealing enough. In this section, let's learn how to make your invitation hard to resist.

You have just learned the "reason" marker *kara*. You can use *kara* to make your question tempting. Let's consider an example. Suppose that there is a restaurant where foods are inexpensive (*yasu-idesu*). Let's ask the listener out to that restaurant to eat:

Track 11
CD-37

*Ano resutoraN-wa yasu-idesu **kara** tabe-ni iki-maseN ka?*

"That restaurant is cheap, **so** won't you go out to eat with me?"

Shortcuts to Success

Do you want to give the listener more than one reason when inviting? The *TE*-form should be used to connect predicates (see Chapter 6). For example, if you want to say that the foods are "cheap" *and* "delicious (*oishi-i*)," you should say:

*Yasuku-te oishi-idesu, **kara** tabe-ni iki-maseN ka?*

"The foods are cheap *and* delicious, so won't you go out to eat with me?"

Let's do some exercises using this pattern. Write convincing invitations based on the following provided information. Make sure that you include *kara*.

Exercise 4

1. _____

   It's fun, so won't you come to the party? ("fun" = *tanoshi-idesu*)

2. _____

   It's interesting, so won't you go to the movie theater to watch XYZ with me? ("interesting" = *omoshiro-idesu*)

3. _____

   It's hot today, so won't you go to the beach to swim? ("hot" = *atsu-idesu*, "today" = *kyō*; "swim" = *oyogi-masu*)

How did you do? Compare your answers with the answer keys at the end of this chapter. Remember that word order is flexible, so even if your answers look different from mine, as long as you use the same words and particles and the verb predicate stays at the end of the sentence, that is perfectly fine.

Huh? _____

The adverb *totemo* means "very," and it modifies an adjective.

There is another way to make your invitation more convincing. In Chapter 9, I introduced *yo*, the sentence-final particle. This particle functions as an "assertion" marker. Let's see an example involving *yo*:

Track 11
CD-38

*Nomi-maseN ka? Totemo oishi-idesu **yo!*** "Won't you drink (this)? It's *very* delicious, **you know!**"

Let's take a mini-quiz again. Using the preceding example sentence as a guide, write (or say) sentences based on the following information.

Exercise 5

1. _____

   Won't you buy this pen? It's cheap! ("buy" = *kai-masu*)

2. _____

   Won't you listen to this CD? It's good! ("listen" = *kiki-masu*)

3. _____

   Won't you watch this *anime?* It's funny! ("funny" = *okashi-i*)

Summary: Essential Expressions

In this chapter, you learned a number of expressions that can be used for asking people out to activities. Let's review some of the most essential expressions you should know:

Verb Stem + *maseN ka?*	"Won't you … (with me)?"
Verb Stem + *mashō!*	"Let's …!"
Verb Stem + *mashō ka?*	"Shall we …?"
Verb Stem + *ni iki-maseN ka?*	"Won't you go out to do …?"
Nani-o shi-mashō ka?	"What shall we do?"
Doko-ni iki-mashō ka?	"Where shall we go?"
I-idesu ne! Verb Stem + mashō!	"Sounds good! Let's …!"
SumimaseN, kyō-wa chotto …	"Sorry, I cannot make it today …"
REASON kara, chotto …	"*REASON*, so I cannot."
Arigatō gozaimasu. *Mata koNdo onegai shimasu.*	"Thank you for asking me. Please ask me next time."
REASON kara, Verb Stem + *maseN ka?*	"*REASON*, so won't you … (with me)?"

With these patterns, you can comfortably ask people out and also reply to people's invitations. Are you skeptical? Be confident! Let's see if you can translate the following dialog by yourself. Again, the answers are at the end of this chapter.

Exercise 6

Translate the following dialog between A and B.

A1: _____

What will you do today? ("today" = *kyō*)

B1: _____

I don't know yet. ("yet" = *mada*)

A2: _____

Won't you go to Tokyo with me to eat delicious sushi?

B2: _____

I'm allergic to fish, so I cannot … ("fish" = *sakana*)

A3: _____

There is also *tempura*, you know! (assertion)

B3: _____

Sounds good! Let's go!

Answers

Exercise 1

Track 11
CD-39–41

1. *Ēga-ni iki-maseN ka?*
2. *Kaimono-ni iki-maseN ka?*
3. *Shokuji-ni iki-maseN ka?*

Exercise 2

Track 11
CD-42–44

1. *BijutsukaN-ni Mona Riza-o mi-ni iki-maseN ka?*
2. *Sushiya-ni oishi-i sushi-o tabe-ni iki-maseN ka?*
3. *Raibu hausu-ni jazu-o kiki-ni iki-maseN ka?*

Exercise 3

Track 11
CD-45–47

1. *Kaeri-mashō!*
2. *Tabe-mashō!*
3. *Koko-de yasumi-mashō!*

Exercise 4

Track 11
CD-48–50

1. *Tanoshi-idesu kara, pāti-ni ki-maseN ka?*
2. *Omoshiro-idesu kara, ēgakaN-ni XYZ-o mi-ni iki-maseN ka?*
3. *Kyō-wa atsu-idesu kara, bīchi-ni oyogi-ni iki-maseN ka?*

Exercise 5

Track 11
CD-51–53

1. *Kono peN-o kai-maseN ka? Yasu-idesu yo!*
2. *Kono CD-o kiki-maseN ka? I-idesu yo!*
3. *Kono anime-o mi-maseN ka? Okashi-idesu yo!*

Exercise 6

Track 11
CD-54

A1: *Kyō-wa nani-o shi-masu ka?*

B1: *Mada wakari-maseN.*

A2: *Tōkyō-ni oishi-i sushi-o tabe-ni iki-maseN ka?*

B2: *Sakana-arerugī-desu kara, chotto …*

A3: *TeNpura-mo ari-masu yo!*

B3: *I-idesu ne! Iki-mashō!*

The Least You Need to Know

◆ Learn as many activity verbs and location words as possible. They are essential for extending invitations.

◆ Use "Shall we …?" (*-mashō ka?*), "Let's …!" (*-mashō!*), and "Won't you …?" (*-maseN ka?*) patterns properly.

◆ Make your invitation tempting by using *kara*, "therefore."

◆ When you must decline someone's invitation, use the *[REASON] kara chotto …* pattern.

Part 4

The Essentials for Traveling

The following chapters will prepare you to travel on your own to Japan and within the country. You will learn how to go through immigration and customs at the airport. You will find out how ground transportation works in Japan. With the phrases you learn in these chapters, you will be able to tell a cab driver, for example, to take you to the hotel of your choice. You will learn step-by-step instructions for check-in and checkout at the hotel. Bank-related phrases and expressions are also covered, in case you want to exchange money.

Just like in the previous chapters, the number of "must-memorize" expressions is minimal. However, with additional vocabulary of your choice, these basic expressions will enable you to say what you need in most travel-related situations.

Chapter **12**

In the Airplane

In This Chapter

- ◆ How to make requests
- ◆ Helpful in-flight expressions

One of the most rewarding aspects of language learning is being able to communicate with people in their native language when you travel. You can go wherever you want, buy things of your own choice (even ask for discounts), and enjoy the best possible local foods. And what's more, you can improve your language skills while having fun!

In Chapters 12 through 21, you will learn important travel-related expressions for activities such as checking in to a hotel, getting around town, dining, and so on. However, you don't have to wait until the plane lands in Japan to practice Japanese. Chances are, on a flight to Japan, the people surrounding you are Japanese speakers. Some of the flight attendants might also be Japanese natives or are fluent in Japanese. Don't waste time; talk to them! By the time you arrive in Japan, you will become more confident about your communication skills.

Making Requests

In Chapter 8 you learned a basic expression to use when making a request. Do you remember it? Here it is:

Track 12
CD-1

Onegai shimasu.   "Please (do it)."

If you want to make your request more polite, add *sumimaseN* at the beginning:

Track 12
CD-2

>   *SumimaseN, onegai shimasu.*   "Excuse me, please (do it)."

> **Green Tea Break**
>
> On non-Japanese airlines, a bi-lingual flight attendant usually wears a different uniform, a scarf, or a special pin (of the Japanese flag, for example).

Onegai shimasu is a multipurpose request expression. If you have a dinner tray in front of you and you want a flight attendant to take it away, you can point to it and gently say *Onegai shimasu*. Simple, isn't it? Using body language and pointing at an object, *onegai shimasu* is a powerful tool for expressing what you want.

XYZ-ni Shi-masu

What would you do in the following situation? As a meal is being served, you are asked which one you would prefer, Japanese tea (*ocha*) or coffee (*kōhī*):

> **Huh?**
>
> *XYZ-ni shi-masu* means "to decide on XYZ." You will often hear this pattern at a restaurant or coffee shop.

Track 12
CD-3

>   *Ocha-ni shi-masu ka, kōhī-ni shi-masu ka?*
>   "Japanese tea, or coffee?"

Suppose that you want to drink Japanese tea, *ocha*. Using *onegai shimasu*, you can make a request as follows:

Track 12
CD-4

>   *Ocha-o onegai shimasu.*   "Japanese tea, please."

> **Green Tea Break**
>
> *Ocha* usually refers to green tea. It is green because it is not roasted—unlike British tea. British tea, or "black tea," is called *kōcha* (literally, "red tea").

By just adding *XYZ-o* to the expression as seen previously, the range of a request can be expanded. You no longer have to point to an object or use body language. With *XYZ-o*, you can even ask an attendant to bring something to you. Suppose that you dropped your fork and you want another one:

Track 12
CD-5

>   *SumimaseN, fōku-o onegai shimasu.*
>   "Excuse me, would you get me a fork?"

When you get what you requested, don't forget to say thank you!

Track 12
CD-6

>   *Dōmo (arigatō).*   "Thank you."

Instead of *onegai shimasu*, you can use the verb *XYZ-o kudasai*, "Please give me XYZ." For example:

Track 12
CD-7

>   *Kōhī-o kudasai.*   "Please give me some coffee."

Green Tea Break

You might recall that as an alternative to *dōmo (arigatō)*, you can use *sumimaseN* to show your appreciation. *SumimaseN* would be more appropriate, especially if you are thanking the listener for the extra work that your request has caused.

Let's look at some realistic situations in which you can use this pattern. When you travel to Japan, you will need to fill out an *Embarkation card* and submit it to an immigration officer at the airport upon arrival. Flight attendants hand these forms out to passengers. Suppose that you were asleep when they came with the form, and you did not get it. Ask for an Embarkation card (*nyūkoku kādo*) as follows:

Track 12
CD-8

> *Nyūkoku kādo-o kudasai.*   "Please give me an Embarkation card."

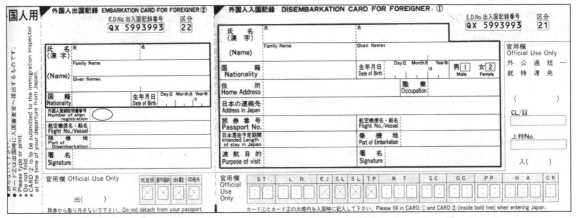

You need to complete a white Embarkation/Disembarkation card in flight and submit it to Japanese Immigration upon arrival.

Green Tea Break

The immigration officer will keep one portion of the Embarkation card and staple the smaller portion to your passport. Don't lose the smaller portion, you will need it to leave the country! For visa or related information, visit the official website of the Japanese Ministry of Foreign Affairs at www.mofa.go.jp.

The *TE*-form Request

Now, let's learn a slightly more sophisticated request expression. Do you remember *TE*-form, the multipurpose conjugation introduced in Chapter 6? If you've forgotten this conjugation, this is a good time to go back to Chapter 6 and review it. The new request pattern you're about to learn makes extensive use of this *TE*-form, as seen here:

> *TE*-form + *kudasai.*   "Please do so-and-so."

With this pattern, you will be able to make a variety of requests. For example, let's ask your friend to come. The verb is *ki-masu* and its *TE*-form is *ki-te*. So the request sentence looks like this:

> *(SumimaseN,) ki-te kudasai.*   "(Excuse me,) please come."

Track 12
CD-9

Now, try taking a mini-test. How would you make a request in each of the following situations? Be prepared, because I will make the exercise a little challenging. I have provided question words in English. Look for these words in Appendix B. Not only that, you need to convert the verb to the *TE*-form. If you aren't sure how to do that, refer to Chapter 6. The answers are at the end of this chapter.

Exercise 1

1. _____

   Please call (= telephone).

2. _____

   Please speak in English. (Hint: The postposition for "in" is *-de.*)

3. _____

   Please wait!

How did you do? Look at the following list of verbs that can be used while in flight:

In-Flight Request Verbs

English	*MASU*-form	*TE*-form
bring	*motte ki-masu*	*motte ki-te*
take X away	*motte iki-masu*	*motte it-te*
clear the tray	*torē-o sage-masu*	*torē-o sage-te*
throw away	*sute-masu*	*sute-te*
take; grab; pick up	*tori-masu*	*tot-te*
go through	*tōshi-masu*	*tōshi-te*
open	*ake-masu*	*ake-te*
close; shut	*shime-masu*	*shime-te*

Let me give you a realistic example of some requests for each of the preceding verbs. It could be a request to a flight attendant or a nearby passenger.

You can probably think of a lot of things that you want a flight attendant to bring to you. Let's ask her to bring water (*mizu*) because you're thirsty:

> *SumimaseN, mizu-o motte ki-te kudasai.*   "Excuse me, please bring water."

Huh?

Motte ki-masu is the verb for "bring" and *motte iki-masu* for "take (away)." These are called "compound" verbs:

> *motte ki-masu* ("bring") = *mochi-masu* ("hold") + *ki-masu* ("come")
>
> *motte iki-masu* ("take away") = *mochi-masu* ("hold") + *iki-masu* ("go")

The first half of such a compound is in *TE*-form. In the rest of this book, you will see more compound verbs in this category.

You finish eating the meal. Suppose that the flight attendants forgot to take your tray away. Using a "pointing" word, *kore* ("this thing"), say the following:

Track 12
CD-10

> (Pointing at the tray) *Kore-o motte it-te kudasai.*   "Please take this away."

You can also use *torē-o sage -masu*, "clear the tray":

> *Torē-o sage-te kudasai.*   "Please clear the tray."

Track 12
CD-11

Yes, *torē* is a loan word for "tray."

Suppose that your seat pocket is full of trash (*gomi*). How would you ask an attendant to throw it away for you? You're causing the attendant to do extra work for you, so be sure you add the magic word, *sumimaseN*:

Track 12
CD-12

> *SumimaseN, gomi-o sute-te kudasai.*   "Excuse me, please throw away the trash."

You can make your request even politer by adding an extra phrase at the end of the *-TE kudasai* pattern:

> *TE*-form + *kudasai maseN ka?*   "Could you please do so-and-so?"

Let's change the previous examples to the more polite version.

Track 12
CD-13

> *SumimaseN, mizu-o motte ki-te kudasai maseN ka?*   "Excuse me, could you please bring water?"

Track 12
CD-14–15

Torē-o sage-te kudasai maseN ka?   "Could you please clear the tray?"

SumimaseN, gomi-o sute-te kudasai maseN ka?   "Excuse me, could you please throw away the trash?"

Making Requests of Your Fellow Passengers

Flight attendants aren't the only people you might have to ask for help. Sometimes it could be passengers sitting near you. What if you sit in a window seat, and you have something in the overhead bin that you want a neighbor passenger to hand to you? You would ask the following question:

SumimaseN, XYZ-o tot-te kudasai.   "Excuse me, please hand XYZ to me."

XYZ could be anything, but in this particular situation, here are things you might put in the overhead bin:

bag	*kabaN* or *baggu*
suitcase	*sūtsu kēsu*
briefcase/attaché case	*atasshu kēsu*

Chances are, there are many bags in the bin and you have to describe your bag. In such a case, the neighbor passenger will ask you *which one* is yours:

Track 12
CD-16

Dore-desu ka?   "Which one is it?"

Shortcuts to Success

When you memorize an adjective, try to pair it with an adjective that is opposite in meaning (antonym), such as:

ōki-i ("big") vs. *chīsa-i* ("small")

kuro-i ("black") vs. *shiro-i* ("white")

taka-i ("expensive") vs. *yasu-i* ("cheap")

omo-i ("heavy") vs. *karu-i* ("light")

This kind of association method makes vocabulary learning easy and meaningful.

Here are helpful description words:

big	*ōki-i*
small	*chīsa-i*
black	*kuro-i*

white	*shiro-i*
blue	*ao-i*
red	*aka-i*
brown	*chairo-i*
yellow	*kīro-i*

If you can't remember color words in Japanese, you can use loan words, as long as they are common colors:

gray	*grē(-no)*
orange	*oreNji(-no)*
beige	*bēju(-no)*
green	*gurīN (-no)*

Lifesavers _____

No matter what their origins are, all loan words are nouns. So *bēju* ("beige"), even though it functions as an adjective, must be attached to the noun connection marker *-no*—as in *bēju-no atasshu kēsu*, "a beige attaché case." If you've forgotten noun description, go back to Chapter 6 and review the section "How to Describe Something or Someone."

In response to *Dore-desu ka?* let's suppose that yours is a small black bag:

Chīsa-i kuro-i kabaN-desu.   "It's the small black bag."

How about a big beige attaché case?

Ōki-i bēju-no atasshu kēsu-desu.   "It's the big beige attaché case."

If you and the neighbor passenger can see your bag, instead of describing it, you can simply say the following using the appropriate "pointing" word:

Are-desu.   "That one."

Track 12
CD-17

The neighbor passenger has finally grabbed your bag and asks you for confirmation:

Kore-desu ka?   "This one (in my hand)?"

Track 12
CD-18

In reply to this question, answer with the following handy expression:

Hai, sō-desu.   "Yes, that's right."

Track 12
CD-19

This expression can be used whenever you agree with the listener's statement.

If you're in a window seat, it isn't fun to disturb your neighbors when you need to go to the

Huh? _____

Remember the four pointing words?

are   "that one away from you and me"

kore   "this one near me" (= speaker's domain)

sore   "that one near you" (= listener's domain)

dore   "which one?"

bathroom, especially when they're asleep. But that's life, and you need to know the phrase for this kind of occasion:

> *SumimaseN, chotto tōshi-te kudasai.*
> "Excuse me, please let me through."

Notice the handy *chotto* here as well. As an alternative to the preceding expression, you can say:

Track 12
CD-20

> *SumimaseN, shitsurē shimasu.*
> "Excuse me, coming through."

When you sit in an aisle seat, on the other hand, *ake-te* ("open") and *shime-te* ("close") might be handy request verbs, too. Suppose that an in-flight movie is on, and you want your neighbor in the window seat to close the blind (*buraiNdo*):

> *BuraiNdo-o shime-te kudasai.* "Please close the blind."

If you want him to open it, then say:

> *BuraiNdo-o ake-te kudasai.* "Please open the blind."

Wow! You've learned a series of "request" patterns. Remember, the sentence formation is [*TE*-form + *kudasai*], and it is a polite request form. In a very casual situation, a *TE*-form alone can be used as a request expression, as in:

> *Sore-o tot-te!* "Get me that one!"

Please note that this is an extremely casual expression. Obviously, in situations in which you are surrounded by strangers, such as in the airplane, the polite version is always preferred.

Polite Requests You Might Hear on the Airplane

Politeness is a very important factor in Japanese, especially in a situation in which service is rendered. You, a passenger, are an important customer, so flight attendants will speak to you very politely, especially when they ask a favor of you. You won't have to say the following expressions, just be familiar with them in case you use a Japanese airline, especially a domestic flight in which Japanese is the primary language.

> *Shīto beruto-o o-shime kudasai.* "Please fasten your seatbelt."
> (*shime-masu* = "fasten")
>
> *Zaseki-o moto-no ichi-ni o-modoshi kudasai.* "Please set the seat back to the original position."
>
> (*zaseki* = seat; *moto-no ichi-ni* "to the original position"; *modoshi-masu* = "set back")

Torē-o moto-no ichi-ni o-modoshi kudasai.   "Please set the tray back to the original position."

Tenimotsu-wa zaseki-no shita-ni o-oki kudasai.   "Please put your carry-on item under the seat."

(*tenimotsu* = carry-on item; *oki-masu* = "put; place")

You might have noticed that the preceding request patterns are different from the one you've learned. The form of this more polite request is …

O + VERB STEM + *kudasai*   "Please do so-and-so." (polite request)

Some requests made by a flight attendant are in negation, as in "Please do not do so-and-so."

Tabako-wa goeNryo kudasai.   "Please refrain from smoking."

Toire-no go-shiyō-wa goeNryo kudasai.   "Please refrain from using the bathroom."
(*goshiyō* = "use")

DeNshi kiki-no go-shiyō-wa goeNryo kudasai.   "Please refrain from using electric devices."

(*deNshi* = "electric"; *kiki* = "device")

XYZ-wa + *goeNryo kudasai*   "Please refrain from XYZ." (polite request)

Before closing this chapter, try a mini-dialog. The dialog is between you and a flight attendant (abbreviated as *FA*). Note that some expressions are from previous chapters.

Exercise 2

FA   *Shīto beruto-o o-shime kudasai.*

     "Please fasten your seatbelt."

YOU 1   _____

     "Ah, excuse me."

FA 1   _____

     "Yes."

YOU 2   _____

     "Excuse me, but could you please get my bag for me?" (Ask politely.)

FA 2   _____

     "Which one?"

YOU 3   _____

     "It's a red bag."

FA 3 _____

"This one?"

YOU 4 _____

"Yes, that's it!"

_____

"Thank you very much."
(The flight attendant is handing out something.)

YOU 5 _____

"What is that (in your hand)?"

FA 5 _____

"This is an Embarkation card. Please fill it in."
("fill in" = *kaki-masu*)

YOU 6 _____

"Yes. Oh, there isn't a pen."
(there is = *ari-masu*)

_____

"Excuse me, please lend me a pen." (Ask politely.)
(lend = *kashi-masu*)

FA 6 _____

"Sure. Here you are."

YOU 7 _____

"Thank you very much."

FA 7 _____

"You're welcome."

Answers

Exercise 1

1. Please call (telephone). *DeNwa shi-te kudasai.*
   (*deNwa shi-masu → deNwa shi-te*)

2. Please speak in English. *Ēgo-de hanashi-te kudasai.*
   (*hanashi-masu → hanashi-te*)

3. Please wait! *Mat-te kudasai.*
   (*machi-masu → mat-te*)

Exercise 2

FA   *Shīto beruto-o o-shime kudasai.*

"Please fasten your seatbelt."

YOU 1   *SumimaseN.*

"Excuse me."

FA 1   *Hai.*

"Yes."

YOU 2   *SumimaseN ga, kabaN-o tot-te kudasai maseN ka?*

"Excuse me, but could you please get my bag for me?"

FA 2   *Dore-desu ka?*

"Which one?"

YOU 3   *Aka-i kabaN-desu.*

"It's a red bag."

FA 3   *Kore-desu ka?*

"This one?"

YOU 4   *Hai, sō-desu!*

"Yes, that's it!"

Dōmo arigatō (gozaimasu).

"Thank you very much."

(The flight attendant is handing out something.)

YOU 5   *Sore-wa naN-desu ka?*

"What is that (in your hand)?"

FA 5   *Nyūkoku kādo-desu.*

"This is an Embarkation card."

Kai-te kudasai.

"Please fill it in."
("fill in" = *kaki-masu*)

YOU 6   *Hai. A, peN-ga ari-maseN.*

"Yes. Oh, there isn't a pen."
(there is = *ari-masu*)

SumimaseN, peN-o kashi-te kudasai maseN ka?

"Excuse me, please lend me a pen."

FA 6   *Hai, dōzo.*

"Sure. Here you are."

YOU 7   *Dōmo arigatō.* or *SumimaseN.*

         "Thank you very much."

FA 7   *Dō itashimashite.*

         "You're welcome."

The Least You Need to Know

- The request form *te kudasai* (or *te kudasai maseN ka*) is extremely useful in conversation. Make sure that you learn the *TE*-form by heart (see Chapter 6).

- Master the pointing words *kore* ("this one"), *sore* ("that one [near the listener]"), *are* ("that one [away from the speaker and listener]"), and *dore* ("which one").

- *Onegai shimasu* is a handy expression to use to request something if you can point at the object.

- Politeness is the key to effective requesting.

- Be able to identify an object using an adjective such as *kuro-i kabaN*, "black bag."

Is the Flight on Time? Time Expressions

In This Chapter

- ◆ Reading the clock
- ◆ Point of time
- ◆ Duration of time

If you're visiting Japan on business, scheduling might be an important matter. Is the flight on time? Will my friend get to the airport to pick me up as scheduled? Can I catch the connecting flight? You can think of numerous situations in which time is essential. In this chapter, you learn how to tell time in Japanese.

Reading the Clock

First, let's learn how to read the clock in Japanese. The word for "o'clock" is *-ji*, and the word for "minutes" is *-fuN*. (Or *-puN* in some cases, as we'll see coming up.) Because you learned the basic numbers in Chapter 7, the following table shouldn't be too difficult for you. Irregular pronunciations are indicated in bold:

Time Expressions

O'clock	-ji	Minutes	-fuN
1 o'clock	*ichi-ji*	**1 minute**	***ip-puN***
2 o'clock	*ni-ji*	2 minutes	*ni-fuN*
3 o'clock	*saN-ji*	**3 minutes**	***saN-puN***
4 o'clock	*yo-ji*	**4 minutes**	***yoN-puN***
5 o'clock	*go-ji*	5 minutes	*go-fuN*
6 o'clock	*roku-ji*	**6 minutes**	***rop-puN***
7 o'clock	*shichi-ji*	7 minutes	*nana-fuN*
8 o'clock	*hachi-ji*	**8 minutes**	***hap-puN***
9 o'clock	*ku-ji*	9 minutes	*kyū-fuN*
10 o'clock	*jū-ji*	**10 minutes**	***jup-puN***
11 o'clock	*jū ichi-ji*	**11 minutes**	***jū ip-puN***
12 o'clock	*jū ni-ji*		
What hour?	*naN-ji*	**What minute?**	*naN-puN*

Let's look at an example. In Japanese, "8:23" is ...

> *Hachi-ji ni-jū saN-puN*

Exercise 1

How would you say the following times in Japanese?

1. 10:52

_____

2. 7:34

_____

3. 6:07

_____

4. 1:00

_____

5. 12:35

_____

If you want to specify A.M. or P.M., add *gozeN*, or *gogo*, respectively, *before you state the time:*

2:55 A.M.	***GozeN*** *ni-ji gojū go-fuN*
3:03 P.M.	***Gogo*** *saN-ji saN-puN*

Useful Time Expressions

First, let's learn how to ask what time it is now.

Q: *NaN-ji-desu ka?*   "What time is it?"

A: *SaN-ji jup-puN-desu.*   "It's 3:10."

If you want to specify the exact point at which something happens, you need to add the time particle *-ni* ("at") to the time, as seen in the following examples:

Q: *NaN-ji-**ni** iki-masu ka?*   "**At** what time are you going?"

A: *Roku-ji-**ni** iki-masu.*   "I am going **at** 6 o'clock."

Do you want to know the departure and arrival times for your flight? The verb for "leave" is *de-masu* and that for "arrive" is *tsuki-masu.* Let's suppose that the departure city is Chicago and the arrival city Tokyo:

*Kono hikōki-wa Shikago-o naN-ji-**ni** de-masu ka?*   "What time will this airplane leave Chicago?"

*Kono hikōki-wa Tōkyō-ni naN-ji-**ni** tsuki-masu ka?*   "What time will this airplane arrive at Tokyo?"

Here are two more important flight schedule words:

shuppatsu   "departure"
Shuppatsu-wa naN-ji-desu ka?
"What time is the departure?"

tōchaku   "arrival"
Tōchaku-wa naN-ji-desu ka?
"What time is the arrival?"

As you know, flight departure/arrival is rarely on schedule, so you really can't ask *exactly* what time the plane leaves or arrives. You might want to attach *goro* ("approximately") to a time expression:

Q: *NaN-ji-**goro** tsuki-masu ka?*   "**About** what time will it arrive?"

A: *Ku-ji-**goro** tsuki-masu.*   "It will arrive **around** 9 o'clock."

Shortcuts to Success

Practice makes perfect and proficient. Whenever you have a chance, say the time in Japanese. All you need is a watch!

Green Tea Break

Japanese people make extensive use of "military time," especially at work or in a publication such as a timetable for public transportation. For example, 7:34 P.M. can be said as …

Jū ku-ji saN jū yoN-puN
"19:34 (7:34 P.M.)"

Or:

Track 13
CD-9

Q: *Tōchaku-wa naN-ji-**goro**-desu ka?*   "What is the **approximate** arrival time?"

A: *Ku-ji-**goro**-desu.*   "It's **around** 9 o'clock."

Lifesavers _____

Here are a couple more useful time expressions:

Ni-ji **chōdo**	"2 o'clock **sharp**"
Ni-ji go-fuN **sugi**	"5 minutes **past** 2 o'clock"
Ni-ji go-fuN **mae**	"5 minutes **before** 2 o'clock"
Go-ji **haN**	"5:30"

Literally, *haN* means "half." Of course, instead of *haN*, you can use *saN jup-puN*, "30 minutes."

Exercise 2

Translate the following dialogs:

1. Q: What time did you wake up today?
   ("wake up" = *oki-masu*)

   _____

   A: I woke up at 7 o'clock.

   _____

2. Q: What time do you go to bed?
   ("go to bed" = *ne-masu*)

   _____

   A: I go to bed around 11 o'clock.

   _____

3. Q: What time will you go to school tomorrow?
   ("school" = *gakkō*)

   _____

   A: I will go at 8 A.M.

   _____

4. Q: What time is the meeting?
   ("meeting" = *kaigi*)

   _____

   A: It's (at) 12 o'clock sharp.

   _____

"From" and "Until"

Having learned the basic time expressions, would you now like to ask a flight attendant what time the in-flight movie starts?

Track 13
CD-10

> *Ēga-wa naN-ji-**kara**-desu ka?*
> "What time does the movie start?" (*Lit.*)
> "From what time is the movie?"

Notice that *-kara* is a particle indicating "from." An equally important time-related particle is *-made*, "until." How would you ask a flight attendant until what time the in-flight movie is? Yes, the answer is …

Track 13
CD-11

> *Ēga-wa naN-ji-**made**-desu ka?*
> "What time does the movie end?"
> (*Lit.*) "Until what time is the movie?"

Huh? _____

The particles *-kara* and *-made* can also be used when referring to the flight origin and destination. In this case, *-made* means "up to." For example:

Tōkyō-kara Nagoya-made iki-masu.
"I'm going from Tokyo to Nagoya (but not beyond)."

Combining these two particles, you can say sentences like the following:

*Ēga-wa naN-ji-**kara** naNji-**made** desu ka?*   "From what time to what time is the movie?"

*Ichi-ji-**kara** ni-ji-**made** terebi-o mi-mashita.*   "I watched TV from 1 o'clock to 2 o'clock."

Exercise 3

Translate the following dialogs:

1. Q: What time does class begin? (*Lit.*) From what time is the class?
   ("class" = *kurasu*)

   _____

   A: It starts at 4 P.M. (*Lit.*) It's from 4 P.M.

   _____

2. Q: Until what time will you be here?
   ("be" = *i-masu*; "here" = *koko-ni*)

   _____

   A: I will be here until about 5 o'clock.

   _____

3. Q: From what time till what time did you study?
   ("study" = *beNkyō shi-masu*)

   _____

A: I studied from 1 o'clock till 2 o'clock.

Duration

So far, you've learned the "point" of time. Now let's move on to the "duration" of time. The good news is that duration in terms of minutes follows exactly the same format as the minutes seen in the following table. Again, irregular pronunciations are indicated in bold:

Duration of Time

Track 13
CD-12

Hours	-jikaN	Minutes	-fuN
1 hour	*ichi-jikaN*	**1 minute**	***ip-puN***
2 hours	*ni-jikaN*	2 minutes	*ni-fuN*
3 hours	*saN-jikaN*	**3 minutes**	***saN-puN***
4 hours	*yo-jikaN*	**4 minutes**	***yoN-puN***
5 hours	*go-jikaN*	5 minutes	*go-fuN*
6 hours	*roku-jikaN*	**6 minutes**	***rop-puN***
7 hours	*nana-jikaN*	7 minutes	*nana-fuN*
8 hours	*hachi-jikaN*	**8 minutes**	***hap-puN***
9 hours	*ku-jikaN*	9 minutes	*kyū-fuN*
10 hours	*jū-jikaN*	**10 minutes**	***jup-puN***
How many hours?	*naN-jikaN*	**How many minutes?**	***naN-puN***
(For) how long?	*donogurai*		

I have included two important question words in the preceding table, *naN-jikaN* ("how many hours") and *donogurai* "(for) how long." Let's ask how long the flight is:

Track 13
CD-13–14

Or:

Furaito-wa naN-jikaN-desu ka?   "How many hours is the flight?"

Furaito-wa donogurai-desu ka?   "How long is the flight?"

You might want to ask how long the flight *takes*. The verb for "take" is *kakari-masu*. To ask how long it takes from Seattle to Tokyo, say:

Q: *Shiatoru-kara Tōkyō-made donogurai kakari-masu ka?*   "How long does it take from Seattle to Tokyo?"

A: *Ku-jikaN-**gurai** kakari-masu.*   "It takes **about** 9 hours."

Did you notice -*gurai* ("about") in the preceding answer? You've already learned -*goro* ("approximately"), but -*goro* is used only for a specific *point* of time, not the *duration* of time. For approximation of duration of time, use -*gurai*.

The sentence patterns you've learned here are extremely useful not only during flight, but anywhere. You can ask a cab driver how long it takes to get to the destination, so you might be able to avoid paying thousands of *yen* for fare!

Before moving on, let's look at one more useful particle, -*de*, "by means of." This particle is useful when you have several choices of transportation and want to compare their speeds. Suppose that you're in Tokyo and wonder what transportation is the best for you to get to Yokohama—*by* bus, *by* train, *by* taxi, and so on. Here is one example:

> *Tōkyō-kara Yokohama-made* **basu-de** *donogurai kakari-masu ka?* "How long does it take **by bus** from Tokyo to Yokohama?"

The following table lists some modes of transportation.

Transportation	
airplane	*hikōki*
bicycle	*jiteNsha*
Bullet Train	*shiNkaNseN*
bus	*basu*
car	*kuruma*
motorcycle	*baiku*
subway	*chikatetsu*
taxi	*takushī*
train	*deNsha*
on foot	*aruite*

A caution is in order regarding *aruite*, "on foot." This phrase does not require the particle -*de*:

> *Aruite iki-masu.* "I'm going on foot."

Green Tea Break

The distance between Tokyo and Yokohama is approximately 25 kilometers (15.5 miles). The Tokyo-Yokohama metropolitan area (a.k.a. the Greater Tokyo area) is probably the most congested in terms of traffic. It sometimes takes three hours to get from Tokyo to Yokohama by car! I would advise you to take the train. It takes only 25 minutes.

Green Tea Break

The Bullet Train, or *shiNkaNseN*, is one of the fastest forms of ground transportation in the world. The Super Express called *Nozomi* can go as fast as 300 kilometers (190 miles) per hour!

Exercise 4

Using the charts for duration of time and modes of transportation, ask the following questions.

1. How long does it take from Tokyo to Osaka by Bullet Train?

   _____

2. How many hours does it take from New York to San Francisco by airplane?

   _____

3. How many minutes does it take from the university to the bookstore on foot?
   ("university" = *daigaku*; "bookstore" = *hoNya*)

   _____

Answers

Exercise 1

Track 13
CD-15

1. 10:52   *jū-ji gojū ni-fuN*
2. 7:34   *shichi-ji saNjū yoN-puN*
3. 6:07   *roku-ji nana-fuN*
4. 1:00   *ichi-ji*
5. 12:35   *jū ni-ji saNjū go-fuN*

Exercise 2

Track 13
CD-16

1. Q: What time did you wake up today?

   NaN-ji-ni oki-mashita ka?

   A: I woke up at 7 o'clock.

   Shichi-ni oki-mashita.

Track 13
CD-17

2. Q: What time do you go to bed?

   NaN-ji-ni ne-masu ka?

   A: I go to bed around 11 o'clock.

   Jū ichi-ji goro ne-masu.

Track 13
CD-18

3. Q: What time will you go to school tomorrow?

   Ashita naN-ji-ni gakkō-ni iki-masu ka?

   A: I will go at 8 A.M.

   GozeN hachi-ji-ni iki-masu.

4. Q: What time is the meeting?

    Kaigi-wa naN-ji-desu ka?

A: It's (at) 12 o'clock *sharp.*

    Jū ni-ji chōdo-desu.

Exercise 3

1. Q: What time does class begin? (*Lit.*) From what time is the class? ("class" = *kurasu*)

    Kurasu-wa naN-ji-kara-desu ka?

A: It starts at 4 P.M. (*Lit.*) It's from 4 P.M.

    Gogo yo-ji-kara-desu.

2. Q: Until what time will you be here?

    NaN-ji-made koko-ni i-masu ka?

A: I will be here until about 5 o'clock.

    Go-ji-goro-made koko-ni i-masu.

3. Q: From what time till what time did you study?

    NaN-ji-kara naN-ji-made beNkyō shi-mashita ka?

A: I studied from 1 o'clock till 2 o'clock.

    Ichi-ji-kara ni-ji-made beNkyō shi-mashita.

Exercise 4

1. "How long does it take from Tokyo to Osaka by Bullet Train?"

    Tōkyō-kara Ōsaka-made shiNkaNseN-de donogurai kakari-masu ka?

2. "How many hours does it take from New York to San Francisco by airplane?"

    Nyūyōku-kara SaN FuraNshisuko-made hikōki-de naN-jikaN kakari-masu ka?

3. "How many minutes does it take from the university to the bookstore on foot?"

    Daigaku-kara hoNya-made aruite naN-puN kakari-masu ka?

The Least You Need to Know

♦ Time expressions require that you know the basic number words covered in Chapter 7.

♦ Note that *-ji* is the counter for "o'clock," *-jikaN* for "hours," and *-fuN* for "minutes."

♦ Particles such as *-kara* ("from") and *-made* ("until") are useful when you want to specify the starting or ending point.

♦ Combine time-related phrases with *X-de*, "by means of X," as in *Basu-de donogurai kakari-masu ka?* ("How long does it take by bus?").

Chapter 14

At the Airport

In This Chapter

- ◆ Airport protocols
- ◆ Counting time length
- ◆ Phone numbers

Now the plane has landed in Japan. It has been a long flight, and you might be a little tired. If you are traveling alone, rather than in a tour group, you will have to go through immigration and customs on your own before you leave the airport. Of course, many immigration and customs officers do speak English, but it is always nice to be able to communicate in Japanese.

At the Immigration Booth

There are several international airports in Japan, but most international flights arrive at either New Tokyo International Airport, also known as Narita Airport (NRT), or Kansai International Airport (KIX) in Osaka.

The first point you will go through is the Immigration booth. There are lines for Japanese nationals and for non-Japanese nationals. By the time you arrive at the booth, you should have your Embarkation card, *nyūkoku kādo*, completely filled out and have your passport in hand. Typical questions that immigration officers ask concern the following:

- ◆ Purpose of visit
- ◆ Length of stay
- ◆ Destination in Japan

"Purpose" is *mokuteki* in Japanese. The officer might first ask you the following:

> *Pasupōto-o mise-te kudasai.* "Please show me your passport."
>
> *Ryokō-no mokuteki-wa naN-desu ka?* "What's the purpose of the trip?"
> (*ryokō* = "travel")

In Chapter 10, you learned some "purpose" words. Let's review some here:

sightseeing	*kaNkō*
business	*shigoto*
business trip	*shucchō*
study abroad	*ryūgaku*

If the purpose of your trip is sightseeing, the answer is simply …

> *Kankō-desu.* "It is sightseeing."

The officer will then ask how long you will stay in Japan:

Track 14
CD-1

> *NihoN-ni-wa donogurai* (or *naN-nichi*) *i-masu ka?*
> "For how long (*or* for how many days) will you stay in Japan?"

You have learned hours and minutes, but not "days" yet. The counter for "days" is *-nichi*. Unfortunately, from "one day" to "10 days," most of the "day" words are irregular and don't make use of this counter. If you can't remember those irregular pronunciations, don't worry! You can still use [Number + *-nichi*]. They are somewhat nonstandard but comprehensible by Japanese people. I list both "authentic" and "survival" versions of counting days in the following table.

Track 14
CD-2

Counting Days

	Authentic Reading	Survival Reading
1 day	*ichi-nichi*	*ichi-nichi*
2 days	*futsuka*	*ni-nichi*
3 days	*mikka*	*saN-nichi*
4 days	*yokka*	*yoN-nichi*
5 days	*itsuka*	*go-nichi*

	Authentic Reading	**Survival Reading**
6 days	*muika*	*roku-nichi*
7 days	*nanoka*	*shichi-nichi*
8 days	*yōka*	*hachi-nichi*
9 days	*kokonoka*	*ku-nichi*
10 days	*tōka*	*jū-nichi*
11 days	*jū ichi-nichi*	*jū ichi-nichi*
How many days?	*naN-nichi*	

Shortcuts to Success

The counting system with *ichi, ni, saN,* and so on was borrowed from Chinese. We also have a traditional Japanese counting system:

1	2	3	4	5	6	7	8	9	10
hi-	*fu-*	*mi-*	*yo-*	*itsu-*	*mu-*	*nana-*	*ya-*	*koko-*	*tō-*

The traditional counting system is used not only for counting days, but also for other items, such as people. In Chapter 10, we saw that "one person" and "two persons" are irregular, but for anything beyond two persons, the counter *-niN* is attached:

hitori	"one person"
futari	"two persons"
saN-niN	"three persons"
yo-niN	"four persons"

You will see some of these counters in the rest of the book, so it's a good idea to become familiar with this system.

If you plan on staying for eight days, your answer looks like this:

Yōka (or hachi-nichi) i-masu.   "I will stay for eight days."

Or simply:

Yōka (or hachi-nichi) desu.   "Eight days."

What if you stay more than just a couple of days, like three weeks, two months, or a year? You will need to know their respective counters. Unlike counting days, these three counters are almost regular. Look at the following table. As usual, irregular instances are indicated in bold.

Track 14
CD-3

Counting Weeks, Months, and Years

	Weeks (-shūkaN)	Months (-kagetsu)	Years (-neN)
1	*is-shūkaN*	*ik-kagetsu*	*ichi-neN*
2	*ni-shūkaN*	*ni-kagetsu*	*ni-neN*
3	*saN-shūkaN*	*saN-kagetsu*	*saN-neN*
4	*yoN-shūkaN*	*yoN-kagetsu*	*yo-neN*
5	*go-shūkaN*	*go-kagetsu*	*go-neN*
6	*roku-shūkaN*	*rok-kagetsu*	*roku-neN*
7	*nana-shūkaN*	*nana-kagetsu*	*nana-neN*
8	*has-shūkaN*	*hachi-kagetsu*	*hachi-neN*
9	*kyū-shūkaN*	*kyū-kagetsu*	*kyū-neN*
10	*jus-shūkaN*	*juk-kagetsu*	*jū-neN*
11	*jū is-shūkaN*	*jū ik-kagetsu*	*jū ichi-neN*
How many?	*naN-shūkaN*	*naN-kagetsu*	*naN-neN*

With the duration words "days," "weeks," "months," and "years," you can express a variety of things. Now let me ask you some questions pertaining to duration. First, figure out what you are being asked, and then answer the question:

Exercise 1

Q1: *Mainichi, nihoNgo-o naN-jikaN benkyō shi-masu ka?*

(*mainichi* = "everyday"; *benkyō shi-masu* = "study")

A1: _____

Q2: *Is-shūkaN-ni, naN-nichi shigoto-o shi-masu ka?*

(*is-shūkaN-ni* = "in one week"; *shigoto* = "work")

A2: _____

Q3: *Ichi-neN-wa, naN-shūkaN ari-masu ka?*

A3: _____

Q4: *Ichi-neN-wa, naN-kagetsu ari-masu ka?*

A4: _____

Q5: *Soko-ni-wa, naN-neN suNde i-masu ka?*

(*soko* = "there," *suNde i-masu* = "live")

A5: _____

Okay, let's get back to the Immigration booth! The immigration officer might ask what your final destination is or where you will stay:

Q: *NihoN-de-wa doko-ni iki-masu ka?* "Where will you go in Japan?"

A: *Kyōto-ni iki-masu.* "I am going to Kyoto."

Q: *Doko-ni tomari-masu ka?* "Where will you stay?"

A: *Puraza Hoteru-ni tomari-masu.* "I will stay at the Plaza Hotel."

If you're staying at your friend's house, and not in a hotel, your answer will be …

Tomodachi-no uchi-ni tomari-masu.
"I will stay at my friend's house."
(*tomodachi* = "friend"; *uchi* = "house")

Remember that the particle *-no* in *tomodachi-no uchi*, "friend's house," is a noun connector (see Chapter 6).

If you stay in a private house, you might be asked to give the officer the address of that house. Suppose that the address is …

800-12 Ogawa-cho
Yokosuka-shi, Kanagawa-ken 238-0004

The suffix *-cho* (or *-machi*) is for "town," *-shi* for "city," and *-ken* for "prefecture." The Japanese way of reading addresses is the mirror image of the Western style:

〒 238-0004
Kanagawa-keN
Yokosuka-shi
Ogawa-chō
800-12 (*hap-pyaku-no jū ni*)

Huh?

In the first example, because the "topic" of the sentence is "in Japan," you need to attach the location particle *-de* to *nihoN*. Note that the particle must be *-de*, not *-ni*, because this sentence has an action verb (*iki-masu*), not an existence verb.

Green Tea Break

The suffix *-keN* is equivalent to "province." There are 43 *keN* total *in* Japan. There are four special districts—Tokyo, Osaka, Kyoto, and Hokkaido—and they have different suffixes:

Tōkyō-to
Ōsaka-fu
Kyōto-fu
Hokkai-dō

〒 is a sign placed in front of a postal code. Postal code, or ZIP code, is called *yūbiN baNgō* in Japanese. 〒 238-0004 should be read as …

YūbiN baNgō ni saN hachi-no zero zero zero yoN "〒 238-0004"

Well, I guess it would be easier to hand it to the officer in the form of a note that has the address (*jūsho*) on it!

Kore-ga jūsho-desu. "This is the address."

Oh, No! My Bag Is Missing! At Baggage Claim

After you go through immigration, you will pick up your luggage and proceed to Customs. What if you can't find your luggage? Don't panic! The good news is that Japanese airports are extremely helpful when your luggage is missing. They will deliver your luggage to your destination by special express as soon as they find it. However, in order to receive this service, you must file a claim.

Green Tea Break

These special delivery services are called *takuhaibiN*, "home delivery express." In the past, one of my bags was lost in the New Tokyo International Airport, so I filed a claim. To my surprise, when I arrived at my parents' house three hours later, my bag had already arrived! Of course, it was free of charge! In Japan, you never have to go back to the airport to pick up your lost luggage.

This service can also be used to send your bags to where you'll be staying. Likewise, you can send your bags to the airport before your departure (one to two days in advance). This way, you don't have to carry your luggage to and from the airport!

To do so, you must first go to an information booth nearby any luggage carousel and tell the officer the following:

Track 14 CD-4

Watashi-no nimotsu-ga ari-maseN.   "My luggage isn't here." (*nimotsu* = "luggage")

Or:

Track 14 CD-5

Watashi-no nimotsu-ga dete ki-maseN.   "My luggage hasn't come out." (*dete ki-masu* = "come out")

Huh? _____

The verb *dete ki-masu* ("come out") is a compound verb that consists of two verbs, *de-masu* ("emerge") and *ki-masu* ("come"). The first half of the compound is in the *TE*-form.

You will be asked for your name, address, flight number, where you are from, and your contact phone number. You know how to say your name and address already. "Flight XYZ" is *XYZ-bin* in Japanese. Suppose that your flight was United 79 and it originated from Chicago:

Q: *BiN-mē-wa naN-desu ka?*
   "What is the name of the flight?"

A: *Yunaiteddo-no nana-jū kyū-biN desu.*
   "United Flight 79."

Q: *Doko-kara nori-mashita ka?*   "Where did you board the airplane?"

A: *Shikago-kara desu.*   "From Chicago."

Giving a phone number is really very simple, if you are already familiar with the basic number words in Japanese. All you need to do is say each number separately. The hyphen is pronounced as *-no*. Let's say that your contact phone number is 03-5860-3715. The number "03" is the area code.

Q: *DeNwa baNgō-wa naN-desu ka?*   "What is the phone number?"
   (*deNwa* = "phone"; *baNgō* = "number")

A: *Zero saN-no go hachi roku zero-no saN nana ichi go-desu.*   "03-5860-3715."

Saying phone numbers helps when remembering basic number words. Try to say your phone number:

Uchi-no deNwa baNgō-wa

_____-desu.

Kaisha-no deNwa baNgō-wa

_____-desu.

Yes, *uchi* is "home" and *kaisha* is "company."

> **Green Tea Break**
>
> Cellular phones are called *kētai deNwa* or simply *kētai*. Cellular phones are extremely popular in Japan, and virtually everyone has one. You can even rent or buy a cellular phone at the airport. These phones are usually operated by prepaid calling cards.

At the Customs Counter

Okay, you've picked up your luggage at the carousel. You have your bags in hand, and proceed to the final checkpoint, Customs. "Customs" is *zēkaN* in Japanese. If you have no taxable items to declare, this is an easy process. However, Customs officers are authorized to check not only for taxable items, but also for illegal objects such as narcotics and firearms. Your bags may be checked here.

Lifesavers _____

The following items are duty-free if they don't exceed the specified quantities:

◆ Alcoholic beverages—three bottles

◆ Cigarettes—two cartons

◆ Perfume—two ounces

◆ Others—200,000 *yen* (U.S.$1,538, provided U.S.$1 = 130 *yen*)

Visit the official website of the Narita Airport Customs at www.narita-airport-customs.go.jp.

If you have nothing to declare, you can proceed to Customs counters indicated by the color green. If you have taxable items or if you don't know whether certain items are taxable, proceed to the Customs counters indicated by the color red. Please note that even in the Green Line, you will be asked by a Customs officer questions similar to those asked at the Immigration booth.

Before learning some Customs-related dialogs, familiarize yourself with important vocabulary.

Customs	*zēkaN*
Customs clearance	*tsūkaN*
declaration	*shiNkoku*
duty-free	*meNzē*
duty-free merchandise	*meNzēhiN*
something to declare	*shiNkoku-suru mono*
souvenir	*omiyage*
tax	*zēkiN*
taxed	*kazē*

Here are some typical questions a Customs officer might ask you at the Customs counter:

Track 14
CD-6–8

KabaN-o ake-te kudasai. "Please open your bag."

Pasupōto-o mise-te kudasai. "Please show me your passport."

Kore-wa doko-de kai-mashita ka? "Where did you buy this?"

If the officer asks you whether there is anything to declare, and you have nothing to declare, the dialog should resemble the following:

Track 14
CD-9

Q: *ShiNkoku-suru mono-wa ari-masu ka?* "Do you have anything to declare?"

A: *Īe, ari-maseN.* "No, I don't."

Suppose that you have a wrapped souvenir for your friends, and the officer asks what it is …

Track 14
CD-10

Q: *Kore-wa naN-desu ka?* "What's this?"

A: *Omiyage-desu. Chokorēto-desu.* "It's a souvenir. It's chocolates."

Track 14
CD-11

Q: *Dare-no desu ka?* "Whose is it? (For whom?)"

A: *Tomodachi-no desu.* "It's for my friend."

Huh?

The question seen in the previous example, *Dare-no desu ka?* ("Whose is it?") is the shortened form of …

Dare-no omiyage-desu ka?   "Whose souvenir is it?"

Likewise, the answer, *Tomodachi-no desu* ("It's my friend's") is the shortened form of …

Tomodachi-no omiyage-desu.   "It's a souvenir for my friend."

Omission of an understood item is common and acceptable in Japanese.

Immigration and Customs clearance at a Japanese airport used to take a lot of time, but because of the simplification of the procedure, now it is very speedy. Although it might depend on how long it takes to get your luggage from the baggage claim, you can usually get out of the airport within 30 to 45 minutes after arrival.

If you are expecting someone to pick you up, she or he is most likely to be right beyond the doors of the Customs section. If you are on your own, you need to secure transportation from the airport to the city. You will learn all the necessary transportation-related expressions in Chapter 15. Bon voyage, or *I-i tabi-o!*

Summary: Essential Expressions

Let's review some of the essential expressions you will find useful at the airport:

NihoN-ni-wa donogurai i-masu ka?   "How long will you stay in Japan?"

NihoN-de-wa doko-ni iki-masu ka?   "Where will you go in Japan?"

Doko-ni tomari-masu ka?   "Where will you stay?"

Watashi-no jūsho-wa XYZ-desu.   "My address is XYZ."

Denwa baNgō-wa XYZ-desu.   "My phone number is XYZ."

KabaN-o ake-te kudasai.   "Please open your bag."

ShiNkoku-suru mono-wa ari-maseN.   "I have nothing to declare."

Dareno-desu ka?   "Whose is it?"

Before moving to the next chapter, do the following review exercise. You are at Immigration and Customs. "Q" stands for questions given by an officer, and "A" stands for your answers.

Exercise 2

At Immigration

Q1: *Pasupōto-o mise-te kudasai.*

A1: _____

"Yes."

Q2: *Ryokō-no mokuteki-wa naN-desu ka?*

A2: _____

"Business."

Q3: *NihoN-ni-wa donogurai i-masu ka?*

A3: _____

"One week."

Q4: *Doko-ni tomari-masu ka?*

A4: _____

"I will stay at the Plaza Hotel."

At Customs

Q5: *KabaN-o ake-te kudasai.*

A5: _____

"Yes."

Q6: *ShiNkoku-suru mono-wa ari-masu ka?*

A6: _____

"No, I don't."

Q7: *Kore-wa naN-desu ka?*

A7: _____

"It's a souvenir."

Q8: *Dareno-desu ka?*

A8: _____

"It's for my friend."

Answers

Exercise 1

Track 14
CD-12

Q1: *Mainichi, nihoNgo-o naN-jikaN benkyō shi-masu ka?*

"How many hours do you study Japanese every day?"

A1: *Mainichi, ichi-jikaN benkyō shi-masu.*

"I study Japanese for one hour every day."

Q2: *Is-shūkaN-ni, naN-nichi shigoto-o shi-masu ka?*

"How many days do you work per week?"

A2: *Is-shūkaN-ni, itsuka shigoto-o shi-masu.*

"I work five days per week."

Q3: *Ichi-neN-wa, naN-shūkaN ari-masu ka?*

"How many weeks does one year have?"

A3: *Ichi-neN-wa, gojū ni-shūkaN ari-masu.*

"One year has 52 weeks."

Q4: *Ichi-neN-wa, naN-kagetsu ari-masu ka?*

"How many months does one year have?"

A4: *Ichi-neN-wa, jū ni-kagetsu ari-masu.*

"One year has 12 months."

Q5: *Soko-ni-wa, naN-neN suNde i-masu ka?*

"How many years have you lived there?"

A5: *Koko-ni-wa, go-neN suNde i-masu.*

"I have lived here for five years." (*koko* = "here")

Exercise 2

Track 14
CD-13

At Immigration

Q1: *Pasupōto-o mise-te kudasai.*

"Please show me your passport."

A1: *Hai.*

"Yes."

Q2: *Ryokō-no mokuteki-wa naN-desu ka?*

"What is the purpose of the trip?"

A2: *Shigoto-desu.* (or *Shuccho-desu.*)

"Business." (or "Business trip.")

Q3: *NihoN-ni-wa donogurai i-masu ka?*

"How long will you stay in Japan?"

A3: *Is-shūkaN-desu.*

"One week."

Q4: *Doko-ni tomari-masu ka?*

Where will you be staying?

A4: *Puraza Hoteru-ni tomari-masu.*

"I will stay at the Plaza Hotel."

Track 14
CD-14

At Customs

Q5: *KabaN-o ake-te kudasai.*

"Open your bag, please."

A5: *Hai.*

"Yes."

Q6: *ShiNkoku-suru mono-wa ari-masu ka?*

"Do you have anything to declare?"

A6: *Īe, ari-maseN.*

"No, I don't."

Q7: *Kore-wa naN-desu ka?*

"What is this?"

A7: *Omiyage-desu.*

"It's a souvenir."

Q8: *Dare-no desu ka?*

"For whom?"

A8: *Tomodachi-no-desu.*

"It's for my friend."

The Least You Need to Know

◆ The questions you will be asked at Immigration and Customs are all predictable, so be prepared.

◆ Be familiar with time duration words so you can answer the immigration officer's questions about the duration of your stay in Japan.

◆ The Japanese way of writing addresses is the mirror image of the Western style.

◆ Saying phone numbers in Japanese is straightforward. Just say each number separately. The hyphen between numbers is pronounced *-no* in Japanese.

Getting to and Around Town

In This Chapter

- ◆ Transportation
- ◆ Directions and locations
- ◆ How to say "I want to …"

Congratulations! You have successfully gone through Immigration and Customs at the airport all by yourself. If someone is waiting to pick you up and take you to your final destination, you can relax! But what if you are on your own and need to get to your destination by yourself? You can no longer follow the crowd. This is the first time you will find yourself completely relying on your own skills. In this chapter, I will show you how to get to your destination without getting lost.

Types of Transportation

As I told you in Chapter 14, most international flights arrive at either the New Tokyo International Airport in Narita (NRT) or the Kansai International Airport in Osaka (KIX). Because both Tokyo and Osaka are extremely overcrowded and have little space within their city limits, their airports are located outside the city. From NRT to Tokyo, it is 60 kilometers (38 miles), and it is 50 kilometers (31 miles) from KIX to Osaka.

To get to the city from the airport, several options are available:

train	*deNsha*
limousine bus	*rimujiN basu*
taxi	*takushī*
limousine car	*haiyā*

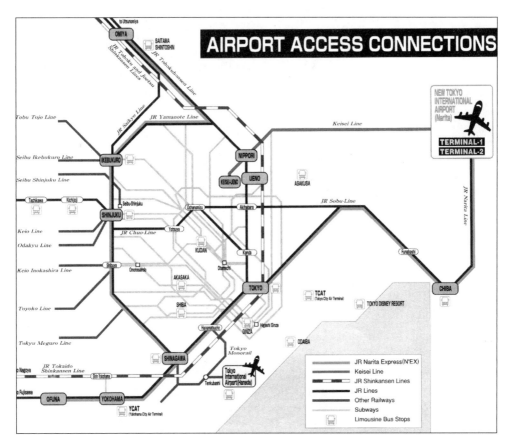

Access to central Tokyo from the New Tokyo International Airport, also known as the Narita Airport (NRT).

(© Japan National Tourist Organization)

Green Tea Break

An "old" international airport is very close to the center of Tokyo, within a 10-mile radius. It's called the Tokyo International Airport, also known as the Haneda Airport. The new airport was built in the late 1970s because Haneda could not accommodate the ever-growing number of incoming flights to Japan. It now mainly serves domestic flights.

Considering the cost and distance from the airport to the city, you probably would want to avoid a taxi or limousine car, so let's focus on a train and limousine bus. Whether you use a train or a limousine bus, you need to do the following:

♦ Go to the ticket counter and state your destination.

♦ Check the departure time and location for the train/bus.

♦ Buy the ticket.

If you are going to stay in a major hotel, I suggest that you take a limousine bus because it stops right in front of major hotels. If not, either limousine bus or train is okay.

I personally prefer the train because it is always on schedule and is not affected by stressful traffic jams. In what follows, let's suppose that we have decided to take the train from Narita Airport to Shinjuku, the hub of the city of Tokyo.

Lifesavers

The following websites provide extensive information on ground transportation at the New Tokyo International Airport and Kansai International Airport. Remember, these website addresses are subject to change!

New Tokyo International Airport (Narita, Tokyo): www.narita-airport.or.jp/airport_e

Kansai International Airport (Osaka): www.kansai-airport.or.jp/english/

Going by Train

There is a vending machine where you can buy a train ticket. It can be a bit too complex for a first-time traveler to use. You will probably feel more comfortable and less stressed buying a ticket the old-fashioned way—by purchasing it at a ticket counter.

Green Tea Break

In Japan, there are a number of private railway companies and a private-sector railway company. The former is called *shitetsu* and the latter *JR* (pronounced as *jē āru*), which stands for *Japan Railways*. *JR* serves much wider areas. Although it depends on exactly where you are heading, in general *JR* is more convenient.

If you are planning to travel around Japan by train, I suggest that you purchase a *JR Pass*. Passes are available in the form of 7, 14, or 21 consecutive days. Because a *JR Pass* is not sold in Japan, you must purchase it at a travel agency prior to departure. You will receive a voucher called an "Exchange Order." Exchange this voucher with a pass at a designated station and specify the starting date. For more information, visit the JR East website at www.jreast.co.jp/e/.

First of all, as shown in the following example, you have to tell the clerk what your destination is. Let's say you are going to the train station called *Shinjuku:*

Track 15
CD-1

> *ShiNjuku Eki-ni iki-tai-N-desu ga ...*   "I want to go to the Shinjuku Station, but ..."
> (*eki* = "station")

You have just seen a very important grammatical pattern, "want to." The formation of this pattern looks like the following:

VERB STEM + *tai-N-desu ga ...*

Huh?

The expression for "I want to" consists of two parts, *tai* ("want") and *N-desu*. The phrase *N-desu* is attached to a predicate when you want to express feelings such as desire, hope, and curiosity, as well as when making an explanation or an excuse. You will see more examples of *-N-desu* later. For the time being, just "swallow" this expression!

Remember, "verb stem" means a verb without *-masu*. This "want to" pattern is very simple and extremely useful. Before we move on, let's practice the pattern here. How would you say the following?

Shortcuts to Success

Did you notice in the previous example that the word *ga* is attached at the end of the sentence, as in …

ShiNjuku Eki-ni iki-tai-N-desu ga … "I want to go to the Shinjuku Station, but …"

This tiny word literally means "but" and is used to soften the tone of a given sentence. You might recall the following expression:

SumimaseN ga … "Excuse me, but …"

This is certainly a "must" expression that makes your Japanese sound natural and polite.

Exercise 1

1. _____

   I want to eat sushi.
   ("eat" = *tabe-masu*)

2. _____

   I want to buy a camera.
   ("buy" = *kai-masu*)

3. _____

   I want to go home!
   ("go home" = *kaeri-masu*)

4. _____

   I want to be a musician.
   ("be XYZ" = *XYZ-ni nari-masu*)

Now, let's get back to the ticket counter. You have just told the counter clerk that you want to go to the Shinjuku Station. The clerk will give you several departure times, as seen next. Suppose that the train leaves at 3 and 4 o'clock.

Huh?

The particle *-to* means "and." This particle connects nouns only.

> *SaN-ji to yo-ji-ga ari-masu.*
> "There are 3 and 4."
>
> *Dochira-ga i-idesu ka?*
> "Which would you prefer?"

You want to take the earlier train:

> *SaN-ji-ga i-idesu.*   "I prefer 3:00."

Don't forget to ask how much the ticket costs. The question word for "how much" is *ikura*.

> *Ikura-desu ka?*   "How much is it?"

As of 2002, the fare from the Narita Airport to the Shinjuku Station is 3,110 *yen*.

> *SaN-zeN hyaku jū eN-desu.*   "It is 3,110 *yen*."

Japanese numbers were introduced in Chapter 7. If you have forgotten them, this is a good time to go back and review them.

In Chapter 13, you learned how to ask how long it takes to get from point X to point Y. The verb for "take" is *kakari-masu*. Let's ask how long it takes to get to the Shinjuku Station.

> *ShiNjuku Eki-made donogurai kakari-masu ka?*   "How long does it take to get to the Shinjuku Station?"

The answer to your question will be …

> *Ichi-jikaN ni-jup-puN-desu.*   "One hour 20 minutes."

Another important question you should ask is from which track the train is leaving. The verb for "leave" is *de-masu* (see Chapter 13).

> *Doko-kara de-masu ka?*   "Where does it leave from?"

Suppose that it leaves from Track #1. "Track" is *-baNseN*.

> *Ichi-baNseN-kara de-masu.*   "It leaves from Track #1."

Instead of *doko* ("where"), you can also use *naN-baNseN* ("which track"):

NaN-baNseN-kara de-masu ka? "Which track does it leave from?"

In addition to these expressions and vocabulary, here are some more useful train-related words:

ticket	*kippu*
reserved seat	*shitēseki*
platform	*hōmu*
for (destination)	*-iki* (for example, *Tokyo-iki*)
to transfer	*norikae-masu*
entrance	*iriguchi*
exit	*deguchi*

Green Tea Break

At every station, there is a gate where your ticket is checked. This is called *kaisatsu-guchi*. This checkpoint is fully automated. You insert your ticket into the machine, and the gate will open if the ticket is validated. If not, the gate will shut in front of you and make an annoying beeping sound (a bit embarrassing if this happens …). Oh, there's one more thing. Your validated ticket will come out from the other side of the gate, so don't forget to pick it up because you will need it at your final destination!

At the kaisatsuguchi, *insert your ticket into the machine to enter or exit a train station.*

If your destination is the last station of the train line, great! But what if you must get off the train at a station before the train's final destination? Suppose that the train is bound for Yokohama, and you need to get off at Shinjuku. The ticket clerk will tell you the following:

ShiNjuku-de ori-te kudasai. "Please get off at Shinjuku."

The verb *ori-te* is the *TE*-form of *ori-masu*, "to get off." (Just in case, the verb for "get on; ride" is *nori-masu*.)

Now you have finally gotten on the train! You want to make sure that you get off at the right station. Why don't you ask your neighbor passenger to signal you when the train approaches the Shinjuku Station? You would want to say: "I want to get off at Shinjuku. Please let me know when we get there." You can say this with all the expressions you have learned and one new verb, *oshie-masu*, "tell."

> *ShiNjuku-de ori-tai-N-desu ga, oshie-te kudasai.*   "I want to get off at Shinjuku, so please let me know."

Did you notice the softening *ga* in the sentence? This would be a perfect setting for you to include the polite marker. You want to sound even more polite? Try the following:

Track 15
CD-2

> *ShiNjuku-de ori-tai-N-desu ga, oshie-te kudasaimaseN ka?*   "I want to get off at Shinjuku, so could you please let me know?"

The pattern of request looks like this:

> *-te kudasaimaseN ka?*   "Could you please do so-and-so?"

If you need to ask a big favor, this pattern is highly recommended.

Train riding can be stressful. But after several experiences, the fear will go away and you will start appreciating its convenience. It is fast, inexpensive, and almost always on time. You can travel virtually anywhere in Japan by train!

Green Tea Break

Big cities also have very extensive subway systems. For example, there are 13 subway lines in Tokyo, and they are closely connected to other subway lines, *JR* lines, and private companies' railways—just like a huge spider web. You can obtain a route map at any subway station. By using a subway system wisely, you can save time and money.

Going by Taxi

Now you have arrived at the station. The original plan was that your friend was supposed to pick you up at the station, but prior to the departure you heard she would not be able to be there. You need to get there by yourself, and it looks like the only means of getting there is by taxi. Taking a taxi on your very first day in Japan? Not a problem!

You have the address of your friend's apartment, which looks like the following:

> My Address
> *Maison Shinjuku* #307
> 700-15 Kita-machi
> Shinjuku-ku
> Landmark: Right next to the library

Lifesavers

When a cab stops, do not stand right in front of the door. Cab doors in Japan open automatically and you certainly would not like to be knocked down on the street! This tip is a lifesaver—kneecap saver, actually!

First, hail a taxi. If you are at a station, there is usually a place where taxis are available. This place is called *takushī noriba*, "taxi stand." There should be a sign with a picture of a taxi.

If you are on the street, look for a taxi that has a red light in the front window because it indicates that the taxi has no passengers. Raise your hand to stop the cab. If the taxi has passengers, the light should be green.

Now you have "safely" gotten into the taxi. The driver will ask you:

Track 15
CD-3

> *Dochira-made (desu ka)?*   "Where to?"

Your destination is *Maison Shinjuku*, right?

> *MezoN ShiNjuku-made onegai shimasu.*   "To *Maison Shinjuku*, please."

Track 15
CD-4   Or:

> *Mezon ShiNjuku-made iki-tai-N-desu ga …*   "I want to go to *Maison Shinjuku* …"

If the driver does not know where the destination is, you might want to give him the address. Recall that Japanese addresses are the mirror image of Western addresses.

Western Style	Japanese Style
Maison Shinjuku #307	Shinjuku-ku
700-15 Kita-machi	Kita-machi 700-15
Shinjuku-ku	*Maison Shinjuku #307*

Green Tea Break

For some reason, apartments in Japan have very fancy names, like French *maison*. Even a mediocre one-bedroom apartment complex can be called *maNshoN* ("mansion") or a little more modestly, *haimu*, derived from the German *Heim*, "apartment."

Remember, on the address card, your friend kindly gave you the landmark so that you can find her apartment easily. According to that note, it is located *next to the library* (*toshokaN*). You can give the directions to the driver as the next example shows:

Track 15
CD-5

> *ToshokaN-no tonari-desu.*
> "It's next to the library."
> (*tonari* = "next")

When you give directions, the following pattern is extremely useful:

[LANDMARK-*no* Direction Word]

The following table lists some "direction" words.

"Direction" Words

above	*ue*
ahead	*saki*
back/behind	*ushiro*
beneath	*shita*
between	*aida*
beyond	*mukō*
front	*mae*
inside	*naka*
right	*migi*
left	*hidari*
next/adjacent	*tonari*
nearby	*chikaku* or *soba*
outside	*soto*

Huh?

An apartment room number ("#") is read as *-gōshitsu*. For example, #307 should be read as *saN-byaku nana-gōshitsu*.

If the destination is *near the library*, you can say:

ToshokaN-no chikaku-desu.   "It's near the library."

Following are some frequently used place names that you might need to use as landmarks when giving directions.

Place Names

post office	*yūbiNkyoku*
public phone	*kōshū deNwa*
library	*toshokaN*
police station	*kēsatsusho*
hospital	*byōiN*
city hall	*shiyakusho*
train station	*eki*
bus stop	*basutē*
school	*gakkō*
kindergarten	*yōchieN*
elementary school	*shōgakkō*
middle school	*chūgaku* or *chūgakkō*
high school	*kōkō*

Place Names

university	*daigaku*
movie theater	*ēgakaN*
theater	*gekijō*
art museum	*bijutsukaN*
Buddhist temple	*otera*
Shinto shrine	*jiNja*
church	*kyōkai*
park	*kōeN*
parking lot	*chūshajō*
restroom	*toire*
shop	*mise*
supermarket	*sūpā*
building	*biru*
department store	*depāto*
convenience store	*koNbini*
bookstore	*hoNya*
fish market	*sakanaya*
vegetable shop	*yaoya*
meat shop	*nikuya*
drugstore	*kusuriya*
barber shop	*tokoya*
sushi bar	*sushiya*
restaurant	*resutoraN*
beauty salon	*biyōiN*

Green Tea Break

A business establishment ending with *-ya*, as in *hoNya* ("bookstore") and *kusuriya* ("drugstore") is often referred to with *-saN*, as in *hoNya-saN* and *kusuriya-saN*. The suffix *-saN* is a "title" that usually is attached to a person's name, as in *Tanaka-saN*, "Mr./Ms. Tanaka." Incidentally, *-saN* is attached to a business establishment, especially when it is privately owned.

Using the words in the previous lists, complete the following exercises. The answers are given at the end of the chapter.

Exercise 2

How would you say the following?

1. "near the bookstore"

   _____

2. "ahead of the city hall"

   _____

3. "in(side) the hospital"

   _____

4. "in front of the high school"

   _____

5. "next to the police station"

   _____

Exercise 3

Look at the map and answer the following questions. The word *doko* means "where."

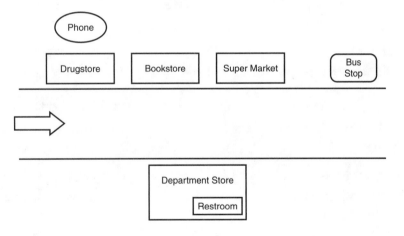

1. Q: *KōshūdeNwa-wa doko-desu ka?*
   A: _____

2. Q: *Basutē-wa doko-desu ka?*
   A: _____

3. Q: *Toire-wa doko-desu ka?*
   A: _____

Huh?

The word for "between" (*aida*) requires the use of two nouns and/or two landmarks. "Between X and Y" in Japanese is …

X *to* Y-*no aida*

For example, if you want to tell the taxi driver that your destination is between the supermarket and meat shop, you should say:

Sūpā-to nikuya-no aida-desu.   "It's between the supermarket and the meat shop."

With the address and simple directions, I am sure that the taxi driver will get you to your friend's apartment. Before ending this section, let me list other expressions that are useful for giving directions.

Track 15
CD-6–11

Koko-desu.   "Right here."

Koko-de tome-te kudasai.   "Please stop here."

Massugu it-te kudasai.   "Please go straight."

Migi-ni magat-te kudasai.   "Please turn to the right."
(*migi*= "right")

Hidari-ni magat-te kudasai.   "Please turn to the left."
(*hidari* = "left")

Ikura-desu ka?   "How much is it?"

Let's do a simulation exercise for giving directions to a taxi driver. Complete the dialog as instructed. The driver is indicated by DR in the dialog.

Exercise 4

DR1:   *Dochira-made?*

YOU1:   _____

I want to go to the Tanaka Building …

DR2:   *Tanaka Biru?*

YOU2:   _____

Yes. It's near Tokyo University, but …

DR3:   *Hai, wakari-mashita.*

YOU3:   _____

Oh, please turn to the left.

DR4:   *Hidari-desu ne.*

YOU4:   _____

Right here. How much is it?

DR5:   *SeN ni-hyaku eN-desu.*

YOU5:   _____

Here you are.

Are You Sure You Want to Drive in Tokyo?

Japan's public transportation system is great! In terms of convenience, areas it serves, and promptness, I believe it is the best system in the world (putting aside the cost). Unless you must live in an extremely rural area, you would not even consider driving in Japan. There are traffic jams wherever you go, and gasoline is incredibly expensive.

What? Do you really want to drive in Japan?

HoNtōni uNteN shi-tai-N-desu ka?   "Do you really want to drive?"
(*hoNtōni* = "really"; *uNteN* = "driving")

Okay, but there are a few things you should be aware of.

First, the driver's seat is located on the right. Unless you are from the United Kingdom, you need some time to get used to the feel of it. It's a strange feeling to maneuver a car on the opposite side. When I go back to Japan, I occasionally drive. Each time, when I intend to use the blinker, I always turn on the wiper instead! Directional orientation is a hard thing to adjust to.

Second, if you are an American, you need to familiarize yourself with the metric system. One mile is equivalent to 1.6 kilometers. So when you see a speed limit sign of "80," do not drive 80 mph; 80kph (kilometers per hour) is only 50 mph!

Third, you need to learn the traffic signs. Sure, many Japanese signs are identical or similar to Western counterparts, but some are unique to Japan and can have Japanese characters on them. Here are some of the signs.

Lifesavers

Here is a mile-kilometer conversion chart:

10km	6.2 miles
20km	12.5 miles
30km	18.8 miles
40km	25 miles
50km	31.2 miles
60km	37.5 miles
70km	43.8 miles
80km	50 miles
90km	56.3 miles
100km	62 miles

Frequently seen traffic signs. If you drive in Japan, be familiar with the Chinese characters written on the STOP sign and SLOW DOWN sign.

Ped Crossing

No Parking

Do Not Enter

School Zone

Stop

One Way

Slow Down

Do Not Pass

No U-Turn

These Directions Only

The warning I want to give to those who want to drive in Japan is this:

Ki-o tsuke-te!   "Be careful!"

Track 15
CD-12

Answers

Exercise 1

1. *Watashi-wa sushi-o tabe-tai-N-desu ga …*

2. *Watashi-wa kamera-o kai-tai-N-desu ga …*

3. *Watashi-wa kaeri-tai-N-desu ga …*

4. *Watashi-wa myūjishaN-ni nari-tai-N-desu ga …*

Exercise 2

1. *hoNya-no soba* or *hoNya-no chikaku*

2. *shiyakusho-no saki*

3. *byōiN-no naka*

4. *kōkō-no mae*

5. *kēsatsusho-no tonari*

Exercise 3

1. *Kusuriya-no ushiro-desu.* "It's behind the drugstore."
2. *Sūpā-no saki-desu.* "It's ahead of the supermarket."

Or:

Sūpā-no chikaku-desu. "It's near the supermarket."

3. *Depāto-no naka-desu.* "It's in the department store."

Exercise 4

Track 15
CD-13

DR 1 *Dochira-made?*

"Where to?"

YOU 1 *Tanaka Biru-made iki-tai-N-desu ga …*

"I want to go to the Tanaka Building …"

DR 2 *Tanaka Biru?*

"Tanaka Building?"

YOU 2 *Ē. Tōkyō Daigaku-no chikaku-desu ga.*

"Yes. It's near Tokyo University."

DR 3 *Hai, wakari-mashita.*

"Yes, I got it."

YOU 3 *A! Hidari-ni magatte kudasai.*

"Oh, please turn to the left."

DR 4 *Hidari-desu ne.*

"Left, okay."

YOU 4 *Koko-desu. Ikura-desu ka?*

Right here. How much is it?

DR 5 *SeN ni-hyaku-eN-desu.*

1,200 *yen.*

YOU 5 *Hai.*

Here you are.

The Least You Need to Know

- In Japan, the most economical way to get to the city from the airport is either by airport limousine bus or train.

- The Japanese train/subway system is extremely reliable and punctual. You can save time and money by using it, especially if you need to get around a big city.

- Be able to buy a train/bus ticket using the handy grammatical pattern "want to" (VERB STEM + *tai-N-desu ga ...*).

- Use the *-te kudasai maseN ka* request pattern if you need to ask a big favor.

- Learn place names and direction words and be able to give directions using the [LANDMARK-*no* Direction Word] pattern.

Chapter 16

At the Hotel

In This Chapter

♦ Making a hotel reservation

♦ Calendar expressions

♦ *RyokaN*—Japanese-style inn

If you are on business or simply plan to do sightseeing in the city, staying in a hotel is not a bad idea. You might want to choose a fancy, rather expensive hotel if your budget allows so that you won't have to worry about communication breakdown because of a lack of English-speaking staff. If you stay in an economy hotel or a hotel in a suburban area, chances are the hotel staff will not understand English.

Making a Hotel Reservation

The easiest way to make a hotel reservation is through the Internet, as you can imagine. There are numerous bilingual sites where you can make an online reservation.

If you are not using online reservations, you probably need to do so either in person at a travel agency or on the phone. For the latter option, you first need to know some basic telephone expressions, covered in more detail in Chapter 22. Let's suppose that you need to make a reservation at a travel agency counter. You can find such facilities at airports and major train stations.

First, you will want to tell an agent that you want to make a hotel reservation. The word for reservation is *yoyaku*. *Yoyaku-o shi-masu* is the verbal form, meaning "make a reservation." Let's say "I want to make a reservation." Remember the "want to" pattern introduced in Chapter 14? You got it! It's [Verb Stem + *tai-N-desu ga* …]. Here is the sentence:

Track 16
CD-1

> *Hoteru-no yoyaku-o shi-tai-N-desu ga* …
> "I want to make a hotel reservation but …"
> (*shi-masu* = ("do"))

You can predict types of questions you will be asked upon making a reservation:

- ◆ Where do you want to stay?
- ◆ From what date to what date?
- ◆ How many people and what kind of room?

For each of these items, let's learn basic expressions.

Huh? _____

> *Yoyaku* is a general word for "reservation." To reserve a concert ticket and restaurant reservation, say the following:
>
> *chiketto-no yoyaku*
>
> *resutoraN-no yoyaku*

Huh? _____

> Remember the function of the sentence-final *ga?* This *ga* is different from the subject marker *-ga* introduced in Chapter 4. Its English equivalent is "but." By adding *ga*, you make your sentence incomplete, allowing the listener to guess what you want. This is a great strategy to make your Japanese sound polite!

Choosing the Hotel

Here are two possible questions you might hear regarding the name of the hotel where you want to stay:

> *Dochira-no hoteru-desu ka?*
> "What hotel is it (that you want to stay)?"
>
> *Hoteru-no namae-wa (naN-desu ka)?*
> "(What is) the name of the hotel?"

For either of the previous questions, you can simply mention the name. Let's say that the hotel you have in mind is the *Plaza Hotel*.

> *Puraza Hoteru-desu.*   "It's Plaza Hotel."

If there is more than one hotel under the same name *Plaza Hotel*, you will be asked:

> *Dochira-no Puraza Hoteru-desu ka?*
> "Which Plaza Hotel is it?"

Or:

> *Dochira-no Puraza Hoteru-deshō ka?*

Let's say you want to stay in the Plaza Hotel located in Shinjuku:

> *ShiNjuku-no Puraza Hoteru-desu.*
> "It's the Plaza Hotel in Shinjuku."

Simple, isn't it? What if you haven't decided which hotel to stay at? The following expressions would be appropriate:

> *Mada kime-te i-maseN.*
> "I haven't decided yet."

> *ShiNjuku-ni tomari-tai-N-desu ga …*
> "I want to stay in Shinjuku, but …"

> *Doko-ga i-idesu ka?*
> "Which one would you recommend?"

In reply to this question, you might hear the following:

> *XYZ Hoteru-wa dō-desu ka?*   "How about XYZ Hotel?"

Or the agent can reply to your question even more politely:

> *XYZ Hoteru-wa ikaga-deshō ka?*   "How about XYZ Hotel?"

The suggestion pattern *-wa dō-desu ka?* (or *-wa ikaga-deshō ka?*—polite version) is extremely useful. You should definitely add this expression to your "must memorize" list!

Huh? _____

When the question word is predictable in a sentence, as seen in the example "What is the name of the hotel?" you can omit that question word and end the sentence with *XYZ-wa?* instead.

Huh? _____

A question ending with *-deshō ka?* is more polite than one ending with *-desu ka?*

Check-In and Checkout Dates

You need to specify the dates of check-in and checkout. Dates are pronounced almost identical to the way you count days, as you saw in Chapter 14. From the first day to the tenth day, they are all irregular. Beyond the eleventh day, however, most of the days are regularly pronounced except for the fourteenth, twentieth, and twenty-fourth days.

Dates

1st day	*tsuitachi*
2nd day	*futsuka*
3rd day	*mikka*
4th day	*yokka*
5th day	*itsuka*
6th day	*muika*

7th day	*nanoka*
8th day	*yōka*
9th day	*kokonoka*
10th day	*tōka*
11th day	*jū ichi-nichi*
12th day	*jū ni-nichi*
13th day	*jū saN-nichi*
14th day	*jū yokka*
20th day	*hatsuka*
24th day	*ni-jū yokka*
What date?	*naN-nichi*

How would you say months? The good news is months are pronounced in a completely regular manner:

**Track 16
CD-7**

Months

January	*ichi-gatsu*
February	*ni-gatsu*
March	*saN-gatsu*
April	*shi-gatsu*
May	*go-gatsu*
June	*roku-gatsu*
July	*shichi-gatsu*
August	*hachi-gatsu*
September	*ku-gatsu*
October	*jū-gatsu*
November	*jū ichi-gatsu*
December	*jū ni-gatsu*
What month?	*naN-gatsu*

Before you forget all the calendar words, answer the following questions. Can you guess what these days are?

1. *Kurisumasu-wa itsu-desu ka?*

2. *Kurisumasu Ibu-wa itsu-desu ka?*

3. *BareNtaiN Dē-wa itsu-desu ka?*

4. *Ēpuriru Fūru-wa itsu-desu ka?*

Shortcuts to Success _____

A useful exercise to practice months and dates is saying people's birthdays, or *taNjōbi*. Ask people this question:

    Q: *TaNjōbi-wa itsu-desu ka?*   "When is your birthday?"

    A: *SaN-gatsu jū ni-nichi-desu.*   "It's March 12."

Now, when is *your* birthday?

_____

Did you get it? Yes, you've been asked when (1) Christmas, (2) Christmas Eve, (3) Valentine's Day, and (4) April Fool's Day are, respectively. Now, answer these questions:

Exercise 1

  1. *Kurisumasu-wa* _____.

  2. *Kurisumasu Ibu-wa* _____.

  3. *BareNtaiN Dē-wa* _____.

  4. *Ēpuriru Fūru-wa* _____.

Let's use this opportunity to learn another important calendar expression, days of the week:

Track 16
CD-8

Days of the Week

Monday	*getsu-yōbi*
Tuesday	*ka-yōbi*
Wednesday	*sui-yōbi*
Thursday	*moku-yōbi*
Friday	*kiN-yōbi*
Saturday	*do-yōbi*
Sunday	*nichi-yōbi*
What day?	*naN-yōbi*

With all these calendar expressions, let's learn how to specify dates of your check-in and checkout. The easiest way to specify these dates is to say "the check-in is so-and-so date and the checkout is so-and-so date." Suppose that you will check in on Tuesday, June 13, and check out on Thursday, June 15:

Track 16
CD-9

Chekku iN-wa roku-gatsu jū saN-nichi ka-yōbi-de,   "Check-in is Tuesday, June 13 and
chekku auto-wa jū go-nichi moku-yōbi-desu.   checkout is Thursday, the 15th."

Huh? _____

Let's not forget another important calendar-related counter, "year." It is *-neN* and can be used for expressing duration and point of time. Here are some examples:

"five years"   *go-neN*

"1985"   *seN kyū-hyaku hachi-jū go-neN*

"2002"   *ni-seN ni-neN*

"what year; how many years"   *naN-neN*

Notice that the day of the week follows the date. Also notice that the two sentences are connected by the *TE*-form, *-de*.

Alternatively, using the "want to" pattern, you can specify the check-in date:

> *Roku-gatsu jū saN-nichi-<u>ni</u> chekku iN shi-tai-N-desu ga …*
> "I want to check in <u>on</u> June 13 …"

The particle *-ni*, which is attached to the date, means "on." Let me give you another way of specifying check-in and checkout dates:

> *Roku-gatsu jū saN-nichi-<u>kara</u>, jū go-nichi-<u>made</u>-desu.*   "It's <u>from</u> June 13 <u>to</u> the 15th."

I think you know by now that particles are extremely important. They make it possible for you to say the same thing in a number of different ways.

Exercise 2

Translate the following by using the expressions you have learned so far.

1. _____
   "I want to check in on Wednesday, March 22."

2. _____
   "Check-in is August 2 and checkout is August 3."

3. _____
   "It's from Monday to Friday."

Number of People and Types of Room

In Chapter 10, we learned how to count people. The counter for people is *-niN*, but "one person" and "two people" are irregular.

Counting People

1	*hitori*
2	*futari*
3	*saN-niN*
4	*yo-niN*
5	*go-niN*
6	*roku-niN*
7	*shichi-niN*
8	*hachi-niN*
9	*kyū-niN*
10	*jū-niN*
11	*jū ichi-niN*
How many?	*naN-niN*

The polite version of the counter *-niN* is *-mēsama*. The clerk at the counter might ask you by using *-mēsama* how many people are staying:

NaN-mēsama-desu ka?   "How many people?"

To reply to this question, just use the regular counter *-niN*:

SaN-niN-desu.   "Three people."

As long as you stay in a Western-style hotel, you can use the same words for room types. But make sure that you *Japanize* them when pronouncing these words!

single	*shiNguru*
twin	*tsuiN*
double	*daburu*
suite	*suīto*

The Japanese word for "room" is *heya* or *oheya* (polite version). Here is a typical dialog between a clerk and a guest regarding selecting a room:

Q: *Donoyōna oheya-ni nasai-masu ka?*
"What kind of room would you like?"

A: *TsuiN-ni shi-masu.*
 "I'll have a twin room."

Huh?

The expression *-ni shi-masu* literally means "decide on ...." This expression is often used when placing an order. By the way, the honorific version of *-ni shi-masu* is *-ni nasai-masu*.

Upon making a reservation, you might be asked to leave a deposit. Major credit cards are widely accepted throughout Japan. This can make reserving a room a lot easier!

Check-In and Checkout

Now you are in the hotel lobby. You're about to check in. First, you need to tell the front desk who you are and indicate that you have made a reservation:

Yoyaku-o shi-te ari-masu XYZ-desu ga.
"I am XYZ. I have a reservation."

> **Lifesavers**
>
> In Japanese hotels, the price for a room might vary depending on how many people stay in the room. For example, the same twin room can cost less if you are staying alone. Make sure that you check the room charge policy prior to making a reservation!

Upon check-in, it is likely that you will be asked the questions covered in the previous section, such as the checkout date, number of people staying, and type of room. There are a couple of things I want to add here that you might find helpful.

If you are a nonsmoker, you should definitely ask for a nonsmoking room because smoking rooms still outnumber nonsmoking rooms in Japanese hotels. "Nonsmoking" is *kiNeN:*

KiNeN-no heya-o onegai shimasu.
"A nonsmoking room, please."

> **Huh?**
>
> The expression *-te ari-masu* is used when talking about something that *has been done in advance.*
>
> Other examples using this pattern are ...
>
> *Kat-te ari-masu.*   "Something has been purchased."
> (*Kat-te* derives from *kai-masu.*)
>
> *TanoN-de ari-masu.*   "Something has been requested."
> (*TanoN-de* derives from *tanomi-masu.*)
>
> *Kai-te ari-masu.*   "Something has been written."
> (*Kai-te* derives from *kaki-masu.*)

You might want to ask what the checkout time is. You learned the time expressions, so you should have no problem saying the following:

Chekku auto-wa naN-ji-desu ka?   "What time is the checkout?"

There is one more thing. You will need to fill out a registration card. It is called *shukuhaku kādo*. It should look similar to a typical registration card used in Western countries. Here are some words you will see on the card:

"Name"	*shimē* or *(o)namae*
"Address"	*jūsho*
"Phone number"	*deNwa baNgō*
"Occupation"	*shokugyō*

You can ask if they have an English version of the registration card:

Ēgo-no kādo-wa ari-maseN ka?	"Don't you have an English card?"

Of course, you can use *ari-masu ka*, instead of the negative version *ari-maseN ka*. The negative question such as this, however, sounds softer and more polite. This is another strategy to make your Japanese sound better!

Lifesavers

You might want to sightsee in the area using the hotel as the hub. Ask the hotel clerk if there are any places to visit in the area. Suppose that the hotel is in Shinjuku:

ShiNjuku-ni-wa nani-ga ari-masu ka?   "What (kinds of things) are in Shijuku?"

This pattern (*XYZ-ni-wa nani-ga ari-masu ka?*) is helpful when you are in a new place by yourself and want to explore the area.

Track 16 CD-14

When you check out, say the by-now-familiar phrase:

Chekku auto, onegai shimasu.   "Checkout, please."

Or:

Kaikē, onegai shimasu.   "Billing, please."
(*kaikē* = bill, account)

You might want to tell the front desk how you want to pay for your room. Suppose that you pay by credit card:

Track 16
CD-15

> *Kādo-de onegai shimasu.* "By credit card, please."

The particle *-de* means "by means of." If paying in cash, say *kyasshu* or *geNkiN*, as in:

> *Kyasshu-de onegai shimasu.* "In cash, please."
> *GeNkiN-de onegai shimasu.* "In cash, please."

If you need a receipt, you should say:

Track 16
CD-16

> *Ryōshūsho-o onegai shimasu.* "Receipt, please."

Instead of *ryōshūsho*, its loan word version *reshīto* can also work!

Staying in a *RyokaN*—a Japanese-Style Inn

It is certainly more convenient to stay in a Western-style hotel because you are familiar with room arrangement, amenities, check-in/checkout procedures, and so forth. However, if you want to enjoy the feel of Japanese tradition, try a Japanese-style inn, or *ryokaN*. In what follows, I will briefly explain the major differences between Western-style hotels and Japanese-style inns.

A *ryokaN* guest room generally has no bed, couch, or carpet. Instead, it has a *futon*, low table, and *tatami* mat. You might know this already, but a *futon* is a foldable mattress with a comforter. A Japanese-style low table is called *chabudai*. *Tatami* is a straw mat, which is about two inches thick.

> **CAUTION**
>
> **Lifesavers**
>
> For more information about *ryokaN*, check out the official website of Japan Ryokan Association at www.ryokan.or.jp.

> **Green Tea Break**
>
> Some larger *ryokaN* have Western-style rooms available. A Japanese-style room is called *washitsu* or *nihoNma*, and a Western-style room is *yōma*.

Perhaps the best part of staying in a *ryokaN* is that breakfast and dinner are included in the accommodations. Typically, a room service person in charge of your room (called *nakaisaN*) takes you to your room after check-in. She will then make nice tea for you and ask what time you want the meal served in your room. The questions look like the following:

> *Oshokuji-wa, naN-ji-goro-ga yoroshi-idesu ka?*
> "Around what time would you like to have the meal?"

Oshokuji is the politer version of *shokuji* ("meal") and *yoroshi-idesu* is a polite equivalent of *i-idesu* ("all right").

If you want the meal served around 6 o'clock, say:

> *Roku-ji-goro onegai shimasu.*
> "Around 6, please."

In general, *nakaisaN*, a person in charge of your room, ensures that you have all you need during your stay.

Before dinner, you might want to relax; take a bath and put on a *yukata*, a casual-style *kimono*.

Here comes dinner! It is usually served on a high tray and placed in front of you as you sit on the *tatami*. Because the food is not at eye level, you have to bend over slightly in order to eat. (If you are not comfortable, you can request that the meal be placed on a *chabudai*, the low table. But you still have to sit on the *tatami*, floor.)

After the meal, the room service person will put away the tray, and then start laying out a *futon*. After you wake up, she will put away the *futon* for you. This is how Japanese people make the best use of their living space.

Lifesavers

If you request in advance, the *ryokaN* will even make lunch for you (for an extra charge). If you plan to venture out and do some activities the following day, you should definitely use this service so you won't have to eat fast food on the street! By the way, the Japanese words for breakfast, lunch, and dinner are …

"breakfast"	*asa-gohaN* or *chō-shoku*
"lunch"	*hiru-gohaN* or *chū-shoku*
"dinner"	*baN-gohaN* or *yū-shoku*

Your room might have a bathtub, but I highly recommend that you use a huge guest bath located away from the guest rooms. This is called *dai-yokujō*, "big bath for guests," or simply *ofuro*. If your travel destination is famous for hot springs (*oNseN*), it would be criminal not to try *dai-yokujō!* Some *ryokaN* inns have several baths, which look like swimming pools. (I first learned how to swim in a *dai-yokujō!*) Some baths are even located outdoors (called *roteNburo*). Taking a bath is definitely serious recreation for Japanese people!

A roteNburo, *or an outdoor* onsen *bath. There is a fence so your privacy is protected!*

(Photo by Tamotsu Hiroi)

There are several manners you should obey when using *ofuro:*

♦ Wash your body thoroughly before dipping.

♦ Do not put your hand towel in the bath water. Put it outside the tub or on your head.

♦ Never use soap in the bath!

♦ Don't drain the bath water after use.

Dipping in a nice and relaxing *oNseN* hot spring and enjoying delicious Japanese cuisine personally served in your room will make staying at a *ryokaN* a memorable experience for you!

Before ending this chapter, take the following review exercise. This is a dialog between you and a hotel clerk upon check-in. I will add the English translation where needed.

Exercise 3

HOTEL 1   *Irasshai mase!*

"Welcome!"

YOU 1   _____

"My name is XYZ. I have a reservation."

HOTEL 2   *XYZ-sama-desu ne. NaN-mēsama-desu ka?*

"Ms./Mr. XYZ. How many people?"

YOU 2   _____

"Two."

HOTEL 3   *Donoyōna oheya-ni nasai-masu ka?*

"What kind of room would you like?"

YOU 3   _____

"Twin room, please."

HOTEL 4   *Hai. Chekku auto-wa?*

"Certainly. When is the checkout date?"

YOU 4   _____

"Saturday, the 17th. What time is the checkout?"

HOTEL 5   *Jū ni-ji-desu. Goyukkuri dōzo.*

"It's 12 o'clock. Make yourself at home, please."

YOU 5   _____

"Thank you."

Answers

Exercise 1

Track 16
CD-17–20

1. *Kurisumasu-wa jū ni-gatsu ni-jū go-nichi-desu.*

2. *Kurisumasu Ibu-wa jū ni-gatsu ni-jū yokka-desu.*

3. *BareNtaiN Dē-wa ni-gatsu jū yokka-desu.*

4. *Ēpuriru Fūru-wa shi-gatsu tsuitachi-desu.*

Exercise 2

Track 16
CD-21–23

1. *SaN-gatsu ni-jū ni-nichi suiyō-bi-ni chekku iN shi-tai-N-desu ga.*

2. *Chekku iN-wa hachi-gatsu futsuka-de, chekku auto-wa hachi-gatsu mikka-desu.*

3. *Getsu-yōbi-kara kiN-yōbi-made desu.*

Exercise 3

HOTEL 1   *Irasshai mase!*

"Welcome!"

Track 16
CD-24

YOU 1   *Yoyaku-o shi-te ari-masu XYZ-desu ga.*

"My name is XYZ. I have a reservation."

HOTEL 2   *XYZ-sama-desu ne. NaN-mēsama-desu ka?*

"Ms./Mr. XYZ. How many people?"

YOU 2   *Futari-desu.*

"Two."

HOTEL 3   *Donoyōna ohaya-ni nasai-masu ka?*

"What kind of room would you like?"

YOU 3   *TsuiN (rūmu)-o onegai shimasu.*

"Twin room, please."

HOTEL 4	*Hai. Chekku auto-wa?*
	"Yes. When is the checkout date?"
YOU 4	*Jū shichi-nichi, do-yōbi-desu.*
	Chekku auto-wa naN-ji-desu ka?
	"Saturday, the 17th. What time is the checkout?"
HOTEL 5	*Jū ni-ji-desu. Goyukkuri dōzo.*
	"It's 12 o'clock. Make yourself at home, please."
YOU 5	*Dōmo arigatō.*
	"Thank you."

The Least You Need to Know

◆ Learn calendar expressions and counting people for making a reservation (*yoyaku*).

◆ Practice basic dialogs for check-in and checkout.

◆ Try a *ryokaN*, a Japanese-style inn. Enjoy delicious meals served in your room and relax in *oNseN*, hot spring bath. Most hot springs are rich in therapeutic minerals.

◆ Here are three points to remember when you take a Japanese-style bath: (1) wash your body before dipping, (2) don't use soap in the bath, and (3) don't drain the bath water after use!

◆ At a *ryokaN*, a *nakaisaN* is in charge of your room and makes sure your stay is comfortable by serving you meals, making a bed, and so on. Tipping a *nakaisaN* (commonly a 1,000 *yen* bill) is a good idea.

Chapter 17

At the Bank

In This Chapter

◆ Japanese bills and coins

◆ Counting money

◆ Currency exchange

◆ Opening a bank account

At least two things have changed the world of traveling in recent years—the Internet and credit cards. Thanks to the Internet, you can find the cheapest possible plane tickets, make a reservation for a hotel, rent a car, and come up with a precise itinerary. And thanks to credit cards, you can travel almost anywhere in the world without carrying a large sum of cash. You can even make an international phone call using a plastic card.

Even though you can rely on your credit card pretty much anywhere in Japan, you should know that Japan is still a cash-oriented society. There are establishments, especially in rural areas, where credit cards are not accepted or a processing charge is added to your purchase. So you'd better know how to deal with *yen*. In this chapter, I will first give you basic facts about Japanese money, and then give you expressions you might use at a bank.

Bills and Coins

In several previous chapters, we dealt with Japanese number words, but they were all small numbers. With money in hand, now we have to deal with bigger numbers. I certainly don't want you to lose your money due to a miscalculation or simply because you don't know how to count Japanese money! To make this chapter easier, I suggest you go back to Chapter 7 and review the counting basics in Japanese.

The monetary unit used in Japan is *yen*, but it is actually pronounced as *eN*. Its international symbol is ¥. First, let's take a look at paper *yen*. There are four kinds of bills: ¥1,000, ¥2,000, ¥5,000, and ¥10,000. Here is how to pronounce each denomination:

Huh? _____

All the denominations of paper *yen* end with the sound *N*, as in *seN*, "1,000." Make sure you pronounce this sound correctly so that you don't pronounce ¥1,000 as *seneN*. It should be *seN eN*. For more details on this sound, refer to Chapter 3.

Track 17
CD-1

Japanese Bills

Denomination	Pronunciation
¥1,000	*seN–eN*
¥2,000	*ni-seN–eN*
¥5,000	*go-seN–eN*
¥10,000	*ichi-maN–eN*

Green Tea Break

Because the bills are slightly different in size (the higher the denomination, the bigger its size!), it is easy to organize your wallet. Also, specially imprinted Braille appears on the left corner, so visually impaired persons can recognize each bill:

¥1,000: One round dot

¥2,000: Three dots (vertical)

¥5,000: Two dots (vertical)

¥10,000: Two dots (horizontal)

1000 yen (front)

1000 yen (back)

Japanese ¥1,000, ¥2,000, ¥5,000, and ¥10,000 bills. The ¥2,000 bills are not widely circulated.

2000 yen (front)

2000 yen (back)

5000 yen (front)

5000 yen (back)

10000 yen (front)

10000 yen (back)

How would you say "coins"? There are six kinds of coins.

Japanese Coins

Track 17
CD-2

Denomination	Pronunciation
¥1	*ichi-eN*
¥5	*go-eN*
¥10	*jū-eN*
¥50	*go-jū-eN*
¥100	*hyaku-eN*
¥500	*go-hyaku-eN*

There are six kinds of coins circulated in Japan. The 1 yen coins are made of aluminum; 5 yen coins are made of copper; 10 yen coins are made of bronze; and 50, 100, and 500 yen coins are all made of nickel.

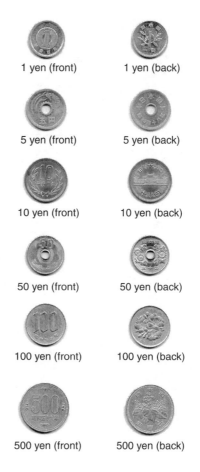

1 yen (front)   1 yen (back)

5 yen (front)   5 yen (back)

10 yen (front)   10 yen (back)

50 yen (front)   50 yen (back)

100 yen (front)   100 yen (back)

500 yen (front)   500 yen (back)

Counting in Japanese can be a challenging task, but it becomes essential when counting your money! If you are not confident about counting, refer back to Chapter 7.

Now, how about a short exercise? How do you say the following in Japanese?

Exercise 1

1. ¥24

_____

2. ¥90

_____

3. ¥805

_____

4. ¥310

_____

5. ¥7,000

_____

6. ¥5,120

_____

7. ¥12,000

_____

8. ¥46,100

_____

9. ¥33,905

_____

10. ¥100,000

_____

Now with all the basics covered, the following sections cover various tasks that are useful at a bank, or *giNkō*:

♦ Currency exchange

♦ Sending money

♦ Opening a bank account

Currency Exchange

The top reason why a foreign traveler uses a bank is to exchange money. The expression for "to exchange" is *ryōgae shi-masu*. Suppose that you have U.S. dollars and want to exchange them to Japanese *yen*. Using the "want to" pattern, say the following:

Track 17
CD-3

> *Amerika doru-o, nihoN eN-ni ryōgae shi-tai-N-desu ga …*   "I want to exchange U.S. *dollars* to Japanese *yen*."

The formula for currency exchange is …

> (Original Currencies)-*o* (Desired Currencies)-*ni ryōgae shi-tai-N-desu ga …*

Note that in the preceding example, "dollar ($)" is pronounced as *doru*.

What do you call other countries' currencies in Japanese?

Track 17
CD-4

Canadian dollar	*Kanada doru*
euro	*yūro*
UK pound	*poNdo*
Mexican peso	*peso*

Now you are at a currency exchange. Exchange your money as instructed:

Exercise 2

1. From Japanese yen to Canadian dollar

2. From euro to Japanese yen

3. From U.S. dollar to UK pound

A bank clerk will ask you how much in U.S. dollars you want to exchange by asking the following:

    Amerika doru-o, ikura-desu ka?   "How much of U.S. dollars?"

Let's say that you have $1,000 to exchange:

    SeN-doru onegai shimasu.   "$1,000, please."

Using the *XYZ-wa ikura-desu ka* pattern, the following expressions can also be useful when exchanging money:

    Tesūryō-wa ikura-desu ka?   "How much is the processing fee?"

    Rēto-wa, ikura-desu ka?   "What is the (exchange) rate?"

Suppose the rate is U.S.$1 = ¥130. Then the answer to the previous rate question is:

    Ichi-doru-wa hyaku saN-jū-eN-desu.   "U.S.$1 = ¥130."

Note that the by-now-familiar *X-wa Y-desu* pattern is just like a "mathematical equation," as explained in Chapter 9.

 Lifesavers ⎯⎯⎯⎯⎯

Usually the processing (or handling) fee for currency exchange is included in the exchange rate.

The word *ryōgae* is used not only for international exchanges, but you can also use it for just breaking a big bill into smaller denominations. Requesting an exchange is easy!

    Ryōgae shi-te kudasai.   "Exchange, please."

Or:

    Ryōgae onegai shimasu.   "Exchange, please."

What if you have a ¥10,000 bill and want to exchange it for ¥1,000 bills?

    Ichi-maN-eN-o seN-eN-ni ryōgae shi-te kudasai.   "Please exchange a ¥10,000 bill to ¥1,000s."

Shortcuts to Success

As of this writing, U.S.$1 is equal to ¥130. However, because the commodity price of Japan is higher than that of the United States, what you can buy with $1 in the United States costs more than ¥130 in Japan. The rule of thumb is U.S.$1 = ¥150. For example, a can of beverage in a vending machine (about 75 cents in the United States) is ¥120. A McDonald's "value set" with Big Mac (about $3.50 in the United States) is about ¥550.

Exercise 3

Ask to break the following bills to smaller bills.

1. A ¥1,000 bill to ¥100s

   _____

2. A ¥5,000 bill to ¥1,000s

   _____

3. A ¥10,000 bill to a ¥5,000 bill *and* ¥1,000s
   (Use *to* for "and.")

   _____

Opening a Bank Account

If you plan to stay in Japan for a longer period of time, you will probably need to open a bank account, or *kōza*. You will be dealing with your money in a foreign country, so you want to be very cautious about bank-related business. If you have a Japanese friend, ask her or him to help you do all the paperwork when opening a new account. If not, I suggest that you go to a branch office of a major Western bank, such as Citibank, where many of the clerks are bilingual. However, if you live in a rural area where there is no Western bank branch and you need to do it on your own, here is how you go about it.

First of all, you should know that in Japanese business, signatures or autographs are not used for identification purpose. Instead, you must use an impression seal (*or* signature stamp) called *haNko* or *iNkaN*. It is about 2.5 inches long (7cm) and its diameter is a half-inch (12mm) to one inch (25mm), usually made of wood or plastic. You can purchase a *haNko* at a local department store in Japan. Unless you are of Japanese descent, you probably don't have a Japanese name. In such a case, it will have to be custom-made, and it will take a couple of days to get your own *haNko*.

Green Tea Break

You can also open your account at a local post office (*yūbiNkyoku*). One of the advantages of using the post office as a "bank" is that you can withdraw your money at any post office in Japan. This way, you won't have to pay a service charge for using other banks' ATMs. On a related note, ATMs might not be open 24 hours, especially in small towns.

A sample impression of haNko *("signature stamp"). It says "Fujita" in* Kanji *(Chinese characters).*

With your *haNko* in hand now, you are ready to open your new account.

> *Atarashi-i kōza-o tsukuri-tai-N-desu ga …*   "I want to make a new account …"

Note that *atarashi-i* means "new" and *tsukuri-masu* means "to make." Also remember the "want to" pattern:

> Verb Stem + *tai-N-desu ga …*   "I want to VERB"

Green Tea Break

If you do not have your *haNko*, you might be asked to use your thumbprint to identify yourself. This method is called *boiN*.

You will be given an application form. (Most major banks have a form written in English.) Next to your name, you will be asked to put a *haNko* impression. This impression is registered in the bank as a means of your identification. Therefore, when you need to withdraw money from your account, you will need your *haNko* (except when you withdraw your money from an ATM, of course).

Here are other important bank-related words:

certificate of deposit (CD) (*or* "term saving")	*tēki yokiN*
regular savings	*futsū yokiN*
interest	*risoku*
cancellation of account	*kaiyaku*
ATM card	*kyasshu kādo*
account number	*kōza baNgō*
account record book	*chokiN tsūchō*

You might be wondering why the list did not include the words for "checking account" or "personal check." In Japan, there is no checking account simply because personal checks are not commonly available. Checks are limited to corporate use in general.

The phrase *chokiN tsūchō* ("account record book") might not be a familiar concept to you. This is a tiny booklet that shows your account record. When you go to your bank to deposit or withdraw money from your account, you need to show this booklet together with your *haNko* ("signature stamp"). After a transaction, the bank clerk will insert the booklet into a machine and print out the transaction activities and balance on it.

Keeping this record of your own bank account makes a few things easier. For example, you can easily cash your traveler's checks or send money to your home country (and receive money by wire to your account from abroad).

First, here is how you request cashing your traveler's check. The expression for "to cash" is *kaNkiN shi-masu*:

Track 17
CD-9

> *Toraberāzu chekku-o kaNkiN shi-tai-N-desu ga …*
> "I want to cash my traveler's checks …"

When you cash traveler's checks, you will be asked to show your ID:

> *MibuN shōmēsho-o mise-te kudasai.*
> "Please show me your ID."
> (*mise-masu* = "to show")

Possible IDs you might have are …

> *pasupōto*
> passport
>
> *kokusai meNkyosho*
> international driver's license

Let's learn some essential phrases for sending (= wiring) money to your home country. The phrase for "send (wire) money" is *sōkiN shi-masu*. Suppose that you want to send money to the United States:

> *Amerika-ni sōkiN shi-tai-N-desu ga …*
> "I want to wire money to the United States …"

You will have to give the bank clerk the following information:

> *Amerika-no XYZ GiNkō-desu.*　"It's the Bank of XYZ in the United States."
> *ABC ShiteN-desu.*　"It's the ABC Branch."
> *UketoriniN-wa John Smith-desu.*　"The recipient is John Smith."
> *Kōza baNgō-wa XXX-desu.*　"The account number is XXX."

Lifesavers _____

If you stay in Japan for more than 90 days, you need to obtain a *gaikokujiN tōrokushō* (Alien Registration Card). It can be obtained at your local city hall (*shiyakusho*). You can use this card as your ID as well.

Lifesavers _____

When you read a series of numbers, such as a phone or account number, say each digit separately, and use *no* for a dash (-). If your account number is 346-2687-1, say:

> *SaN yoN roku <u>no</u> ni roku hachi nana <u>no</u> ichi*

Learning Japanese number words can be a lot of work, but it will make your life much less stressful when it comes to money and banking.

Answers

Track 17
CD-10

Exercise 1

1. ¥24 *ni-jū yo-eN*

2. ¥90 *kyū-jū-eN*

3. ¥805 *hap-pyaku go-eN*

4. ¥310 *saN-byaku jū-eN*

5. ¥7,000 *nana-seN-eN*

6. ¥5,120 *go-seN hyaku ni-jū-eN*

7. ¥12,000 *ichi-maN ni-seN-eN*

8. ¥46,100 *yoN-maN roku-seN hyaku-eN*

9. ¥33,905 *saN-maN saN-zeN kyū-hyaku go-eN*

10. ¥100,000 *jū-maN-eN*

Exercise 2

1. From Japanese yen to Canadian dollar

   NihoN eN-o, Kanada doru-ni ryōgae shi-tai-N-desu ga …

2. From euro to Japanese yen

   Yūro-o, nihoN eN-ni ryōgae shi-tai-N-desu ga …

3. From U.S. dollar to UK pound

   Amerika doru -o, poNdo-ni ryōgae shi-tai-N-desu ga …

Track 17
CD-11–13

Exercise 3

1. A ¥1,000 bill to ¥100s

   SeN-eN-o hyaku-eN-ni ryōgae shi-te kudasai.

2. A ¥5,000 bill to ¥1,000s

   Go-seN-eN-o seN-eN-ni ryōgae shi-te kudasai.

3. A ¥10,000 bill to a ¥5,000 bill *and* ¥1,000s

   Ichi-maN-eN-o go-seN-eN to seN-eN-ni ryōgae shi-te kudasai.

The Least You Need to Know

- Familiarize yourself with Japanese bills and coins. There are four kinds of bills—¥1,000, ¥2,000, ¥5,000, and ¥10,000—and there are six kinds of coins: ¥1, ¥5, ¥10, ¥50, ¥100, and ¥500.

- The ability to count numbers in Japanese is a true lifesaver!

- Be able to ask for currency exchange and know how to cash your traveler's checks.

- In Japan, a *haNko*, or seal impression, is used for bank transactions in place of a signature.

Part 5

Japanese for Fun

This part covers four fun activities: shopping, dining, home stay, and leisure time. You will learn all the "must-know" shopping phrases and expressions. Dining is also a fun part of traveling—especially in Japan. With the expressions covered in these chapters, you can decide what to eat and order your favorite dishes, not to mention learn about Japanese dining etiquette.

If at all possible, try arranging a home stay. Nothing is a more exciting and authentic experience than living in a real Japanese house with Japanese people. I will take you on a virtual house tour and explain in detail what you are or are not expected to do in a Japanese home.

If you're an independent person and want to explore Japan on your own, Chapter 21 is for you. After reading the chapter, you will be able to make plans for a short trip. You will also discover what kinds of popular events are held during each season.

Chapter 18

Let's Go Shopping!

In This Chapter

- ◆ Buying what you want
- ◆ Four basic counters
- ◆ Use of adjectives

We dealt with Japanese money in Chapter 17. While your memory is still fresh, let's move on to shopping! There is no doubt that shopping is one of the best parts of traveling. If you like shopping, you will find this chapter very helpful.

Types of Shops

One thing I noticed when I first came to the United States was that supermarkets in the United States are so big that you can buy almost anything there. Consequently, I noticed that specialty shops such as vegetable shops, meat shops, and small general stores are extremely scarce in the States, compared to Japan.

In Japan, the number of supermarkets (*sūpā*) has grown rapidly in recent years, but there are still many traditional small retail stores. Here is a list of the Japanese names for common retail stores:

Shops

shop (in general)	*mise*
general store	*zakkaya*

convenience store	*koNbini*
bookstore	*hoNya* (or *hoNya-saN*)
fish market	*sakanaya* (or *sakanaya-saN*)
vegetable shop	*yaoya* (or *yaoya-saN*)
meat shop	*nikuya* (or *nikuya-saN*)
drug store	*kusuriya* (or *kusuriya-saN* or *yakkyoku*)
shoe store	*kutsuya* (or *kutsuya-saN*)
office supply store	*buNbōguya* (or *buNbōguya-saN*)
florist	*hanaya* (or *hanaya-saN*)
bakery	*paNya* (or *paNya-saN*)
cleaner	*kurīniNguya* (or *kurīniNguya-saN*)
liquor store	*sakaya* (or *sakaya-saN*)

Huh?

You might have noticed that many of the shop names end in *ya*, "shop." So by looking at *hoNya* ("bookstore") you know that the Japanese word for "book" is *hoN*. There are two exceptions: *yaoya* ("vegetable shop") and *sakaya* ("liquor shop"). The words for "vegetable" and "liquor" are *yasai* and *sake*, respectively, not *yao* and *saka*. Also, as seen in the list, businesses ending with *ya* often end with *-saN*, as in *hoNya-saN*. This way, these names sound more personable.

Lifesavers

A convenience store, or *koNbini*, does more than just sell a variety of goods. You can use dry-cleaning services, send packages via an express home delivery service called *takuhaibiN*, use a photocopier, buy a concert ticket, and so on. Even in rural areas, you can find at least one *koNbini* near you!

As you know, shopping at a supermarket is easy. You just put merchandise in your shopping cart, take it to the cashier, and then pay. But what if the item you are looking for can only be found in a small retail shop? If so, you will need to converse with a shop clerk to get what you want.

Let's learn some basic dialogs that contain essential shopping expressions.

Shop Talk

When you enter a shop, you will be greeted with …

Track 18
CD-1

Irasshai mase. "Welcome!"

This is a ritualized expression, so you don't have to reply to this greeting. The shop clerk will then ask you if she or he can be of assistance:

> *Nanika osagashi-desu ka?*
> "Looking for something?"

The basic expression that you should use when you buy something is very simple, as shown here:

> *XYZ-o kudasai.* "Please give me XYZ."

Alternatively, you can say "I *want* XYZ":

> *XYZ-ga hoshi-i-N-desu ga …*
> "I want XYZ …"

These expressions will suffice if you purchase just one item, but what if you want to buy more than one? You should know how to attach the desired number to a noun.

Basic Counters

One of the notable characteristics of Japanese is that when you count objects, you must attach an appropriate counter to the number. In English, when you count "uncountable" substances such as paper, salt, and water, you use phrases such as "three sheets of paper," "a pinch of salt," or "two glasses of water." Japanese counters are in a sense similar to "sheet," "pinch," and "glass," but they are not limited to uncountable objects.

Lifesavers _____

If you are just looking, the following phrase can be handy:

> *Mi-te iru dake-desu.*
> "Just looking."

Huh? _____

If you use "want" with a verb (as in "want to do so-and-so"), use the following pattern:
Verb Stem + *tai*-N-desu ga …

Huh? _____

The word *hoshi-i* ("want") is an adjective in Japanese. So "I don't want (it)" should be …

> *Hoshi-kuna-idesu.*
> "I don't want (it)."

Refer to Chapter 5 for adjective conjugation.

We have already seen two counters in Chapter 10: *-niN* for counting people and *-sai* for ages. In this chapter, you will learn four types of counters that are useful when counting objects for shopping: *-mai*, *-satsu*, *-hoN*, and *-tsu/-ko*.

Counter	Used For	Examples
-mai	flat objects	paper, CDs, pizza, stamps, plates
-satsu	bound objects	books, magazines
-hoN	long objects	pens, bananas, bottles
-tsu/-ko	miscellaneous objects	vegetables, eggs, erasers, paper clips, fruits, chairs

I referred to *-tsu* as the counter for miscellaneous objects. This is the general counter, so if you are not sure exactly which counter to use, you can always use it as a default. This counter behaves in a slightly complicated way. But don't worry about that now! We will look at how it works shortly. Just remember that these four counters should cover most merchandise you might need to buy at Japanese shops.

Now, let's look at each of the first three counters from 1 to 11. The pronunciation pattern of words from 11 on is just the same as that for words between 1 and 10. As always, irregular pronunciation is indicated in bold face.

Track 18
CD-5

Three "Basic" Counters

	Flat	**Bound**	**Long**
One	*ichi-mai*	***is-satsu***	***ip-poN***
Two	*ni-mai*	*ni-satsu*	*ni-hoN*
Three	*saN-mai*	*saN-satsu*	***saN-boN***
Four	*yoN-mai*	*yoN-satsu*	*yoN-hoN*
Five	*go-mai*	*go-satsu*	*go-hoN*
Six	*roku-mai*	*roku-satsu*	***rop-poN***
Seven	*nana-mai*	*nana-satsu*	*nana-hoN*
Eight	*hachi-mai*	***has-satsu***	***hap-poN***
Nine	*kyū-mai*	*kyū-satsu*	*kyū-hoN*
Ten	*jū-mai*	***jus-satsu***	***jup-poN***
Eleven	*jū ichi-mai*	***jū is-satsu***	***jū ip-poN***
How many?	*naN-mai*	*naN-satsu*	***naN-boN***

When you want to specify the quantity of an object, you should use the following sentence pattern:

[ITEM-*particle* QUANTITY-*counter* … Predicate]

With this pattern in mind, let's say both "Please give me five pens" and "I want five pens."

Track 18
CD-6–7

PeN-o go-hoN kudasai.   "Please give me five pens."

PeN-ga go-hoN hoshi-i-N-desu ga. …   "I want five pens. …"

Now answer the following questions for practice. An item and its quantity are provided. The answers are given at the end of this chapter.

Exercise 1

1. _____

   "Please give me three (3) bananas." (Hint: banana = long)

2. _____

   "Please give me two (2) telephone cards." (Hint: cards = flat)

3. _____

   "I want five (5) Japanese language books." (Hint: books = bound)

4. _____

   "I want seven (7) DVDs." (Hint: DVDs = flat)

5. _____

   "I bought eleven (11) blue pencils." ("blue" = *aoi*; "pencil" = *eNpitsu*)

6. _____

   "I ate one (1) cookie." (Hint: cookie = flat)

7. _____

   "There are thirteen (13) books." ("there are X" = *X-ga ari-masu*)

8. _____

   "Please buy six (6) bottles of beer." (Hint: beer bottle = long)

9. _____

   "There are four (4) shirts." (Hint: shirt = flat)

10. _____

    "Eight (8) '10 *yen*' stamps, please." ("10 *yen* stamps" = *jū-eN kitte*)

Let's move on to the counters used for miscellaneous objects—*-tsu* and *-ko*. Miscellaneous objects are things such as (lumpy) vegetables, eggs, erasers, paper clips, (lumpy) fruits, chairs, and so on.

Track 18
CD-8

The Counters for Miscellaneous Objects

	-tsu	*-ko*
One	*hito-tsu*	**ik-ko**
Two	*futa-tsu*	*ni-ko*
Three	*mit-tsu*	*saN-ko*
Four	*yot-tsu*	*yoN-ko*
Five	*itsu-tsu*	*go-ko*
Six	*mut-tsu*	**rok-ko**
Seven	*nana-tsu*	*nana-ko*

Eight	*yat-tsu*	**hak-ko**
Nine	*kokono-tsu*	*kyū-ko*
Ten	*tō*	**juk-ko**
Eleven	*jū ichi*	**jū ik-ko**
Twelve	*jū ni*	*jū ni-ko*
How many?	*iku-tsu*	*naN-ko*

Note 1: For "ten," the counter -tsu *does not accompany the number.*

Note 2: For "eleven" and beyond, the counter -tsu *is not used. Instead, regular numbers such as* jū ichi, *"eleven,"* jū ni, *"twelve,"* jū saN, *"thirteen," and so on are used.*

Lifesavers

Although *-tsu* and *-ko* are interchangeable, *-ko* cannot be used for counting age. See Chapter 10 for more details.

As you see in the chart, the *-tsu* counter is complicated. I was tempted to teach you just the *-ko* counter because it's much simpler. However, you will hear the *-tsu* counter often, so you should at least know how it works. It's perfectly okay to stick to *-ko* when you count objects.

Let's do an exercise, focusing on the *-tsu* counter. Again, an item and its quantity are provided. How would you say the following?

Exercise 2

1. _____

Please give me three (3) apples. ("apple" = *riNgo*)

2. _____

I want four (4) balls. ("ball" = *bōru*)

3. _____

I ate nine (9) sushi!

4. _____

I want seven (7) donuts. ("donut" = *dōnattsu*)

5. _____

There are five (5) clips on the table. ("on the table" = *tēburu-ni*; "clip" = *kurippu*)

Huh?

The general counters *hito-tsu, futa-tsu,* and so on are the native Japanese version of the by now familiar counting system starting with *ichi, ni, saN,* and so on, which is actually of Chinese origin. If you recall, this native counting system was already introduced in counters for people (see Chapter 10) and counters for days and reading a calendar (see Chapters 14 and 16).

I Want *This* One, Not *That* One!

You should be able to let the shop clerk know exactly what you want. The easiest way is just to point at the item and say "this one." If you recall, I introduced "pointing words" in Chapter 9. Let's review them:

Pointing Words: Nouns

kore	this one
sore	that one (near the listener)
are	that one (away from the speaker and listener)
dore	which one

If the item of interest is near you, point at it and say:

Track 18
CD-9

    Kore-o kudasai.   "Please give me this one."

If the item is on the clerk's side, use *sore* instead:

Track 18
CD-10

    Sore-o kudasai.   "Please give me that one (near you)."

On the other hand, if it is away from you and the clerk, use *are:*

Track 18
CD-11

    Are-o kudasai.   "Please give me that one over there (away from both of us)."

The use of *kore, sore,* and *are* is illustrated in the following figure:

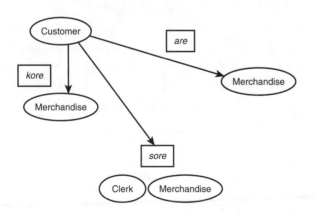

The pointing words, kore, "this one (near the speaker)," sore, "that one (near the listener)," and are, "that one (away from the speaker and listener)."

If the clerk still cannot figure out which one you mean, she or he will ask you:

Track 18
CD-12

    Dore-desu ka?   "Which one?"

Green Tea Break

If you love shopping or even window shopping, try a department store, or *depāto*. Japanese department stores have virtually everything—clothes, bags, shoes, jewelry, books, toys, furniture, food court, and restaurants. Interestingly, all department stores look alike in terms of their floor plan, so you can expect to find the same setup at any store.

Basement: Food court, coffee shops

First floor: Ladies' accessories, shoes, and so on

Second and third floors: Ladies' clothes, bags, cosmetics, and so on

Fourth floor: Children's and babies' clothes, ladies clothes', and so on

Fifth floor: Men's clothes, eyeglasses, sporting goods, and so on

Sixth floor: Furniture, household goods, jewelry, and so on

Seventh floor: Restaurants, special sales, toys, office supplies, books, CDs, and so on

Rooftop: Pet shop, gardening, game center, and so on

In summer, department stores have a "beer garden" on the rooftop. Last but not least, try checking out the food court in the basement. You will have a good time not only looking at a variety of foods, but also trying free samples. (You can have a light meal there!) This is where you can practice the "pointing" words like *kore*, *sore*, and *are*. It can be a free Japanese lesson with free food! A department store is one of the best places for a student of Japanese.

Sometimes, instead of using just "this <u>one</u>" or "that <u>one</u>," you might want to be more specific. Suppose that you want a pen, but there are many kinds of items other than pens in the showcase—pencils, erasers, notebooks, ink, and so on. In such a case, you need to use an appropriate pointing word as an "adjective":

Pointing Words: Adjectives

kono X	this X
sono X	that X (near the listener)
ano X	that X (away from the speaker and listener)
dono X	which X

Here is an example:

Sono peN-o kudasai.   "Please give me that pen (near you)."

Here is another useful expression when you look for something at a shop. If you just want to take a look at the item, try this request pattern:

Track 18
CD-14

> *XYZ-o mise-te kudasai.*   "Please show me XYZ."

If you have found what you really want to buy, ask the clerk how much it is:

Track 18
CD-15

> *Ikura-desu ka?*   "How much is it?"

Or:

Track 18
CD-16

> *XYZ-wa ikura-desu ka?*   "How much is XYZ?"

You might think that just pointing is not enough. Do you want to be more specific in describing the item of interest? Okay, then you need to learn more adjectives. Here is a list of adjectives frequently used in shopping.

Shopping-Related Adjectives

big	*ōki-i*
small	*chīsa-i*
long	*naga-i*
short	*mijika-i*
black	*kuro-i*
white	*shiro-i*
red	*aka-i*
yellow	*kīro-i*
brown	*chairo-i*
new	*atarashi-i*
light	*karu-i*
heavy	*omo-i*
thin	*usu-i*
thick	*atsu-i*

Now, combining everything you have learned so far, translate the following.

Exercise 3

1. _____

   Please give me that black pencil (near you).
   ("pencil" = *eNpitsu*)

2. _____

Please give me two of these NIKE shirts.
("shirts" = *shatsu*)

3. _____

I want two of those white bags over there.
("bag" = *kabaN*)

4. _____

I want that small clock (near you).
("clock" = *tokē*)

5. _____

How much is this yellow pen?
("how much?" = *ikura-desu ka*)

6. _____

Please show me those big suitcases over there.
("show me" = *mise-masu*; "suitcase" = *sūtsu kēsu*)

7. _____

Please give me this jacket.
("jacket" = *jaketto*)

8. _____

How much are those brown shoes (near you)?
("shoes" = *kutsu*)

9. _____

Please show me that thin case (near you).
("case" = *kēsu*)

10. _____

Please give me three sheets of that red paper over there.
("paper" = *kami*)

Here's one more important word! The word for "change" is *otsuri*.

Lifesavers _____

Don't forget to add 5 percent government sales tax! "Sales tax" is *shōhi zē*.

Don't You Have a *Cheaper* One?

Compromise isn't a good thing when it comes to shopping because you don't want to end up buying something you are not really happy with! In this section, you will learn how to ask a shop clerk whether there is anything else of a similar kind.

Suppose that you are looking for a pair of shoes, *kutsu*. The pair you tried on is a little too tight, so you want to ask the clerk for a bigger size.

Track 18
CD-17

> *Mō sukoshi ōki-i no-wa ari-maseN ka?*   "Isn't there (*or* Don't you have) a little bigger one?"

Remember two important phrases here:

mō sukoshi	"a little more"
no	"one"

Note that the tiny word *no* attaches to an adjective. What if you don't like the color and want a red one instead?

> *Aka-i no-wa ari-maseN ka?*   "Isn't there (*or* Don't you have) a red one?"

Lifesavers

When you are asked a negative question such as "*Aka-i no-wa ari-maseN ka?*" ("Don't you have a red one?"), you must be careful how you answer with *hai* or *īe*. *Hai* means that "what you said is *right*," whereas *īe* means that "what you said is *not right*." So when you are asked "Don't you have a red one?" if you *do* have it, you should use *īe*, as in:

> *Īe, ari-masu.* "(What you said is not right.) I do have it."

On the other hand, if you *don't* have it, you should use *hai*, as in:

> *Hai, ari-maseN.* "(What you said is right.) Right, I don't have it."

Now how would you say the following?

Exercise 4

1. _____

   Don't you have a little cheaper one?
   ("cheap" = *yasu-i*)

2. _____

   Please show me a little lighter one.
   ("light" = *karu-i*)

3. _____

   Please give me a black one.
   ("black" = *kuro-i*)

Here is another important word, *hoka* ("other"). If you want to see other kinds of merchandise, this word is very useful:

Track 18
CD-18–19

Hoka no-wa ari-masu ka? "Do you have other ones?"

Hoka no-o mise-te kudasai. "Please show me other ones."

While showing you other items, the clerk will say either one of the following:

Track 18
CD-20–21

Kore-wa dō-desu ka? "How about this one?"

Kore-wa ikaga-desu ka? "How about this one?"

The word *ikaga* is the polite version of *dō*. If you still do not like what the clerk has suggested, it's perfectly okay to say so, but the following reply would sound very polite:

Shortcuts to Success

The [*X-wa dō-desu ka?*] pattern is extremely useful for any situation in which you need to make a suggestion.

Track 18
CD-22

Ē … chotto … "Well …"

When you decide on something, say either one of the following:

Track 18
CD-23–24

Kore-o kudasai. "This one, please."

Kore-ni shi-masu. "I'll take this one."

(*X-ni shi-masu* = "decide on X")

Before wrapping up this chapter, I want you to take part in the following rather lengthy dialog. Don't panic! You can do it! This dialog contains some materials from the previous chapters, so it is a good review exercise, too. Good luck!

Exercise 5

SHOP 1 _____

"Welcome!"

YOU 1 _____

"I want (some) paper."

("paper" = *kami*)

SHOP 2 _____

"What kind of paper?"

("what kind" = *doNna*)

YOU 2 _____

"Blue one."

SHOP 3 _____

"How about this one?"

YOU 3 _____

"How much is it?"

SHOP 4 _____

"It's 20 yen per sheet. (Lit. One sheet, 20 yen.)"

YOU 4 _____

"Isn't there a little cheaper one?"

SHOP 5 _____

"Yes. This is 10 yen per sheet."

YOU 5 _____

"I'll take this one. Please give me 10 sheets."

SHOP 6 _____

"100 yen."

YOU 6 _____

"Here, 1,000 yen."

SHOP 7 _____

"The change, 900 yen. Thank you very much."

YOU 7 _____

"Thanks!"

Answers

Track 18
CD-25–28

Exercise 1

1. "Please give me three (3) bananas."

   Banana-o saN-boN kudasai.

2. "Please give me two (2) telephone cards."

   TerefoN kādo-o ni-mai kudasai.

3. "I want five (5) Japanese language books."

   NihoNgo-no hoN-ga go-satsu hoshi-i-N-desu ga.

4. "I want seven (7) DVDs."

   DVD-ga nana-mai hoshi-i-N-desu ga.

5. "I bought eleven (11) blue pencils."

   (Watashi-wa) ao-i eNpitsu-o jū ip-poN kai-mashita.

6. "I ate one (1) cookie."

   (Watashi-wa) kukkī-o ichi-mai tabe-mashita.

7. "There are thirteen (13) books."

   HoN-ga jū saN-satsu ari-masu.

8. "Please buy six (6) bottles of beer."

   Bīru-o rop-poN kat-te kudasai.

9. "There are four (4) shirts."

   Shatsu-ga yoN-mai ari-masu.

10. "Eight '10 *yen*' stamps, please."

    Jū-eN kitte-o hachi-mai onegai shimasu.

Exercise 2

1. "Please give me three (3) apples."

   RiNgo-o mit-tsu kudasai.

2. "I want four (4) balls."

   Bōru-ga yot-tsu hoshi-i-N-desu ga.

3. "I ate nine (9) sushi!"

   (Watashi-wa) sushi-o kokono-tsu tabe-mashita.

4. "I want seven (7) donuts."

   Dōnattsu-ga nana-tsu hoshi-i-N-desu ga.

5. "There are five (5) clips on the table."

   Tēburu-ni kurippu-ga itsu-tsu ari-masu.

Exercise 3

1. "Please give me that black pencil (near you)."

   Sono kuro-i eNpitsu-o kudasai.

2. "Please give me two of these NIKE shirts."

   Kono NIKE-no shatsu-o ni-mai kudasai.

3. "I want two of those white bags over there."

   Ano shiro-i kabaN-ga futa-tsu hoshi-i-N-desu ga.

4. "I want that small clock (near you)."

   Sono chīsa-i tokē-ga hoshi-i-N-desu ga.

5. "How much is this yellow pen?"

Kono kīro-i peN-wa ikura-desu ka?

6. "Please show me those big suitcases over there."

Ano ōki-i sūtsu kēsu-o mise-te kudasai.

7. "Please give me this jacket."

Kono jaketto-o kudasai.

8. "How much are those brown shoes (near you)?"

Sono chairo-i kutsu-wa ikura-desu ka?

9. "Please show me that thin case (near you)."

Sono usu-i kēsu-o mise-te kudasai.

10. "Please give me three sheets of that red paper over there."

Ano aka-i kami-o saN-mai kudasai.

Exercise 4

1. "Don't you have a little cheaper one?"

Mō sukoshi yasu-i no-wa ari-maseN ka?

2. "Please show me a little lighter one."

Mō sukoshi karu-i no-o mise-te kudasai.

3. "Please give me a black one."

Kuro-i no-o kudasai.

Exercise 5

Track 18
CD-40

SHOP 1   *Irasshai mase.*

         "Welcome!"

YOU 1   *Kami-ga hoshi-i-N-desu ga.*

         "I want (some) paper."

SHOP 2   *DoNna kami-desu ka?*

         "What kind of paper?"

YOU 2   *Ao-i no-desu.*

         "Blue one."

SHOP 3   *Kore-wa ikaga-desu ka?*

         "How about this one?"

YOU 3   *Ikura-desu ka?*

         "How much is it?"

SHOP 4   *Ichi-mai, ni-jū-eN-desu.*

"It's 20 *yen* per sheet."

YOU 4   *Mō sukoshi yasu-i no-wa ari-maseN ka?*

"Isn't there a little cheaper one?"

SHOP 5   *Hai, kore-wa ichi-mai, jū-eN-desu.*

"Yes. This is 10 *yen* per sheet."

YOU 5   *Kore-ni shi-masu. Jū-mai kudasai.*

"I'll take this one. Please give me 10 sheets."

SHOP 6   *Hyaku-eN-desu.*

"100 *yen*."

YOU 6   *Hai, seN-eN.*

"Here, 1,000 *yen*."

SHOP 7   *Otsuri, kyū-hyaku-eN-desu. Arigatō gozai mashita.*

"The change, 900 *yen*. Thank you very much."

YOU 7   *Dōmo (arigatō).*

"Thanks!"

The Least You Need to Know

◆ Four types of counters—-*mai*, -*satsu*, -*hoN*, and -*tsu*/-*ko*—will take care of your basic shopping needs.

◆ Pointing words (such as *kore, sore,* and *are*) and adjectives are useful for specifying the item of interest.

◆ Don't compromise! Use the phrases you learned in this chapter to keep asking until you find what you want.

◆ A department store is an ideal place for a student of Japanese to practice the language, shop, and taste free Japanese food samples!

More Than Just Sushi: Dining Out in Japan

In This Chapter

◆ Likes and dislikes

◆ Making a comparison

◆ How to order food

◆ Tips for eating at a Japanese restaurant

Japanese people take eating seriously. They don't mind paying a fortune at a restaurant if the food is great. Customers expect excellence in cooking, and their high standard has brought about the high quality of dining establishments. Please note that dining can be expensive in Japan, but of course, you can find fine moderately priced restaurants, too.

If you want to enjoy dining in Japan, take a close look at the useful dining vocabulary and phrases in this chapter. Okay, *tabe-ni iki-mashō!* Let's go out to eat!

Likes and Dislikes

Japanese cuisine is called *nihoN ryōri* or *washoku*. You might be curious about what other cuisines are called in Japanese:

Western food	*Sēyō ryōri* or *Yōshoku*
Chinese food	*Chūka ryōri*
Korean food	*KaNkoku ryōri*
French food	*FuraNsu ryōri*
Italian food	*Itaria ryōri*
Spanish food	*SupeiN ryōri*
Indian food	*INdo ryōri*
Mexican food	*Mekishiko ryōri*
German food	*Doitsu ryōri*
American food	*Amerika ryōri*
British food	*Igirisu ryōri*

As you can see, you can be specific about cuisine by adding the country name to the word *ryōri*, such as *Burajiru ryōri* ("Brazilian food"). The word for "restaurant" is *resutoraN*, but for Asian food restaurants, either *ryōri-ya* or *ryōri-teN* is preferred.

If you are going out to eat with other people, you might have to decide what kind of food you will eat.

Track 19
CD-1

> *DoNna ryōri-ga suki-desu ka?*   "What kind of cuisine do you like?"

Lifesavers _____

Here is how to say "I'm hungry!" and "I'm thirsty!":

Onaka-ga suki-mashita.   "I'm hungry!"

Nodo-ga kawaki-mashita.   "I'm thirsty!"

If you are talking with your friends in a casual setting, I recommend the following alternatives:

Onaka-ga suita!   "I'm hungry!"

Nodo-ga kawaita!   "I'm thirsty!"

Instead of *ryōri*, you can use *tabemono*, "food."

> *DoNna tabemono-ga suki-desu ka?*   "What kind of food do you like?"

What if you are determined to eat Japanese food, particularly *sushi*, and you want to see if your Japanese friend also feels like eating *sushi*?

Track 19
CD-2

> *Sushi-wa suki-desu ka?*   "Do you like sushi?"

If your friend does not like sushi, she will say either one of the following:

Track 19
CD-3–5

Māmā-desu.   "So-so."

Amari suki-jana-idesu.   "I don't like it very much."

Kirai-desu!   "I hate it!"

Note that *kirai* is a very strong word for dislike, so I suggest that you not use it as a reply.

If you want your Japanese to sound natural, keep in mind that the key to success is "indirectness." Don't hesitate to use "vague" expressions such as *māmā*, "so-so" and *amari*, "(not) very." I recommend putting *Sō-desu nē* …, "Well, let's see …," at the beginning of your reply, as shown here:

Track 19
CD-6

Q: *Sushi-wa suki-desu ka?*
"Do you like sushi?"

A: *Sō-desu nē … Amari suki-jana-idesu.*
"Well, let's see … not very much …"

Huh? _____

The word *sushi* is marked by *-wa* because it is the conversation topic. For the function of *-wa* as the topic, refer to Chapter 4.

This way doesn't sound self-centered, but emphatic!

If, on the other hand, your friend likes sushi very much, the reply will be:

Track 19
CD-7

Daisuki-desu!   "I love it!"

Totemo suki-desu.   "I like it very much."

Even though Japanese food is delicious, there might be something you cannot eat. In such a case, you will find the like/dislike expressions in this section very helpful.

Lifesavers _____

Chapter 11 has extensive coverage of helpful expressions you can use when you ask people to go out to eat.

Exercise 1

Complete the following dialogs.

1. Q: "What kind of sports do you like?"

   _____

   A: "I like tennis."

   _____

2. Q: "What kind of Japanese food do you like?"

   _____

   A: "I like sukiyaki."

   _____

3. Q: "Do you like Spanish cuisine?"

_____

A: "I love it!"

_____

4. Q: "Do you like natto (fermented soybeans)?"

_____

A: "Well, let's see … not very much …"

_____

Making Comparison

Let's learn another useful pattern called "comparative question." If you and your friend have not decided between the two choices, say, Japanese or Chinese food, ask her the following:

NihoN ryōri-to, chūka ryōri-to,   "Between Japanese and Chinese food,
dochira-no hō-ga i-idesu ka?   which is better?"

The schematic pattern is …

X-to, Y-to, dochira-no hō-ga PREDICATE _ka?_

The predicate part does not have to be an adjective like _i-idesu_, "is good," as shown here:

Track 19
CD-8

Sushi-to, teNpura-to, dochira-no hō-ga suki-desu ka?

"Between _sushi_ and _tempura_, which do you like better?"

Answering this question is easy! Remember, when you answer a question in Japanese, all you need to do is replace the question word with your answer. If you like _sushi_ better, you would say:

Track 19
CD-9

Sushi-no hō-ga suki-desu.
"I like _sushi_ better."

Lifesavers

Because a number of vegetables and fruits are of foreign origin, they are pronounced as loan words, such as _asparagasu_, "asparagus," and _painapppuru_, "pineapple." Make sure that you Japanize the words!

Huh?

If you have three or more items to compare, the pattern looks slightly different:

X-to, Y-to, Z-<u>de</u>, dore-ga ichibaN <u>PREDICATE</u> ka? "Among X, Y, and Z, which is the most ...?"

Here is an example:

Q: *Sushi-to, teNpura-to, sukiyaki-de, dore-ga ichibaN oishi-idesu ka?* "Among *sushi, tempura,* and *sukiyaki,* which is the most delicious?"

A: *Sushi-ga ichibaN oishi-idesu!* "*Sushi* is the most delicious!"

The question word *dore* is used when comparing three or more items, whereas *dochira-no hō* is used when comparing two items.

Before we move on to the next section, here are some common foods in Japanese:

Foods

meat	*niku*	fruits	*furūtsu*
beef	*gyū-niku/bīfu*	apple	*riNgo*
pork	*buta-niku/pōku*	watermelon	*suika*
chicken	*tori-niku/chikiN*	cantaloupe	*meroN*
fish	*sakana*	grape	*budō*
shrimp/prawn	*ebi*	tangerine	*mikaN*
crab	*kani*	peach	*momo*
egg	*tamago*	beverage	*nomimono*
rice	*kome*	milk	*gyūnyū/miruku*
bread	*paN*	water	*mizu*
tofu	*tōfu*	liquor (and *sake*)	*sake*
vegetable	*yasai*	condiment	*chōmiryō*
(round) onion	*tamanegi*	salt	*shio*
scallion	*negi*	sugar	*satō*
potato	*jagaimo*	pepper	*koshō*
sweet potato	*satsumaimo*	soy sauce	*shōyu*
cabbage	*kyabetsu*	vinegar	*osu*
garlic	*niNniku*	oil	*abura/oiru*
carrot	*niNjiN*	horseradish	*wasabi*
green pepper	*pīmaN*	mustard	*karashi/masutādo*
squash	*kabocha*		

Exercise 2

Using the given words, make a comparative question and answer. Use the English-Japanese dictionary in Appendix B for vocabulary.

1. Q: _____

   [apples, peaches, like better?]

   A: _____

   [I like peaches better.]

2. Q: _____

   [ski, skate, more fun?]

   A: _____

   [ski is more fun]

3. Q: _____

   [Japanese, Chinese, easier]

   A: _____

   [Japanese is easier]

Ordering

You and your friend have decided on Japanese food, and here you are in a Japanese restaurant! Many Japanese restaurants have Japanese-style rooms with *tatami* (straw) mats. This individually separated room is called *ozashiki*. You take your shoes off before you sit on the *tatami* mat. If you prefer an *ozashiki* room, say the following to the waiter:

> *Ozashiki-wa aite i-masu ka?*
> "Is the ozashiki available?"
> (*aite i-masu* = "vacant")

Upon being seated, you will be given a hot steamed towel to wipe your hands (and face, if you wish). It is so refreshing, especially on a hot, muggy summer day!

If reading a Japanese menu is challenging for you, ask for an English version:

> *Ēgo-no menyū-wa ari-masu ka?*
> "Do you have an English menu?"
> (*Ēgo* = "English")

Track 19
CD-10

Green Tea Break

Most restaurants have a nicely decorated display case next to the entrance. In the display, there are realistic food models made out of wax. You can point to the dish you would like when ordering if you don't want to order from the menu. These food models look so real that you are tempted to eat them! Many tourists actually buy these wax models as souvenirs.

Here is a list of popular dishes you will find on the menu.

Japanese Dishes

sushi	sushi
makizushi	sushi role
sashimi	sashimi (sliced raw fish)
udoN	thick noodle
soba	thin noodle
yakisoba	fried noodle
yakiniku	grilled meat
katsu	cutlet
katsudoN	rice bowl with cutlet
gohaN	steamed rice
onigiri	rice ball
teNpura	battered deep-fried fish/vegetable
teNdoN	rice bowl with tempura
tōfu	tofu
yakizakana	broiled fish
nabe	a dish served in the pot
sukiyaki	sukiyaki (Japanese pot sticker)
rāmeN	ramen (Japanized Chinese noodle)
tsukemono	pickled vegetable
misoshiru	miso soup (with soybean paste base)
tsukidashi or *otōshi*	assorted appetizer
ocha	green tea

Mmmm! Aren't you getting hungry? Let's order some dishes! The Japanese word for "ordering" is *chūmoN*. After a short while, the waiter will ask you whether you have decided:

Track 19
CD-11

> *Go-chūmoN-wa okimari-desu ka?*
> "Have you decided what you would like to order?"

In Chapters 12 and 18, you learned an important expression that can be used when making a decision:

> *XYZ-ni shi-masu.*   "I've decided on XYZ."

Green Tea Break

As defined in the previous list, *tsukidashi* or *otōshi* is an assorted appetizer, like Italian *antipasto*. Each restaurant has its own *tsukidashi*, ranging from pickled vegetables to broiled fish. It is usually served complimentary, especially when you order an alcoholic beverage.

Huh? _____

The prefix *go-*, as seen in *go-chūmoN*, "order," is another marker to indicate politeness.

If you want to order *sushi*, say

Track 19
CD-12

Sushi-ni shi-masu. "I'll have sushi."

Of course, you can use the handy *onegai shimasu:*

Track 19
CD-13

Sushi-o onegai shimasu. "Sushi, please."

The waiter will ask if you want anything to drink (*nomimono* = "beverage"):

Track 19
CD-14

O-nomimono-wa? "Anything to drink?"

If you are thirsty and want something, use either the preceding *XYZ-ni shi-masu* pattern or the *XYZ-o onegai shimasu* pattern. If you don't want anything, here is what you should say:

Track 19
CD-15

Kekkō-desu or *I-idesu.* "No, thanks."

When you order sushi, a plate comes with assorted sushi. If there is any particular sushi you cannot eat, you should tell the waiter so that he will get you something different. Suppose that you are allergic to shrimp (*ebi*). Here is a very easy way to say "I cannot eat shrimp":

Track 19
CD-16

Ebi-wa dame-naN-desu. "I cannot eat shrimp."

The word *dame* literally means "no good." In general, the *XYZ-wa dame-naN-desu* pattern can be used when you cannot do *XYZ*. For example, if you cannot speak Spanish, you can say *SupeiN-go-wa dame-naN-desu.* You should definitely memorize this handy expression!

Alternatively, you can say "I'm allergic to shrimp," as in:

Track 19
CD-17

Ebi arerugī-naN-desu. "I'm allergic to shrimp."
(*arerugī* = "allergy")

XYZ arerugī-naN-desu is also a handy expression when you want to let people know that you are allergic to XYZ.

Huh? _____

In *dame-naN-desu* and *arerugī-naN-desu*, *naN* does not have grammatical meaning because it is an emphatic idiomatic expression.

Even if you are not comfortable using chopsticks (*hashi*), don't feel embarrassed! Tell the waiter you cannot use them and ask for a fork. Here again, you should use the *XYZ-wa dame-naN-desu* pattern:

Hashi-wa dame-naN-desu ga … Fōku-wa ari-maseN ka? "I cannot use chopsticks. Isn't there a fork?"

Actually, it is perfectly acceptable to eat *sushi* using your hand, so you might not need a fork after all!

> **Green Tea Break**
>
> Sushi is raw fish served on a rice ball, whereas sashimi is sliced raw fish without rice. Sushi or sashimi definitely tastes better with only a small amount of soy sauce. This way, you can appreciate the texture of the fish. Don't soak it in the sauce! Dip only the fish side, not the rice, into the sauce. This is another reason why it's better to use your hand rather than chopsticks—you could easily drop the sushi on the sauce plate with chopsticks!

Learning the Etiquette

The food is now served. It would be nice if you said the following ritual expression before eating:

Itadakimasu.

Track 19
CD-18

Itadakimasu literally means "I humbly accept the food."

By the way, when you finish eating, don't forget to say the following:

Gochisōsama (deshita).

Track 19
CD-19

Gochisōsama (deshita) literally means "That was a feast!"

If you would like seconds of something such as rice or *miso* soup or a refill of tea or coffee, you can use the following handy phrase:

Okawari (onegai shimasu).   "May I have another bowl (or cup)?"

Track 19
CD-20

Here is another useful phrase. If you'd like your friend to pass you something like soy sauce or salt, use the following pattern:

XYZ-o tot-te kudasai.   "Please pass me XYZ."

Here is an example:

Shōyu-o tot-te kudasai.   "Please pass me the soy sauce."

Track 19
CD-21

If you are with Japanese people, or there is a waiter/waitress nearby, go ahead and ask them manner-related questions. The first step of asking such questions is to find out whether a certain behavior is acceptable. Here is a perfect sentence pattern that can be used to ask these questions:

-TE-mo i-idesu ka?   "Is it okay to …?"

I explained the *TE*-form in Chapter 6 and introduced several usages of this form in the previous chapters. Again, this form is used for the "Is it okay?" pattern. For example, if you want to ask whether it's okay to use a fork to eat sushi, say the following:

Track 19
CD-22

>*Fōku-o tsukat-te-mo i-idesu ka?*   "Is it okay to use a fork?"
>(*tsukai-masu* = "to use")

Or:

>*Te-de tabe-te-mo i-idesu ka?*   "Is it okay to eat with my hands?"
>(*te* = "hand"; *-de* = "with")

If it is acceptable, your Japanese friend or the waiter will say:

Track 19
CD-23   Or:

>*Ē, i-idesu yo!*   "Sure, it's okay!"

>*Ē, mochiroN!*   "Yes, of course!"

Track 19
CD-24   If it is not acceptable, she or he will say:

Track 19
CD-25

>*Chotto ...*   "Well ..."

When you hear *chotto* in a hesitant tone, that's an indirect way of saying "no."

Asking manner-related questions with the food in front of you should be a lot of fun, and your Japanese friend or waiter will be happy to answer your questions! This is a much better way to learn the etiquette than reading a book on manners.

Here are some things you should or should not do at a Japanese restaurant:

- Don't drink the soup first. Drink it as you eat the main dish.
- Don't use a spoon when drinking soup. Bring the bowl to your mouth and sip it.
- It's okay to make subtle noises when eating.
- Don't leave your chopsticks sticking up in your rice! This is a taboo! The only time you can do so is when making offerings for the spirits of the dead in front of the family altar (*butsudaN*).

Shortcuts to Success

The *TE-mo i-desu ka* pattern can also be used when you ask for permission, as seen in the following example:

Q: *Tabako-o sut-te-mo i-idesu ka?*   "May I smoke?"
(*sui-masu* = "to smoke")
A: *Ē, dōzo.*   "Sure."

Green Tea Break

Slurping is perfectly okay when you eat noodles, especially when they are hot. It's difficult not to eat without slurping anyway, so why not? A friend of mine who owns a noodle shop even told me that he checks the quality of the noodle by carefully listening to customers' slurping! It's true!

- When you eat rice from a bowl, never pour soy sauce on it! It's culturally unacceptable and considered uneducated.
- "Doggie bagging" is not a common practice.
- Tipping is not necessary.

Just by observing people around you, you will learn the culture of eating in Japan. But don't spend too much time on observation. Take time to appreciate the food, too!

Exercise 3

Translate the following permission sentences.

1. "Is it okay to drink?"
   ("drink" = *nomi-masu*)

   _____

2. "Is it okay to go home?"
   ("go home" = *kaeri-masu*)

   _____

3. "Excuse me. Is it okay to go to the bathroom?"
   ("go to the bathroom" = *toire-ni iki-masu*)

   _____

Taste Words

If you have never eaten a certain food, you might want to ask how it tastes. The word for "taste" is *aji*. The following question will be helpful:

Track 19
CD-26

> *DoNna aji-desu ka?*   "How does it taste?"

Here is a list of commonly used taste words:

Taste Words

sweet	*ama-i*
spicy hot	*kara-i*
salty	*shiokara-i* or *shoppa-i*
sour	*suppa-i*
bitter	*niga-i*

If it is a little bit sour, say:

> *Chotto suppa-i-desu.* "It is a little bit sour."

If you want to be more specific in explaining what the food tastes like, use *mitai-desu:*

> *ChikiN mitai-desu.* "It tastes like chicken."

The *mitai-desu expression* can be used in any situation when you make an analogy. For example, if your friend looks like a movie star, give him a compliment using this form:

> *Ēga sutā mitai-desu ne!* "You look like a movie star!"

Check, Please!

Now you have just finished eating. If you are ready for your check, you must ask for it. Here is how to ask for a check:

> *OkaNjō-o, onegai shimasu.* "Check, please."

If you forget the word *okaNjō*, you can use the loan word *chekku* as the last resort.

In a Japanese restaurant, generally your waiter/waitress is not your cashier. Instead, you take the check to the cashier at the door and pay there. By the way, as I mentioned previously, you do not have to leave a tip for the waiter.

Huh? _____

Note that *oishi-kattadesu* is the past tense of the adjective *oishi-idesu*. Refer to Chapter 5 if you want to review the adjective conjugation.

Unless they are students, Japanese people hardly go dutch, or pay 50-50. For example, suppose that you and I go to eat and I decide to pay. You don't have to feel that you owe me. You can pay the next time we go out to eat. This is how we break even! Sometimes you will see people fighting over a check at a restaurant, saying "No, I will pay!" or "You paid last time, so let me pay this time!" If you would like to pay, when the waiter brings a check to the table, quickly grab it and tell your friends the following:

> *Watashi-ga harai-masu.* "I will pay."
> (*harai-masu* = "to pay")

After you pay the cashier, the shop host/hostess will say to you upon leaving the restaurant:

> *Dōmo arigatō gozai-mashita.* "Thank you very much (for coming)!"

You can reply by saying *gochisōsama*. In addition, if the food was delicious, give them a compliment:

> *Oishi-kattadesu!* "It was delicious!"

With the expressions introduced in this chapter, you should be able to have a stress-free dining experience. After all, dining should be fun. So enjoy Japanese food!

Exercise 4

Complete the dialog between you and the waiter (abbreviated as WTR).

WTR 1   *Go-chūmoN-wa okimari-desu ka?*

          "Have you decided what you would like to order?"

YOU 1   _____

          "I'll have tempura."

WTR 2   *O-nomimono-wa?*

          "Anything to drink?"

YOU 2   _____

          "Do you have sake?"

WTR 3   *SumimaseN, o-sake-wa arimaseN ga … Bīru-wa ikaga-desu ka?*

          "Sorry, we don't have sake. How about beer?"

YOU 3   _____

          "No, thank you. I cannot drink beer."

Answers

Exercise 1

Track 19
CD-32

1. Q: "What kind of sports do you like?"

   DoNna supōtsu-ga suki-desu ka?

   A: "I like tennis."

   Tenisu-ga suki-desu.

2. Q: "What kind of Japanese food do you like?"

   DoNna NihoN-no tabemono-ga suki-desu ka?

   A: "I like *sukiyaki*."

   Sukiyaki-ga suki-desu.

Track 19
CD-34

3. Q: "Do you like Spanish cuisine?"

   SupeiN ryōri-ga suki-desu ka?

   A: I love it!

   Daisuki-desu.

4. Q: "Do you like *natto* (fermented soybeans)?"

   Nattō-ga suki-desu ka?

   A: Well, not very much …

   Sō-desu nē … Amari suki-jana-idesu.

Exercise 2

1. Q: "Which do you like better, apples or peaches?"

   RiNgo-to, momo-to dochira-no hō-ga suki-desu ka?

   A: "I like peaches better."

   Momo-no hō-ga suki-desu.

2. Q: "Which is more fun, skiing or skating?"

   Sukī-to, sukēto-to dochira-no hō-ga tanoshi-idesu ka?

   A: "Skiing is more fun."

   Skī-no hō-ga tanoshi-idesu.

3. Q: "Which is easier, Japanese or Chinese?"

   NihoNgo-to, Chūgokugo-to dochira-no hō-ga yasashi-idesu ka?

   A: "Japanese is easier."

   NihoNgo-no hō-ga yasashi-idesu.

Exercise 3

1. "Is it okay to drink?"

   NoN-de mo i-idesu ka?

2. "Is it okay to go home?"

   Kaet-te mo i-idesu ka?

3. "Excuse me. Is it okay to go to the bathroom?"

   SumimaseN. Toire-ni it-te mo i-idesu ka?

Exercise 4

WTR 1   *Go-chūmoN-wa okimari-desu ka?*

       "Have you decided what you would like to order?"

YOU 1   *TeNpura-ni shi-masu.*

       "I'll have tempura."

WTR 2   *O-nomimono-wa?*

       "Anything to drink?"

YOU 2   *O-sake-wa ari-masu ka?*

         "Do you have sake?"

WTR 3   *SumimaseN, o-sake-wa arimaseN ga … Bīru-wa ikaga-desu ka?*

         "Sorry, we don't have sake. How about beer?"

YOU 3   *Kekkō-desu. Bīru-wa dame-naN-desu.*

         "No, thank you. I cannot drink beer."

The Least You Need to Know

◆ Be familiar with Japanese names for food.

◆ *Kirai* is a very strong word for expressing dislike. It's better to use an expression such as *Māmā-desu*, "So-so."

◆ Learn the pattern for asking a comparative question—*X-to, Y-to, dochira-no hō-ga* PREDICATE *ka*—which gives the listener a wider range of choices when answering.

◆ Order food using *X-ni shi-masu*, "I decide on X."

◆ Learn etiquette for dining in Japan by using the pattern *-TE-mo i-idesu ka …?* "Is it okay to …?"

Chapter 20

Touring a Japanese House

In This Chapter

◆ Get to know the structure of a Japanese house

◆ Making yourself at home

◆ Important Japanese household items

Staying in a fancy hotel is worry free and can be great if you plan to just do sightseeing. But those who want to know the lifestyle of ordinary Japanese people should try a home stay program. This is the best way to improve your Japanese, too, because you will be totally immersed in a Japanese-speaking environment 24 hours a day while getting accustomed to the way Japanese people live.

Even if the primary purpose of your trip is conventional sightseeing, there are a number of "short home stay" programs available in Japan. Such information can be obtained via the Internet or at a travel agency specializing in Japan. Alternatively, you can stay in a home-style inn called *miNshuku*. This is similar to a B&B (bed and breakfast), but unlike a B&B, a *miNshuku* offers supper as well.

Let's imagine that you are now home staying at your host family's house and are learning what a typical Japanese house looks like and how Japanese people live.

A Typical Japanese Household

Many things in Japan are now Westernized, and houses are no exception. It's hard to see a 100 percent pure traditional Japanese house nowadays unless you go to a rural region. A typical contemporary Japanese house is wooden and two story. There are both Western-style rooms and traditional Japanese-style rooms in one house. Here is a list of house-related words in Japanese:

Rooms

room	*heya*
Japanese-style room	*nihoNma*
Western-style room	*yōma*
living room	*ribiNgu nūmu*
family room	*ima* or *chanoma*
bedroom	*beddo nūmu*
entrance hall	*geNkaN*
kitchen	*kicchiN* or *daidokoro*
bathroom	*ofuro* or *basu nūmu*
toilet	*toire* or *otearai*
hallway	*rōka*
futon storage	*oshīre*
stairs	*kaidaN*
slide door	*fusuma*

Shortcuts to Success _____

A number of Internet sites explain what a Japanese household looks like. Here are two:

www.japan-guide.com

www.nipponliving.com

Better research will make you psychologically prepared so that you can avoid culture shock!

Okay, here you are! You have just arrived at your host family's house. You are welcomed by the family at the door. Let's have a virtual home stay experience around the clock. Along with information about each room, I will give you helpful tips as well as do's and don'ts.

Entering the House—GeNkaN

When you enter the house, you will see a tiny area called the *geNkaN*, where you take off your shoes and leave them before entering the house. Even a completely Western-style house has a *geNkaN*. Remember that in Japan, you cannot enter the house with your shoes on! The *geNkaN* floor is one step lower than the rest of the house, so you can sit in the hallway and easily take off or put on your shoes there. Here are the words for "take off" and "put on" shoes (*kutsu*):

kutsu-o nugi-masu	"to take off shoes"
kutsu-o haki-masu	"to put on shoes"

When you leave your shoes in the *geNkaN*, make sure that you put the heels of your shoes against the wall. Indoor slippers (*surippa*) might also be available for you.

Take off your shoes at the geNkaN *before entering the house. As seen in this figure, place your shoes with the heels against the wall.*

(Photo courtesy Agency for Cultural Affairs of Japan)

If you recall, in Chapter 8 I introduced several ritualized expressions to be uttered when entering the house. Upon entering the house, say either one of the following:

Track 20
CD-1–2

Shitsurē shimasu.	"(*Lit.*) Excuse me."
Ojama shimasu.	"(*Lit.*) Sorry to intrude upon your privacy."

After you become introduced to the host family, you are part of the family. From that time on, upon returning home, you should say something different:

Track 20
CD-3

Tadaima.	"I'm home."

Your family will welcome you home by saying:

Track 20
CD-4

Okaeri nasai.	"Welcome back."

By the way, when you leave home for work, school, or errands, say the following fixed expression:

Track 20
CD-5

Itte kimasu. "(Lit.) I am going and coming back."

Your (host) family will send you off by saying:

Itte rasshai. "(Lit.) Please go and come back."

Track 20
CD-6

Japanese-Style Room—*NihoNma*

By the time you are taken to your room, you and your host family should have exchanged greetings and self-introductions. You might want to go back to Chapter 9 to review useful expressions for meeting people.

Your room might be either a Western-style room (*yōma*) or a Japanese-style room (*nihoNma*). In the latter case, keep these points in mind. A *nihoNma* is a multipurpose room. In general, it simply has *tatami* mats on the floor, a Japanese dresser called *taNsu*, an easily removable low table called *chabudai*, and floor cushions called *zabutoN*. Each *nihoNma* has a built-in *futon* storage called *oshīre*.

> **Huh?**
>
> A Japanese-style room is also called *washitsu*. *Wa* is a prefix whose meaning is "Japanese." For example, *washoku* means "Japanese food," and *wafuku* means "*kimono*."

The main concept of a *nihoNma* is that, by making everything removable, you can convert the room into any type of room, like a guest room, a bedroom, or even a temporary storage room. You can even make more space by removing the *fusuma* sliding doors between the rooms.

Family Room—*Ima* or *Chanoma*

It's dinner time! The dinner might be served in the *ima* (or *chanoma*), "family room." In the *ima*, you must sit on the *tatami* floor. You might find this practice a little challenging. Here is a tip. Try not to sit straight because your legs will probably go numb within five minutes. Dinner time should be fun, not a pain, so you are allowed to be relaxed. If you are male, you can sit with your legs crossed "Indian style." If you are female, you can extend your legs to the side (not forward), "side saddle."

> **Green Tea Break**
>
> Many houses have a Western-style dining room. It usually shares the kitchen space and is called *dainiNgu kicchiN*, "dining kitchen."

In winter, instead of an ordinary low table (*chabudai*), a heated table called *kotatsu* is used. There is an infrared heater inside the *kotatsu*. You remove the tabletop, put a thin *futon* over the table frame, and place the tabletop back on top of the *futon*. The thin *futon* is designed to trap the heat in the table frame, so you can warm your legs. This is quite comfortable especially on a cold winter night because most Japanese homes do not have central heating.

At meals, always remember that you must say something before and after you eat:

Track 20
CD-7–8

[Before the meal] *Itadakimasu.*
[After the meal] *Gochisōsama deshita.*

Your host might offer you something to eat or drink by saying:

Track 20
CD-9

Kore, dō-desu ka?   "How about this?"

Or:

Track 20
CD-10

Dōzo.   "Here you are."

If you want it, say either *Itadakimasu* or …

Onegai shimasu.   "Yes, please."

If you don't want it, politely decline the offer:

Track 20
CD-11

Arigatō gozaimasu. Demo, kekkō-desu.   "Thank you for the offer, but no thank you."
(*demo* = "but")

The expression "I'm full!" also works in Japanese:

Track 20
CD-12

Onaka-ga ippai-desu! Arigatō gozaimasu.   "I'm full! Thank you."
(*onaka* = "stomach"; *ippai* = "full")

If the meal was fantastic, don't forget to give your host mother a compliment on her cooking:

Track 20
CD-13

Totemo oishi-kattadesu!   "It was very delicious!"

"Bathroom"—*Ofuro*

The concept of a Japanese bathtub, or *ofuro*, is quite different from that of a Western bathtub. It is a place to warm yourself, not to wash your body. The tub is deep enough to dip into the water up to your shoulders. So the word for "take a bath" in Japanese is actually "enter a bath":

ofuro-ni hairi-masu   "take a bath"
(*hairi-masu* = [*Lit.*] "to enter")

Because warming your body and relaxing are the most important concepts of taking a bath "Japanese style," most people take a bath before going to bed.

Unlike a Western-style bath, you do not pour hot water into the bathtub. There is a tiny water heater (or boiler) attached to the bath. To conserve energy, your host family might not set up the bath in the morning, even if you have a habit of taking a bath in the morning. You might be able to take only a shower in the morning, however. You might want to ask the family if it is okay to do so. Remember the "permission" pattern introduced in Chapter 19? Using -*TE-mo i-idesu ka*, ask the following question:

> ### Green Tea Break
>
> Nowadays, more and more houses have a 24-hour-ready bath. The water heater has a thermostat, so the bath water can remain comfortably warm.

Track 20
CD-14

Asa, shawā-o abi-te-mo i-idesu ka?
"May I take a shower in the morning?"
(*asa* = "morning")

Just like at an *oNseN* (hot spring), as explained in Chapter 16, before you dip in, you wash yourself outside the tub using either the bath water or a shower. This "washing area" is called *araiba*. This is to keep the bath water clean so that the water can be shared. Important things to note are that you neither use soap in the water nor empty the bathtub after use!

Ofuro consists of a bathtub and washing area.

(Photo courtesy Agency for Cultural Affairs of Japan)

Many Western people feel uncomfortable sharing bath water with other people because it is considered unsanitary. I think, however, that this is based on the misconception that Japanese people wash themselves in the bath water, which is not true, as mentioned previously. Consider a Japanese bath to be like a swimming pool. You don't mind sharing pool water and you certainly don't empty the pool after use, right? The Japanese bath is the same thing!

The room next to the bathroom is the *datsuijo*, (un)dressing room. The expression for "to undress" is *nugi-masu*. As for the expression for "to dress; to put on (clothes)," there are two verbs. For wearing clothes above the waist line, use *ki-masu*, and for wearing clothes below the waist line, use *haki-masu*. Although most clothes-related items are loan words, let's see how they are pronounced in Japanese.

Clothes

shirt	*shatsu*
blouse	*burausu*
coat	*kōto*
sweater	*sētā*
jacket	*jaketto*
skirt	*sukāto*
pants	*paNtsu* or *zuboN*
jeans	*jīNzu*
underwear	*shitagi*
men's underwear	*paNtsu*
panty	*paNti*
bra	*burajā*
socks	*kutsushita*
pantyhose	*paNti sutokkiNgu*
stockings	*sutokkiNgu*

For example, you use *ki-masu* for sweaters and *haki-masu* for jeans:

> *Sētā-o ki-masu.*   "I wear a sweater."
>
> *JīNzu-o haki-masu.*   "I wear a pair of jeans."

While staying with a home stay family, there will be many occasions when you go out with the host family and need to change your clothes or get dressed. You will find the following expressions handy:

> *Kigaete ki-masu.*
> "I'm going to change my clothes."
>
> *Fuku-o ki-te ki-masu.*
> "I'm going to get dressed."

Green Tea Break

In case you home stay, it's comforting to know that most host families are aware that Western people are not comfortable sharing bath water, so they will let you take a bath first. Plus, you're their guest, and Japanese families will offer the bath to their guests first anyway!

For the second pattern, you can substitute *fuku* ("clothes") with a specific item. For example, on a very cold day, you might want to say:

> *Kōto-o ki-te ki-masu.*   "I'm going to put my coat on."

Bedtime

Before you go to bed, make sure that you say "good night" to your host family:

Track 20
CD-15

> *Oyasumi nasai.*   "Good night."

Your host family might have laid out a futon for you before you go to your room. If not, just remember that a futon is stored in the *oshīre* storage attached to your room. Make sure that you fold the futon and put it back in the *oshīre* storage the next morning.

The futon is stored in the oshīre. *After waking up, fold the futon and put it back into the* oshīre.

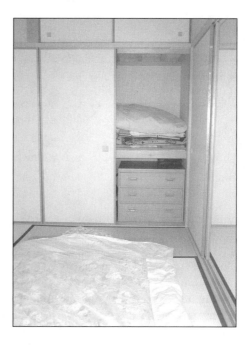

Perhaps you want to use the bathroom before going to bed. You might have heard from somebody a horrifying story about Japanese toilets. That is, you don't sit on the toilet seat but step over the toilet and squat. Or you might have heard that Japanese toilets do not use the "flushing" method but the "dropping" method instead. Sure, if you go to the countryside of Japan and stay in a 50-year-old house, you might be able to see a non-flushing, squat-type toilet. But Japan is more civilized than you might think!

It is more than 95 percent probable that your host family's house has a Western-style toilet. Even more amazingly, Japanese toilets have undergone a revolution in the past decade: More and more houses now have a paperless toilet called a "washlet," or *uosshuretto*.

A washlet looks like an ordinary Western-style toilet, but an adjustable nozzle does the cleaning. In a sense, it's like an automatic *bidet*. By using the control panel, you can change the direction of water, water pressure, and water temperature. You can even heat the toilet seat in winter! Make sure that you flush the toilet before using the washlet. For those who are not comfortable using it or are simply unfamiliar with the instructions, of course, you can use the old-fashioned paper method!

> **CAUTION**
>
> **Lifesavers**
>
> In public restrooms such as those in stations or department stores, the majority of toilets are still squat-type (flushing, of course). But Western-style toilets are usually available in at least one or two stalls.
>
> Although it might not be "intuitive" to Westerners, when you enter the stall, face the rear of the stall.

Green Tea Break

There are a couple more toilet-related cautions. First, it is best that women not flush feminine products because they might plug up the toilets easily (perhaps because of narrower plumbing pipes).

Second, in the toilet area, there is a pair of slippers you must change into as you enter. Don't continue to wear them outside of the toilet room! Likewise, don't forget to remove your house slippers when entering the toilet room.

Now the morning comes. Did you have a good sleep? Oh, don't forget to say "Good morning" when you see your host family in the morning!

Track 20
CD-22

Ohayō gozaimasu.   "Good morning."

Okay, this is it for the virtual house tour! The most important thing is not to hesitate to ask questions whenever you are not sure about something. There is an old proverb in Japanese that says:

Kiku-wa ittoki-no haji.   "Better to ask the way than go astray."

Asking is the fastest way to learn the culture and language. Don't spend too much time on looking at a dictionary or guidebook, just ask Japanese people around you!

Household Items

Let's finish the chapter with some lists of Japanese words for important household items (room by room).

Kitchen Items

plate	*osara*
rice bowl/tea cup	*chawaN*
glass	*koppu*
Japanese tea pot	*kyūsu*
chopsticks	*hashi*
knife	*hōchō* or *naifu*
rice cooker	*suihaNki*
deep pan	*nabe*
frying pan	*furaipaN*
refrigerator	*rēzōko*
microwave oven	*deNshireNji*
detergent	*seNzai*
cleaning cloth	*fukiN*
cutting board	*manaita*
rice (uncooked)	*okome*
rice (cooked)	*gohaN*
(Japanese) tea	*ocha*
cupboard	*shokkidana* (Western style) or *chadaNsu* (Japanese syle)
cooking range	*reNji*
sink	*nagashi*

Bathroom Items

soap	*sekkeN*
hot water	*oyu*
cold water	*mizu*
water faucet	*jaguchi*
water heater (for bathtub)	*yuwakashiki*
wash bowl/wash basin	*seNmeNki*
shampoo	*shaNpū*
conditioner	*riNsu*

towel	*taoru*
laundry basket	*datsuikago*
washing machine	*seNtakuki*
toothbrush	*haburashi*
toothpaste	*hamigakiko*
mirror	*kagami*
blow dryer	*doraiyā*

Room Items

desk	*tsukue*
chair	*isu*
trash can	*gomibako*
bookcase	*hoNdana*
chest	*taNsu*
futon	*futoN*
pillow	*makura*
blanket	*mōfu*
vacuum cleaner	*sōjiki*
iron	*airoN*
clock	*tokē*
alarm clock	*mezamashi dokē*

Items Outside the House

yard; garden	*niwa*
garage	*garēji*
gate	*moN*
pond	*ike*
porch	*pōchi*
mail box	*yūbiN uke* or *yūbiN bako*
plants	*ueki*
bonsai plants	*boNsai*
dog	*inu*
doghouse	*inugoya*
cat	*neko*

As I said at the beginning of this chapter, home staying is definitely an invaluable experience. By living in a traditional house with "real" people, you can get the feel of how Japanese people live. And most importantly, you can learn Japanese at a much faster speed. So if there is an opportunity, try living in a house with a host family!

The Least You Need to Know

◆ You will gain a lot from home stay experiences, especially insight into the way Japanese people communicate. Home stay is a great way to improve your Japanese!

◆ Always leave your shoes in the *geNkaN* when entering a Japanese house.

◆ Get to know culturally specific things about Japanese houses such as how to use a Japanese bath, lay out a futon, and so on.

◆ Be familiar with basic household items, especially daily-used items such as utensils, bathroom items, and so on.

◆ Remember the old Japanese proverb, *Kiku-wa ittoki-no haji*—"Better to ask the way than go astray."

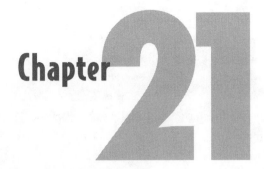

Chapter 21

Spending Leisure Time

In This Chapter

 ◆ Planning activities in chronological order

 ◆ Weather and climate

 ◆ Annual traditional events in Japan

Even if you are traveling in Japan with a large tour group, you might have a day off, which you can spend with a few good friends. You should go out and explore the country. It's a lot of fun to make a travel plan by yourself, without relying on a group tour. This chapter gives you tips that will make your day trip enjoyable.

Where Do You Wanna Go?

If you have a day off, where can you possibly go? You know by now that the Japanese public transportation system is so great that you can go anywhere. Here is a list of places you might want to consider going:

Places to Go

amusement park	*yūeNchi* or *amyūzumeNto pāku*
shopping center	*shoppiNgu seNtā*
shopping mall	*mōru*
department store	*depāto*

kabuki (theater)	*kabuki*
sumo (stadium)	*sumō*
sea	*umi*
mountain	*yama*
movie theater	*ēgakaN*
museum	*hakubutsukaN*
art museum	*bijutsukaN*
Buddhist temple	*otera*
Shinto shrine	*jiNja*
castle	*oshiro*
festival	*(o)matsuri*
bowling alley	*bōriNgujō*
swimming pool	*pūru*
restaurant	*resutoraN*
coffee shop	*kissateN*
beer garden	*bia gādeN*
shopping	*kaimono*
bus tour	*basu tsuā*

If you're going with someone else (especially a Japanese person), the following questions might be helpful. All these questions have been introduced in the previous chapters. Do you remember them? I've also provided a sample answer to each question:

> Q: *Doko-ni iki-mashō ka?* "Where shall we go?"
>
> A: *Mōru-wa dō-desu ka?* "How about the shopping mall?"
>
> Q: *NaN-yōbi-ni shi-mashō ka?* "What day shall we decide on?"
>
> A: *Do-yōbi-ni shi-maseN ka?* "Won't we go on Saturday?"
>
> Q: *NaN-de iki-masu ka?* "How will we get there?" (*Lit.*) "By what means will we go there?"
>
> A: *DeNsha-de iki-mashō!* "Let's go by train!"

Shortcuts to Success

In addition to *naN-de*, "by what means," *nani-de* is also acceptable.

If you've forgotten the words for days of the week, refer to Chapter 16.

It is important to decide by what means you will go to your destination. I introduced some forms of transportation in Chapter 13; let's review them here.

Means of Transportation

bus	*basu*
sightseeing bus	*kaNkō basu*
train	*deNsha*
subway	*chikatetsu*
Bullet Train	*shiNkaNseN*
monorail	*monorēru*
airplane	*hikōki*
car	*kuruma*
taxi	*takushī*
on foot	*aruite*

Caution: aruite *("on foot") does not require the particle -de.*

Lifesavers

If you want to have a worry-free short trip, try a guided tour, or *gaido tsuā*, a bus tour with a tour guide. You can find such tours in most major cities, and you can obtain information about a special tour for foreign visitors with a bilingual tour guide. If you are staying in a major hotel, chances are they will pick you up at the hotel.

In Tokyo, there is a sightseeing tour company called *Hato Basu*. It provides a wide variety of day, half-day, or evening tours to various destinations. Many such tours include a famous Japanese restaurant in the itinerary so that you can enjoy the traditional cuisine! You can make a reservation at major hotels, train terminals, or travel agencies.

Let's suppose that you and your friends have decided to take a day trip to Mt. Fuji (*Fuji-saN*) on Saturday, by means of a highway bus:

Do-yōbi-ni kōsoku basu-de Fuji-san-ni iki-masu.   "We will go to Mt. Fuji by highway bus on Saturday."

Make a Plan

One of the fun aspects of traveling is planning. Let's make a travel schedule in Japanese for our day trip to Mr. Fuji.

06:00	Wake up	*Oki-masu*
06:30	Breakfast	*AsagohaN-o tabe-masu*

07:00	Leave the hotel	*Hoteru-o de-masu*
07:15	Go to Shinjuku by train	*DeNsha-de ShiNjuku-ni iki-masu*
08:00	Buy tickets	*Kippu-o kai-masu*
08:30	Ride the highway bus	*Kōsoku basu-ni nori-masu*
11:30	Arrive at Mt. Fuji	*Fuji-saN-ni tsuki-masu*
12:00	Lunch	*HirugohaN-o tabe-masu*
01:00 to 04:00	Free time	*Jiyū jikaN*
04:00	Buy souvenirs	*Omiyage-o kai-masu*
04:30	Ride the bus	*Basu-ni nori-masu*
07:30	Arrive at Shinjuku	*ShiNjuku-ni tsuki-masu*
08:00	Dinner	*BaNgohaN-o tabe-masu*
09:00	Go back to the hotel by taxi	*Takushī-de hoteru-ni kaeri-masu*
10:00	Take a shower	*Shawā-o abi-masu*
11:00	Go to bed	*Ne-masu*

This schedule might look a little detailed, but there are two reasons for that. The first reason is that I want you to remember all the important vocabulary. The second reason is that I want to introduce a new grammatical pattern for listing activities in chronological order.

You can connect "activity" verbs using the *TE*-form, and when you do so, the connected sentences show a chronological sequence. (If you have forgotten the formation of the *TE*-forms, refer to Chapter 6.)

Huh?

In Chapter 10, you learned how to connect "nonactivity" verbs using the *TE*-form. Here is an example:

Watashi-wa kekkoN shite i-te, kanai-no namae-wa Risa-desu.

"I am married, and my wife's name is Lisa."

"Being married" is not an "activity" verb. When the *TE*-form connects "nonactivity" verbs or predicates, chronological order is not specified.

Looking at the schedule, let's connect the first three activities, "waking up at 6," "eating breakfast at 6:30," and "leaving the hotel at 7." The sentence should look like this:

Track 21
CD-1

Roku-ji-ni oki-te, roku-ji haN-ni asagohaN-o tabe-te, shichi-ji-ni hoteru-o de-masu.
"I will wake up at 6, eat breakfast at 6:30, and leave the hotel at 7."

Remember, for "half an hour," you can simply say *haN* (see Chapter 13). Now, for your exercise, connect the following activities with the times. The answers are provided at the end of the chapter.

Exercise 1

1. Go to Shinjuku by train (at 7:15)—Buy tickets (at 8)—Ride the highway bus (at 8:30)

   _____

2. Buy souvenirs (at 4)—Ride bus (at 4:30)—Arrive at Shinjuku (at 7:30)

   _____

3. Go back to the hotel by taxi (at 9)—Take a shower (at 10)—Go to bed (at 11)

   _____

The *TE*-forms are probably the most challenging grammatical pattern introduced in this book. However, they are also one of the most important and useful grammatical concepts: They appear in various patterns, such as "making requests," "connecting sentences," and "asking permission." Because of the limitation of space in this book, I cannot include all the patterns of the *TE*-form. If you want to continue to study Japanese and go beyond this book (I hope you will do so), the mastery of the *TE*-forms will definitely help you grasp the grammar more easily!

Huh?

According to the explanation given in Chapter 6 for the formation of the *TE*-forms, you might suppose that the *TE*-form of *oki-masu* ("wake"), *iki-masu* ("go"), and *abi-masu* ("take [a shower]") would be *oi-te*, *ii-te*, and *aN-de*, respectively. However, these are exceptions, and *oki-te*, *it-te*, and *abi-te* are the correct forms. These are irregular *TE*-forms you'll need to memorize.

Weather and Climate

For any type of outdoor activities, it is important to know what weather and climate your destination has. Let's learn some basic vocabulary for weather and climate.

Before getting into these topics, however, let's learn the words for "seasons":

Track 21
CD-2

season	*kisetsu*
spring	*haru*
summer	*natsu*
autumn	*aki*
winter	*fuyu*

Now answer the following question:

Track 21
CD-3

> *Dono kisetsu-ga suki-desu ka?*

Did you get it? The words *dono* and *suki-desu* mean "which" and "to like," respectively. So the question is, "What is your favorite season?" My answer would be …

Track 21
CD-4

> *(Watashi-wa) haru-ga suki-desu.*   "I like spring."

If you want to ask a "superlative" question—such as "Which season do you like *the most?*"—just add *ichibaN* to the predicate:

Track 21
CD-5

> Q: *Dono kisetsu-ga ichibaN suki-desu ka?*   "Which season do you like the most?"
> A: *Haru-ga ichibaN suki-desu.*   "I like spring the most."

In the next two subsections, you will learn some essential vocabulary and expressions for weather and climates.

Weather

The Japanese word for "weather" is *teNki.* Here is a list of basic weather nouns:

Track 21
CD-6

sunny (weather)	*hare*
cloudy (weather)	*kumori*
rainy (weather)	*ame*
snowy (weather)	*yuki*

If you want to ask how today's weather is, say the following:

> *Kyō-no teNki-wa dō-desu ka?*   "How's today's weather?"

Lifesavers _____

Usually from mid-June to mid-July, there is a rainy season called *tsuyu* all over Japan, except Hokkaido. Because the weather is not very predictable during this season, avoid traveling if possible, especially if you plan to do outdoor activities.

Because the preceding weather words are all nouns, your answer should end with *-desu:*

> *Ame-desu.*   "It's rainy."

Nobody can predict the weather with 100 percent accuracy. If you want to sound presumptive, use *-deshō* instead of *-desu:*

Track 21
CD-7

> Q: *Kyō-no teNki-wa dō-deshō ka?*
>   "How will today's weather be?"
> A: *Ame-deshō.*   "I suppose it'll be rainy."

The verbal forms of the preceding weather words are shown next. Note that when they end with -*masu*, they usually refer to a future event:

Track 21
CD-8

Hare-masu.   "It will become sunny."

Kumori-masu.   "It will become cloudy."

Ame-ga furi-masu.   "It will rain."

Yuki-ga furi-masu.   "It will snow."

How do you say "It will snow tomorrow"?

Track 21
CD-9

Ashita-wa yuki-ga furi-masu.   "It will snow tomorrow."

Huh?

Weather words ending with -*masu* also refer to a general weather trend. For example, say the following when you mean "It snows a lot in Alaska":

Arasuka-wa yuki-ga takusaN furi-masu. "It snows a lot in Alaska." (*takusaN* = "a lot")

Similarly:

NihoN-wa roku-gatsu-ni ame-ga takusaN furi-masu. (*roku-gatsu* = "June")   "In Japan, it rains a lot in June."

You have just seen the time reference words for "today" (*kyō*) and "tomorrow" (*ashita*). Let's learn time reference words for days, weeks, months, and years.

In the following pattern, "0" means present, "+" means future, and "-" means past. The accompanying number is an indication of how far into the past or future we're talking about. For example "-2" day (*ototoi*) is "the day before yesterday," "-1" day (*kinō*) is "yesterday," "0" day (*kyō*) is "today," "+1" day (*ashita*) is "tomorrow," and "+2" day (*asatte*) is "the day after tomorrow":

Lifesavers

In Japan, temperature is indicated by Celsius (= °C), *sesshi*, not Fahrenheit (= °F), *kashi*. (Refer to Chapter 2 for Celsius-Fahrenheit conversion.) Whether Celsius or Fahrenheit, the word for "degree" is -*do*, as in *sesshi ni-jū-do*, "20°C."

	-2	-1	0	+1	+2
Day	*ototoi*	*kinō*	*kyō*	*ashita*	*asatte*
Week	*seNseNshū*	*seNshū*	*koNshū*	*raishū*	*saraishū*
Month	*seNseNgetsu*	*seNgetsu*	*koNgetsu*	*raigetsu*	*saraigetsu*
Year	*ototoshi*	*kyoneN*	*kotoshi*	*raineN*	*saraineN*

But let's get back to the weather! When you describe the current weather, you must change the verb form to the *TE*-form and attach *i-masu* to the verb:

Hare-te i-masu.   "It is sunny (now)."

Kumot-te i-masu.   "It is cloudy (now)."

Ame-ga fut-te i-masu.   "It is raining (now)."

Yuki-ga fut-te i-masu.   "It is snowing (now)."

Climates

Most of the climate words are adjectives and end with *-idesu*:

"It's hot."   *Atsu-idesu.*

"It's warm."   *Atataka-idesu.*

"It's humid."   *Mushiatsu-idesu.*

"It's cold."   *Samu-idesu.*

"It's cool."   *Suzushi-idesu.*

Huh? _____

The word for "cold" is *samu-i,* but this refers to *cold air.* When you want to refer to "cold substances," such as liquids, use *tsumeta-i.* On a related note, *tsumeta-i* also refers to personality, as in …

tsumeta-i hito   "a cold person"

Watashi-wa tsumeta-idesu.   "I am a cold person." (personality)

Compare the second sentence with the following:

Watashi-wa samu-idesu.   "I am cold." (temperature)

By the way, *atsu-i* ("hot") refers to temperature only. When it refers to "spicy hot," use *kara-i,* as introduced in Chapter 19.

Now, using "season" and "climate" words, answer the following questions. As usual, the answers are at the end of this chapter.

Exercise 2

1. *Arasuka-no fuyu-wa dō-desu ka?*
   (*Arasuka* = "Alaska")

   (Cold)

2. *Furorida-no natsu-wa dō-desu ka?*
   (*Furorida* = "Florida")
   (Humid)

   _____

3. *Kariforunia-no haru-wa dō-desu ka?*
   (*Kariforunia* = "California")
   (Warm)

   _____

4. *NihoN-no aki-wa dō-desu ka?*
   (Cool)

   _____

Annual Events

If your schedule fits, you should definitely check out some traditional cultural events. They are not only fun, but also educational!

Traditional annual events are called *nenchū gyōji*. Each region has unique local events; you can easily check out what events are available at the place you are staying. In the rest of this chapter, I will explain some major annual events season by season.

Green Tea Break

When you visit somewhere, why don't you send a postcard to your family? Here is a list of postal vocabulary:

postcard	*ehagaki*
letter	*tegami*
stamps	*kitte*
package	*kozutsumi*
post office	*yūbiNkyoku*

If you have a stamped postcard, you can just drop it in a nearby postbox called *yūbiN posuto* or simply *posuto*. It is painted red and has the "〒" postal symbol on it, so you can't miss it!

It's easy to locate a yūbiN
posuto, *or postbox, because it
is painted red.*

*(Photo courtesy Agency for
Cultural Affairs of Japan)*

Spring Events

The most notable spring event is *Hanami*, Cherry Blossom Festival. The cherry tree is
the national tree of Japan. When cherry trees bloom in April, Japanese people gather
under the trees and have picnic parties while appreciating the arrival of spring. After all,
Hanami literally means "flower watching" (*hana* = "flowers"; *mi* = "to see").

> ### Green Tea Break
>
> In order to get the best spots at a
> *hanami* festival, people come to
> the park early in the morning and
> mark their "territories" by leaving
> picnic mats or even surrounding
> the area by ropes! They are that
> serious! Where legally allowed,
> you can even drink *sake* at a
> *hanami*.

March 3 is *Hina Matsuri*, Princess Festival or Girl's
Day. This is the day to celebrate the growth of girls at
home. Historically speaking, this was an important
event held at the Imperial Palace some 1,000 years ago.
It is still celebrated, not only by the imperial family but
by everyone, especially families with little girls. They
display dolls of a prince and princess and many other
court nobles on a five- to seven-step decorated stand.
Because *Hina Matsuri* is basically a family celebration,
you might be able to see what it is like if you visit
someone's house on that day, or you can find these doll
sets on display at department stores.

Summer Events

Right after the rainy season, or *tsuyu*, there are hundreds of firework festivals everywhere
in Japan, usually sponsored and organized by local governments. The firework festival is
called *hanabi taikai* in Japanese. The word *hanabi* literally means "flowers of fire" (*hana* =
"flowers"; *bi* = "fire"). Japanese fireworks are some of the very best in the world, in terms
of arrangement, beauty, and size of the "flowers of fire." Firework festivals are usually
held near a big river or ocean beach. There are many street vendors at these festivals, so
you can enjoy traditional Japanese (junk) foods such as *riNgo ame* ("candy apple"), *yaki
tōmorokoshi* ("roasted corn with soy sauce flavor"), *yakisoba* ("fried noodle"), and *yaki ika*
("roasted squid with soy sauce").

In July or August (depending on whether the event is based on the old "moon" calendar or modern "solar" calendar), there is a very important cultural (and religious) event called *o-boN*. This is when the spirits of deceased family members are believed to come back to this world. So *o-boN* is comparable to Halloween in a sense. (But children don't go trick or treating, and they don't wear a costume or mask.) *BoN* is a Buddhist term for "memorial."

During *o-boN*, there are community festivals called *natsu matsuri*, "summer festival." There is a huge tower-like stand in the middle of a field, and on the stand people play the traditional *taiko* drums like crazy, along with traditional dance music. Many people wear a *yukata* (casual *kimono*) and dance in a circle around the stand. This dance is called *boN odori*, "bon dance."

You definitely should check this out because you can see real people and experience real culture. Like firework festivals, hundreds of vendors are on the street, where you can buy food, toys, and also perfect souvenir gadgets!

Autumn Events

Autumn is a calm, but beautiful, season. One of the autumn events is *tsukimi*, "Moon Watching" (*tsuki* = "moon"; *mi* = "to see"), a very ancient but still practiced cultural event. On the night of a full moon in September (or occasionally October), people go out and appreciate the beauty of the moon and sky. Try *tsukimi dango*, rice cake served while watching the moon.

The majority of Japanese trees are broad-leaved, and their leaves turn red or yellow in the autumn. These beautiful autumn leaves are called *kōyō*. Because of this natural wonder, mid-October to early November is the most popular season for driving: Japanese people go out to beautiful mountains by car and enjoy hiking. Even if you do not drive in Japan, you can easily find a bus or train tour, which will take you to a beautiful mountain that is famous for *kōyō*. You can enjoy the scenery, and you just might come across delicious local cuisines there. Keep in mind that autumn is known as the "season of appetite" in Japan.

Winter Events

The biggest events of winter are New Year's Eve and New Year's Day. Many businesses (especially government offices and companies) are closed from December 28 to January 4. (Some grocery stores and most convenience stores are open during this period.)

The Japanese word for New Year's Eve is *ōmisoka*. At Buddhist temples, priests start tolling the bells a couple of hours before midnight. They toll the bell 108 times that night. Do you know why? In Buddhism, it is believed that we have 108 worldly desires, so 108 times of bell tolling renounces the desires at the end of the year.

Green Tea Break

Despite the fact that the population of Christians in Japan is only about 1 percent, Christmas (*Kurisumasu*) is very popular, although highly commercialized. On Christmas Day, particularly among young people, gift giving is quite popular. For some unknown reason, young Japanese people eat "Christmas cake." (Until I came to the United States, I had believed every American ate "Christmas cake" on Christmas!) *Kurisumasu* is spent with friends or your boy- or girlfriend. It is not a family gathering holiday like it is in the West. Oh, by the way, Christmas is not a national holiday in Japan.

Similarly, for a commercial reason, St. Valentine's Day (*BareNtaiN Dē*) is extremely popular in Japan. However, Japanese people redefined this day with a new ritual. In Japan, February 14 is the day when women give chocolate to the men they like, their male family members, and/or their male co-workers. Men are not supposed to give a gift to women on this day. On March 14, exactly one month later, it is time for men to give a gift (usually something more expensive than what they received, such as a handkerchief) to the women in return! This day is called *Howaito Dē*, "White Day."

Right after midnight, many people go to either a Buddhist temple or *Shinto* shrine to pray for the prospective year, good health, and fortune. This is called *hatsu mairi*. Many of them dress up, often wearing traditional *kimonos*. Most public transportation is open 24 hours from New Year's Eve to New Year's Day for those who pay a visit to shrines or temples. Bear in mind that wherever you go, it is extremely crowded. If you plan to take children there, make sure that you hold their hands tight!

New Year's Days are called *oshōgatsu*, and the very first day of January is called *gaNtaN*. If you missed the midnight visitation to a temple or shrine, try going there during the first three days of the New Year. Don't forget to buy a "lucky charm," or *omamori*.

There is another reason why you should not miss New Year's Day—the traditional New Year food called *osechi ryōri*. If you stay at someone's house for New Year's, you will be treated with delicious homemade foods. Even if you stay at a hotel, it will offer a special holiday treat on New Year's Day.

Green Tea Break

It's amazing that about 70 percent of the entire Japanese population (80 million people) visit a temple or shrine during the first three days of the New Year!

Planning your own short trip can be fun because you don't have to worry about someone else's schedule. You might need a little courage to go out to explore Japan on your own, but it's definitely worth it. Do some research and preparation in advance: This makes your own leisure time even more successful and memorable!

Answers

Exercise 1

1. Go to Shinjuku by train (at 7:15)—Buy tickets (at 8:00)—Ride the highway bus (at 8:30)

   Shichi-ji jū go-fuN-ni deNsha-de ShiNjuku-ni it-te,

   hachi-ji-ni kippu-o kat-te,

   hachi-ji haN-ni kōsoku basu-ni nori-masu.

2. Buy souvenirs (at 4:00)—Ride bus (at 4:30)—Arrive at Shinjuku (at 7:30)

   Yo-ji-ni omiyage-o kat-te,

   yo-ji haN-ni basu-ni not-te,

   shichi-ji haN-ni ShiNjuku-ni tsuki-masu.

3. Go back to the hotel by taxi (at 9:00)—Take a shower (at 10:00)—Go to bed (at 11:00)

   Ku-ji-ni takushī-de hoteru-ni kaet-te,

   jū-ji-ni shawā-o abi-te,

   jū ichi-ji-ni ne-masu.

Exercise 2

1. Q: *Arasuka-no fuyu-wa dō-desu ka?*

   "How is the winter in Alaska?"

   A: *Arasuka-no fuyu-wa samu-idesu.*

2. Q: *Furorida-no natsu-wa dō-desu ka?*

   "How is the summer in Florida?"

   A: *Furorida-no natsu-wa mushiatsu-idesu.*

3. Q: *Kariforunia-no haru-wa dō-desu ka?*

   "How is the spring in California?"

   A: *Kariforunia-no haru-wa atataka-idesu.*

4. Q: *NihoN-no aki-wa dō-desu ka?*

   "How is the autumn in Japan?"

   A: *NihoN-no aki-wa suzushi-idesu.*

The Least You Need to Know

◆ Using the *TE*-form, you can connect sentences in chronological order.

◆ Knowing weather/climate expressions will help you plan wisely. Important weather-related words are: *hare* ("sunny"), *ame* ("rainy"), *kumori* ("cloudy"), and *yuki* ("snowy"). Some climate-related words are: *atsu-idesu* ("hot"), *atataka-idesu* ("warm"), *samu-idesu* ("cold"), and *suzushi-idesu* ("cool").

◆ Experience Japanese culture and tradition by checking out various annual events. Local festivals especially are a great opportunity to understand the traditional values of Japan.

Part 6

Troubleshooting

Life is full of unexpected events, sometimes good and sometimes challenging. The chapters in this part provide useful information for those challenging events.

Chapter 22 covers all the facts and expressions you need to make a phone call, domestic or international. Chapter 23 provides information should you need to seek medical assistance, and Chapter 24 is for other kinds of emergencies. Chapter 25 contains helpful phrases and tips in case you experience inconveniences at a hotel, restaurant, or shop.

Better preparation makes you feel secure and confident. Even if you are not in trouble, the expressions you will learn in these chapters will be lifesavers for you.

Talking on the Phone

In This Chapter

- ◆ The telephone system in Japan
- ◆ Calling home from Japan
- ◆ A sample phone conversation

I bet you spend quite a lot of time on the phone every day, making business calls, talking with friends, and so on. It's easy and convenient, but when it comes to making a phone call in a foreign country, it's a different story!

In this chapter, you will first learn some basic facts about Japanese phones and then learn two useful tasks—making an international call to your home country and having a simple telephone conversation.

Japanese Phone Facts

First of all, here is a list of essential telephone vocabulary:

telephone; telephone call	*deNwa*
cellular telephone	*kētai deNwa* or *kētai*
public pay phone	*kōshū deNwa*
telephone number	*deNwa baNgō*
make a phone call	*deNwa-o shi-masu*

collect call	*korekuto kōru*
operator	*operētā*
phone book	*deNwachō*

Public telephones, or kōshū deNwa, *are both coin- and telephone card–operated.*

(Photo courtesy Agency for Cultural Affairs of Japan)

Green Tea Break

In Japan, almost everyone has a cellular phone, or *kētai*. Use of a *kētai* is a serious public concern nowadays. It's wise to turn off your *kētai* in a public place such as in a train, at a train station, or at a movie theater. At a hospital, it is mandatory to turn off your *kētai* so as to not disturb patients with pacemakers.

CAUTION Lifesavers

You can find a *terefoN kādo* vending machine in which there are many public phones, such as a train station, or you can buy them at convenience stores (*koNbini*).

If you go to Japan on a business trip, you will find a cellular phone, or *kētai*, essential. You might already have a special calling plan or calling card that allows you to use your existing phone for international calls from abroad. If your cellular phone does not work in Japan and you want to have one, you have two options: You can rent a *kētai* phone with a prepaid calling plan, or you can purchase a package of a *kētai* phone and a prepaid calling card. For either option, you can find vendors at the airport.

Let's move on to Japanese public pay phones, or *kōshū deNwa*. How do they work? Most public phones accept coins (10 *yen* coin or 100 *yen* coin) and a prepaid calling card called *terefoN kādo*. If you use coins, please note that it is not an unlimited call even if you are making a local call. With 10 *yen*, you can make a local call for 3 minutes.

When you use a prepaid calling card in the United States or Canada, you enter your PIN. Japanese prepaid cards work different. In Japan, you insert a prepaid *terefoN kādo* into the upper slot of a telephone. There is no PIN because the telephone reads your card and verifies its remaining time. After use, your card will be ejected from the lower slot, leaving a punch hole indicating how many minutes remain on the card.

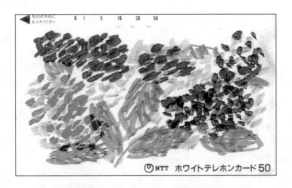

Use a Japanese calling card (terefoN kādo) by inserting it into a payphone. Remaining minutes are indicated by a punch hole.

Pronouncing telephone numbers is quite easy. You just say each number separately and use *no* for a hyphen between numbers. For example, 0423-41-8796 is pronounced as …

Track 22
CD-1

> *Zero yoN ni saN nō yoN ichi nō hachi nana kyū roku*

Area codes such as "0423" in the preceding example are called *shigai kyokubaN*. Note that all Japanese area codes start with 0. If you are making a local call, you don't have to dial the area code.

Lifesavers

When "0" appears in a phone number (other than at the beginning), it can be pronounced as *maru*, instead of *zero*, as in:

41-8096   *YoN ichi no hachi maru kyū roku*

Exercise 1

Write the following phone numbers in Japanese.

1. 25-4325

   _____

2. 045-286-2091

   _____

3. 0426-63-2154

   _____

4. 03-3950-4672

   _____

Now you are ready to make a phone call. The most important phrase in a telephone conversation is …

Track 22
CD-2

Moshi moshi. "Hello."

Shortcuts to Success _____

English speakers tend to pronounce this phrase like *mòshi MÓshi,* putting a strong accent on the second *mo* and a weak accent on the first *mo.* As explained in Chapter 3, the Japanese accent does not work like the English accent. Make sure that you do not give a strong intonation to the word, but put a slight stress on the first *mo.* Calmness in pronunciation will make your Japanese more natural.

Let's Call Home!

If you are staying in a hotel, there should be detailed instructions in your room as to how to make an international call from the room phone.

If you are calling from an ordinary hotel room telephone, you must first dial the selected phone company's access number. For example, the telephone company access code of *KDD* (a Japanese phone company) is "001." Then you would dial the country code, the area code, and the rest of the phone number:

001 + COUNTRY CODE + AREA CODE + NUMBER

Here are the country codes of some English-speaking countries:

United States	1
Canada	1
United Kingdom	44
Australia	61
New Zealand	64

Lifesavers _____

The country code of Japan is 81. If you are making an international call to Japan from the United States, and the phone number you are calling is 0425-76-2795, dial the following:

011-81-425-76-2795

The access number from the United States to other countries is 011. Note that you do not dial the first digit of the area code, 0.

What if you want to call collect to your home country? Again, let's use *KDD* because it is probably the most foreigner-friendly phone company, and many operators are bilingual. The number to remember for a collect call is …

Collect Call (KDD): 0051

When you call, the operator will answer like this:

Hai, KDD-desu. "This is KDD."

You could speak in English because the operator will probably be bilingual:

Ēgo-de onegai shimasu. "In English, please."

You might want to try your Japanese first! You can always switch to English later. First tell the operator that you want to make a collect call:

Korekuto kōru-o shi-tai-N-desu ga … "I want to make a collect call …"

Or simply:

Korekuto kōru-o onegai shimasu. "Collect call, please."

You can make your request more specific by adding which country you want to call:

<u>*Amerika-ni*</u> *korekuto kōru-o onegai shimasu.* "Collect call to the USA, please."

The operator will ask you several questions, which I list here:

Dochira-no kuni-ni okake-desu ka? "Which country are you calling?" (*kuni* = country)

Aite-no deNwa baNgō-wa naN-baN-desu ka? "What is the phone number of the other party?"

Aite-no o-namae-wa naN-desu ka? "What is the name of the other party?"

An important word is *aite*, literally meaning "the other party"—in this case, "the person you are calling."

A telephone conversation can be a challenging task because, unlike in an ordinary conversation, you cannot see the listener. So even if you do not understand what the operator says, you should not be ashamed about asking the operator to repeat himself! The following expressions might be useful:

SumimaseN, wakari-maseN. "Sorry, I don't understand."

SumimaseN, kikoe-maseN. "Sorry, I cannot hear you."

Mō ichido it-te kudasai. "Please say it again." (*mō ichido* = "one more time")

Track 22
CD-7

Mō sukoshi yukkuri hanashi-te kudasai. "Please speak a little more slowly."
(*mō sukoshi* = "little more"; *yukkuri* = "slow")

Track 22
CD-8

Mō sukoshi ōki-i koe-de hanashi-te kudasai.
"Please speak a little louder."
(*koe* = "voice")

Huh?

Remember the permission pattern [*TE-mo i-desu ka*] that was introduced in Chapter 18? This can be used not only with a verb but also a noun, as in *Ēgo-de-mo i-desu ka*, "Would English be acceptable?" Note that the *TE*-form of a noun is *XYZ-de*.

If you really cannot communicate in Japanese any further, say the following as the last resort:

Track 22
CD-9

Ēgo-de i-idesu ka?
"Would English be okay?"

Or:

Track 22
CD-10

Ēgo-de onegai shimasu.
"In English, please."

When You Must Call Someone's House

Suppose that there is an urgent matter that you must let your Japanese friend, *Yumiko*, know about, so you are calling her house. Yumiko is fluent in English, but what if she is not at home and someone in the family, who does not understand English, picks up the phone? Leaving an accurate message in Japanese might be a little too challenging at this point, so let's focus on the following simpler tasks:

◆ Ask if your friend is at home.

◆ Provided that she is not at home, ask the family member to tell your friend to call you.

◆ Identify yourself and leave your phone number.

Let's look at a simulated telephone conversation. Here is the situation:

◆ Yumiko's family name is Tanaka.

◆ Yumiko's mother picks up the phone.

◆ Your name is John Brown (*JoN BurauN*).

◆ Your phone number is 03-4213-8267.

Study the whole conversation first. Then we'll divide it into parts and examine it more closely.

Telephone Dialog

Track 22
CD-11

TANAKA 1   *Moshi moshi, Tanaka-desu ga.*

"Hello, this is the Tanaka's."

YOU 1   *Moshi moshi, JoN BurauN to mōshi-masu ga, Yumiko-saN onegai shimasu.*

                   "Hello, my name is John Brown. May I talk to Yumiko?"

TANAKA 2   *SumimaseN, Yumiko-wa rusu-desu ga …*

                   "Sorry, Yumiko is out."

YOU 2   *Sō-desu ka.*

                   Jā, atode deNwa shi-te hoshi-i-N-desu ga …

                   "I see. Then, I would like her to call me later."

TANAKA 3   *Hai. DeNwa baNgō-wa naN-baN-desu ka?*

                   "Certainly. What is your phone number?"

YOU 3   *Zero saN no yoN ni ichi saN no hachi ni roku nana-desu.*

                   "03-4213-8267."

TANAKA 4   *Hai, wakari-mashita.*

                   "Yes, I got it."

YOU 4   *Onegai shimasu. Shitsurē shimasu.*

                   "Thank you. Good-bye."

TANAKA 5   *Shitsurē shimasu.*

                   "Good-bye."

In what follows, I will explain the dialog in detail segment by segment.

Segment 1

> **Shortcuts to Success**
>
> When you memorize a dialog, listen to the CD and try to work with one short segment at a time. For example, in this telephone dialog, pay attention to only the Tanaka 1–You 1 segment until you become fully comfortable. Then move on to the next segment.

TANAKA 1   *Moshi moshi, Tanaka-desu ga.*

                   "Hello, this is the Tanaka's."

YOU 1   *Moshi moshi, JoN BurauN to mōshi-masu ga, Yumiko-saN onegai shimasu.*

                   "Hello, my name is John Brown. May I talk to Yumiko?"

> **Lifesavers**
>
> In a telephone conversation, it is wise to avoid the verb *i-masu*, as in *Yumiko-saN-wa i-masu ka*, "Is Yumiko there?" This might sound a little rude.

What is important in this segment is your self-introduction. Because you are not sure who you are talking with at this point, you need to be polite. As discussed in Chapter 9, the pattern *NAME to mōshi-masu* is a very polite expression for self-introduction.

Instead of *Yumiko-saN onegai shimasu*, you could ask a much more formal question such as the following:

Track 22
CD-12

> *Yumiko-saN-wa irasshai-masu ka?* "Is Yumiko at home?"

The verb *irasshai-masu* is the super-polite version of *i-masu*, "to be."

Segment 2

TANAKA 2   *SumimaseN, Yumiko-wa rusu-desu ga.* ...

"Sorry, Yumiko is out."

YOU 2   *Sō-desu ka.*

Jā, atode Yumiko-san-ni deNwa shi-te hoshi-i-N-desu ga ...

"I see. Then, I would like her to call me later." (*atode* = "later")

The word *rusu* means "not at home." Note that this sentence ends with the familiar *ga* ..., the conversation softening marker. Instead of *rusu-desu*, you could say ...

Shortcuts to Success

As you know, in Japanese, you can omit items that are known to both the speaker and listener. So if I want *you* to call me later, I can omit both *watashi* ("I") and *anata* ("you"):

Atode deNwa shi-te hoshi-i-N-desu ga ...
"I want you to call me later."

Track 22
CD-13

> *SumimaseN, Yumiko-wa ori-maseN ga* ...
> "Sorry, Yumiko is not here."

This segment contains a very important expression pattern:

> PERSON-*ni* VERB-*te hoshi-i-N-desu ga* ...
> "I want PERSON to do so-and-so."

In Segment 2, you want Yumiko to call you later. This expression is very handy when you indirectly ask someone to do something. Let's practice using this pattern. The answers are at the end of this chapter.

Huh?

Remember in Segment 1, you learned *irasshai-masu*, "to be." Now you learned *ori-masu*, which also means "to be." Both are polite verbs, but *irasshai-masu* is used when you refer to "someone besides you or your family member," whereas *ori-masu* is used when you refer to yourself or your family member. In the previous case, because Yumiko is a family member of Mrs. Tanaka, she uses *ori-masu*. On the other hand, in Segment 1, you used *irasshai-masu* because Yumiko is not your family member.

Exercise 2

1. I want Ms. Yamamoto to call (me) at 7 o'clock.

_____

2. I want you to bring a newspaper.

("bring" = *mot-te ki-masu*; "newspaper" = *shiNbuN*)

_____

3. I want Mr. Tanaka to come to my party.

("come" = *ki-masu*)

_____

4. I want you to speak in English.

("speak" = *hanashi-masu*; "in English" = *ēgo-de*)

_____

5. I want Ms. Yamada to photocopy this.

("to photocopy" = *kopī shi-masu*)

_____

Segments 3, 4, and 5

TANAKA 3	*Hai. DeNwa baNgō-wa naN-baN-desu ka?*
	"Certainly. What is your phone number?"
YOU 3	*Zero saN no yoN ni ichi saN no hachi ni roku nana-desu.*
	"03-4213-8267."
TANAKA 4	*Hai, wakari-mashita.*
	"Yes, I got it."
YOU 4	*Onegai shimasu. Shitsurē shimasu.*
	"Thank you. Good-bye."
TANAKA 5	*Shitsurē shimasu.*
	"Good-bye."

These segments are relatively straightforward. Make sure that you say your phone number clearly, digit by digit. Here again, there is a handy expression, *onegai shimasu*. Use this phrase when you ask someone to take care of a certain task.

Shortcuts to Success

The adjective *hoshi-i* literally means "desirable." Besides the usage that I have just introduced here, it can be used when you want something (noun), as explained in Chapter 18.

Watashi-wa riNgo-ga hoshi-i-N-desu ga …

"I want an apple …"

Important Numbers

You should know some important phone numbers in Japan:

Ambulance (*kyūkyūsha*)	119
Fire (*shōbōsho*)	119
Police (*kēsatsu*)	110

Chapter 23 covers useful Japanese expressions for medical emergencies, and Chapter 24 covers other kinds of emergencies.

Here are some more nonemergency, but useful, phone numbers:

Time (*jihō*)	117
Weather forecast (*teNki yohō*)	177
Phone directory (*baNgō aNnai*)	104

Here is information for English-speaking countries' embassies in Tokyo. The area code (03) is not necessary if you're calling within the metropolitan Tokyo area.

American (U.S.) Embassy
Phone: (03) 3224-5000 (Tokyo)
Website: usembassy.state.gov/tokyo
Address: 1-10-5 Akasaka, Minato-ku, Tokyo 107-8420

Canadian Embassy
Phone: (03) 5412-6200 (Tokyo)
Website: www.dfait-maeci.gc.ca/ni-ka
Address: 7-3-38 Akasaka, Minato-ku, Tokyo 107-8503

British Embassy
Phone: (03) 5211-1183 (Tokyo)
Website: www.uknow.or.jp/be/index_e.html
Address: 1 Ichibancho, Chiyoda-ku, Tokyo 102-8381

Australian Embassy
Phone: (03) 5232-4111 (Tokyo)
Website: www.australia.or.jp/english/seifu/index.html
Address: 2-1-14 Mita, Minato-ku, Tokyo 108-8361

New Zealand Embassy
Phone: (03) 3467 2271 (Tokyo)
Website: www.nzembassy.com
Address: 20-40 Kamiyama-cho, Shibuya-ku, Tokyo 150-0047

You might have noticed that talking on the phone does not require a lot of new vocabulary. However, you really have to listen carefully to the person on the other end because you cannot see her or him. Remember, nothing is wrong or inappropriate about asking the other party to repeat something or to speak slowly or louder.

Answers

Exercise 1

Track 22
CD-14–17

1. 25-4325

   ni go no yoN saN ni go

2. 045-286-2091

   zero yoN go no ni hachi roku no ni zero kyū ichi

3. 0426-63-2154

   zero yoN ni roku no roku saN no ni ichi go yoN

4. 03-3950-4672

   zero saN no saN kyū go zero no yoN roku nana ni

Exercise 2

Track 22
CD-18-22

1. "I want Ms. Yamamoto to call (me) at 7 o'clock."

   Yamamoto-saN-ni shichi-ji-ni deNwa shi-te hoshi-i-N-desu ga …

2. "I want you to bring a newspaper."

   ShiNbuN-o mot-te ki-te hoshi-i-N-desu ga …

3. "I want Mr. Tanaka to come to my party."

   Tanaka-saN-ni watashi-no pāti-ni ki-te hoshi-i-N-desu ga…

4. "I want you to speak in English."

   Ēgo-de hanashi-te hoshi-i-N-desu ga …

5. "I want Ms. Yamada to photocopy this."

   Yamada-saN-ni kore-o kopī shi-te hoshi-i-N-desu ga …

The Least You Need to Know

- Most public phones in Japan accept 10 yen coins or 100 yen coins and a prepaid calling card called *terefoN kādo*. With 10 yen, you can make a local call for 3 minutes.

- Pronouncing telephone numbers is quite easy. You just say each number separately and use *no* for a hyphen between numbers.

◆ Say *Moshi moshi* ("hello") when answering the telephone in Japan. Remember not to accent any of the syllables.

◆ As always, politeness is important. The pattern *NAME to mōshi-masu* is a very polite expression for self-introduction over the telephone.

◆ Remember, nothing is wrong or inappropriate about asking the other party to repeat something or to speak slowly or louder.

Chapter 3

I'm Sick! Call 911?
No, Call 119!

In This Chapter

- ◆ Health-related and body-part vocabulary
- ◆ Telling a doctor how you feel
- ◆ Buying medicine

Sickness is the last thing you want to encounter when traveling abroad. But this can happen to anyone, and I want you to be prepared. In this chapter, I will introduce health-related expressions you will find helpful if you get sick.

Health-Related Expressions

First of all, let's take a look at some important health-related expressions:

Health-Related Vocabulary

sickness	*byōki*
hospital	*byōiN*
emergency hospital	*kyūkyū byōiN*
first aid	*ōkyū shochi*
first aid room	*imushitsu*

doctor/doctor's office	*isha*
medicine	*kusuri*
pharmacy	*kusuriya* or *yakkyoku*
pharmacist	*yakuzaishi*
take medicine	*kusuri-o nomi-masu*
ambulance	*kyūkyūsha*
hospitalization	*nyūiN*
be hospitalized	*nyūiN shi-masu*
injury	*kega*
take a lab test	*keNsa-o shi-masu*
see a doctor	*isha-ni iki-masu*
prescription	*shohōseN*
health insurance	*keNkō hokeN*
insurance card	*hokeNshō*
handicapped person	*shiNshōsha*
I feel sick.	*KibuN-ga waru-i-N-desu.*
I'm injured.	*Kega-o shi-mashita.*

If you don't feel well, you should let people know by saying …

> *Guai-ga waru-i-N-desu ga …*   "I am not feeling well …"

Track 23 CD-1

If you are on your own and want to find out where the hospital is, say

> *ByōiN-wa doko-desu ka?*   "Where is the hospital?"

Track 23 CD-2

Huh?

The word *byōiN* refers to a hospital as well as a doctor's office. On a street map, a *byōiN* is indicated by a "cross" symbol.

If you are staying in a fairly large hotel, it might have a medical room where first aid is available. This is called an *imushitsu*, "first aid room."

In case of a medical emergency, say the following to someone near you:

> *Kyūkyūsha-o yoN-de kudasai.*
> "Please call an ambulance."

Track 23 CD-3

If you must call an ambulance yourself, call "119." Don't confuse it with "911"!

Lifesavers _____

The emergency number "119" is for both medical emergencies and fire. In case of fire, say *Kaji-desu,* "Fire." In case of a medical emergency, say *Kyūkyūsha onegai shimasu,* "Ambulance, please." The number for the police is "110."

You can obtain hospital information in English at the following phone numbers:

03-5285-8181

03-3212-2323

Both of these are Tokyo numbers. If you are calling within the city of Tokyo, you do not have to dial the area code "03."

At a Doctor's Office

Before seeing a doctor at a hospital, you will need to check in. The check-in booth is called *uketsuke*. They will ask you several questions, such as:

name	*(o)namae* or *shimē*
address	*(go)jūsho*
phone number	*deNwa baNgō*
age	*neNrē*
occupation	*shokugyō*
birth date	*sēneN gappi*

You might be asked to fill out a registration form with the preceding information. Many hospitals have an English registration form. Here is how you ask for an English version:

Ēgo-no fōmu-wa ari-masu ka? "Do you have an English form?"

Upon check-in, you will be asked to show your insurance card to the receptionist:

HokeNshō-o mise-te kudasai. "Please show me your insurance card."

Lifesavers _____

If your trip to, or stay in, Japan is less than one year, I strongly suggest that you obtain short-term travel health insurance before leaving for Japan. Your existing health insurance might cover medical expenses incurred in a foreign country; however, it requires a tremendous amount of paperwork and also documentation written by your doctor. If it is written in Japanese, it must be translated into English! Travel health insurance might be slightly expensive, but it is definitely less of a hassle.

Shortcuts to Success

It's effective to categorize body-part vocabulary according to areas and memorize them. For example, memorize all the face-related words at once.

If your situation is not an emergency, you might have to wait in a waiting room near the examination room until you are called. The waiting room is called *machiai shitsu*; the examination room is *shiNsatsu shitsu*.

Parts of the Body

When you see a doctor, you will need to describe your medical condition. You should be familiar with the Japanese words for parts of the body.

Parts of the Body

head	*atama*	chest	*mune*
face	*kao*	belly	*onaka*
hair	*kami*	back	*senaka*
forehead	*hitai*	waist	*koshi*
eye	*me*	crotch; groin	*mata*
eyelid	*mabuta*	buttocks	*oshiri*
ear	*mimi*	thigh	*momo*
nose	*hana*	knee	*hiza*
mouth	*kuchi*	leg/foot	*ashi*
lip	*kuchibiru*	ankle	*ashikubi*
teeth	*ha*	toe	*tsumasaki*
gum	*haguki*	heart	*shiNzō*
tongue	*shita*	lung	*hai*
chin	*ago*	stomach	*i*
cheek	*hō*	liver	*kaNzō*
neck	*kubi*	kidney	*jiNzō*
throat	*nodo*	appendix	*mōchō*
shoulder	*kata*	lymph node	*riNpaseN*
arm	*ude*	intestines	*chō*
armpit	*wakinoshita*	genitals	*sēki*
hand	*te*	saliva	*tsuba*
finger	*yubi*	blood	*chi*
elbow	*hiji*	perspiration	*ase*

Huh?

The name of each finger is as follows:

thumb	*oya-yubi*
index finger	*hitosashi-yubi*
middle finger	*naka-yubi*
ring finger	*kusuri-yubi*
little finger	*ko-yubi*

By the way, *oya* means "parent," *hitosashi* means "pointing at people," *naka* means "middle," *kusuri* means "medicine," and *ko* means "child." The ring finger is the "medicine finger" in Japanese because this finger was used to mix a certain kind of medicine in old days.

Symptoms

Before examining you, your doctor will ask you the following question:

Track 23
CD-4

Dō shi-mashita ka? "What is the problem?"

Let's familiarize ourselves with some common symptoms.

Symptoms

X hurts.	*X-ga ita-i-N-desu.*
I got a cut on X.	*X-o kiri-mashita.*
I feel itchy in the X.	*X-ga kayu-i-N-desu.*
I have a headache.	*Atama-ga ita-idesu.*
I have a stomachache.	*Onaka-ga ita-idesu.*
I have a toothache.	*Ha-ga ita-idesu.*
I have back pain.	*Koshi-ga ita-idesu.*
I caught a cold.	*Kaze-o hiki-mashita.*
I have a fever.	*Netsu-ga ari-masu.*
I cough.	*Seki-ga de-masu.*
I'm sweating.	*Ase-o kai-te i-masu.*
I have a sore throat.	*Nodo-ga ita-idesu.*
I have a runny nose.	*Hana-ga de-te i-masu.*
I have a stuffy nose.	*Hana-ga tsumat-te i-masu.*
I vomited.	*Haki-mashita.*

I have nausea.	*Hakike-ga shi-masu.*
I feel dizzy.	*Memai-ga shi-masu.*
I feel a chill.	*Samuke-ga shi-masu.*
I feel tired.	*Tsukare-te i-masu.*
I don't have an appetite.	*Shokuyoku-ga ari-maseN.*
I have diarrhea.	*Geri-o shi-te i-masu.*
I'm constipated.	*BeNpi-o shi-te i-masu.*
I'm bleeding.	*Shukketsu shi-te i-masu.*
I broke a bone.	*Hone-o ori-mashita.*
I have a sprain.	*NeNza shi-mashita.*
I got burnt.	*Yakedo shi-mashita.*
I'm pregnant.	*NiNshiN shi-te i-masu.*
I'm having my period.	*Sēri-desu.*
I have cramps.	*Sēritsū-ga ari-masu.*
I have a heavy discharge.	*Orimono-ga hido-idesu.*
My period is late.	*Sēri-ga okure-te i-masu.*

The first two expressions in the preceding table are particularly useful when you describe your symptom. All you need to do is replace "X" with the appropriate part of the body.

Track 23
CD-5–6

X-ga ita-i-N-desu.   "X hurts."

Atama-ga ita-i-N-desu ga …   "I have a headache."

X-o kiri-mashita.   "I got a cut on X."

Yubi-o kiri-mashita.   "I got a cut on my finger."

Huh?

Notice that the word *ita-i* ends with *N-desu*. This <u>N</u> is a "feeling" marker. When you want to emphasize the expression of a feeling, this marker is effective. Other than *ita-i*, this emotion marker <u>N</u> is also seen in "desire" constructions:

NihoN-ni <u>iki-ta-i</u>-N-desu.   "I want to go to Japan."

RiNgo-ga <u>hoshi-i</u>-N-desu.   "I want an apple."

"Wanting" is an internal feeling of the speaker.

You might want to describe to the doctor what kind of pain you are experiencing:

I have a dull pain.   *Nibuku ita-i-N-desu.*

I have a slight pain.   *Sukoshi ita-i-N-desu.*

I have an intense pain.   *Totemo ita-i-N-desu.*

I have a pricking pain.   *Chiku-chiku ita-i-N-desu.*

I have a throbbing pain.   *Zuki-zuki ita-i-N-desu.*

I have a burning sensation.   *Hiri-hiri ita-i-N-desu.*

I have an itchy pain.   *Itagayu-i-N-desu.*

I have a massive headache.   *Atama-ga gaN-gaN.*

Common Requests a Doctor Makes

Your doctor might make the following requests during the examination:

Track 23
CD-7-17

Yoko-ni nat-te kudasai.   "Please lie down."
(*yoko-ni nari-masu* = "lie down")

Aomuke-ni nat-te kudasai.   "Please lie on your back."
(*aomuke-ni nari-masu* = "lie on your back")

Utsubuse-ni nat-te kudasai.   "Please lie on your stomach."
(*utsubuse-ni nari-masu* = "lie on your stomach")

Fuku-o nui-de kudasai.   "Please take off your clothes."
(*fuku* = "clothes"; *nugi-masu* = "take off")

Fuku-o ki-te kudasai.   "Please put on your clothes."
(*ki-masu* = "wear")

Iki-o sut-te kudasai.   "Please breathe."
(*iki* = "breath"; *sui-masu* = "inhale")

Iki-o hai-te kudasai.   "Please exhale."
(*haki-masu* = "exhale")

Kuchi-o ake-te kudasai.   "Please open your mouth."
(*ake-masu* = "open")

Tat-te kudasai.   "Please stand up."
(*tachi-masu* = "stand up")

Suwat-te kudasai.   "Please sit down."
(*suwari-masu* = "sit down")

Ā-to it-te kudasai.   "Please say 'ah.'"
(*ii-masu* = "say")

Whether at a hospital or a doctor's office, if a prescription is given, you must purchase the medicine prescribed at the same office. Pharmacies you find in town sell only over-the-counter drugs.

Last, but not least, if you are in a general hospital, you need to know which medical department you are supposed to go to, such as "internal medicine," "dermatology," or someplace else.

Medical Departments

internal medicine	*naika*
surgery	*geka*
dentist	*shika*
pediatrics	*shōnika*
dermatology	*hifuka*
gynecology	*fujiNka*
radiology	*hōshaseNka*
otolaryngology (ears, nose, and throat)	*jibika*
urology	*hinyōkika*
neurology	*shiNkēka*
psychiatric	*sēshiNka*

Before moving on to the next section, here is a list of names of diseases.

Names of Medical Problems

common cold	*kaze*
flu	*iNfurueNza*
headache	*zutsū*
migraine	*heNzutsū*
food poisoning	*shokuchūdoku*
food poisoning (mild)	*shokuatari*
ear infection	*chūjieN*
cavity (tooth decay)	*mushiba*
sinus (infection)	*bieN*
muscle sprain	*neNza*
fracture	*kossetsu*
pneumonia	*haieN*
appendicitis	*mōchōeN*
hemorrhoid	*ji*

gastritis	*ieN*
stroke	*nōsocchū*
heart attack	*shiNzō hossa*
miscarriage	*ryūzaN*
cancer	*gaN*
burn	*yakedo*
sexually transmitted disease	*sēbyō*

> **Green Tea Break**
>
> An x-ray is called *reNtogeN* (in honor of the inventor of x-rays, Wilhelm K. Roentgen).

At the Pharmacy

If your medical problem is a rather minor one and you think that over-the-counter medicine will take care it, the best place to go is a *kusuriya* or *yakkyoku*, which both mean "pharmacy."

Because thousands of drugs are available at a pharmacy and their directions and indications are written in Japanese, I think that the best way to find the most suitable medicine for you is to ask a pharmacist, or *yakuzaishi*. You have just learned in the previous section how to describe your medical condition, right?

> **Green Tea Break**
>
> In Japan, many prescribed medicines come in powder form in packets rather than in capsules. You pour the powder into your mouth and use water to help you swallow.

When you find the right medicine, ask the pharmacist questions such as how many times a day to take it, how many tablets to take each time, and so on. Here is how to ask these questions:

Track 23
CD-18-19

> *Ichi-nichi naN-kai-desu ka?* "How many times a day?"
> (*naN-kai* = "how many times")
>
> *Ik-kai naN-jō-desu ka?* "How many tablets each time?"
> (*naN-jō* = "how many tablets")

You have just seen two new counters, *-kai* ("times; rounds") and *-jo* ("tablets"). What if you should take the medicine three times a day?

Track 23
CD-20

> *Ichi-nichi saN-kai-desu.* "Three times a day."

Likewise, what if you should take two tablets each time?

> *Ik-kai ni-jō-desu.* "Two tablets each time."

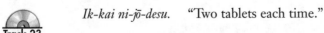
Track 23
CD-21

Some medicine should be taken before or after a meal.

> *ShokuzeN-ni noN-de kudasai.*   "Take (it) before a meal." (*shokuzeN* = "before meal")
>
> *Shokugo-ni noN-de kudasai.*   "Take (it) after a meal." (*shokugo* = "after meal")

You might have noticed that the verb for "take (medicine)" is *nomi-masu*, which literally means "drink; swallow." This verb applies to liquid, tablets, or powder.

Okay, before closing this chapter, let's list some common drugs.

Common Drugs and Medical Supplies

for cold/flu	*kazegusuri*
for coughing	*seki-no kusuri*
for headache	*zutsūyaku*
for stomachache	*onaka-no kusuri*
for motion sickness	*yoidome*
for itchiness	*kayumidome*
for reducing fever	*genetsuzai*
antibiotics	*kōsē busshitsu*
compress (for muscle pain)	*shippu*
eyedrop	*megusuri*
painkiller	*itamidome*
disinfectant solution	*shōdokuyaku*
Band-Aid	*baNsōkō*
bandage	*hōtai*
eye patch	*gaNtai*
cream	*kurīmu*
vitamin	*bitamiN*
cough drop	*nodoame*
women's sanitary products	*sēri yōhiN*
sanitary napkin	*napukiN*
tampon	*taNpoN*
contraceptive	*hiniNgu*
cast	*gipusu*
wheelchair	*kurumaisu*
crutch	*matsubazue*
cane	*tsue*

I hope your trip is safe, fun, and most importantly, that you won't have to count on this chapter. But it is better to be prepared, just in case. Have a safe trip!

Green Tea Break

If you visit Japan in the winter, you will be surprised to see many people on the street wearing surgical masks, or *masuku*. No, they aren't surgeons! They wear these cotton masks to prevent the spread of germs. They might appear bizarre to you at first, but remember their motive and be grateful for their thoughtfulness!

The Least You Need to Know

- The Japanese number for medical emergencies is 119, not 911!
- Body-part words are essential in daily conversations, too.
- Master the pattern *[Body part]-ga ita-i-N-desu,* "X hurts."
- Be familiar with the words for basic medicines.
- Pharmacies in town sell only over-the-counter drugs. So if a doctor gives you a prescription, you must purchase the medicine right there at the doctor's office.

Chapter 24

I Lost My Wallet! Nonmedical Emergencies

In This Chapter

◆ Important facts for your safety

◆ Reporting a lost or stolen item

◆ Use of "if"

◆ Describing an activity in the past

◆ What to do when you get lost on the street

I know you are a wise traveler, but no matter how careful you are, unexpected things can happen, such as getting sick (discussed in Chapter 23). In this chapter, I will talk about other kinds of emergencies like lost articles or theft. I'm sure that your trip will be safe and fun, but this chapter is just for your peace of mind.

Safety Facts and Japanese Police

Japan is quite a safe country. The crime rate is very low compared with that in many Western countries. You can walk alone at night in downtown Tokyo without worrying about being robbed or attacked. Public transportation is also safe and clean, so getting around town is a piece of cake.

One unique thing contributing to community safety in Japan is the presence of KOBAN (pronounced *kōbaN*), or "community police stands." A *kōbaN* is a small house-like building where two or three police officers are stationed and patrol the neighboring community.

You can report any matters such as theft, lost articles, or criminal offences you might have witnessed at a nearby *kōbaN*. For travelers, a *kōbaN* is especially helpful when you get lost and want to find your destination. Huge local maps are available there. The officers know the area very well. If your destination is near, she or he will even take you there!

There is a sign written in romanized characters, KOBAN, so you can't miss the nearest police office.

(Photo courtesy Agency for Cultural Affairs of Japan)

When you have a nonmedical emergency and need immediate attention, you should call the police. The phone number is 110. It is not 911. Also remember, as noted in Chapter 23, you should dial 119 for a medical emergency or fire.

Lifesavers

There are two phone numbers at which you can talk with the police in English:

Police (General Information in English): 03-3501-0110

Police Foreign Language Hotline: 03-3503-8484

The 03 is the area code for the City of Tokyo. If you're calling within Tokyo, dial without 03.

Because I introduced a few police-related words, let me list some more:

police	*kēsatsu*
police station	*kēsatsusho*
police officer	*kēkaN* or *omawarisaN*
police car	*patokā*

Just in case you experience any trouble, I want to make sure that you can speak or understand enough to have the problem taken care of. In the following sections, I will talk about three possible emergencies:

Huh?

The word *omawarisaN* is an informal and frequently used term for a police officer. This literally means "a person who patrols."

◆ You lost something.

◆ Your belonging was stolen.

◆ You got lost in town.

Lost and Found

The word for a "lost article" is *otoshimono*. What kinds of belongings are you likely to lose while walking? Here are some possible items:

wallet; purse	*saifu*
passport	*pasupōto*
credit card	*kurejitto kādo*
ticket (for theater)	*chiketto*

ticket (for transportation)	*kippu*
camera	*kamera*
handbag	*haNdobaggu*
bag	*baggu* or *kabaN*
jacket	*jaketto* or *uwagi*
hat	*bōshi*
umbrella	*kasa*
sunglasses	*saN gurasu*
eyeglasses	*megane*
ring	*yubiwa*
pen	*peN*
wrist watch	*tokē*
day planner	*techō*
electronic organizer	*deNshi techō*
cellular phone	*kētai deNwa* or *kētai*
laptop computer	*nōto pasokoN*

If you lost something on the street, I suggest that you go to a nearby police stand (*kōbaN*) or police station (*kēsatsu*). On the other hand, if you lost something in a public place such as a train station (*eki*), department store (*depāto*), or theater (*gekijō*), the place to go is an information booth. (There is hardly any place called "Lost and Found" in Japan.) The word for "information booth" is either *aNnaijo* or *iNfomēshoN*.

You should tell the police officer or information officer that you lost, say, your wallet:

Track 24
CD-1

> *Saifu-o otoshi-mashita.* "I lost my wallet."

Then ask her or him whether it has been reported to the station or booth:

Track 24
CD-2

> *Koko-ni ki-te i-maseN ka?* "Hasn't it been reported here?"
> (*ki-te i-masu* = [*Lit.*] "has come")

She or he might ask you what your wallet looks like:

> *DoNna saifu-desu ka?* "What kind of wallet is it?"

Suppose that your wallet is a black, leather one.

> *Kuro-i kawa-no saifu-desu.* "It's a black leather wallet." (*kawa* = "leather")

Does this answer sound familiar? Yes, in Chapter 12 you learned how to describe a noun in terms of color and size. Now, given the following description, describe the lost article, using the preceding answer as a template. You can find all the description items in Appendix B. As usual, the answers are given at the end of this chapter.

Huh? _____

The word for "leather" is *kawa*. Because it is a noun, when it describes the noun *saifu* ("wallet"), it must be marked by *-no*, as in *kawa-no saifu*.

Exercise 1

1. "It's a red cloth bag."
   ("cloth" = *nuno*)

   _____

2. "It's a blue American passport."

   _____

3. "It's a small Nikon camera."
   ("*Nikon*" = *nikoN*)

   _____

4. "It's a ticket for the Bullet Train."

   _____

5. "It's a white, small day planner."

   _____

If they have your wallet, their answer will be …

> *Hai, ari-masu yo.*   "Yes, we have it."

If not, unfortunately, it will be …

> *SumimaseN, ari-maseN (nē).*
> "No, we don't."

Even if the wallet is yours, they won't give it to you unless you prove that it's yours. They might ask you a question that only the real owner of the wallet would be able to answer:

**Track 24
CD-3**

> *Saifu-ni-wa nani-ga hait-te i-masu ka?*
> "What is in the wallet?" (*hait-te i-masu* = "be put [in]")

Huh? _____

Besides leather (*kawa*) and cloth (*nuno*), here are other common materials:

vinyl	*binīru*
plastic	*purasuchikku*
rubber	*gomu*
gold	*kiN*
silver	*giN*
aluminum	*aruminiumu*
metal	*kiNzoku*

Your answer should be as specific as possible. Suppose that your wallet contains your driver's license and a Citibank credit card:

Track 24
CD-4

> *MeNkyoshō-to Shitī BaNku-no kurejitto kādo-ga hait-te i-masu.*

Here are the words for items commonly found in one's wallet:

driver's license	*meNkyoshō*
international driver's license	*kokusai meNkyoshō*
photograph	*shashiN*
credit card	*kurejitto kādo*
business card	*mēshi*
ID card	*mibuNshōmēshō*
money	*okane*

Now look at your own bag. What do you find in your bag? Write down your answer using the preceding sentence pattern:

Answer: _____

Other than the identification question seen previously, the police or information officer might also ask you basic questions such as your name, address, age, and occupation. Refer to Chapter 23, where these words are listed, for a review.

If ... Then

If, unfortunately, you cannot find your wallet, leave your phone number so that they will be able to contact you when they receive it. Let's learn how to say "Please call me when (*or* if) you find it."

> *Mitsukari-mashita ra deNwa shi-te kudasai.*   "When (*or* If) you find it, then please
> (*mitsukari-masu* = "find")   call me."

Lifesavers

As mentioned in Chapter 22, pronouncing telephone numbers is easy. Just pronounce each digit separately and use *no* for each hyphen.

Notice that the word *ra* follows the past tense of the verb, as in *mitsukari-mashita ra,* "when you find it, then." *Ra* literally means "when/if ... then." Here are some more examples of *ra.*

> *Yamamoto-saN-ga ki-mashita ra shirase-te kudasai.*
> "When Ms. Yamamoto comes, then please let me know."
> (*shirase-masu* = "inform")

Tanaka-saN-ga kaeri-mashita <u>ra</u> oshie-te kudasai.   "When Ms. Tanaka comes home, then please tell me."
(*kaeri-masu* = "come/go home")

Let's practice the *ra* pattern. Translate the following sentences.

Exercise 2

1. "When I arrive at the hotel, then I will call you." ("arrive at X" = *X-ni tsuki-masu)*

   _____

2. "If it rains, then I will not go." ("it rains" = *ame-ga furi-masu)*

   _____

3. "If there is a ticket (available), then I want to go." ("there is X" = *X-ga ari-masu;* "want to VERB" = *Verb Stem + ta-i-N-desu ga")*

   _____

Theft!

As I mentioned at the beginning of this chapter, Japan is a relatively safe country, but this doesn't mean it is completely crime free. There is still a chance you might encounter a pickpocket (*suri*) when you walk in a crowded place like a shopping center or ride a packed train. Also, don't leave your luggage unattended, to avoid a baggage thief (*okibiki*).

Imagine this scenario. After you leave a department store, you notice that your purse or wallet, which was in your backpack, is gone! So you go to a nearby police stand, or *kōbaN*, to talk with a police officer (*kēkaN*). Now, let's take a look at a likely conversation between you and the police officer step by step.

Huh? _____

Here are the words for other theft crimes:

stealing (general term)
dorobō or *nusumi*

purse snatching   *hittakuri*

robbery   *gōtō*

shoplifting   *maNbiki*

Like a medical doctor, the officer will ask you what brought you there. Do you remember the expression?

Dō shi-mashita ka?   "What is the problem?"

**Track 24
CD-5**

You want to tell the officer that your wallet was stolen. An important expression you should know is …

XYZ-o nusumare-mashita.   "My XYZ was stolen."

In this case, you should say:

> *Saifu-o nusumare-mashita.* "My purse was stolen."

Other than basic questions about your identification, which have just been mentioned, the officer will ask you *where* it was stolen. Now, can you answer the following question? Suppose the name of the department store you were at is Mitsukoshi Department Store in Ginza:

> Officer: *Doko-de nusumare-mashita ka?* "Where was it stolen?"
> You: _____

How did you do? The answer is …

> You: *GiNza-no Mitsukoshi Depāto-* "It was stolen at the Mitsukoshi Department
> *de nusumare-mashita.* Store in Ginza."

The officer will then ask you the following question. Can you figure out what he is asking?

> Officer: *Itsu-desu ka?*

Yes, good job! The word *itsu* means "when." You think it happened about 2 o'clock.

> You: *Ni-ji-goro-desu.* "Around 2 o'clock."
> (*goro*= "around")

Because this incident happened in the department store, the next likely question will be on what floor it happened. The counter for "floor" is *-kai*. Look at the following counter chart for "floors." Irregular pronunciation is indicated in bold.

Counters for "Floor" (*-kai*)

1st floor	**ik-kai**
2nd floor	*ni-kai*
3rd floor	*saN-kai*
4th floor	*yoN-kai*
5th floor	*go-kai*
6th floor	**rok-kai**
7th floor	*nana-kai*
8th floor	**hak-kai**
9th floor	*kyū-kai*
10th floor	**juk-kai**
11th floor	**jū ik-kai**
What floor?	*naN-kai*

If you think it happened on the seventh floor, a dialog between the officer and you should look like this:

Lifesavers _____

Refer to Chapter 18 for more information on the floor setting of a department store.

> Officer: *NaN-kai-desu ka?*   "Which floor?"
>
> You: *Nana-kai-desu.*   "Seventh floor."

What Were You *Doing* That Time?

The officer might be curious about what you were doing at that time. Suppose that you *were browsing* the bookstore. Here is another important pattern, an expression that allows you to say "I *was doing* so-and-so." (It's a past progressive pattern, technically speaking.) Note that this pattern makes use of the *TE*-form:

> *-te i-mashita.*   "was doing -"

Huh? _____

Of course, the progressive pattern can be used for the present tense as well.

> *-te i-masu*   "is doing"

An example is:

> Q: *Ima, nani-o shi-te i-masu ka?*   "What are you doing now?"
> A: *Terebi-o mi-te i-masu.*   "I'm watching TV."

A typical dialog regarding this question might resemble the following:

> Officer: *Nani-o shi-te i-mashita ka?*   "What were you doing (then)?"
>
> You: *HoN-o mi-te i-mashita.*   "I was looking at books."

Let's practice this past progressive pattern.

Exercise 3

Translate both questions and answers into Japanese. Use Appendix B for help with vocabulary.

1. Q: What were you doing yesterday?

   _____

   A: I was sleeping all day. ("all day" = *ichinichijū*)

   _____

2. Q: What were you doing from 1:00 to 2:00 today?

   _____

   A: I was studying Japanese!

   _____

After a series of questions, a police officer or information officer will ask for your contact address or phone number:

contact person	_reNrakusaki_
contact address	_reNrakusaki-no jūsho_
contact phone number	_reNrakusaki-no deNwa baNgō_

Well, I suppose rather than memorizing all these expressions, it might be more efficient to just be cautious when traveling!

Help! I Think I'm Lost!

Do you have a good sense of direction? If you don't, you will need to pay extra attention when traveling in Japan not only because of language barriers but also because many signs are written only in Japanese.

Green Tea Break

In Western countries, addresses are given in reference to a street such as 345 Baker Street. So once you find Baker Street, it's easy to find the house because it is _on_ the street. The Japanese address system is not based on reference to a street. Instead, it is area-based, for example:

Tokyo	"Tokyo"
Shinjuku-ku	"Shinjuku District"
Kita-machi 700	"Kita Town 700"

This "700" could be in the middle or at the end of the _Kita_ area. Before you visit someone's house, make sure that you ask her or him to draw a map for you!

In Chapter 15, you learned how to ask for directions. In this section, we will look at the same issue from a different angle. Suppose that you get lost somewhere in a busy town. You want to go to your destination, but you don't have time to ask people for detailed directions.

You know how to ask where a certain thing is ...

Track 24
CD-14

   XYZ-wa doko-desu ka?   "Where is XYZ?"

Using this pattern, you can ask where you are now:

Track 24
CD-15

> *Koko-wa doko-desu ka?* "Where am I?"
> (*koko* = "here")

Or you can say that you are lost:

Track 24
CD-16

> *Michi-ni mayoi-mashita!* "I'm lost!"

If you are truly desperate, the following sentence might also be appropriate:

Track 24
CD-17

> *SumimaseN, chotto komatte i-masu.* "Excuse me, I'm in trouble."
> (*komatte i-masu* = "be in trouble")

Okay, maybe you are not that desperate. Perhaps you still want to find the way out on your own. Good for you! However, even if that's the case, I think it's wise to ask whether your destination is near or far away from where you are now.

Track 24
CD-18–19

> *Chika-idesu ka?* "Is it near?"
> *Tō-idesu ka?* "Is it far away?"

If it is near but seems hard to get to by yourself, try the following question:

Track 24
CD-20

> *SumimaseN, tsure-te it-te kudasai maseN ka?* "Excuse me, but could you please take
> (*tsure-te iki-masu* = "take [someone]")   me there?"

If your destination is far away, why don't you ask her or him to draw you a map?

Track 24
CD-21

> *SumimaseN, chizu-o kai-te kudasai maseN ka?* "Excuse me, could you draw a map
> (*chizu* = "map")   for me?"

CAUTION **Lifesavers** _____

If you desperately need help and need to communicate in English, you can count on the free telephone consultation service called Japan Helpline. The following telephone number is toll-free (only within Japan):

Japan Helpline: 0120-46-1997

The number 0120 is equivalent to 800 in the United States. Numbers beginning with 0120 are toll-free (*furī daiaru*, "free dial").

There is an online help service operated by a nonprofit organization called jhelp.com:

www.jhelp.com

This site also provides a number of useful telephone numbers.

Because this is a Japanese textbook, I encourage you to use Japanese, but if you are seriously in need of help, use the wild card:

Track 24
CD-22

Ēgo-ga hanase-masu ka? "Do you speak English?" (*hanase-masu* = "can speak")

> **Shortcuts to Success**
>
> Because English is a mandatory subject in junior high school and senior high school (six years total), many Japanese people understand basic English. However, because speaking and listening are not emphasized in school, you might want to either speak English slowly and clearly or even write down your questions.

Having read this chapter and Chapter 23, I bet you are well prepared and worry free. Enjoy your stay in Japan. And remember, when something unexpected happens, don't panic. Panicking makes you forget all the Japanese expressions you have learned. Only a calm state of mind will help you in an emergency!

Answers

Exercise 1

1. "It's a red cloth bag."

   Aka-i nuno-no kabaN-desu.

2. "It's a blue American passport."

   Ao-i Amerika-no pasupōto-desu.

3. "It's a small *Nikon* camera."

   Chīsa-i nikoN-no kamera-desu.

4. "It's a ticket for the Bullet Train."

   ShiNkaNseN-no kippu-desu.

5. "It's a small, white day planner."

   Shiro-i chīsa-i techō-desu.

Exercise 2

Track 24
CD-23–24

1. "When I arrive at the hotel, then I will call you."

   Hoteru-ni tsuki-mashita ra deNwa shi-masu.

2. "If it rains, then I will not go."

   Ame-ga furi-mashita ra iki-maseN.

3. "If there is a ticket (available), then I want to go."

   Chiketto-ga ari-mashita ra iki-tai-N-desu ga …

Exercise 3

1. Q: *Kinō, nani-o shi-te i-mashita ka?*

   A: *Ichinichijū ne-te i-mashita.*

2. Q: *Kyō, ichi-ji-kara ni-ji-made nani-o shi-te i-mashita ka?*

   A: *NihoNgo-o beNkyō shi-te i-mashita!*

The Least You Need to Know

◆ A *kōbaN* is a community police box. You can report any lost articles or crime. You can also use a *kōbaN* when you need directions.

◆ When you are in trouble, remain calm so that you can tell people exactly what's happened.

◆ Be able to describe a past event using *–te imashita*, "I was doing X."

◆ The word *-ra* ("if") broadens your language capability.

◆ When you are seriously in need of help, don't hesitate to count on English. *Ēgo-ga hanase-masu ka?* ("Do you speak English?") is a handy expression. When you speak English to Japanese people, speak slowly and clearly.

Chapter 25

Making Complaints

In This Chapter

- ◆ Dealing with poor services at a hotel, restaurant, and shop
- ◆ How to make a complaint
- ◆ Making a request without being blunt

I have mentioned from time to time throughout this book that Japanese people tend to not show their emotions in public, especially frustration or anger. This does not mean, however, that the Japanese are always content and never make complaints. They do complain when necessary. While you are in Japan, you might encounter some inconveniences or frustrating circumstances. In this chapter, I will teach you how to make complaints without being blunt
or offending people.

As a traveler or business person, the following are likely settings in which you might have to make a complaint:

- ◆ Hotels
- ◆ Restaurants
- ◆ Shops

Let's look at each one and learn some useful complaint expressions.

Staying at a Not-So-Great Hotel

Not everyone stays in a luxurious, five-star hotel when traveling. If your travel budget is tight, the first thing cut is probably the accommodation budget. Inconveniences are likely to occur at an economy hotel. Let's suppose that you are staying at a so-so hotel and are facing various inconveniences.

Room-Related Problems

You come back to your room at the end of the day and you notice that the room has not been cleaned. You should call the operator, or *furoNto*. This word is a shortened form of *furoNto desuku*, the front desk. Call him or her and say your room number first. Saying your room number is just like saying telephone numbers—pronounce each digit separately. Make sure that your room number is followed by *-gōshitsu*. If your room number is #423, say:

Track 25
CD-1

> *Moshi moshi, yoN ni saN-gōshitsu-desu ga …*   "Hello, this is #423 …"

Tell him or her the room is not clean:

> *Heya-ga yogore-te i-masu.*   "The room is not clean."
> (*heya* = "room"; *yogore-te i-masu* "is dirty")

Or you can say that there has not been maid service yet:

> *Mēdo sābisu-gamada-desu ga …*   "There has not been any maid service yet …"
> (*mada* = "not yet")

As explained in Chapters 11 and 16, the phrase *mada* ("not yet") is very useful when you want to mention that something is not done or ready.

Huh? _____

The opposite of *mada* ("not yet") is *mō* ("already"). See these words in action in the following dialog:

Q: *Mō tabe-mashita ka?*   "Did you eat already?"
A: *Mada-desu.*   "Not yet."

Track 25
CD-2

Here is how you ask for maid service. Yes, use the familiar *onegai shimasu*:

> *Mēdo sābisu-o onegai shimasu.*   "Maid service, please."

If something in your room is broken, the following pattern will be useful:

XYZ-ga koware-te i-masu.   "XYZ is broken."

An example would be …

Terebi-ga koware-te i-masu.   "The TV is broken."

Here's a list of things that can break in your hotel room:

TV	*terebi*
radio	*rajio*
clock	*tokē*
alarm	*arāmu*
air conditioner	*eakoN*
heater	*hītā*
shower	*shawā*
toilet	*toire*
bathtub	*basutabu*
hair dryer	*doraiyā*
refrigerator	*rēzōko*
lamp	*raNpu*
lightbulb	*deNkyū*
door	*doa*
lock	*kagi*
window	*mado*
bed	*beddo*
water faucet	*jaguchi*
sink	*nagashi*
table	*tēburu*
chair	*isu*
desk	*tsukue*
closet	*kurōzetto*

> **CAUTION**
>
> **Lifesavers**
>
> Another expression for "broken" is *koshō shi-te i-masu*—"is out of order."

The word for "fix; repair" is *naoshi-masu.* Say the following when you want someone to come fix it:

Naoshi-ni ki-te kudasai.   "Please come fix it."

Green Tea Break

One of the items in the list is *eakoN*. This is a shortened form of *ea koNdishonā*. Japanese people are crazy about shortening words, especially loan words. Here are some more examples:

"personal computer"   *pasokoN* (shortened from *p<u>ā</u>sonaru <u>koN</u>pyūtā*)

"car navigator"   *kānabi* (shortened from *kā <u>nabi</u>gētā*)

"digital camera"   *dejikame* (shortened from *<u>deji</u>taru <u>kame</u>ra*)

Remember that *-te kudasai* is a pattern used when making a request.

In Chapter 12, you learned a more formal pattern, as seen here:

Naoshi-ni ki-te kudasai maseN ka?   "Could you please come fix it?"

Because you're making a complaint here, *-te kudasai maseN ka* would sound "too" polite. Here is another useful pattern that is less formal than *-te kudasai maseN ka* but more appropriate than *-te kudasai* in this particular circumstance:

-Te kure maseN ka?   "Would you do so-and-so for me?"

With this pattern, "Please come fix it" would be …

Naoshi-ni ki-te kure maseN ka?   "Would you come fix it for me?"

Let's stick to this pattern for the rest of this section.

Rather than fixing it, you could ask him or her to replace it:

Torikae-te kure maseN ka?   "Would you replace it?"
(*torikae-masu* = "replace")

What if there is an amenity that is supposed to be in your room, but isn't? Here is a list of typical hotel room amenities:

soap	*sekkeN*
shampoo	*shaNpū*
conditioner	*riNsu*
toothbrush	*haburashi*
toothpaste	*hamigaki*
shower cap	*shawā kyappu*
bath towel	*basu taoru*
facial towel	*taoru*

Track 25
CD-4

Track 25
CD-5

extra towel	*kae-no taoru*
comb	*kushi*
razor	*kamisori*
shaving cream	*shēbu kurīmu*
body lotion	*rōshoN*
hair brush	*hea burashi*
sewing set	*saihō setto*
laundry bag	*seNtakubukuro*
iron	*airoN*
ironing board	*airoN dai*
hanger	*haNgā*

Tell the front desk operator that you don't have, say, shampoo, and you want some brought to your room:

Track 25
CD-6–7

> *ShaNpū-ga ari-maseN.*   "There is no shampoo."
> (*ari-masu* = "there is")

> *Mot-te ki-te kure maseN ka?*   "Would you bring it to me?"
> (*mot-te ki-masu* = "bring")

Other Problems

Let's look at some other hotel-related complaints. Suppose that you ordered room service for breakfast, and you've been waiting for half an hour. Let's let the front desk operator know:

> *Rūmu sābisu-o tanomi-mashita ga, mada ki-maseN.*   "I requested room service, but it
> (*tanomi-masu* = "to request")   hasn't come yet."

Notice that the handy *mada* ("not yet") is used here again.

Noises are another common complaint. I remember staying in a cheap hotel once. I realized when I lay down to sleep that my room was sandwiched between groups of high school basketball players! They were partying and playing at all hours of the night! Sound familiar? I think you can easily imagine how irritating that could be. In such a case, you should call the front desk and hope that they will take care of the problem. This might not always solve the problem, but it's worth a try!

> *Tonari-no heya-ga urusa-i-N-desu ga ...*   "The (room) next door is noisy ..."
> (*tonari* = "next door")

Huh?

The adjective *urusa-i* ("noisy") can also be used for "Shut up!" Because the emphasis is placed on *sa*, as in *uru<u>sa</u>i*, it sounds like *SAi!*

If you want to tell people nicely to be quiet, use the following phrase:

> *SumimaseN ga, shizuka-ni shi-te kure maseN ka?*
> "Excuse me. Would you be quiet?"
> (*shizuka* = "quietness")

Before leaving this section, let's look at another important matter, an error on the bill. The word for "bill; invoice" is *sēkyūsho*. If you find a discrepancy on your bill, bring it to the appropriate person's attention!

> *Sēkyūsho-ga machigat-te i-maseN ka?*   "Isn't there an error on the bill?"

The verb *machigat-te i-masu* literally means "incorrect." What if you got the bill for a different room?

> *Watashi-no heya-no-jana-idesu.*   "This is not my room's."

For other important hotel-related matters, refer to Chapter 16.

Inconveniences at a Restaurant

Besides satisfying your appetite, one of the reasons for dining out is convenience: You don't have to go grocery shopping or cook or wash dishes. So you are buying a service at a restaurant; however, you might occasionally come across a restaurant that does not give you adequate service. In this section, we will look at common problems you might experience at a restaurant and learn how to make a complaint. Remember, because you are buying a service, it's perfectly okay to make a complaint! But let's learn how to do so in a polite way.

I am sure that you have experienced waiting for your food for what seems like an eternity! Here is a useful expression you can say to the waitress or waiter:

Shortcuts to Success

Making a complaint is a tough task because you might fear offending people. Try to say the "magic" word *sumimaseN* at the beginning of your sentence. You will be amazed at how effectively this little word softens the tone of your speech.

> *Watashi-no ryōri-wa mada-desu ka?*
> "Is my food coming yet?"

Track 25
CD-10

Of course, you can make your complaint more specific:

> *SaN-jup-puN mae-ni chūmoN shi-mashita ga ...*   "I ordered 30 minutes ago."
> (*mae-ni* = "ago")

You are dining with your friends. Everyone is served but you, and they are waiting for your food to arrive. Even though this is not at all your fault, I'm sure that you feel guilty because it makes your friends uncomfortable to start eating without you! To avoid this, you might want to make the following request when placing an order:

> *MiNna issho-ni mot-te ki-te kudasai.*
> "Please bring everything together."
> (*miNna* = "everything"; *issho-ni* = "together")

What if the waitress or waiter brings something you didn't order? Here is how to say "I didn't order this!" The word for "to order" is *chūmoN shi-masu.*

Track 25
CD-11

> *SumimaseN, kore-wa chūmoN shi-te i-maseN ga ...*   "Excuse me. I didn't order this, but ..."

Green Tea Break
Nowadays—particularly in Western-style restaurants or bars—instead of *chūmoN shi-masu* ("to order"), you can use the loan word *ōdā shi-masu.* This is used mostly among young people.

Just like Western countries, a good, reputable restaurant in Japan (serving Japanese or non-Japanese cuisines) is hard to get into without a reservation. Let's say that you made a reservation on the phone and got there at the specified time, 6 P.M. However, because of their mistake, they did not have your table ready. How would you convey your frustration to them?

> *Machigainaku, roku-ji-ni yoyaku-o shi-mashita kedo ...*   "I'm absolutely sure I made a reservation for 6 P.M.!"
> (*machigainaku* = "I'm absolutely sure"; *yotaku* = "reservation")

To make your argument even more convincing, mention the name of the person who received your reservation request:

> *Tanaka-saN-ni onegai shi-mashita ga ...*
> "I asked Ms./Mr. Tanaka to take care of my reservation, but ..."

Huh?
The sentence-final particle *kedo* literally means "but." Use this particle when you are in disagreement with the listener. For example, in *Machigainaku, roku-ji-ni yoyaku-o shi-mashita kedo ...* ("I'm absolutely sure I made a reservation for 6 P.M.!"), you are in disagreement with the restaurant receptionist's assumption that you did not make a reservation.

Lifesavers

When you make a business call, it is a good habit to ask who you are talking with, so you can later refer to that person by name. Be sure you ask politely:

SumimaseN ga, o-namae-o itadake-masu ka?
"Excuse me, but may I have your name?"
(*itadake-masu* = "can receive")

Refer to Chapter 19 for other important restaurant-related matters, such as placing an order.

Although we have looked at several problematic scenarios, it is comforting to know that overall service in Japan is excellent. You will probably not encounter any major problems.

Shopping-Related Problems

When you get into the refund-and-return aspect of shopping, it can be frustrating. Because you are visiting Japan, all such problems related to your purchases must be resolved before leaving the country!

Damaged Items

Now you've bought a camera. You left the store and opened the box, only to find that the camera is broken. You must return it to the shop and express that it is broken:

Kore-o kai-mashita ga, koware-te i-masu.   "I bought this, but it's broken."
(*koware-te i-masu* = "is broken")

Besides *koware-te i-masu* ("is broken"), here are some more words for "defects":

torn (fabric)	*yabure-te i-masu*
does not function/work	*ugoki-maseN*
broken (plates, glasses)	*ware-te i-masu*
manufacturer's defect	*furyōhiN-desu*
spoiled (food)	*itaN-de i-masu*
rotten (food)	*kusat-te i-masu*

Lifesavers

A warranty on products purchased in Japan, or *hoshōsho,* is usually good only within Japan. If you want your product covered in your home country, I suggest that you go to a designated duty-free shop. You can find duty-free shops in department stores and at the airport as well.

Do you want to buy a camera with a warranty? Then try Shinjuku if you are in Tokyo, and Nihonbashi if you are in Osaka. If you are looking for any electronics, try Akihabara in Tokyo. In Osaka, Nihonbashi is also the place for electronics.

To replace the broken camera with a new one, say the following:

Track 25
CD-12

> *Atarashi-i no-to torikae-te kure maseN ka?*
> "Would you replace it with a new one?"
> (*atarashi-i* = "new", *no* = "one")

Don't forget to take the receipt with you! The word for "receipt" in Japanese is either *ryōshūsho* or *reshīto*.

Huh?

The phrase for "to return (merchandise)" is *heNpiN shi-masu*. A common expression would be ...

> *HeNpiN shi-tai-N-desu ga* ....
> "I want to return (this) ..."

This Is Not What I Bought!

What if they gave you something you didn't buy?

Track 25
CD-13

> *Kat-ta mono-to chigai-masu!*   "This is different from what I bought!"
> (*chigai-masu* = "different")

Even if it is the same product, it might be the wrong size:

Track 25
CD-14

> *Saizu-ga chigai-masu!*   "Wrong size!"
> (*chigai-masu* = "different; wrong")

Let me introduce an important expression here, which means "too [ADJECTIVE]":

> [*ADJECTIVE STEM*] + sugi-masu = "It is too [ADJECTIVE]."

For example, if the jacket you got is too big, say:

> *Ōki sugi-masu!*   "It is too big!"
> (*ōki* = "big" [derived from *ōki-i*])

Track 25
CD-15

If, on the other hand, it is too small, say:

> *Chīsa sugi-masu!*   "It is too small!"
> (*chīsa* = "small" [derived from *chīsa-i*])

Track 25
CD-16

Huh?

An adjective stem is one *without -i*. For example, the stem for *taka-i* ("expensive") is *taka*.

If they don't have a replacement item in stock, ask them to send it to you:

> *Okut-te kure maseN ka?*   "Would you send it to me?"
> (*okuri-masu* = "send")

Track 25
CD-17

Because competition among retail stores is so fierce, Japanese shops are famous for quality customer service. I am sure that they will send it to you by express delivery at no cost to you!

Green Tea Break

The word for "customer service" is *afutā sābisu,* a Japanized loan word ("after service"). I guess this means that the Japanese provide good service to a customer even *after* the purchase.

We have looked at only three situations, but I am sure that you can apply the same principles to other situations. Don't be too hesitant to complain when you believe you are right. You pay for services, and you deserve satisfaction. They will listen to you, I promise. In Japan, the customer is treated as a "god." There is a phrase to express this sentiment: *Okyakusama-wa kamisama-desu!* "Customers are gods!"

So you are almighty!

The Least You Need to Know

- Don't hesitate to complain when the situation requires. You deserve the best possible customer service!

- *X-ga mada-desu ga* ("X hasn't come yet") is a handy phrase to use when you wait too long for the service you requested.

- Know how to make a complaint without offending people. When you must make a request, *-Te kuremaseN ka?* is a handy expression, which is neither too rude nor too polite.

- Be familiar with basic words for problems, such as *Koware-te i-masu* ("It's broken") and *Kat-ta mono-to chigai-masu!* ("This is different from what I bought!").

- Be familiar with the pattern Adjective Stem + *sugi-masu* ("It's too X"), as in *Chīsa sugi-masu!* ("It's too small!")

Appendix

Written Japanese: A Brief Introduction

There are two kinds of writing systems in Japanese, *kana* (syllable characters) and *kanji* (Chinese characters). *Kana* represents Japanese syllables. Remember that Japanese has 102 possible syllables (see Chapter 3). Each syllable has its corresponding *kana*. That is, *kana* can represent any Japanese sound. For example, the Japanese word *kawa*, which consists of two syllables (*ka* and *wa*), can be represented by two *kana* characters, as in かわ.

Kana is useful, but the problem with this system is that it only represents syllable sounds, not meanings. For example, *kawa* has two meanings in Japanese, "river" and "skin," but the *kana* representation of this word, namely かわ, does not distinguish the meanings.

Kanji, or Japanized Chinese characters, resolve this shortcoming of *kana*. The *kanji* for *kawa*, "river," is 川, and the *kanji* for *kawa*, "skin," is 皮. *Kanji* provides both sound and meaning.

Japanese speakers mix both *kana* and *kanji* systems in written Japanese. For example, if a Japanese newspaper were written entirely in *kana*, it would be difficult for readers because of the many possible synonyms. However, by using *kanji* characters where appropriate, writers can ensure that readers can read the newspaper without ambiguity.

In the sections that follow, I will introduce the complete set of kana and briefly discuss the *kanji* system.

Kana

As mentioned, *kana* represents Japanese syllables. *Kana* includes two subsystems, *hiragana* and *katakana*. *Hiragana* characters represent native Japanese words such as *omoshiroi*, "interesting," *kotoba*, "language," and so on. On the other hand, *katakana* characters represent (1) foreign words such as *kamera*, "camera," *waiN*, "wine," and so on and (2) sound mimics such as *nyānyā* "meow," *bataN*, "slam!" and so on. First, let's look at hiragana.

Hiragana: For Native Japanese Words

In Chapter 3 we learned that Japanese has 102 syllables. Here are all of the syllables with their corresponding *hiragana*.

Hiragana

	ø	k	s	t	n	h	m	y	r	w
a	あ	か	さ	た	な	は	ま	や	ら	わ
	a	*ka*	*sa*	*ta*	*na*	*ha*	*ma*	*ya*	*ra*	*wa*
i	い	き	し	ち	に	ひ	み		り	
	i	*ki*	*shi*	*chi*	*ni*	*hi*	*mi*		*ri*	
u	う	く	す	つ	ぬ	ふ	む	ゆ	る	
	u	*ku*	*su*	*tsu*	*nu*	*fu*	*mu*	*yu*	*ru*	
e	え	け	せ	て	ね	へ	め		れ	
	e	*ke*	*se*	*te*	*ne*	*he*	*me*		*re*	
o	お	こ	そ	と	の	ほ	も	よ	ろ	[を]*
	o	*ko*	*so*	*to*	*no*	*ho*	*mo*	*yo*	*ro*	*(o)*

*The character [を] (o) is a special grammatical marker that indicates a direct object. For a full explanation of the grammatical function of this -o, see Chapter 4.

	g	z	d	b	p
a	が	ざ	だ	ば	ぱ
	ga	*za*	*da*	*ba*	*pa*
i	ぎ	じ	(ぢ)*	び	ぴ
	gi	*ji*	*(ji)*	*bi*	*pi*
u	ぐ	ず	(づ)*	ぶ	ぷ
	gu	*zu*	*(zu)*	*bu*	*pu*

	g	z	d		b	p
e	げ	ぜ	で		べ	ぺ
	ge	ze	de		be	pe
o	ご	ぞ	ど		ぼ	ぽ
	go	zo	do		bo	po

The characters ち and づ in parentheses are pronounced exactly the same as じ (ji) and ず (zu), respectively. These are classical characters and are hardly used in the contemporary Japanese writing system.

	ky	sh	ch	ny	hy	my	ry
a	きゃ	しゃ	ちゃ	にゃ	ひゃ	みゃ	りゃ
	kya	sha	cha	nya	hya	mya	rya
u	きゅ	しゅ	ちゅ	にゅ	ひゅ	みゅ	りゅ
	kyu	shu	chu	nyu	hyu	myu	ryu
o	きょ	しょ	ちょ	にょ	ひょ	みょ	りょ
	kyo	sho	cho	nyo	hyo	myo	ryo

	gy	j (= zy)		by	py
a	ぎゃ	じゃ		びゃ	ぴゃ
	gya	ja		bya	pya
u	ぎゅ	じゅ		びゅ	ぴゅ
	gyu	ju		byu	pyu
o	ぎょ	じょ		びょ	ぴょ
	gyo	jo		byo	pyo

Stand-Alone Consonants

Double consonant: っ *(smaller than* つ*)*

N: ん

You might have noticed that some characters are a little smaller in size than others. Y sounds such as *kya*, *myo*, and *byu* are written as きゃ, みょ, and びゅ, respectively. Even though these are written as two attached characters, these are all one-syllable sounds. The other small character is the double consonant sound っ (as opposed to つ). For example, *sotto*, "gently," should be written そっと.

It's important to remember that *hiragana* represents ordinary Japanese words—words such as *nihoN*, "Japan" (にほん), *sakana*, "fish" (さかな), *neko*, "cat" (ねこ), and *Fuji-saN*, "Mt. Fuji" (ふじさん). *Hiragana* is not used for sound effects or words imported from other languages.

Now let's do a couple of exercises. Using the preceding tables, convert the following words into *hiragana*. Remember, to convert to *hiragana*, you combine the symbols for each syllable. The answers are at the end of this appendix.

Exercise 1

Ex. "shoulder"	*kata*	かた	
1. "nose"	*hana*	_____	
2. "shoes"	*kutsu*	_____	
3. "kimono"	*kimono*	_____	
4. "head"	*atama*	_____	
5. "teacup"	*chawaN*	_____	
6. "dictionary"	*jisho*	_____	
7. "pencil"	*eNpitsu*	_____	
8. "telephone"	*deNwa*	_____	
9. "stamp"	*kitte*	_____	
10. "meal"	*shokuji*	_____	

How about trying it the other way around now? I'll list some well-known Japanese words in *hiragana*. Your task is to figure out what the words are.

Exercise 2

Ex. きもの	kimono	
1. てんぷら	_____	
2. すきやき	_____	
3. すし	_____	
4. つなみ	_____	
5. さけ	_____	
6. かぶき	_____	
7. からて	_____	
8. ふとん	_____	
9. ぜん	_____	
10. よこはま	_____	

Katakana: For Loan Words and Sound Mimics

Katakana is the other *kana* system. As *hiragana* is used to represent native Japanese vocabulary, *katakana* is used to represent foreign (particularly Western) words and sound mimics.

First, let's take a look at the *katakana* tables. You will notice that many *katakana* characters, such as カ (ka) and セ (se), resemble their *hiragana* counterparts, か and せ, respectively.

Katakana

	ø	k	s	t	n	h	m	y	r	w
a	ア	カ	サ	タ	ナ	ハ	マ	ヤ	ラ	ワ
	a	*ka*	*sa*	*ta*	*na*	*ha*	*ma*	*ya*	*ra*	*wa*
i	イ	キ	シ	チ	ニ	ヒ	ミ		リ	
	i	*ki*	*shi*	*chi*	*ni*	*hi*	*mi*		*ri*	
u	ウ	ク	ス	ツ	ヌ	フ	ム	ユ	ル	
	u	*ku*	*su*	*tsu*	*nu*	*fu*	*mu*	*yu*	*ru*	
e	エ	ケ	セ	テ	ネ	ヘ	メ		レ	
	e	*ke*	*se*	*te*	*ne*	*he*	*me*		*re*	
o	オ	コ	ソ	ト	ノ	ホ	モ	ヨ	ロ	
	o	*ko*	*so*	*to*	*no*	*ho*	*mo*	*yo*	*ro*	

	g	z	d	b	p
a	ガ	ザ	ダ	バ	パ
	ga	*za*	*da*	*ba*	*pa*
i	ギ	ジ	(ヂ)*	ビ	ピ
	gi	*ji*	*(ji)*	*bi*	*pi*
u	グ	ズ	(ヅ)*	ブ	プ
	gu	*zu*	*(zu)*	*bu*	*pu*
e	ゲ	ゼ	デ	ベ	ペ
	ge	*ze*	*de*	*be*	*pe*
o	ゴ	ゾ	ド	ボ	ポ
	go	*zo*	*do*	*bo*	*po*

The characters ヂ and ヅ in parentheses are pronounced exactly the same as ジ (ji) and ズ (zu), respectively. These are classical characters and are hardly used in the contemporary Japanese writing system.

	ky	sh	ch	ny	hy	my	ry
a	キャ	シャ	チャ	ニャ	ヒャ	ミャ	リャ
	kya	*sha*	*cha*	*nya*	*hya*	*mya*	*rya*
u	キュ	シュ	チュ	ニュ	ヒュ	ミュ	リュ
	kyu	*shu*	*chu*	*nyu*	*hyu*	*myu*	*ryu*
o	キョ	ショ	チョ	ニョ	ヒョ	ミョ	リョ
	kyo	*sho*	*cho*	*nyo*	*hyo*	*myo*	*ryo*

	gy	j (= zy)		by	py
a	ギャ	ジャ		ビャ	ピャ
	gya	*ja*		*bya*	*pya*
u	ギュ	ジュ		ビュ	ピュ
	gyu	*ju*		*byu*	*pyu*
o	ギョ	ジョ		ビョ	ピョ
	gyo	*jo*		*byo*	*pyo*

Stand-Alone Consonants

Double consonant: ッ *(smaller than* ツ*)*

N: ン

We find frequent use of loan words in Japanese daily life in areas like fashion, information technology, and entertainment such as movies and music. But don't forget food! Japanese people are crazy about eating foods from all over the world. They Japanize not only the tastes but also the names of foods.

In the following exercise, 10 international foods are given in *katakana*. Using the preceding tables, pronounce the words and try to figure out what they are. This may be a bit challenging, so I will give you a hint for each question by adding the name of the country the food comes from. The answers are at the end of this appendix.

In questions 8, 9, and 10, you'll see a new symbol, ー. This is a character for a long vowel, a convention seen only in *katakana*.

Exercise 3

   Ex. カラマリ (Spain)　　　　　　　"calamari"

    1. エスカルゴ (France)　　　　　_____

    2. エンチラダ (Mexico)　　　　　_____

    3. ペキンダック (China)　　　　　_____

    4. サンドイッチ (United Kingdom)　　_____

5. リングイニ (Italy)　　　　　_____

6. パエリア (Spain)　　　　　_____

7. キムチ (Korea)　　　　　_____

8. メープルシロップ (Canada)　_____

9. カレー (India)　　　　　_____

10. ハンバーガー (United States)　_____

Now, try the opposite. Can you convert the following place names into *katakana*? This is a more challenging task than the transcription you did in the *hiragana* section, because first you need to Japanize these loan words. For example, if you wanted to transcribe "France" into *katakana*, you would first need to Japanize it (*furaNsu*), then transcribe each syllable into *katakana*, as in フランス. The words used in the exercise are all relatively simple words, so you can transcribe them as they are pronounced in English.

Exercise 4

Ex. France	*furaNsu*	フランス
1. America	_____	_____
2. Canada	_____	_____
3. Poland	_____	_____
4. Morocco	_____	_____
5. Brazil	_____	_____
6. Florida	_____	_____
7. Spain	_____	_____
8. Monaco	_____	_____
9. Panama	_____	_____
10. Africa	_____	_____

Foreign words are written in *katakana*. You're now familiar with *katakana*, so why not try to write your name? Remember the steps: First Japanize your name, then transcribe it using *katakana*. Following are some common English names in *katakana*. I hope you find yours here!

Names in *Katakana*

Female Names			**Male Names**		
Alice	アリス	*(Arisu)*	Alex	アレックス	*(Arekkusu)*
Amy	エイミー	*(Eimī)*	Andy	アンディー	*(ANdi)*
Angela	アンジェラ	*(ANjera)*	Ben	ベン	*(BeN)*
Anne	アン	*(AN)*	Bill	ビル	*(Biru)*
Barbara	バーバラ	*(Bārbara)*	Bob	ボブ	*(Bobu)*
Carol	キャロル	*(Kyaroru)*	Chris	クリス	*(Kurisu)*
Christy	クリスティ	*(Kurisuti)*	Colin	コリン	*(KoriN)*
Cindy	シンディ	*(ShiNdi)*	David	デービッド	*(Dēbiddo)*
Diana	ダイアナ	*(Daiana)*	Derek	デレク	*(Dereku)*
Ellen	エレン	*(EreN)*	Ed	エド	*(Edo)*
Hanna	ハンナ	*(HaNna)*	Eric	エリック	*(Erikku)*
Julie	ジュリー	*(Jurī)*	George	ジョージ	*(Jōji)*
Kate	ケイト	*(Keito)*	Jack	ジャック	*(Jakku)*
Kathy	キャシー	*(Kyashī)*	Jim	ジム	*(Jimu)*
Laurie	ローリー	*(Rōrī)*	John	ジョン	*(JoN)*
Lisa	リサ	*(Risa)*	Ken	ケン	*(KeN)*
Mary	メアリー	*(Mearī)*	Mark	マーク	*(Māku)*
Meg	メグ	*(Megu)*	Mike	マイク	*(Maiku)*
Melissa	メリッサ	*(Merissa)*	Pete	ピート	*(Pīto)*
Paula	ポーラ	*(Pōra)*	Phil	フィル	*(Firu)*
Rebecca	レベッカ	*(Rebekka)*	Robert	ロバート	*(Robāto)*
Sammy	サミー	*(Samī)*	Sam	サム	*(Samu)*
Sandy	サンディ	*(SaNdi)*	Sean	ショーン	*(ShōN)*
Sara	サラ	*(Sara)*	Tim	ティム	*(Timu)*
Vanessa	バネッサ	*(Banessa)*	Tom	トム	*(Tomu)*

Lifesavers

In native Japanese vocabulary, the following sounds do not exist:

ti as in "<u>Ti</u>m" *fo* as in "<u>Fo</u>rd"
di as in "San<u>dy</u>" *she* as in "<u>She</u>lly"
fa as in "<u>Fa</u>ust" *che* as in "<u>Che</u>lsea"
fi as in "<u>Phi</u>l" *je* as in "<u>Je</u>n"
fe as in "<u>Fe</u>llini"

To transcribe these foreign sounds as accurately as possible, special notations are used in *katakana*:

ti	ティ as in ティム "Tim"
di	ディ as in サンディ "Sandy"
fa	ファ as in ファウスト "Faust"
fi	フィ as in フィル "Phil"
fe	フェ as in フェリーニ "Fellini"
fo	フォ as in フォード "Ford"
she	シェ as in シェリー "Shelly"
che	チェ as in チェルシー "Chelsea"
je	ジェ as in ジェン "Jen"

There are two characters combined to make one syllable. Note that the companion vowel such as イ should be written smaller, as in ィ.

Katakana also represents sound mimics. It's interesting to compare English sound mimics with their Japanese counterparts. You may be surprised how different the Japanese mimic sounds are.

English Sound Mimics	Japanese Sound Mimics
slam!	バタン！ *(bataN)*
tap tap	トントン *(toNtoN)*
ding-dong	ピンポーン *(piNpōN)*
cock-a-doodle-doo	コケコッコー *(kokekokkō])*
moo	モー *(mō)*
bowwow	ワンワン *(waNwaN)*
meow	ニャーニャー *(nyānyā)*
oink oink	ブーブー *(b⁻ub-u)*

Kanji

There is one last writing convention in Japanese, called kanji, or Japanized Chinese characters. As mentioned earlier, unlike kana, each kanji character represents not only a sound, but also a word meaning. For example, the character 山 is pronounced ya-ma and means "mountain." The beauty of kanji is that it is so visual you get the word meaning at first glance.

Kana actually evolved as a simplification of Chinese characters. This invention was brilliant, but the Japanese didn't abandon Chinese kanji characters even after the invention of kana; kanji were important to keep because of their convenience. As a result of not discarding kanji, written Japanese can express highly abstract ideas. This is great unless you're one of many young Japanese students having to memorize all the basic kanji! I remember taking hundreds and thousands of kanji quizzes when I was in school.

The Japanese Ministry of Education and Science says the mastery of a little fewer than 2,000 kanji characters would be sufficient to read more than 90 percent of daily Japanese words. Japanese publications, except children's books, are written in a combination of both kana and kanji. For example, with the recommended number of kanji, you will be able to read a Japanese newspaper without any difficulty.

Comprehensive coverage of kanji is beyond the scope of this book. Interested readers should refer to textbooks or exercise books available in bookstores. I recommend the following books for beginning learners of the Japanese writing system:

Henshall, K., and T. Takagaki. *A Guide to Learning Hiragana and Katakana*. Rutland, VT: Charles E. Tuttle Company, 1990.

Association for Japanese-Language Teaching, ed. *Japanese for Busy People—Kana Workbook*. New York: Kodansha International, 1996.

Henshall, K. *A Guide to Remembering Japanese Characters*. Rutland, VT: Charles E. Tuttle Company, 1988.

Foerster, A., and N. Tamura. *Kanji ABC: A Systematic Approach to Japanese Characters*. Rutland, VT: Charles E. Tuttle Company, 1994.

Answers

Exercise 1

1. "nose"	*hana*	はな
2. "shoes"	*kutsu*	くつ
3. "kimono"	*kimono*	きもの
4. "head"	*atama*	あたま
5. "teacup"	*chawaN*	ちゃわん
6. "dictionary"	*jisho*	じしょ
7. "pencil"	*eNpitsu*	えんぴつ
8. "telephone"	*deNwa*	でんわ
9. "stamp"	*kitte*	きって
10. "meal"	*shokuji*	しょくじ

Exercise 2

1. てんぷら   *tenpura* ("tempura")
2. すきやき   *sukiyaki*
3. すし   *sushi*
4. つなみ   *tsunami* (tidal wave)
5. さけ   *sake*
6. かぶき   *kabuki*
7. からて   *karate*
8. ふとん   *futoN* (futon)
9. ぜん   *zeN*
10. よこはま   *Yokohama*

Exercise 3

1. エスカルゴ   (France)   escargot
2. エンチラダ   (Mexico)   enchilada
3. ペキンダック   (China)   Peking duck
4. サンドイッチ   (United Kingdom)   sandwich
5. リングイニ   (Italy)   linguine
6. パエリア   (Spain)   paella
7. キムチ   (Korea)   kim chee
8. メープルシロップ   (Canada)   maple syrup
9. カレー   (India)   curry
10. ハンバーガー   (United States)   hamburger

Exercise 4

1. America   *Amerika*   アメリカ
2. Canada   *Kanada*   カナダ
3. Poland   *PōraNdo*   ポーランド
4. Morocco   *Morokko*   モロッコ
5. Brazil   *Burajiru*   ブラジル

6. Florida	*Furorida*	フロリダ
7. Spain	*SupeiN*	スペイン
8. Monaco	*Monako*	モナコ
9. Panama	*Panama*	パナマ
10. Africa	*Afurika*	アフリカ

English to Japanese Dictionary

This mini English-Japanese dictionary contains most of the words introduced in this book, as well as other frequently used basic words.

The English entries are listed in alphabetical order in the leftmost column. For each entry, its Japanese corresponding word or words are provided in romanized characters in the second column. When there are two Japanese words, they are divided by a semicolon (;).

The Japanese word or words in each entry are transcribed into Japanese *kana* characters in the rightmost column. For a more detailed explanation of *kana* characters, see Appendix A.

The *kanji* (Chinese characters) counterpart of a Japanese word is provided in square brackets [ ]. Note that not every Japanese word has a *kanji* counterpart. (For example, see the entry for "able.")

The Japanese characters in the rightmost column may be helpful when you need to let a Japanese speaker know which word you are referring to.

A

able	*deki-masu*	できます
above	*ue*	うえ［上］
absence	*yasumi*	やすみ［休み］
absent	*yasumi-masu*	やすみます［休みます］
accident	*jiko*	じこ［事故］
across	*mukō*	むこう［向こう］
address	*jūsho*	じゅうしょ［住所］
adult	*otona*	おとな［大人］
afraid	*kowa-i*	こわい［怖い］
after	*ato(de)*	あと（で）［後（で）］
afternoon	*gogo*	ごご［午後］
again	*mō ichido*	もう いちど［もう一度］
age	*toshi; neNrē*	とし［年］；ねんれい［年齢］
ago	*mae*	まえ［前］
ahead	*saki*	さき［先］
airplane	*hikōki*	ひこうき［飛行機］
airport	*kūkō*	くうこう［空港］
all	*zeNbu*	ぜんぶ［全部］
all day	*ichinichijū*	いちにちじゅう［一日中］
all night	*hitobaNjū*	ひとばんじゅう［一晩中］
all right	*i-i*	いい
almost	*hotoNdo*	ほとんど
already	*mō*	もう
although -	*- kedo*	～けど
always	*itsumo*	いつも
A.M.	*gozeN*	ごぜん［午前］
ambulance	*kyūkyūsha*	きゅうきゅうしゃ［救急車］
American people	*AmerikajiN*	アメリカじん［アメリカ人］
among -	*- no nakade*	～の なかで［～の中で］
animal	*dōbutsu*	どうぶつ［動物］

another	*betsu(no)*	べつ（の）［別（の）］
answer (verb)	*kotae-masu*	こたえます［答えます］
apple	*riNgo*	りんご
appointment	*yakusoku*	やくそく［約束］
April	*Shi-gatsu*	しがつ［四月］
arm	*ude*	うで［腕］
around	*mawari*	まわり
arrive	*tsuki-masu*	つきます［着きます］
ask	*kiki-masu*	ききます［聞きます］
August	*Hachi-gatsu*	はちがつ［八月］
aunt	*obasaN*	おばさん
autumn	*aki*	あき［秋］

B

baby	*akachaN*	あかちゃん［赤ちゃん］
back	*ushiro*	うしろ［後ろ］
back (body part)	*senaka*	せなか［背中］
bad	*waru-i*	わるい［悪い］
bag	*baggu; kabaN*	バッグ; かばん
bake	*yaki-masu*	やきます［焼きます］
bank	*giNkō*	ぎんこう［銀行］
barber shop	*tokoya*	とこや［床屋］
bath (tub)	*ofuro*	おふろ［お風呂］
bathroom (toilet)	*toire; otearai*	トイレ; おてあらい［お手洗い］
beard	*hige*	ひげ
beautiful	*utsukushi-i*	うつくしい［美しい］
beauty salon	*biyōiN*	びよういん［美容院］
become	*nari-masu*	なります
beer	*bīru*	ビール
before	*mae*	まえ［前］
begin	*hajime-masu*	はじめます［始めます］

behind	*ushiro*	うしろ［後ろ］
bend	*mage-masu*	まげます［曲げます］
best	*ichibaN*	いちばん［一番］
between - and -	*- to - no aida*	〜と〜の あいだ［〜と〜の間］
beverage	*nomimono*	のみもの［飲み物］
big	*ōki-i*	おおきい［大きい］
bill (invoice)	*sēkyūsho*	せいきゅうしょ［請求書］
bird	*tori*	とり［鳥］
birth date	*sēneNgappi*	せいねんがっぴ［生年月日］
birthday	*taNjōbi*	たんじょうび［誕生日］
black	*kuro-i*	くろい［黒い］
blanket	*mōfu*	もうふ［毛布］
blood	*chi*	ち［血］
blue	*ao-i*	あおい［青い］
body	*karada*	からだ［体］
book	*hoN*	ほん［本］
bookstore	*hoNya*	ほんや［本屋］
boring	*taikutsu(na)*	たいくつ（な）［退屈（な）］
born	*umare-masu*	うまれます［生まれます］
box	*hako*	はこ［箱］
boy	*otokonoko*	おとこのこ［男の子］
bread	*paN*	パン
break (destroy)	*kowashi-masu*	こわします［壊します］
breakfast	*asagohaN; chōshoku*	あさごはん［朝ご飯］；ちょうしょく［朝食］
bridge	*hashi*	はし［橋］
bright	*akaru-i*	あかるい［明るい］
bring (person)	*tsure-te ki-masu*	つれて きます［連れてきます］
bring (thing)	*mot-te ki-masu*	もって きます［持ってきます］
British people	*IgirisujiN*	イギリスじん［イギリス人］
broken (machine, etc.)	*koware-te i-masu; koshō shi-te i-masu*	こわれて います［壊れています］；こしょう して います［故障しています］

broken (plate, etc.)	*ware-te i-masu*	われて います［割れています］
brother (older)	*onīsaN*	おにいさん［お兄さん］
brother (younger)	*otōto*	おとうと［弟］
brown	*chairo-i*	ちゃいろい［茶色い］
Buddhism	*Bukkyō*	ぶっきょう［仏教］
build	*tate-masu*	たてます［建てます］
building	*biru*	ビル
Bullet Train	*ShiNkaNseN*	しんかんせん［新幹線］
bus stop	*basutē*	バスてい［バス停］
business	*shigoto*	しごと［仕事］
business card	*mēshi*	めいし［名刺］
business trip	*shucchō*	しゅっちょう［出張］
busy	*isogashi-i*	いそがしい［忙しい］
but	*demo*	でも
buttocks	*oshiri*	おしり［お尻］
buy	*kai-masu*	かいます［買います］
by - (time)	*- madeni*	〜までに

C

cake	*kēki*	ケーキ
call (to address; to invite)	*yobi-masu*	よびます［呼びます］
call (telephone)	*deNwa shi-masu*	でんわ します［電話します］
can (do)	*deki-masu*	できます
Canadian people	*KanadajiN*	カナダじん［カナダ人］
car	*kuruma*	くるま［車］
cat	*neko*	ねこ［猫］
cellular phone	*kētai (deNwa)*	けいたい（でんわ）［携帯（電話）］
center	*maNnaka*	まんなか［真ん中］
chair	*isu*	いす
change (verb)	*kae-masu*	かえます
change (money)	*otsuri*	おつり［お釣り］

cheap	*yasu-i*	やすい［安い］
child	*kodomo*	こども［子供］
China	*Chūgoku*	ちゅうごく［中国］
Chinese language	*Chūgokugo*	ちゅうごくご［中国語］
choose	*erabi-masu*	えらびます［選びます］
chopsticks	*hashi*	はし［箸］
Christ	*Kirisuto*	キリスト
Christian	*KurisuchaN*	クリスチャン
Christianity	*Kirisutokyō*	キリストきょう［キリスト教］
church	*kyōkai*	きょうかい［教会］
cigarette	*tabako*	タバコ
city	*machi*	まち［町 or 街］
clean (adjective)	*kirē(na)*	きれい（な）
clean up (verb)	*sōji shi-masu*	そうじ します［掃除します］
climb	*nobori-masu*	のぼります［登ります］
clock	*tokē*	とけい［時計］
close	*shime-masu*	しめます［閉めます］
clothes	*fuku*	ふく［服］
cloudy	*kumori*	くもり［曇］
coffee	*kōhī*	コーヒー
coffee shop	*kissateN*	きっさてん［喫茶店］
cold	*samu-i*	さむい［寒い］
cold (illness)	*kaze*	かぜ［風邪］
color	*iro*	いろ［色］
come	*ki-masu*	きます［来ます］
company	*kaisha*	かいしゃ［会社］
company employee	*kaishaiN*	かいしゃいん［会社員］
conference	*kaigi*	かいぎ［会議］
consulate	*ryōjikaN*	りょうじかん［領事館］
continue	*tsuzuke-masu*	つづけます［続けます］
convenience store	*koNbini*	コンビニ
convenient	*beNri(na)*	べんり（な）［便利（な）］

conversation	*kaiwa*	かいわ［会話］
cooking	*ryōri*	りょうり［料理］
cool	*suzushi-i*	すずしい［涼しい］
count	*kazoe-masu*	かぞえます［数えます］
country	*kuni*	くに［国］
cousin	*itoko*	いとこ
cry	*naki-masu*	なきます［泣きます］
Customs (office)	*zēkaN*	ぜいかん［税関］
cut	*kiri-masu*	きります［切ります］

D

dance (verb)	*odori-masu*	おどります［踊ります］
dangerous	*abuna-i*	あぶない［危ない］
dark	*kura-i*	くらい［暗い］
date (going out)	*dēto*	デート
date (on a calendar)	*hizuke*	ひづけ［日付］
daughter	*musume*	むすめ［娘］
day off	*yasumi*	やすみ［休み］
day planner	*techō*	てちょう［手帳］
December	*Jū ni-gatsu*	じゅう にがつ［十二月］
decide	*kime-masu*	きめます［決めます］
deep	*fuka-i*	ふかい［深い］
delicious	*oishi-i*	おいしい
depart (leave)	*de-masu*	でます［出ます］
department store	*depāto*	デパート
desk	*tsukue*	つくえ［机］
dictionary	*jisho*	じしょ［辞書］
die	*shini-masu*	しにます［死にます］
different	*chigai-masu*	ちがいます［違います］
difficult	*muzukashi-i*	むずかしい
dining	*shokuji*	しょくじ［食事］

dinner	baNgohaN; yūshoku	ばんごはん［晩ご飯］；ゆうしょく［夕食］
dirty	kitana-i	きたない［汚い］
dislike	kirai(na)	きらい（な）［嫌い（な）］
do	shi-masu; yari-masu	します; やります
doctor; doctor's office	isha	いしゃ［医者］
dog	inu	いぬ［犬］
dollar	doru	ドル
down	shita	した［下］
draw	kaki-masu	かきます［描きます］
drink	nomi-masu	のみます［飲みます］
drive	uNteN shi-masu	うんてん します［運転します］
driver's license	meNkyoshō	めんきょしょう［免許証］
drop	otoshi-masu	おとします［落とします］
drugstore	kusuriya; yakkyoku	くすりや［薬屋］；やっきょく［薬局］
dry (verb)	kawakashi-masu	かわかします［乾かします］
during -	- no aida	～の あいだ［～の間］
duty-free merchandise	meNzēhiN	めんぜいひん［免税品］

E

ear	mimi	みみ［耳］
early	haya-i	はやい［早い］
east	higashi	ひがし［東］
easy	yasashi-i	やさしい
eat	tabe-masu	たべます［食べます］
egg	tamago	たまご［卵 or 玉子］
eight	hachi	はち［八］
elbow	hiji	ひじ
electricity	deNki	でんき［電気］
elementary school	shōgakkō	しょうがっこう［小学校］

embassy	*taishikaN*	たいしかん［大使館］
employed	*tsutome-te i-masu*	つとめて います［勤めています］
English language	*Ēgo*	えいご［英語］
enjoy	*tanoshimi-masu*	たのしみます［楽しみます］
enjoyable	*tanoshi-i*	たのしい［楽しい］
enter	*hairi-masu*	はいります［入ります］
entrance	*iriguchi*	いりぐち［入口］
errand	*yōji*	ようじ［用事］
evening	*baN*	ばん［晩］
everybody	*miNna*	みんな
everything	*zeNbu*	ぜんぶ［全部］
exchange (money)	*ryōgae*	りょうがえ［両替］
exit	*deguchi*	でぐち［出口］
expensive	*taka-i*	たかい［高い］
eye	*me*	め［目］

F

face	*kao*	かお［顔］
family	*kazoku*	かぞく［家族］
far away	*tō-i*	とおい［遠い］
father	*otōsaN*	おとうさん［お父さん］
favorite	*daisuki(na)*	だいすき（な）［大好き（な）］
February	*Ni-gatsu*	にがつ［二月］
feel	*kaNji-masu*	かんじます［感じます］
festival	*matsuri*	まつり［祭］
few	*sukoshi*	すこし［少し］
find	*mitsuke-masu*	みつけます
finger	*yubi*	ゆび［指］
finish	*owarase-masu*	おわらせます［終わらせます］
fire (flame; blaze)	*hi*	ひ［火］
fire (a fire; on fire)	*kaji*	かじ［火事］

firework	*hanabi*	はなび［花火］
first	*hajime*	はじめ
fishing	*tsuri*	つり［釣り］
five	*go*	ご［五］
fix	*naoshi-masu*	なおします［直します］
flower	*hana*	はな［花］
follow (someone)	*tsui-te iki-masu*	ついて いきます
food	*tabemono*	たべもの［食べ物］
foot	*ashi*	あし［足］
for the sake of -	*- no tameni*	〜の ために
forest	*mori*	もり［森］
forget	*wasure-masu*	わすれます［忘れます］
four	*yoN; shi*	よん; し［四］
free (of charge)	*tada*	ただ
freezer	*rētōko*	れいとうこ［冷凍庫］
Friday	*KiN-yōbi*	きんようび［金曜日］
friend	*tomodachi*	ともだち［友達］
from -	*- kara*	〜から
front	*mae*	まえ［前］
fun	*tanoshi-i*	たのしい［楽しい］
function (verb)	*ugoki-masu*	うごきます［動きます］

G

get (obtain)	*morai-masu*	もらいます
get off (vehicle)	*ori-masu*	おります［降ります］
get on (vehicle)	*nori-masu*	のります［乗ります］
girl	*oNnanoko*	おんなのこ［女の子］
give	*age-masu*	あげます
give birth	*umi-masu*	うみます［産みます］
glass	*garasu*	ガラス
go	*iki-masu*	いきます［行きます］

go home	*kaeri-masu*	かえります［帰ります］
God	*Kamisama*	かみさま［神様］
gold	*kiN*	きん［金］
good	*i-i*	いい
graduate school	*daigakuiN*	だいがくいん［大学院］
grandchild	*mago*	まご［孫］
grandfather	*ojīsaN*	おじいさん
grandmother	*obāsaN*	おばあさん

H

half	*haNbuN*	はんぶん［半分］
hand	*te*	て［手］
happy	*ureshi-i*	うれしい
hard (difficult)	*muzukashi-i*	むずかしい
hard (stiff)	*kata-i*	かたい［堅い］
hat	*bōshi*	ぼうし［帽子］
have	*mot-te i-masu*	もって います［持っています］
he	*kare*	かれ［彼］
head	*atama*	あたま［頭］
health insurance	*keNkō hokeN*	けんこう ほけん［健康保険］
healthy	*geNki(na);keNkō(na)*	げんき（な）［元気（な）］；けんこう（な）［健康（な）］
hear	*kikoe-masu*	きこえます［聞こえます］
heavy	*omo-i*	おもい［重い］
help (assist)	*tetsudai-masu*	てつだいます［手伝います］
help (rescue)	*tasuke-masu*	たすけます［助けます］
here	*koko*	ここ
high	*taka-i*	たかい［高い］
high school	*kōkō*	こうこう［高校］
hobby	*shumi*	しゅみ［趣味］
home	*uchi*	うち［家］

homemaker	*shufu*	しゅふ［主婦］
hospital	*byōiN*	びょういん［病院］
hospitalization	*nyūiN*	にゅういん［入院］
hot (spicy)	*kara-i*	からい［辛い］
hot (temperature)	*atsu-i*	あつい［暑い *or* 熱い］
hot water	*oyu*	おゆ［お湯］
hour	*jikaN*	じかん［時間］
house	*ie; uchi*	いえ［家］；うち［家］
how	*dōyatte*	どうやって
how long	*donogurai*	どのぐらい
how many	*ikutsu*	いくつ
how much (money)	*ikura*	いくら
how much (quantity)	*donogurai*	どのぐらい
how old (age)	*ikutsu; naNsai*	いくつ; なんさい［何歳］
humid	*mushiatsu-i*	むしあつい［むし暑い］
hundred	*hyaku*	ひゃく［百］
hurt (painful)?	*ita-i*	いたい［痛い］
husband (my husband)	*shujiN; otto*	しゅじん［主人］；おっと［夫］
husband (someone's husband)	*goshujiN*	ごしゅじん［ご主人］

I

I	*watashi*	わたし［私］
ice	*kōri*	こおり［氷］
idea	*kaNgae*	かんがえ［考え］
illness	*byōki*	びょうき［病気］
important	*taisetsu(na)*	たいせつ（な）［大切（な）］
in what way	*dōyatte*	どうやって
inconvenient	*fubeN(na)*	ふべん（な）［不便（な）］
information booth	*aNnaijo*	あんないじょ［案内所］
injury	*kega*	けが

inn (Japanese style)	*ryokaN*	りょかん［旅館］
inside	*naka*	なか［中］
insurance	*hokeN*	ほけん［保険］
interesting	*omoshiro-i*	おもしろい
international driver's license	*kokusai meNkyoshō*	こくさい めんきょしょう ［国際免許証］
intersection	*kōsateN*	こうさてん［交差点］
it	*sore*	それ
itchy	*kayu-i*	かゆい

J

January	*Ichi-gatsu*	いちがつ［一月］
Japan	*NihoN; NippoN*	にほん［日本］；にっぽん［日本］
Japanese language	*NihoNgo*	にほんご［日本語］
Japanese people	*NihoNjiN*	にほんじん［日本人］
Jesus Christ	*Iesu Kirisuto*	イエス キリスト
job	*shigoto*	しごと［仕事］
July	*Shichi-gatsu*	しちがつ［七月］
June	*Roku-gatsu*	ろくがつ［六月］

K

keep	*tot-te oki-masu*	とって おきます
kind (gentle)	*shiNsetsu(na); yasashi-i*	しんせつ（な）［親切（な）］；やさしい［優しい］
kindergarten	*yōchieN*	ようちえん［幼稚園］
knee	*hiza*	ひざ［膝］
know	*shitte i-masu*	しって います［知って います］
Korea	*KaNkoku*	かんこく［韓国］

L

lake	mizūmi	みずうみ［湖］
language	kotoba	ことば［言葉］
laptop computer	nōto pasokoN	ノート パソコン
large	ōki-i	おおきい［大きい］
last	saigo	さいご［最後］
last month	seNgetsu	せんげつ［先月］
last week	seNshū	せんしゅう［先週］
last year	kyoneN	きょねん［去年］
late	oso-i	おそい［遅い］
later	atode	あとで［後で］
laugh	warai-masu	わらいます［笑います］
laundry	seNtaku	せんたく［洗濯］
lawyer	beNgoshi	べんごし［弁護士］
learn	narai-masu	ならいます［習います］
leave (depart)	de-masu	でます［出ます］
leave (something)	nokoshi-masu	のこします［残します］
left (direction)	hidari	ひだり［左］
leg	ashi	あし［足］
letter	tegami	てがみ［手紙］
library	toshokaN	としょかん［図書館］
light (electric)	deNki	でんき［電気］
light (weight)	karu-i	かるい［軽い］
like	suki-desu	すきです［好きです］
lip	kuchibiru	くちびる［唇］
liquor	sake	さけ［酒］
listen	kiki-masu	ききます［聞きます］
little (amount)	sukoshi	すこし［少し］
live (reside)	sumi-masu	すみます［住みます］
lock	kagi	かぎ［鍵］
lonely	sabishi-i	さびしい［寂しい］

long	*naga-i*	ながい［長い］
look	*mi-masu*	みます［見ます］
look for	*sagashi-masu*	さがします［探します］
lose	*nakushi-masu*	なくします
lost article	*otoshimono*	おとしもの［落とし物］
love (noun)	*ai*	あい［愛］
love (verb)	*aishi-te i-masu*	あいして います［愛しています］
low	*hiku-i*	ひくい［低い］
luggage	*nimotsu*	にもつ［荷物］
lunch	*hirugohaN; chūshoku*	ひるごはん［昼ご飯］； ちゅうしょく［昼食］

M

make	*tsukuri-masu*	つくります［作ります］
man	*otoko; otoko-no hito*	おとこ［男］；おとこの ひと ［男の人］
many	*takusaN*	たくさん
map	*chizu*	ちず［地図］
March	*SaN-gatsu*	さんがつ［三月］
marriage	*kekkoN*	けっこん［結婚］
May	*Go-gatsu*	ごがつ［五月］
mean (attitude)	*ijiwaru(na)*	いじわる（な）
meaning	*imi*	いみ［意味］
meat	*niku*	にく［肉］
medicine	*kusuri*	くすり［薬］
meet	*ai-masu*	あいます［会います］
meeting	*kaigi*	かいぎ［会議］
menstruation	*sēri*	せいり［生理］
messy	*yogore-te i-masu*	よごれて います［汚れています］
microwave oven	*deNshi reNji*	でんし レンジ［電子レンジ］
middle	*maNnaka*	まんなか［真ん中］
middle school	*chūgakkō*	ちゅうがっこう［中学校］

mind	*kokoro*	こころ［心］
mirror	*kagami*	かがみ［鏡］
missionary	*seNkyōshi*	せんきょうし［宣教師］
mistake	*machigae-masu*	まちがえます［間違えます］
Monday	*Getsu-yōbi*	げつようび［月曜日］
money	*okane*	おかね［お金］
month	*tsuki*	つき［月］
moon	*tsuki*	つき［月］
morning	*asa*	あさ［朝］
mother	*okāsaN*	おかあさん［お母さん］
mountain	*yama*	やま［山］
mouth	*kuchi*	くち［口］
move	*ugoki-masu*	うごきます［動きます］
movie	*ēga*	えいが［映画］
movie theater	*ēgakaN*	えいがかん［映画館］
music	*oNgaku*	おんがく［音楽］
mustache	*hige*	ひげ

N

name	*namae; shimē*	なまえ［名前］；しめい［氏名］
near	*chika-i*	ちかい［近い］
nearby (location)	*chikaku*	ちかく［近く］
neck	*kubi*	くび［首］
need	*iri-masu*	いります
nephew	*oi*	おい［甥］
new	*atarashi-i*	あたらしい［新しい］
newspaper	*shiNbun*	しんぶん［新聞］
New Year	*Shōgatsu*	しょうがつ［正月］
New Year's Eve	*ōmisoka*	おおみそか［大みそか］
next	*tsugi*	つぎ［次］
next door	*tonari*	となり［隣］
next month	*raigetsu*	らいげつ［来月］

next week	*raishū*	らいしゅう［来週］
next year	*raineN*	らいねん［来年］
nice	*i-i*	いい
niece	*mei*	めい［姪］
night	*yoru*	よる［夜］
nine	*kyū; ku*	きゅう；く［九］
no	*īe*	いいえ
no smoking	*kiNeN*	きんえん［禁煙］
noisy	*urusa-i*	うるさい
north	*kita*	きた［北］
nose	*hana*	はな［鼻］
not yet	*mada*	まだ
notebook	*nōto*	ノート
November	*Jū ichi-gatsu*	じゅう いちがつ［十一月］
now	*ima*	いま［今］
number	*baNgō*	ばんごう［番号］
nurse	*kaNgofu*	かんごふ［看護婦］

O

October	*Jū-gatsu*	じゅうがつ［十月］
of course	*mochiroN*	もちろん
okay	*i-i*	いい
old	*furu-i*	ふるい［古い］
old (age)	*toshi-o totta*	としを とった［年をとった］
one	*ichi*	いち［一］
only -	*- dake*	〜だけ
open	*ake-masu*	あけます［開けます］
order (food)	*chūmoN shi-masu*	ちゅうもん します［注文します］
other	*hoka(no)*	ほか（の）［他（の）］
out of order	*koshōchū*	こしょうちゅう［故障中］
outside	*soto*	そと［外］

P

pain	*itami*	いたみ［痛み］
painful	*ita-i*	いたい［痛い］
paper	*kami*	かみ［紙］
parcel	*kozutsumi*	こづつみ［小包み］
parent	*oya*	おや［親］
parents	*ryōshiN*	りょうしん［両親］
park	*kōeN*	こうえん［公園］
pass (through)	*tōri-masu*	とおります［通ります］
passport	*pasupōto*	パスポート
pastor	*bokushi*	ぼくし［牧師］
pay	*harai-masu*	はらいます［払います］
peach	*momo*	もも［桃］
pencil	*eNpitsu*	えんぴつ［鉛筆］
people	*hito*	ひと［人］
pepper	*koshō*	こしょう
period (menstruation)	*sēri*	せいり［生理］
person	*hito*	ひと［人］
pharmacy	*kusuriya; yakkyoku*	くすりや［薬屋］； やっきょく［薬局］
phone book	*deNwachō*	でんわちょう［電話帳］
photograph	*shashiN*	しゃしん［写真］
picture	*e*	え［絵］
pillow	*makura*	まくら［枕］
place	*basho; tokoro*	ばしょ［場所］；ところ［所］
plate	*osara*	おさら［お皿］
platform (station)	*hōmu*	ホーム
play (have fun)	*asobi-masu*	あそびます［遊びます］
play (sports)	*shi-masu; yari-masu*	します；やります
plenty	*takusaN*	たくさん

P.M.	*gogo*	ごご［午後］
police	*kēsatsu*	けいさつ［警察］
police car	*patokā*	パトカー
police officer	*omawarisaN; kēkaN*	おまわりさん; けいかん［警官］
police station	*kēsatsusho*	けいさつしょ［警察署］
pond	*ike*	いけ［池］
poor (poverty)	*biNbō(na)*	びんぼう（な）［貧乏（な）］
poor (unskilled)	*heta(na)*	へた（な）［下手（な）］
post office	*yūbiNkyoku*	ゆうびんきょく［郵便局］
postcard	*ehagaki*	えはがき［絵はがき］
practice	*reNshū*	れんしゅう［練習］
president (company)	*shachō*	しゃちょう［社長］
pretty	*kirē(na)*	きれい（な）
price	*nedaN*	ねだん　　［値段］
problem	*moNdai*	もんだい［問題］
professor	*kyōju*	きょうじゅ［教授］
promise	*yakusoku*	やくそく［約束］
province	*shū*	しゅう［州］
public telephone	*kōshū deNwa*	こうしゅう でんわ［公衆電話］
pull	*hippari-masu*	ひっぱります［引っぱります］
push	*oshi-masu*	おします［押します］
put (place)	*oki-masu*	おきます［置きます］

Q

question	*shitsumoN*	しつもん［質問］
quick	*haya-i*	はやい［速い］
quickly	*hayaku*	はやく［速く］
quiet	*shizuka(na)*	しずか（な）［静か（な）］

R

radio	*rajio*	ラジオ
rain (noun)	*ame*	あめ［雨］
rain (verb)	*ame-ga furi-masu*	あめが ふります［雨が 降ります］
read	*yomi-masu*	よみます［読みます］
real	*hoNtō(no)*	ほんとう（の）［本当（の）］
really	*hoNtō(ni)*	ほんとうに［本当に］
receive	*morai-masu*	もらいます
receptionist	*uketsuke*	うけつけ［受付］
red	*aka-i*	あかい［赤い］
refrigerator	*rēzōko*	れいぞうこ［冷蔵庫］
remember (memorize)	*oboe-masu*	おぼえます［覚えます］
remember (recall)	*omoidashi-masu*	おもいだします［思い出します］
remove	*tori-masu*	とります［取ります］
repair	*naoshi-masu*	なおします［直します］
replace	*torikae-masu*	とりかえます［取り換えます］
request	*tanomi-masu*	たのみます［頼みます］
reservation	*yoyaku*	よやく［予約］
rest (relax)	*yasumi-masu*	やすみます［休みます］
restaurant (Asian)	*ryōriya; ryōriteN*	りょうりや［料理屋］； りょうりてん［料理店］
restaurant (Western)	*resutoraN*	レストラン
restroom	*toire; otearai*	トイレ；おてあらい［お手洗い］
return	*kaeshi-masu*	かえします［返します］
rice (steamed)	*gohaN*	ごはん［ご飯］
rice bowl	*chawaN*	ちゃわん［茶碗］
rich	*okanemochi(no)*	おかねもち（の）［お金持ち（の）］
ride	*nori-masu*	のります［乗ります］
right (correct)	*tadashi-i*	ただしい［正しい］
right (direction)	*migi*	みぎ［右］
ring	*yubiwa*	ゆびわ［指輪］

river	*kawa*	かわ［川］
room	*heya*	へや［部屋］
run	*hashiri-masu*	はしります［走ります］

S

sad	*kanashi-i*	かなしい［悲しい］
safe	*aNzeN(na)*	あんぜん（な）［安全（な）］
sake (rice wine)	*sake*	さけ［酒］
sales tax	*shōhizē*	しょうひぜい［消費税］
salt	*shio*	しお［塩］
same	*onaji*	おなじ［同じ］
sanitary product (for women)	*sēri yōhiN*	せいり ようひん［生理用品］
Saturday	*Do-yōbi*	どようび［土曜日］
say	*ī-masu*	いいます［言います］
scary	*kowa-i*	こわい［怖い］
school	*gakkō*	がっこう［学校］
sea	*umi*	うみ［海］
search	*sagashi-masu*	さがします［探します］
season	*kisetsu*	きせつ［季節］
seat	*seki*	せき［席］
see	*mi-masu*	みます［見ます］
sell	*uri-masu*	うります［売ります］
send	*okuri-masu*	おくります［送ります］
September	*Ku-gatsu*	くがつ［九月］
seven	*nana; shichi*	なな; しち［七］
she	*kanojo*	かのじょ［彼女］
Shintoism	*ShiNtō*	しんとう［神道］
ship	*fune*	ふね［船］
ship (send)	*okuri-masu*	おくります［送ります］
shoe	*kutsu*	くつ［靴］

shop (store)	*mise*	みせ［店］
shopping	*kaimono*	かいもの［買い物］
short	*mijika-i*	みじかい［短い］
short (person's height)	*se-ga hiku-i*	せがひくい［背が低い］
shoulder	*kata*	かた［肩］
show (verb)	*mise-masu*	みせます［見せます］
shrimp	*ebi*	えび
shrine (Shinto)	*jiNja*	じんじゃ［神社］
sibling	*kyōdai*	きょうだい
sickness	*byōki*	びょうき［病気］
side	*yoko*	よこ［横］
sightseeing	*kaNkō*	かんこう［観光］
silver	*giN*	ぎん［銀］
since -	*- kara*	〜から
sing	*utai-masu*	うたいます［歌います］
sister (older)	*onēsaN*	おねえさん［お姉さん］
sister (younger)	*imōto*	いもうと［妹］
sit	*suwari-masu*	すわります［座ります］
six	*roku*	ろく［六］
skillful	*jōzu(na)*	じょうず（な）［上手（な）］
sky	*sora*	そら［空］
sleep	*ne-masu*	ねます［寝ます］
sleepy	*nemu-i*	ねむい［眠い］
small	*chīsa-i*	ちいさい［小さい］
smell	*nioi*	におい［匂い］
smelly	*kusa-i*	くさい［臭い］
smoke	*tabako-o sui-masu*	タバコを すいます
snow (noun)	*yuki*	ゆき［雪］
snow (verb)	*yuki-ga furi-masu*	ゆきが ふります［雪が降ります］
soap	*sekkeN*	せっけん
soft	*yawaraka-i*	やわらかい［柔らかい］
someone	*dareka*	だれか

something	*nanika*	なにか
sometime	*itsuka*	いつか
somewhere	*dokoka*	どこか
son	*musuko*	むすこ［息子］
song	*uta*	うた［歌］
so-so	*māmā*	まあまあ
sound	*oto*	おと［音］
sour	*suppa-i*	すっぱい
south	*minami*	みなみ［南］
souvenir	*omiyage*	おみやげ
soy sauce	*shōyu*	しょうゆ
speak	*hanashi-masu*	はなします［話します］
spend (money)	*okane-o tsukai-masu*	おかねを つかいます ［お金を使います］
spicy	*kara-i*	からい［辛い］
spring	*haru*	はる［春］
stairs	*kaidaN*	かいだん［階段］
stamp	*kitte*	きって［切手］
stand (up)	*tachi-masu*	たちます［立ちます］
start	*hajime-masu*	はじめます［始めます］
state	*shū*	しゅう［州］
station	*eki*	えき［駅］
stay	*i-masu*	います
stay (overnight)	*tomari-masu*	とまります［泊まります］
still	*mada*	まだ
stop (halt)	*tome-masu*	とめます［止めます］
stop (quit)	*yame-masu*	やめます
store (shop)	*mise*	みせ［店］
story (tale)	*hanashi*	はなし［話］
straight	*massugu*	まっすぐ
street	*tōri*	とおり［通り］
strong	*tsuyo-i*	つよい［強い］

student	*gakusē*	がくせい［学生］
study	*beNkyō shi-masu*	べんきょう します［勉強します］
study abroad	*ryūgaku*	りゅうがく［留学］
subway	*chikatetsu*	ちかてつ［地下鉄］
sugar	*satō*	さとう［砂糖］
summer	*natsu*	なつ［夏］
sun	*taiyō*	たいよう［太陽］
Sunday	*Nichi-yōbi*	にちようび［日曜日］
sunny	*hare*	はれ［晴］
supermarket	*sūpā*	スーパー
sushi bar	*sushiya*	すしや［寿司屋］
sweet	*ama-i*	あまい［甘い］
swim	*oyogi-masu*	およぎます［泳ぎます］

T

take (obtain)	*tori-masu*	とります［取ります］
take (someone) to somewhere	*tsure-te iki-masu*	つれて いきます［連れて いきます］
take (something) to somewhere	*mot-te iki-masu*	もって いきます［持って いきます］
take a bath	*ofuro-ni hairi-masu*	おふろにはいります ［お風呂に入ります］
take a picture	*shashiN-o tori-masu*	しゃしんを とります ［写真を撮ります］
take a shower	*shawā-o abi-masu*	シャワーを あびます
take medicine	*kusuri-o nomi-masu*	くすりを のみます［薬を飲みます］
take off (clothes)	*nugi-masu*	ぬぎます［脱ぎます］
talk	*hanashi-masu*	はなします［話します］
tall	*taka-i*	たかい［高い］
tall (person's height)	*se-ga taka-i*	せがたかい［背が高い］
taste	*aji*	あじ［味］
taxi stand	*takushī noriba*	タクシー のりば［タクシー乗り場］
tea (British)	*kōcha*	こうちゃ［紅茶］

tea (Japanese)	*ocha*	おちゃ［お茶］
tea cup (green tea)	*chawaN*	ちゃわん［茶碗］
teach	*oshie-masu*	おしえます［教えます］
teacher	*kyōshi; seNsē*	きょうし［教師］；せんせい［先生］
telephone	*deNwa*	でんわ［電話］
telephone number	*deNwa baNgō*	でんわ ばんごう［電話番号］
television	*terebi*	テレビ
tell	*ī-masu*	いいます［言います］
temple (Buddhist)	*otera*	おてら［お寺］
ten	*jū*	じゅう［十］
than -	*- yori*	～より
that (adjective; near listener)	*sono*	その
that (adjective; over there)	*ano*	あの
that one (near listener)	*sore*	それ
that one over there	*are*	あれ
there (away from speaker and listener)	*asoko*	あそこ
there (near listener)	*soko*	そこ
there is (a person)	*i-masu*	います
there is (a thing)	*ari-masu*	あります
they	*karera*	かれら
thick	*atsu-i*	あつい［厚い］
thin	*usu-i*	うすい［薄い］
thing (intangible)	*koto*	こと［事］
thing (tangible)	*mono*	もの［物］
think (contemplate)	*kaNgae-masu*	かんがえます［考えます］
think (suppose)	*omoi-masu*	おもいます［思います］
this (adjective)	*kono*	この
this month	*koNgetsu*	こんげつ［今月］
this one	*kore*	これ
this week	*koNshū*	こんしゅう［今週］

this year	*kotoshi*	ことし［今年］
thousand	*seN*	せん［千］
three	*saN*	さん［三］
throat	*nodo*	のど
throw away	*sute-masu*	すてます［捨てます］
Thursday	*Moku-yōbi*	もくようび［木曜日］
ticket (for admission)	*chiketto*	チケット
ticket (for transportation)	*kippu; jōshakeN*	きっぷ［切符］；じょうしゃけん［乗車券］
time	*jikaN*	じかん［時間］
tip	*chippu*	チップ
tired	*tsukare-masu*	つかれます［疲れます］
to -	*- ni*	～に
today	*kyō*	きょう［今日］
together	*isshoni*	いっしょに［一緒に］
tomorrow	*ashita*	あした［明日］
tongue	*shita*	した［舌］
tonight	*koNya*	こんや［今夜］
tooth	*ha*	は［歯］
toothbrush	*haburashi*	ハブラシ
toothpaste	*hamigaki*	ハミガキ
top	*ue*	うえ［上］
traffic signal	*shiNgō*	しんごう［信号］
train	*deNsha*	でんしゃ［電車］
transfer (train, bus)	*norikae-masu*	のりかえます［乗り換えます］
trash	*gomi*	ごみ
trash can	*gomibako*	ごみばこ［ごみ箱］
travel/trip	*ryokō*	りょこう［旅行］
tree	*ki*	き［木］
true	*hoNtō(no)*	ほんとう（の）［本当（の）］
Tuesday	*Ka-yōbi*	かようび［火曜日］

turn	*magari-masu*	まがります［曲がります］
two	*ni*	に［二］
typhoon	*taifū*	たいふう［台風］

U

unappetizing	*mazu-i*	まずい
uncle	*ojisaN*	おじさん
under	*shita*	した［下］
understand	*wakari-masu*	わかります
underwear	*shitagi*	したぎ［下着］
United Kingdom	*Igirisu*	イギリス
university	*daigaku*	だいがく［大学］
until -	*- made*	〜まで
up	*ue*	うえ［上］
use	*tsukai-masu*	つかいます［使います］

V

various	*iroiro(na)*	いろいろ(な)
vegetable	*yasai*	やさい［野菜］
vinegar	*osu*	おす［お酢］
visit	*tazune-masu*	たずねます［訪ねます］
voice	*koe*	こえ［声］
vomit	*haki-masu*	はきます［吐きます］

W

waist	*koshi*	こし［腰］
wait	*machi-masu*	まちます［待ちます］
wake up	*oki-masu*	おきます［起きます］
walk	*aruki-masu*	あるきます［歩きます］
wallet	*saifu*	さいふ［財布］

want (something)	*hoshi-i*	ほしい［欲しい］
war	*seNsō*	せんそう［戦争］
warm	*atatakai*	あたたかい［暖かい］
warranty (product)	*hoshōsho*	ほしょうしょ［保証書］
wash	*arai-masu*	あらいます［洗います］
washing machine	*seNtakuki*	せんたくき［洗濯機］
watch (clock)	*tokē*	とけい［時計］
watch (look)	*mi-masu*	みます［見ます］
water	*mizu*	みず［水］
water faucet	*jaguchi*	じゃぐち［蛇口］
water heater	*yuwakashiki*	ゆわかしき［湯沸かし器］
we	*watashitachi*	わたしたち［私達］
weak	*yowa-i*	よわい［弱い］
wear (above waist line)	*ki-masu*	きます［着ます］
wear (below waist line)	*haki-masu*	はきます
weather	*teNki*	てんき［天気］
wedding (ceremony)	*kekkoNshiki*	けっこんしき［結婚式］
Wednesday	*Sui-yōbi*	すいようび［水曜日］
week	*shū*	しゅう［週］
west	*nishi*	にし［西］
when	*itsu*	いつ
where	*doko; dochira*	どこ; どちら
which (adjective)	*dono; dochira*	どの; どちら
which one	*dore*	どれ
white	*shiro-i*	しろい［白い］
why	*dōshite*	どうして
wife (my wife)	*kanai; tsuma*	かない［家内］;つま［妻］
wife (someone's wife)	*okusaN*	おくさん［奥さん］
wind	*kaze*	かぜ［風］
window	*mado*	まど［窓］
winter	*fuyu*	ふゆ［冬］
with - (person)	*- to*	～と

with - (thing)	*- de*	〜で
woman	*oNna; oNna-no hito*	おんな［女］；おんなの ひと ［女の人］
word	*kotoba; taNgo*	ことば［言葉］；たんご［単語］
work (noun)	*shigoto*	しごと［仕事］
work (verb)	*shigoto-o shi-masu; hataraki-masu*	しごとを します［仕事をします］；はたらきます［働きます］
write	*kaki-masu*	かきます［書きます］
wrong	*machigat-te i-masu*	まちがって います［間違っています］

X-Y

year	*neN; toshi*	ねん；とし［年］
yellow	*kīro-i*	きいろい［黄色い］
yen (currency)	*eN*	えん［円］
yes	*hai; ē*	はい；ええ
yesterday	*kinō*	きのう［昨日］
you	*anata*	あなた
young	*waka-i*	わかい［若い］

Z

zero	*zero; rei*	ゼロ；れい［零］
zip code	*yūbiN baNgō*	ゆうびん ばんごう［郵便番号］
zoo	*dōbutsueN*	どうぶつえん［動物園］

Japanese to English Dictionary

This mini Japanese-English dictionary contains most of the words introduced in this book, as well as other frequently used basic words.

The Japanese entries are listed in alphabetical order in the leftmost column. They are written in romanized characters. In the second column, each entry is transcribed into Japanese *kana* characters. The *kanji* (Chinese characters) counterpart of a Japanese word is provided in square brackets [ ]. Note that not every Japanese word has a *kanji* counterpart. (For example, see the entry for *age-masu*, "give.")

The English meaning of each Japanese entry is listed in the rightmost column.

There are numerous words whose pronunciations are identical, such as *hashi*, "bridge," and *hashi*, "chopsticks." Since these words are totally different in meaning, they are listed as separate entries. The difference is indicated by their *kanji* (Chinese characters) representations.

A

abuna-i	あぶない［危ない］	dangerous
age-masu	あげます	give
ai	あい［愛］	love (noun)
ai-masu	あいます［会います］	meet
aishi-te i-masu	あいして います［愛しています］	love (verb)
aji	あじ［味］	taste
akachaN	あかちゃん［赤ちゃん］	baby
akaru-i	あかるい［明るい］	bright
ake-masu	あけます［開けます］	open
aki	あき［秋］	autumn
ama-i	あまい［甘い］	sweet
ame	あめ［雨］	rain (noun)
ame-ga furi-masu	あめが ふります［雨が降ります］	rain (verb)
AmerikajiN	アメリカじん［アメリカ人］	American people
anata	あなた	you
aNnaijo	あんないじょ［案内所］	information booth
ano	あの	that (adjective; over there)
aNzeN(na)	あんぜん（な）［安全（な）］	safe
ao-i	あおい［青い］	blue
arai-masu	あらいます［洗います］	wash
are	あれ	that one (over there)
ari-masu	あります	there is (a thing)
aruki-masu	あるきます［歩きます］	walk
asa	あさ［朝］	morning
asagohaN	あさごはん［朝ご飯］	breakfast
ashi	あし［足］	foot; leg
ashita	あした［明日］	tomorrow
asobi-masu	あそびます［遊びます］	play (have fun)
asoko	あそこ	there (away from speaker and listener)

atama	あたま［頭］	head
atarashi-i	あたらしい［新しい］	new
atatakai	あたたかい［暖かい］	warm
ato(de)	あと（で）［後（で）］	after; later
atsu-i	あつい［暑い *or* 熱い］	hot (temperature)
atsu-i	あつい［厚い］	thick

B

baggu	バッグ	bag
baN	ばん［晩］	evening
baNgō	ばんごう［番号］	number
baNgohaN	ばんごはん［晩ご飯］	supper
basho	ばしょ［場所］	place
basutē	バスてい［バス停］	bus stop
beNgoshi	べんごし［弁護士］	lawyer
beNkyō shi-masu	べんきょうします［勉強します］	study
beNri(na)	べんり（な）［便利（な）］	convenient
betsu(no)	べつ（の）［別（の）］	another
biNbō(na)	びんぼう（な）［貧乏（な）］	poor (poverty)
biru	ビル	building
bīru	ビール	beer
biyōiN	びよういん［美容院］	beauty salon
biza	ビザ	visa
bokushi	ぼくし［牧師］	pastor
bōshi	ぼうし［帽子］	hat
Budda	ブッダ	Buddha
Bukkyō	ぶっきょう［仏教］	Buddhism
byōiN	びょういん［病院］	hospital
byōki	びょうき［病気］	sickness

C

chairo-i	ちゃいろい ［茶色い］	brown
chawaN	ちゃわん ［茶碗］	rice bowl; tea cup (green tea)
chi	ち ［血］	blood
chigai-masu	ちがいます ［違います］	different; wrong
chika-i	ちかい ［近い］	near
chikaku	ちかく ［近く］	nearby (location)
chikatetsu	ちかてつ ［地下鉄］	subway
chiketto	チケット	ticket (for admission)
chippu	チップ	tip
chīsa-i	ちいさい ［小さい］	little; small
chizu	ちず ［地図］	map
chōshoku	ちょうしょく ［朝食］	breakfast
chūgakkō	ちゅうがっこう ［中学校］	middle school
Chūgoku	ちゅうごく ［中国］	China
Chūgokugo	ちゅうごくご ［中国語］	Chinese language
chūmoN shi-masu	ちゅうもん します ［注文します］	order (food)
chūshoku	ちゅうしょく ［昼食］	lunch

D

daidokoro	だいどころ ［台所］	kitchen
daigaku	だいがく ［大学］	university
daigakuiN	だいがくいん ［大学院］	graduate school
daisuki(na)	だいすき（な）［大好き（な）］	favorite
- dake	〜だけ	only -
dareka	だれか	someone
- de	〜で	at -; with - (thing)
deguchi	でぐち ［出口］	exit
deki-masu	できます	able; can (do)
de-masu	でます ［出ます］	leave; depart

demo	でも	but
deNki	でんき［電気］	electricity; light
deNsha	でんしゃ［電車］	train
deNshi reNji	でんし レンジ［電子レンジ］	microwave oven
deNwa	でんわ［電話］	telephone
deNwa baNgō	でんわ ばんごう［電話番号］	telephone
deNwa shi-masu	でんわ します［電話します］	make a phone call
deNwachō	でんわちょう［電話帳］	phone book
depāto	デパート	department store
dēto	デート	date (going out)
dōbutsu	どうぶつ［動物］	animal
dōbutsueN	どうぶつえん［動物園］	zoo
dochira	どちら	where; which
doko	どこ	where
dokoka	どこか	somewhere
dono	どの	which (adjective)
donogurai	どのぐらい	how long; how much (quantity)
dore	どれ	which one
doru	ドル	dollar
dōshite	どうして	why
dōyatte	どうやって	how; in what way
Do-yōbi	どようび［土曜日］	Saturday

E

e	え［絵］	picture
ē	ええ	yes
ebi	えび	shrimp/prawn
ēga	えいが［映画］	movie
ēgakaN	えいがかん［映画館］	movie theater
Ēgo	えいご［英語］	English language

ehagaki	えはがき ［絵はがき］	postcard
eki	えき ［駅］	station
eN	えん ［円］	yen (currency)
eNpitsu	えんぴつ ［鉛筆］	pencil
erabi-masu	えらびます ［選びます］	choose

F

fubeN(na)	ふべん（な）［不便（な）］	inconvenient
fuka-i	ふかい ［深い］	deep
fuku	ふく ［服］	clothes
fune	ふね ［船］	ship
furu-i	ふるい ［古い］	old
fuyu	ふゆ ［冬］	winter

G

gakkō	がっこう ［学校］	school
gakusē	がくせい ［学生］	student
garasu	ガラス	glass
geNki(na)	げんき（な）［元気（な）］	healthy
Getsu-yōbi	げつようび ［月曜日］	Monday
giN	ぎん ［銀］	silver
giNkō	ぎんこう ［銀行］	bank
go	ご ［五］	five
Go-gatsu	ごがつ ［五月］	May
gogo	ごご ［午後］	P.M.; afternoon
gohaN	ごはん ［ご飯］	rice (steamed)
gomi	ごみ	trash
gomibako	ごみばこ ［ごみ箱］	trash can
goshujiN	ごしゅじん ［ご主人］	someone's husband
gozeN	ごぜん ［午前］	A.M.
gyūnyū	ぎゅうにゅう ［牛乳］	milk

H

ha	は［歯］	tooth
haburashi	ハブラシ	toothbrush
hachi	はち［八］	eight
Hachi-gatsu	はちがつ［八月］	August
hai	はい	yes
hairi-masu	はいります［入ります］	enter
haisha	はいしゃ［歯医者］	dentist
hajime	はじめ	first
hajime-masu	はじめます［始めます］	begin; start
haki-masu	はきます［吐きます］	vomit
haki-masu	はきます	wear (below waist line)
hako	はこ［箱］	box
hamigaki	ハミガキ	toothpaste
hana	はな［花］	flower
hana	はな［鼻］	nose
hanabi	はなび［花火］	firework
hanashi	はなし［話］	story (tale)
hanashi-masu	はなします［話します］	speak; talk
haNbuN	はんぶん［半分］	half
harai-masu	はらいます［払います］	pay
hare	はれ［晴］	sunny
haru	はる［春］	spring
hashi	はし［橋］	bridge
hashi	はし［箸］	chopsticks
hashiri-masu	はしります［走ります］	run
hataraki-masu	はたらきます［働きます］	work (verb)
haya-i	はやい［早い；速い］	early; quick
hayaku	はやく［速く］	quickly
heta(na)	へた（な）［下手（な）］	poor (unskilled)
heya	へや［部屋］	room

hi	ひ ［火］	fire (flame; blaze)
hidari	ひだり ［左］	left (direction)
higashi	ひがし ［東］	east
hige	ひげ	mustache; beard
hiji	ひじ	elbow
hikōki	ひこうき ［飛行機］	airplane
hiku-i	ひくい ［低い］	low
hippari-masu	ひっぱります ［引っぱります］	pull
hirugohaN	ひるごはん ［昼ご飯］	lunch
hito	ひと ［人］	people/person
hitobaNjū	ひとばんじゅう ［一晩中］	all night
hiza	ひざ ［膝］	knee
hizuke	ひづけ ［日付］	date (on a calendar)
hoka(no)	ほか（の）［他（の）］	other
hokeN	ほけん ［保険］	insurance
hōmu	ホーム	platform (station)
hoN	ほん ［本］	book
hoNtō(ni)	ほんとうに ［本当に］	really
hoNtō(no)	ほんとう（の）［本当（の）］	true; real
hoNya	ほんや ［本屋］	bookstore
hoshi-i	ほしい ［欲しい］	want (something)
hotoNdo	ほとんど	almost
hyaku	ひゃく ［百］	hundred

I

ichi	いち ［一］	one
ichibaN	いちばん ［一番］	best
Ichi-gatsu	いちがつ ［一月］	January
ichinichijū	いちにちじゅう ［一日中］	all day
ie	いえ ［家］	house
īe	いいえ	no

Iesu Kirisuto	イエス キリスト	Jesus Christ
Igirisu	イギリス	United Kingdom
IgirisujiN	イギリスじん［イギリス人］	British people
i-i	いい	all right; good; nice; okay
ijiwaru(na)	いじわる（な）	mean (attitude)
ike	いけ［池］	pond
iki-masu	いきます［行きます］	go
ikura	いくら	how much (money)
ikutsu	いくつ	how many; how old (age)
ima	いま［今］	now
i-masu	います	there is (a person)
ī-masu	いいます［言います］	say; tell
imi	いみ［意味］	meaning
imōto	いもうと［妹］	sister (younger)
inu	いぬ［犬］	dog
iriguchi	いりぐち［入口］	entrance
iri-masu	います	need
iro	いろ［色］	color
iroiro(na)	いろいろ（な）	various
isha	いしゃ［医者］	doctor; doctor's office
isogashi-i	いそがしい［忙しい］	busy
isshoni	いっしょに［一緒に］	together
isu	いす	chair
ita-i	いたい［痛い］	painful; hurts
itami	いたみ［痛み］	pain
itoko	いとこ	cousin
itsu	いつ	when
itsuka	いつか	sometime
itsumo	いつも	always

J

jikaN	じかん［時間］	time; hour
jiko	じこ［事故］	accident
jiNja	じんじゃ［神社］	shrine (Shinto)
jisho	じしょ［辞書］	dictionary
jōshakeN	じょうしゃけん［乗車券］	ticket (for transportation)
jōzu(na)	じょうず（な）［上手（な）］	skillful
jū	じゅう［十］	ten
Jū ichi-gatsu	じゅう いちがつ［十一月］	November
Jū ni-gatsu	じゅう にがつ［十二月］	December
Jū-gatsu	じゅうがつ［十月］	October
jūsho	じゅうしょ［住所］	address

K

kabaN	かばん	bag
kae-masu	かえます	change (verb)
kaeri-masu	かえります［帰ります］	go home
kaeshi-masu	かえします［返します］	return
kagami	かがみ［鏡］	mirror
kagi	かぎ［鍵］	lock
kaidaN	かいだん［階段］	stairs
kaigi	かいぎ［会議］	meeting; conference
kai-masu	かいます［買います］	buy
kaimono	かいもの［買い物］	shopping
kaisha	かいしゃ［会社］	company
kaishaiN	かいしゃいん［会社員］	company employee
kaiwa	かいわ［会話］	conversation
kaji	かじ［火事］	fire (a fire; on fire)
kami	かみ［紙］	paper
Kamisama	かみさま［神様］	God
KanadajiN	カナダじん［カナダ人］	Canadian people

kanai	かない ［家内］	my wife
kanashi-i	かなしい ［悲しい］	sad
kaNgae	かんがえ ［考え］	idea
kaNgae-masu	かんがえます ［考えます］	think (contemplate)
kaNgofu	かんごふ ［看護婦］	nurse
kaNji-masu	かんじます ［感じます］	feel
kaNkō	かんこう ［観光］	sightseeing
KaNkoku	かんこく ［韓国］	Korea
kanojo	かのじょ ［彼女］	she
kao	かお ［顔］	face
- kara	〜から	since -; from -
karada	からだ ［体］	body
kara-i	からい ［辛い］	spicy; hot (taste)
kare	かれ ［彼］	he
karera	かれら	they
karu-i	かるい ［軽い］	light (weight)
kata	かた ［肩］	shoulder
kata-i	かたい ［堅い］	hard; stiff
kawa	かわ ［川］	river
kawakashi-masu	かわかします ［乾かします］	dry (verb)
Ka-yōbi	かようび ［火曜日］	Tuesday
kayu-i	かゆい	itchy
kaze	かぜ ［風邪］	cold (illness)
kaze	かぜ ［風］	wind
kazoe-masu	かぞえます ［数えます］	count
kazoku	かぞく ［家族］	family
kega	けが	injury
kēkaN	けいかん ［警官］	police officer
kēki	ケーキ	cake
kekkoN	けっこん ［結婚］	marriage
kekkoNshiki	けっこんしき ［結婚式］	wedding (ceremony)
keNkō hokeN	けんこう ほけん ［健康保険］	health insurance

keNkō(na)	けんこう（な）［健康（な）］	healthy
kēsatsu	けいさつ［警察］	police
kēsatsusho	けいさつしょ［警察署］	police station
kētai (deNwa)	けいたい（でんわ） ［携帯（電話）］	cellular phone
ki	き［木］	tree
kiki-masu	ききます［聞きます］	listen; ask
kikoe-masu	きこえます［聞こえます］	hear
ki-masu	きます［来ます］	come
ki-masu	きます［着ます］	wear (above waist line)
kime-masu	きめます［決めます］	decide
kinō	きのう［昨日］	yesterday
kiN	きん［金］	gold
kiNeN	きんえん［禁煙］	no smoking
KiN-yōbi	きんようび［金曜日］	Friday
kippu	きっぷ［切符］	ticket (for transportation)
kirai(na)	きらい（な）［嫌い（な）］	dislike
kirē(na)	きれい（な）	clean; pretty
kiri-masu	きります［切ります］	cut
Kirisuto	キリスト	Jesus Christ
Kirisutokyō	キリストきょう［キリスト教］	Christianity
kīro-i	きいろい［黄色い］	yellow
kisetsu	きせつ［季節］	season
kissateN	きっさてん［喫茶店］	coffee shop
kita	きた［北］	north
kitana-i	きたない［汚い］	dirty
kitte	きって［切手］	stamp
kōcha	こうちゃ［紅茶］	tea (British)
kodomo	こども［子供］	child
koe	こえ［声］	voice
kōeN	こうえん［公園］	park
kōhī	コーヒー	coffee

koko	ここ	here
kōkō	こうこう［高校］	high school
kokoro	こころ［心］	mind
kokusai meNkyoshō	こくさい めんきょしょう［国際免許証］	international driver's license
koNbini	コンビニ	convenience store
koNgetsu	こんげつ［今月］	this month
kono	この	this (adjective)
koNshū	こんしゅう［今週］	this week
koNya	こんや［今夜］	tonight
kore	これ	this one
kōri	こおり［氷］	ice
kōsateN	こうさてん［交差点］	intersection
koshi	こし［腰］	waist
koshō	こしょう	pepper
koshō shi-te i-masu	こしょう して います［故障しています］	broken (machine, etc.)
koshōchū	こしょうちゅう［故障中］	out of order
kōshū deNwa	こうしゅう でんわ［公衆電話］	public telephone
kotae-masu	こたえます［答えます］	answer (verb)
koto	こと［事］	thing (intangible)
kotoba	ことば［言葉］	language; word
kotoshi	ことし［今年］	this year
kowa-i	こわい［怖い］	afraid; scary
koware-te i-masu	こわれて います［壊れています］	broken (machine, etc.)
kowashi-masu	こわします［壊します］	break (destroy)
ku	く［九］	nine
kubi	くび［首］	neck
kuchi	くち［口］	mouth
kuchibiru	くちびる［唇］	lip
Ku-gatsu	くがつ［九月］	September
kūkō	くうこう［空港］	airport

kumori	くもり ［曇］	cloudy
kuni	くに ［国］	country
kura-i	くらい ［暗い］	dark
KurisuchaN	クリスチャン	Christian
kuro-i	くろい ［黒い］	black
kuruma	くるま ［車］	car
kusa-i	くさい ［臭い］	smelly
kusuri	くすり ［薬］	medicine
kusuri-o nomi-masu	くすりを のみます ［薬を飲みます］	take medicine
kusuriya	くすりや ［薬屋］	drugstore; pharmacy
kutsu	くつ ［靴］	shoe
kutsushita	くつした ［靴下］	socks
kyō	きょう ［今日］	today
kyōdai	きょうだい	sibling
kyōju	きょうじゅ ［教授］	professor
kyōkai	きょうかい ［教会］	church
kyoneN	きょねん ［去年］	last year
kyōshi	きょうし ［教師］	teacher
kyū	きゅう ［九］	nine
kyūkyūsha	きゅうきゅうしゃ ［救急車］	ambulance

M

machi	まち ［町 *or* 街］	city
machigae-masu	まちがえます ［間違えます］	mistake
machigat-te i-masu	まちがって います ［間違っています］	wrong
machi-masu	まちます ［待ちます］	wait
mada	まだ	not yet; still
- made	〜まで	until -
- madeni	〜までに	by - (time)
mado	まど ［窓］	window

mae	まえ［前］	ago; before; front
magari-masu	まがります［曲がります］	turn
mage-masu	まげます［曲げます］	bend
mago	まご［孫］	grandchild; grandson
Mahometto	マホメット	Muhammad
makura	まくら［枕］	pillow
māmā	まあまあ	so-so
maNnaka	まんなか［真ん中］	center; middle
massugu	まっすぐ	straight
matsuri	まつり［祭］	festival
mawari	まわり	around
mazu-i	まずい	unappetizing
me	め［目］	eye
mei	めい［姪］	niece
meNkyoshō	めんきょしょう［免許証］	driver's license
meNzēhiN	めんぜいひん［免税品］	duty-free merchandise
mēshi	めいし［名刺］	business card
michi	みち［道］	road
midori	みどり［緑］	green
migi	みぎ［右］	right (direction)
mijika-i	みじかい［短い］	short
mi-masu	みます［見ます］	look; see; watch
mimi	みみ［耳］	ear
minami	みなみ［南］	south
miNna	みんな	everybody
mise	みせ［店］	shop (store)
mise-masu	みせます［見せます］	show (verb)
mitsuke-masu	みつけます	find
mizu	みず［水］	water
mizūmi	みずうみ［湖］	lake
mō	もう	already
mō ichido	もういちど［もう一度］	again

mochiroN	もちろん	of course
mōfu	もうふ［毛布］	blanket
Moku-yōbi	もくようび［木曜日］	Thursday
moNdai	もんだい［問題］	problem; trouble
mono	もの［物］	thing (tangible)
morai-masu	もらいます	receive; get; obtain
mori	もり［森］	forest
mot-te i-masu	もっています［持っています］	have; possess
mot-te iki-masu	もっていきます ［持っていきます］	take (something) somewhere
mot-te ki-masu	もってきます［持ってきます］	bring (thing)
mukō	むこう［向こう］	across
mushiatsu-i	むしあつい［むし暑い］	humid
musuko	むすこ［息子］	son
musume	むすめ［娘］	daughter
muzukashi-i	むずかしい	difficult; hard

N

naga-i	ながい［長い］	long
naka	なか［中］	inside
naki-masu	なきます［泣きます］	cry
nakushi-masu	なくします	lose
namae	なまえ［名前］	name
nana	なな［七］	seven
nanika	なにか	something
naNsai	なんさい［何歳］	how old (age)
naoshi-masu	なおします［直します］	fix; repair
narai-masu	ならいます［習います］	learn
nari-masu	なります	become
natsu	なつ［夏］	summer
nedaN	ねだん［値段］	price

neko	ねこ［猫］	cat
ne-masu	ねます［寝ます］	sleep
nemu-i	ねむい［眠い］	sleepy
neN	ねん［年］	year
neNrē	ねんれい［年齢］	age
ni	に［二］	two
- ni	～に	to -
Nichi-yōbi	にちようび［日曜日］	Sunday
Ni-gatsu	にがつ［二月］	February
NihoN	にほん［日本］	Japan
NihoNgo	にほんご［日本語］	Japanese language
NihoNjiN	にほんじん［日本人］	Japanese people
niku	にく［肉］	meat
nimotsu	にもつ［荷物］	luggage
nioi	におい［匂い］	smell
NippoN	にっぽん［日本］	Japan
nishi	にし［西］	west
- no aida	～の あいだ［～の間］	during -
- no nakade	～のなかで［～の中で］	among -
- no tameni	～の ために	for the sake of -
nobori-masu	のぼります［登ります］	climb
nodo	のど	throat
nokoshi-masu	のこします［残します］	leave (something)
nomi-masu	のみます［飲みます］	drink
nomimono	のみもの［飲み物］	beverage
nori-masu	のります［乗ります］	ride; get on (vehicle)
norikae-masu	のりかえます［乗り換えます］	transfer (train, bus)
nōto	ノート	notebook
nōto pasokoN	ノート パソコン	laptop computer
nugi-masu	ぬぎます［脱ぎます］	take off (clothes)
nyūiN	にゅういん［入院］	hospitalization

O

obasaN	おばさん	aunt
obāsaN	おばあさん	grandmother
oboe-masu	おぼえます ［覚えます］	remember (memorize)
ocha	おちゃ ［お茶］	tea (Japanese)
odori-masu	おどります ［踊ります］	dance (verb)
ofuro	おふろ ［お風呂］	bath (tub)
ohashi	おはし ［お箸］	chopsticks
oi	おい ［甥］	nephew
oishi-i	おいしい	delicious
ojisaN	おじさん	uncle
ojīsaN	おじいさん	grandfather
okane	おかね ［お金］	money
okanemochi(no)	おかねもち（の）［お金持ち（の）］	rich
okane-o tsukai-masu	おかねを つかいます ［お金を使います］	spend (money)
okāsaN	おかあさん ［お母さん］	mother
ōki-i	おおきい ［大きい］	big
oki-masu	おきます ［置きます］	put; place
oki-masu	おきます ［起きます］	wake up
okuri-masu	おくります ［送ります］	send; ship
okusaN	おくさん ［奥さん］	someone's wife
omawarisaN	おまわりさん	police officer
ōmisoka	おおみそか ［大みそか］	New Year's Eve
omiyage	おみやげ	souvenir
omo-i	おもい ［重い］	heavy
omoidashi-masu	おもいだします ［思い出します］	remember (recall)
omoi-masu	おもいます ［思います］	think (suppose)
omoshiro-i	おもしろい	interesting
onaji	おなじ ［同じ］	same

onēsaN	おねえさん［お姉さん］	sister (older)
onīsaN	おにいさん［お兄さん］	brother (older)
oNgaku	おんがく［音楽］	music
oNna	おんな［女］	woman
oNna-no hito	おんなの ひと［女の人］	woman
oNnanoko	おんなのこ［女の子］	girl
ori-masu	おります［降ります］	get off (vehicle)
osara	おさら［お皿］	plate
oshie-masu	おしえます［教えます］	teach
oshi-masu	おします［押します］	push
oshiri	おしり［お尻］	buttocks
oso-i	おそい［遅い］	late
osu	おす［お酢］	vinegar
otearai	おてあらい［お手洗い］	bathroom (toilet)
otera	おてら［お寺］	temple (Buddhist)
oto	おと［音］	sound
otoko	おとこ［男］	man
otoko-no hito	おとこの ひと［男の人］	man
otokonoko	おとこのこ［男の子］	boy
otona	おとな［大人］	adult
otōsaN	おとうさん［お父さん］	father
otoshi-masu	おとします［落とします］	drop
otoshimono	おとしもの［落とし物］	lost article
otōto	おとうと［弟］	brother (younger)
otsuri	おつり［お釣り］	change (money)
otto	おっと［夫］	my husband
owarase-masu	おわらせます［終わらせます］	finish
oya	おや［親］	parent
oyogi-masu	およぎます［泳ぎます］	swim
oyu	おゆ［お湯］	hot water

P

patokā	パトカー	police car
paN	パン	bread

R

raigetsu	らいげつ［来月］	next month
raineN	らいねん［来年］	next year
raishū	らいしゅう［来週］	next week
rajio	ラジオ	radio
rei	れい［零］	zero
reNji	レンジ	stove (for cooking)
reNshū	れんしゅう［練習］	practice
resutoraN	レストラン	restaurant
rētōko	れいとうこ［冷凍庫］	freezer
rēzōko	れいぞうこ［冷蔵庫］	refrigerator
roku	ろく［六］	six
Roku-gatsu	ろくがつ［六月］	June
ryōgae	りょうがえ［両替］	exchange (money)
ryōjikaN	りょうじかん［領事館］	consulate
ryokaN	りょかん［旅館］	inn (Japanese style)
ryokō	りょこう［旅行］	travel/trip
ryōri	りょうり［料理］	cooking
ryōriteN	りょうりてん［料理店］	restaurant (Asian)
ryōriya	りょうりや［料理屋］	restaurant (Asian)
ryōshiN	りょうしん［両親］	parents
ryōshūsho	りょうしゅうしょ［領収書］	receipt
ryūgaku	りゅうがく［留学］	study abroad

S

sabishi-i	さびしい［寂しい］	lonely
sagashi-masu	さがします［探します］	look for; search

saifu	さいふ［財布］	wallet
saigo	さいご［最後］	last
sakana	さかな［魚］	fish
sake	さけ［酒］	liquor
saki	さき［先］	ahead
samu-i	さむい［寒い］	cold
saN	さん［三］	three
SaN-gatsu	さんがつ［三月］	March
satō	さとう［砂糖］	sugar
se-ga hiku-i	せがひくい［背が低い］	short (person's height)
se-ga taka-i	せがたかい［背が高い］	tall (person's height)
seki	せき［席］	seat
sekkeN	せっけん	soap
sēkyūsho	せいきゅうしょ［請求書］	bill (invoice)
senaka	せなか［背中］	back (body part)
sēneNgappi	せいねんがっぴ［生年月日］	birth date
sēri	せいり［生理］	period; menstruation
sēri yōhiN	せいり ようひん［生理用品］	sanitary product (for women)
seN	せん［千］	thousand
seNgetsu	せんげつ［先月］	last month
seNkyōshi	せんきょうし［宣教師］	missionary
seNsē	せんせい［先生］	teacher
seNshū	せんしゅう［先週］	last week
seNtaku	せんたく［洗濯］	laundry
seNtakuki	せんたくき［洗濯機］	washing machine
shachō	しゃちょう［社長］	president (company)
shashiN	しゃしん［写真］	photograph
shashiN-o tori-masu	しゃしんを とります［写真を撮ります］	take a picture
shawā-o abi-masu	シャワーを あびます	take a shower
shi	し［四］	four
shichi	しち［七］	seven

Shichi-gatsu	しちがつ［七月］	July
Shi-gatsu	しがつ［四月］	April
shigoto	しごと［仕事］	work (noun); job; business
shigoto-o shi-masu	しごとを します［仕事を します］	work (verb)
shikeN	しけん［試験］	exam
shi-masu	します	do; play (sports)
shimē	しめい［氏名］	name
shime-masu	しめます［閉めます］	close
shini-masu	しにます［死にます］	die
shiNbun	しんぶん［新聞］	newspaper
shiNgō	しんごう［信号］	traffic signal
ShiNkaNseN	しんかんせん［新幹線］	Bullet Train
shiNsetsu(na)	しんせつ（な）［親切（な）］	kind; gentle
ShiNtō	しんとう［神道］	Shintoism
shio	しお［塩］	salt
shiokara-i	しおからい［塩辛い］	salty
shiro-i	しろい［白い］	white
shita	した［舌］	tongue
shita	した［下］	under; down
shitagi	したぎ［下着］	underwear
shitsumoN	しつもん［質問］	question
shitte i-masu	しって います［知って います］	know
shizuka(na)	しずか（な）［静か（な）］	quiet
shōgakkō	しょうがっこう［小学校］	elementary school
Shōgatsu	しょうがつ［正月］	New Year
shōhizē	しょうひぜい［消費税］	sales tax
shokuji	しょくじ［食事］	dining; meal
shōyu	しょうゆ	soy sauce
shū	しゅう［州］	state; province
shū	しゅう［週］	week
shucchō	しゅっちょう［出張］	business trip
shufu	しゅふ［主婦］	homemaker

shujiN	しゅじん［主人］	my husband
shumi	しゅみ［趣味］	hobby
sōji shi-masu	そうじします［掃除します］	clean up (verb)
soko	そこ	there (near listener)
sono	その	that (adjective; near the listener)
sora	そら［空］	sky
sore	それ	that one (near the listener)
soto	そと［外］	outside
Sui-yōbi	すいようび［水曜日］	Wednesday
suki-desu	すきです［好きです］	like
sukoshi	すこし［少し］	few; little (amount)
sumi-masu	すみます［住みます］	live (reside)
sūpā	スーパー	supermarket
suppa-i	すっぱい	sour
sushiya	すしや［寿司屋］	sushi bar
sute-masu	すてます［捨てます］	throw away
suwari-masu	すわります［座ります］	sit
suzushi-i	すずしい［涼しい］	cool

T

tabako	タバコ	cigarette
tabako-o sui-masu	タバコを すいます	smoke
tabe-masu	たべます［食べます］	eat
tabemono	たべもの［食べ物］	food
tachi-masu	たちます［立ちます］	stand (up)
tada	ただ	free (of charge)
tadashi-i	ただしい［正しい］	right (correct)
taifū	たいふう［台風］	typhoon
taikutsu(na)	たいくつ（な）［退屈（な）］	boring
taisetsu(na)	たいせつ（な）［大切（な）］	important

taishikaN	たいしかん［大使館］	embassy
taiyō	たいよう［太陽］	sun
taka-i	たかい［高い］	tall; high; expensive
takusaN	たくさん	many; plenty
takushī noriba	タクシー のりば ［タクシー乗り場］	taxi stand
tamago	たまご［卵 or 玉子］	egg
taNgo	たんご［単語］	word
taNjōbi	たんじょうび［誕生日］	birthday
tanomi-masu	たのみます［頼みます］	request
tanoshi-i	たのしい［楽しい］	enjoyable; fun
tanoshimi-masu	たのしみます［楽しみます］	enjoy
tasuke-masu	たすけます［助けます］	rescue; help
tate-masu	たてます［建てます］	build
tazune-masu	たずねます［訪ねます］	visit
te	て［手］	hand
teNki	てんき［天気］	weather
terebi	テレビ	television
tetsudai-masu	てつだいます［手伝います］	assist
- *to*	〜と	with - (person)
- *to - no aida*	〜と〜の あいだ［〜と〜の間］	between - and -
tō-i	とおい［遠い］	far away
toire	トイレ	bathroom (toilet)
tokē	とけい［時計］	clock; watch
tokoro	ところ［所］	place
tokoya	とこや［床屋］	barber shop
tomari-masu	とまります［泊まります］	stay (overnight)
tome-masu	とめます［止めます］	stop (halt)
tomodachi	ともだち［友達］	friend
tonari	となり［隣］	next door
tori	とり［鳥］	bird
tōri	とおり［通り］	street

tori-masu	とります［取ります］	remove; take (obtain)
tōri-masu	とおります［通ります］	pass (through)
torikae-masu	とりかえます［取り換えます］	replace
toshi	とし［年］	age; year
toshi-o totta	としを とった［年をとった］	old (age)
toshokaN	としょかん［図書館］	library
tot-te oki-masu	とって おきます	keep
tsugi	つぎ［次］	next
tsui-te iki-masu	ついて いきます	follow (someone)
tsukai-masu	つかいます［使います］	use
tsukare-masu	つかれます［疲れます］	tired
tsuki	つき［月］	month; moon
tsuki-masu	つきます［着きます］	arrive
tsukue	つくえ［机］	desk
tsukuri-masu	つくります［作ります］	make
tsuma	つま［妻］	my wife
tsure-te iki-masu	つれて いきます ［連れていきます］	take (a person) to somewhere
tsure-te ki-masu	つれてきます［連れてきます］	bring (person)
tsutome-te i-masu	つとめて います［勤めています］	employed
tsuyo-i	つよい［強い］	strong
tsuzuke-masu	つづけます［続けます］	continue

U

uchi	うち［家］	home; house
ude	うで［腕］	arm
ue	うえ［上］	above; up; top
ugoki-masu	うごきます［動きます］	move; function
uketsuke	うけつけ［受付］	receptionist
umare-masu	うまれます［生まれます］	born
umi	うみ［海］	sea
umi-masu	うみます［産みます］	give birth

uNteN shi-masu	うんてん します ［運転します］	drive
ureshi-i	うれしい	happy
uri-masu	うります ［売ります］	sell
urusa-i	うるさい	noisy
ushiro	うしろ ［後ろ］	back; behind
usu-i	うすい ［薄い］	thin
uta	うた ［歌］	song
utai-masu	うたいます ［歌います］	sing
utsukushi-i	うつくしい ［美しい］	beautiful

W

waka-i	わかい ［若い］	young
wakari-masu	わかります	understand
warai-masu	わらいます ［笑います］	laugh
ware-te i-masu	われて います ［割れています］	broken (plate, etc.)
waru-i	わるい ［悪い］	bad
wasure-masu	わすれます ［忘れます］	forget
watashi	わたし ［私］	I
watashitachi	わたしたち ［私達］	we

X–Y

yaki-masu	やきます ［焼きます］	bake
yakusoku	やくそく ［約束］	appointment; promise
yama	やま ［山］	mountain
yame-masu	やめます	stop (quit)
yari-masu	やります	do; play (sports)
yasai	やさい ［野菜］	vegetable
yasu-i	やすい ［安い］	cheap
yasumi	やすみ ［休み］	absence; day off
yasumi-masu	やすみます ［休みます］	rest (relax); absent
yawaraka-i	やわらかい ［柔らかい］	soft

yobi-masu	よびます ［呼びます］	call (to address); invite
yōchieN	ようちえん ［幼稚園］	kindergarten
yogore-te i-masu	よごれて います ［汚れています］	messy
yōji	ようじ ［用事］	errand
yoko	よこ ［横］	side
yomi-masu	よみます ［読みます］	read
yoN	よん ［四］	four
- yori	〜より	than -
yoru	よる ［夜］	night
yowa-i	よわい ［弱い］	weak
yoyaku	よやく ［予約］	reservation
yubi	ゆび ［指］	finger
yubiwa	ゆびわ ［指輪］	ring
yūbiN	ゆうびん ［郵便］	letter; mail
yūbiN baNgō	ゆうびん ばんごう ［郵便番号］	zip code
yūbiN uke	ゆうびん うけ ［郵便受け］	mailbox
yūbiNkyoku	ゆうびんきょく ［郵便局］	post office
yuki	ゆき ［雪］	snow (noun)
yuki-ga furi-masu	ゆきが ふります ［雪が降ります］	snow (verb)
yūshoku	ゆうしょく ［夕食］	dinner

Z

zēkaN	ぜいかん ［税関］	Customs (office)
zeNbu	ぜんぶ ［全部］	all; everything
zero	ゼロ	zero

Index

Symbols

-*de* ("by means of" and "at"), 36, 40
-*ga* particle (subject marker), 35-38
-*ka* (questions), 73-74
-*kara* ("from"), 36, 39
-*made* ("up to" and "until"), 36, 39
-*mo* ("also"), 36, 39
-*ni* ("toward" and "in"), 35-36, 38-39
-*o* object marker, 35-36, 38
-*to* ("together with"), 36, 40-41
-*wa* (topic), 36, 41-42

A

addresses, writing, 186
adjective predicate conjugation, 50-52
adjectives, 38, 69-70
    conjugation, 50-52
        suffixes, 50
    i-idesu (irregular adjective), 52
    na- adjectives, 71-73
    pointing adjectives, 109
    predicates
        TE-form, 67
affirmative present tense, 47
ages, 125-126
Ainu people, 12
airplanes, making requests, 145-156
airports, 179
    expressions, 175-178
        baggage claim, 172-173
        Customs counter, 173-175
        immigration booths, 167-171

Alien Registration Cards, obtaining, 217
also (-*mo*), 39
animals, counters, 89
anime ("animation") videos, renting, 4
annual events in Japan, 275-278
archipelago countries, 12
articulating sound, 20
asking questions, 73-75
at (-*de*), 40
autumn events in Japan, 277

B

bank accounts, opening, 215-217
bargaining, shopping, 232-234
bat-to, pronunciation, 25
bathrooms, 259-262
bedrooms, 262-263
bilingual flight attendants, attire, 146
bills, 210-213
body parts, vocabulary, 298-299
bound objects, counters, 89
bowing, 104
    greetings, 95
buffer expressions, 96
Bullet Train (*shiNkaNseN*), 163
by means of (-*de*), 40

C

calls (telephone), making, 286-293
cellular phones, popularity of, 284
Celsius (C), 13
checking in/out of hotels, 202-204

Chinese vs. Japanese, 14
Christmas, 278
climate, vocabulary, 271-274
coins, 210-213
comparative questions, 242-244
complaints, making
    hotels, 322-326
    restaurants, 326-328
    shopping, 328-330
compound words, 21
confidence, exhibiting, 4-5
conjugation, 45-46
    adjective predicate conjugation, 50-52
    adjectives, suffixes, 50
    nouns, 53-56
        suffixes, 53
    suffixes, 47
    verb predicate conjugation, 46-50
consonants, 20-23
    double consonants, 25
    standalone consonants, 23-26
conversation partners, finding, 6
counters, 88-89, 225-228
    animals, 89
    bound objects, 89
    days, 168
    long objects, 89
    machinery, 89
    people, 89, 124-125
    small objects, 89
    thin and flat objects, 88
counting people, 201
counting units, progression of, 87
courteous expressions, 97-98
creativity, 6
crime rate in Japan, 308
cultural rituals, 15
currency, 210-213
    bank accounts, opening, 215-217
    exchange rate, 213-215

D

dates, 197
days, 199
    counters, 168
denominations, monetary
    bills, 210
    coins, 211
departing expressions, 98-99
department stores, floor plans, 230
descriptive words, 69-70
dialogs, memorizing, 289
dining, expressions, 94-95
dining out, expressions, 239-241
    comparative questions, 242-244
    etiquette, 247-249
    ordering, 244-246
    paying, 250-251
    taste, 249-250
direct objects, 35
directions, asking for, 316-318
double consonants, 25
dōmo, 97
driving in Tokyo, 191-193
drugs, vocabulary, 303-305
duration, expressions, 162-165

E

eating
    complaints, making, 326-328
    dining, 248
    display cases, 244
    expressions, 239-241
        comparative questions, 242-244
        etiquette, 247-249
        ordering, 244-246
        paying, 250-251
        taste, 249-250
    menus, 245
    slurping, 248

eb, 16
embassies, contact information, 292
emergency telephone numbers (Japan), 292-293
endings, verbs, 63
English
    fixed word order, 34
    schools, requirements, 318
ethnicity, Japan, 14
etiquette, restaurants, 247-249
events in Japan, 275-278
exchange rate, currency, 213-215
expressions (common), 93, 101-103
    airports, 175-178
        baggage claim, 172-173
        Customs counter, 173-175
        immigration booths, 167-171
    buffer expressions, 96
    complaints
        hotels, 322-326
        restaurants, 326-328
        shopping, 328-330
    courteous, 97-98
    departing, 98-99
    dining, 94-95
    dining out, 239-241
        comparative questions, 242-244
        etiquette, 247-249
        ordering, 244-246
        paying, 250-251
        taste, 249-250
    directions, 316-318
    giving and receiving, 100
    greetings, 94
        leaving and coming home, 95-96
        night, 96
        time of day, 94
    health-related, 295-305
    introductions, 103-110
    invitations, 129-135
        declining, 135-137
        promoting, 137-138
    "let's ...," 134
    personal information, 113-115

    background, 115
    family, 122
    hobbies, 119-127
    marital status, 116
    occupation, 116-118
    residence, 115
requests, 99-100
    flights, 145-156
"shall we ...?," 134-135
shopping, 224-232
    haggling, 232-234
telephones, 283-293
time, 157-161
    duration, 162-165

F

Fahrenheit (F) scale, converting to Celsius (C), 13
fall events in Japan, 277
family rooms, 258-259
fixed expressions (common), 101-103
    airports, 175-178
        baggage claim, 172-173
        Customs counter, 173-175
        immigration booths, 167-171
    buffer expressions, 96
    courteous, 97-98
    departing, 98-99
    dining, 94-95
    giving and receiving, 100
    greetings, 94
        leaving and coming home, 95-96
        night, 96
        time of day, 94
    introductions, 103-110
    invitations, 129-135
        declining, 135-137
        promoting, 137-138
    "let's ...," 134
    personal information, 113-115
        background, 115
        family, 122

hobbies, 119-127
marital status, 116
occupation, 116-118
residence, 115
requests, 99-100
"shall we ...?," 134-135
time, 157-161
duration, 162-165
fixed word order, English, 34
flat objects, counters, 88
flights, requests, 145-156
formal conversation, 15
from (-*kara*), 39
fruits, 242
fu, pronunciation, 23
futons, 205

G

gairaigo, 27-28
geography of Japan, 11-14
grammar, word order, 35-36
greetings, 94
bowing, 95, 104
dining, 94-95
introductions, 103-110
leaving and coming home, 95-96
night, 96
time of day, 94
guided tours, taking, 269

H

haggling, shopping, 232-234
hai, 16
Haneda Airport, 180
health-related expressions, 295-305
Hokkaido people, 12
holidays in Japan, 275-278
homes, 256
entering, 257-258

household items, 264-266
rooms, 258
bathrooms, 259-262
bedrooms, 262-263
family rooms, 258-259
homogeneous societies, 15
hospitals, medical departments, 302
hotels
checking in/out, 202-204
choosing, 196
complaints
making, 322-326
reservations, making, 195-201
houses, 256
entering, 257-258
household items, 264-266
rooms, 258
bathrooms, 259-262
bedrooms, 262-263
family rooms, 258-259
hyaku ("hundred"), 84

I

i-idesu, 52
idioms (common), 93, 101-103
airports, 175-178
baggage claim, 172-173
Customs counter, 173-175
immigration booths, 167-171
buffer expressions, 96
courteous, 97-98
departing, 98-99
dining, 94-95
giving and receiving, 100
greetings, 94
leaving and coming home, 95-96
night, 96
time of day, 94
health-related, 295-305
introductions, 103-110

invitations
    declining, 135-137
    promoting, 137-138
"let's ...," 134
personal information, 113-115, 129-135
    background, 115
    family, 122
    hobbies, 119-127
    marital status, 116
    occupation, 116-118
    residence, 115
requests, 99-100
    flights, 145-156
"shall we ...?," 134-135
time, 157-161
    duration, 162-165
illnesses, vocabulary, 302
immigration booths, expressions to use,
    167-171
in (-*ni*), 38-39
indirect objects, 35
interjections, 108
intonation patterns, 28-30
introductions, 103-110
    bowing, 104
    exchanging names, 103-106
    occupations, 107
    parties, 108-110
    residence, 107-108
invitations, 129-135
    declining, 135-137
    promoting, 137-138
itineraries, trips to Japan, 269-271

J

Japan, geography, 11-14
Japan Railways (JR), 181
Japan Ryokan Association, 204
Japanese vs. Chinese, 14
JR (Japan Railways), 181

K

kana, 12
kanji, 12
Kansai International Airport in Osaka (KIX),
    179
karaoke, 21
kimonos, 205
KIX (Kansai International Airport in Osaka),
    179
kōbaN (community police), 308
Koreans, immigration to Japan, 12

L

large animals, counters, 89
listening skills, 17
loan words, 27-28
    acting as nouns, 151
long objects, counters, 89
long vowels, 26
lost items, retrieving, 309-313

M

machinery, counters, 89
medical departments, vocabulary, 302
menus, restaurants, 245
months, 198

N

N, pronunciation, 25
na- adjectives, 71-73
namae, 105
National Seclusion Policy, 14
New Tokyo International Airport in Narita
    (NRT), 179-180
New Year's Day, 277
Nihon, 12
Nippon, 12

nouns, 70
  conjugation, 53-56
    suffixes, 53
  loan words, 151
  predicates, *TE*-form, 66-67
NRT (New Tokyo International Airport in
  Narita), 179-180
numbers, 81
  ages, 125-126
  counters, 88-89, 225-228
    people, 124-125
  eleven through ninety-nine, 82-83
  one through ten, 81-82
  one hundred through nine thousand,
    ninety-nine, 83-86
  practicing, 82
  ten thousand and above, 86-87

O

object marker (*-o*), 38
objects, 38-39
  counters
    animals, 89
    bound objects, 89
    long objects, 89
    machinery, 89
    people, 89
    small objects, 89
    thin and flat objects, 88
  lack of, 42-43
ocha ("green tea"), 146
oNseN, 205-206
opening bank accounts, 215-217
ordering in restaurants, 244-246

P

particles, 35-36
  -de ("by means of" and "at"), 40
  -ga (subject marker), 37-38
  -kara ("from"), 39
  -made ("up to" and "until"), 39
  -mo ("also"), 39
  -ni ("toward" and "in"), 38-39
  -o (object marker), 38
  -to ("together with"), 40-41
  -wa (topic), 41-42
  objects, 38-39
  sentence-final particles, 108
  verbs, 37-38
past affirmative conjugation, nouns, 56
past negative conjugation, nouns, 56
paying in restaurants, expressions, 250-251
people
  counters, 89, 124-125
  counting, 201
persistence, 6
personal information, sharing, 113-115
  background, 115
  family, 122
  hobbies, 119-127
  marital status, 116
  occupation, 116-118
  residence, 115
pharmaceuticals, vocabulary, 303-305
phones, vocabulary, 283-293
phrases (common), 93, 101-103
  airports, 175-178
    baggage claim, 172-173
    Customs counter, 173-175
    immigration booths, 167-171
  buffer expressions, 96
  complaints
    hotels, 322-326
    restaurants, 326-328
    shopping, 328-330
  courteous, 97-98
  departing, 98-99
  dining, 94-95
  dining out, 239-241
    comparative questions, 242-244
    etiquette, 247-249
    ordering, 244-246
    paying, 250-251
    taste, 249-250

directions, 316-318
giving and receiving, 100
greetings, 94
   leaving and coming home, 95-96
   night, 96
   time of day, 94
health-related, 295-305
introductions, 103-110
invitations, 129-137
   promoting, 137-138
"let's …," 134
personal information, 113-115
   background, 115
   family, 122
   hobbies, 119-127
   marital status, 116
   occupation, 116-118
   residence, 115
requests, 99-100
   flights, 145-156
"shall we …?," 134-135
shopping, 224-232
   haggling, 232-234
telephones, 283-293
time, 157-161
   duration, 162-165
pointing adjectives, 109
pointing words, 109-110
police
   Japan, 307-309
   thefts, reporting, 313-316
politeness, 16
pop-pu, pronunciation, 25
population of Japan, 13
post offices, opening accounts in, 216
predicates, 35, 46
   adjective predicate conjugation, 50-52
   adjectives, *TE*-form, 67
   nouns, *TE*-form, 66-67
   verb predicate conjugation, 46-50
prepositions, 35
present negative conjugation, nouns, 56
prices, writing out, 85

pronunciation
   consonants, 23-26
      double, 25
      standalone, 23-24
   intonation patterns, 28-30
   loan words, 27-28
   vowels, 21
      long, 26
public transportation, 181-185
   vocabulary, 267-269

Q

question words, 197
questions, asking, 73-75

R

ra, pronunciation, 24
rainy season in Japan, 272
re, pronunciation, 24
requests
   expressions, 99-100
   on flights, 145-156
   TE-form of, 147-150
reservations, hotels, making, 195-201
restaurants
   complaints, making, 326-328
   display cases, 244
   expressions, 239-241
      comparative questions, 242-244
      etiquette, 247-249
      ordering, 244-246
      paying, 250-251
      taste, 249-250
   menus, 245
   slurping, 248
ri, pronunciation, 24
ritualized expressions (common), 101-103
   buffer expressions, 96
   courteous, 97-98
   departing, 98-99

dining, 94-95
giving and receiving, 100
greetings, 94
    leaving and coming home, 95-96
    night, 96
    time of day, 94
introductions, 103-110
requests, 99-100
rituals, 15
ro, pronunciation, 24
rooms, 258
    bathrooms, 259-262
    bedrooms, 262-263
    family rooms, 258-259
rop-pyaku, 84
ru, pronunciation, 24
rugby, popularity of, 121
ryokaN, 204-205
    staying in, 204-206

S

salutations, 94
    dining, 94-95
    introductions, 103-110
    leaving and coming home, 95-96
    night, 96
    time of day, 94
sashimi, 247
sayōnara, 99
seasons, 271
    Japan, 13
sentence-final particles, 108
sentences
    simplicity of, 42-43
    word order, 34-36
shiNkaNseN (Bullet Train), 163
shitsurē shimasu, 98
shopping
    complaints, making, 328-330
    department store floor plans, 230
    expressions, 224-232
        haggling, 232-234
    types of, 223-224

sickness, vocabulary, 302
situations, anticipating, 7
slurping in restaurants, 248
small animals, counters, 89
small objects, counters, 89
society (Japanese), 15-16
sounds
    articulating, 20
    consonants, 23
        standalone, 23-26
    English vs. Japanese, 5
    intonation patterns, 28-30
    loan words, 27-28
    syllables, 20-21
    vowels, 21
        long, 26
sports, rugby, popularity of, 121
spring events in Japan, 276
St. Valentine's Day, 278
standalone consonants, 23-26
stores
    department, floor plans, 230
    expressions, 224-232
        haggling, 232-234
    types of, 223-224
subject marker (*-ga*), 37-38
subjects, lack of, 42-43
subway systems, 185
suffixes (conjugation)
    adjectives, 50
    nouns, 53
    verbs, 47
summer events in Japan, 276-277
sushi, 247
syllabication, 20-21
syllables, 20-21
    vowels, 20
symptoms, illness, vocabulary, 299-305
synonyms, 6

T

taste, expressions, 249-250
taxis, 185-190
TE-form, 68-69
  adjective predicates, 67
  noun predicates, 66-67
  requests, 147-150
  verbs, 62-65, 270-271
telephones, vocabulary, 283-293
thefts, reporting, 313-316
thin objects, counters, 88
time, expressions, 94-96, 157-161
  duration, 162-165
Time, Place, Occasion (TPO), 17-18
tipping, 205
together with (*-to*), 40-41
Tokyo, Japan, 13
Tokyo International Airport, 180
topic (*-wa*), 41-42
toward (*-ni*), 38-39
TPO (Time, Place, Occasion), 17-18
trains
  stations, 184
  transportation, 181-185
transportation, 163
  driving, 191-193
  public transportation, 181-185
    vocabulary, 267-269
  subway systems, 185
  taxis, 185-190
  trains, 181-185
  types of, 179-181
traveling in Japan, planning, 269-271
tsu, pronunciation, 23

U

U.S. dollars, exchange rates, 213-215
until (*-made*), 39
up to (*-made*), 39

V

Valentine's Day, 278
vegetables, 242
verb predicate conjugation, 46-50
verbs, 37-38, 46
  affirmative present tense, 47
  conjugation, 45-46
    adjective predicate conjugation, 50-52
    nouns, 53-56
    suffixes, 47
    verb predicate conjugation, 46-50
  endings, 63
  predicates, 46
  TE-form, 62-65, 270-271
vowels, 20-21
  long, 26
  syllables, 20

W

wa, pronunciation, 24
watashi-wa XYZ-desu, 105
weather, vocabulary, 271-274
wh-questions, 74-75
winter events in Japan, 277-278
word order, 34-36

X-Y-Z

X-wa Y-desu pattern, 104
XYZ-ni shi-masu, 146

y, pronunciation, 24
years, writing out, 85
yen, 212-213
  exchange rate, 213-215

CD Track List

Track 1: Welcome
Track 2: Instructions
Track 3: Selected examples from Chapter 3
Track 4: Selected examples from Chapter 4
Track 5: Selected examples from Chapter 5
Track 6: Selected examples from Chapter 6
Track 7: Selected examples from Chapter 7
Track 8: Selected examples from Chapter 8
Track 9: Selected examples from Chapter 9
Track 10: Selected examples from Chapter 10
Track 11: Selected examples from Chapter 11
Track 12: Selected examples from Chapter 12
Track 13: Selected examples from Chapter 13
Track 14: Selected examples from Chapter 14
Track 15: Selected examples from Chapter 15
Track 16: Selected examples from Chapter 16
Track 17: Selected examples from Chapter 17
Track 18: Selected examples from Chapter 18
Track 19: Selected examples from Chapter 19
Track 20: Selected examples from Chapter 20
Track 21: Selected examples from Chapter 21
Track 22: Selected examples from Chapter 22
Track 23: Selected examples from Chapter 23
Track 24: Selected examples from Chapter 24
Track 25: Selected examples from Chapter 25

Working with Your CD

The CD that accompanies this book gives you an opportunity to hear Japanese words, phrases, and dialogs as they are spoken so you can practice intonation, inflections, and sounds. The track list helps coordinate the CD with the book. Exercises contained on the CD are marked in the book by the CD icon.

CD credits:

Female voice: Yuko Takahashi
Male voice: Niroyuki Nakia

Producers: Alex Kent, Context Communications, Amherst, Massachusetts, and The Language Lab, New York, New York

Script: Dr. Naoya Fujita

Recording Engineer: Wes Talbot of Music Media, Northampton, Massachusetts